Long Title: Looking For
The Good Times
Examining the Monkees' Songs, One By One

by Michael A. Ventrella
and Mark Arnold

Long Title: Looking for the Good Times; Examining the Monkees' Songs, One by One
By Michael A. Ventrella and Mark Arnold

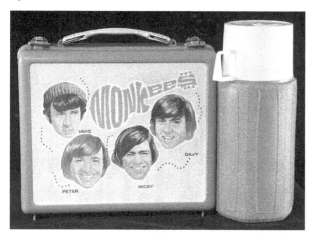

For information, address:
BearManor Media
P.O. Box 71426
Albany, GA 31708
bearmanormedia.com

Cover artwork by Scott Shaw!
Permission is granted to other publications or media to excerpt the contents contained herein for review purposes provided that the correct credit and copyright information is included for any materials reproduced.
Live concert photos by Stephanie Fine and used with permission.
Typesetting and layout by Robbie Adkins.
Published in the USA by BearManor Media.

Library of Congress Cataloging-in-Publication Data
Ventrella, Michael A., and Mark Arnold
Long Title: Looking for the Good Times; Examining the Monkees' Songs, One by One / by Michael A. Ventrella and Mark Arnold
Includes index.
ISBN 978-1-62933-176-8

Books by Mark Arnold:
The Best of the Harveyville Fun Times!
Created and Produced by Total TeleVision productions (BearManor)
If You're Cracked, You're Happy, Part Won (BearManor)
If You're Cracked, You're Happy, Part Too (BearManor)
Mark Arnold Picks on The Beatles
Frozen in Ice: The Story of Walt Disney Productions (BearManor)
Think Pink: The Story of DePatie-Freleng (BearManor)
Pocket Full of Dennis the Menace (BearManor)

Books by Michael A. Ventrella:
Arch Enemies (Double Dragon)
The Axes of Evil (Double Dragon)
Bloodsuckers: A Vampire Runs for President (Double Dragon)
Tales of Fortannis: A Bard's Eye View (editor) (Double Dragon)
Tales of Fortannis: A Bard in the Hand (editor) (Double Dragon)
Tales of Fortannis: A Bard Day's Knight (editor) (Double Dragon)
Tales of Fortannis: A Bard Act to Follow (editor) (Double Dragon)
Baker Street Irregulars (editor; with Jonathan Maberry) (Diversion Books)

SPECIAL THANKS TO all the people who agreed to be interviewed for this book: Gene Cornish, Ron Dante, Dean Friedman, Tommy James, Howard Kaylan, Peter Noone, Butch Patrick, David Peel, Stu Phillips, and to Scott Shaw! for his incredible cover (with coloring by Dan Nakrosis), and to everyone who worked with The Monkees and of course, to the Pre-Fab Four themselves.

DEDICATED TO the memory of David Thomas Jones (December 30, 1945 - February 29, 2012). Your talent and commitment as an entertainer and as a member of The Monkees is missed and will be remembered forever.

CONTENTS:

FOREWORD
by Jerry Beck

"Wanting to Feel... To Know What is Real..."

The Monkees may have been "manufactured" but their music was real.

As a child of the 1960s, my love for comic books, cartoons and all things television has no peer (that is, with the exception of the guys who wrote this book). Rock and Roll changed the world during that decade too (the highlight event of my ninth birthday (I was born on February 9th) was watching the 1964 Beatles debut on The Ed Sullivan Show — with a segment which also featured the US TV debut of Davy Jones... but I digress).

The 1966 NBC television show *The Monkees* combined all my interests in one place — comedy, rock music, and a cartoon-like break-the-fourth-wall sensibility in the plotlines and mayhem. On the show they even occasionally dressed as comic book superheroes ("Monkee-Men") and used their real names in character (only Abbott and Costello and Roy Rogers ever did that — back in the 1950s).

It occurred to me early on that while it was possible a band like The Monkees *could* have existed, the group (as presented on screen) just couldn't *be* real. Four out-of-work musicians with a four bedroom Malibu beach pad (the rent on that today would be upwards of $10k per month) and a customized "Monkeemobile" (not to mention their specially tailored cavalry 'bib' shirts, as band uniforms).

I loved the 'fantasy' of it all. Four college-aged guys — the dreamboat from England, the cowboy from from Texas, a folkie from the East coast, and a drummer from L.A. — How could they have gotten together? Where would they have met? This union could *only* be manufactured.

But I never had any doubt they were a real rock group. Their first two albums sounded pretty legitimate to me. In fact, the music was sweet and the songs were damn good. I soon began to appreciate the "sound" The Monkees produced.

So convincing was the act, that it became a cause célèbre in 1967 when it was revealed that 'they didn't play their own instruments'. But The Monkees themselves wanted to be a real music group and fought for the right to be one. And ultimately — spoiler alert — they succeeded. Their third, fourth, fifth and sixth albums are masterpieces of 60s California pop rock.

For all the backlash toward the early Don Kirshner tracks — I say "nay". Kirshner defined the sound of the show and for the group. He curated the Neil Diamond, Carole King, Neil Sedaka and Boyce & Hart material (and even tolerated a few Nesmith compositions) to set the tone. When you understand that the early backing tracks were produced by the legendary Wrecking Crew (who played under The Beach Boys,

The Byrds, The Mamas and the Papas, among many others) it's easier to appreciate the qualities of the sound — and the craft — on these first two albums.

The "real" Monkees come through on their next four albums in 1967 and 1968. I bought all these when they were new and loved them. The Monkees weren't following The Beatles or any other group — they were doing their own thing, and it was wonderful.

Their songwriting collaborators (who, in addition to those named above, now included Harry Nilsson, Micky Dolenz and Peter Tork) crafted appealing songs with meaning and heart, that really spoke to the younger generation at the time. The Monkees had a unique "voice" — it was sometimes pop, sometimes retro, sometimes experimental and always progressive.

By the time it was over in 1969-70, their sound standardized into the bubble gum pop of the time — and that wasn't a bad thing either — but you could feel the ambition had drained away (the departure of Tork and Nesmith didn't help).

No matter. I've remained a fan ever since. I have always been proud of my faith and fandom of all things Monkee — and nothing Dolenz, Jones, Tork and Nesmith did in suceeding years has tarnished my opinion. In fact, all four have made great tracks in the decades since. 2016's **GOOD TIMES!** perfectly encapsulates their talents and the music they will always be known for.

It's a blast to re-listen to my vintage Monkees albums these days (via mp3 files on flash drive, usually when I'm driving) — and it's been more fun to read the opinions of Mike and Mark in this book. The fact that we are still talking about the music all these years later says it all.

It took 50 years — but The Monkees now matter. Their music was always real — and has found new audiences unprejudiced by the sitcom or any controversy over a manufactured image. Their songs have stood the test of time.

Jerry Beck is a film industry executive, an author and a journalist who teaches animation history at Cal Arts and lives in Los Angeles, CA. He blogs at CartoonResearch.com

INTRODUCTION
by Howard Kaylan

I was, oh, so prepared to hate The Monkees. Who the hell did these guys think they were? We, The Turtles, had worked *hard* in the miraculous two years after high school, eking out three top twenty records, in our Beatle haircuts and living our hippy dippy lifestyles.

Tour bus and hotel time, man.

And then these clowns come along — actors, damned actors, pretending they were a band — and the world drops its pants.

Sure, they were cute — we weren't — but everyone knew that The Wrecking Crew had played on all of their sessions — they didn't play their own instruments — and that they huge corporate money behind them, two major studios, and ubiquitous interviews to precede their launch.

We waited.

Clarksville came out.

Damn! That was good.

The show debuted. Really funny. *A Hard Day's Night* but even dumber. I loved it.

They were funny too. And just when the world needed a good laugh.

They were imitation Beatles — just like we were — but with the benefit of some of the greatest songwriters and producers in rock history.

So I gained respect for these actors.

Because the music worked. Still does.

Hey, the Fabs loved these guys. As did Zappa, who famously appeared in *Head*.

And all these years later, what's *not* to love?

When they began playing their own instruments and writing their own songs, it signaled the growth of the "group" and the end of an era.

The TV show may have ended but the music was only beginning to deeply root itself in our collective DNA.

Despite early naysayers and lowly pessimists such as I, The Monkees wound up being far more than just the Boob Tube's contribution to the Woodstock generation. Their songs and their humor will never fade from the public consciousness.

Their four personalities define us all. Which one are you?

I think I'm a Mike.

Howard Kaylan is the founder of The Turtles, and later was one half of Flo and Eddie and one of Frank Zappa's Mothers of Invention. His memoir Shell Shocked *has some great stories that you should all read!*

DON'T DO THAT!
by Mark Arnold

Another Monkees book? I hear you cry. What possible insight could this book possibly have for a pop group that's been around for over 50 years and has been maligned (and also M.I.A. off and on) for much of that time? They are apparently permanently barred from The Rock and Roll Hall of Fame for not writing or performing their own material, yet Elvis Presley gets a free pass. Despite that fact that later on, all of The Monkees *did* write *and* perform their own material at times, the myth remains that they didn't write their own songs or play their own instruments and so what? Until The Beatles made it standard operating procedure for a band to virtually always write and perform their own material, most singers didn't. If that was a requirement, we would not regard Frank Sinatra or Bing Crosby or Barbra Streisand with much fondness.

The Monkees are still considered by some to not be a real group because they did not come together by their own volition. However, since they have come together to undertake major rock concert tours every few years since 1967, they have actually been a *real* rock band far, far longer than being a fake one. Micky Dolenz summed it up best in an interview for *CBS This Morning* in May 2016, "I've often said that it was like Leonard Nimoy really becoming a vulcan."

Most Monkees books and histories seem to cover the years 1965-1971 and tend to focus on their 1966-1968 TV series with little regard that they reunited for tours, albums, TV specials and other reasons from 1975-1977, 1986-1989, 1993-1998, 2001-2002, and most recently from 2010-2016. This book will focus more on their music as that is the one lasting legacy The Monkees have to offer. There is magic in the recording. Surprising and amazing since the group didn't have complete control over everything, but it's the "getting by with a little help from their friends" (to paraphrase a phrase) that makes The Monkees music so magical.

This has always been kind of a mystery to me. If the four were never totally enamored with each other beyond the two seasons of the TV series, then why (again, with the exception of Nesmith) didn't they try harder to prove themselves as viable solo acts over the years until the off times later on between reunion tours?

My take on it is that they realize that even two Monkees is a greater force than Monkees on their own, plus The Monkees name holds a certain sort of cache. Since this book is really not about their solo endeavors, I will take this opportunity to discuss their solo works and my surprise that none of them achieved any real lasting solo success, even as television actors.

I first became aware of The Monkees when they were in Saturday morning reruns around 1970 or 1971 when I was 3 and 4 years old. Even then, I didn't care for the "wacky" antics of the Pre-Fab Four and apart from the opening title theme, rarely watched the show beyond the opening titles. I had no idea that these shows were reruns and figured that they were one in a long-line of Saturday morning TV shows featuring musical groups and songs including *The Archies*, *H.R. Pufnstuf*, *The Banana Splits*, *The Globetrotters*, *The Hardy Boys*, *The Cattanooga Cats*, *The Groovie Goolies*, *Josie and the Pussycats* and even *The Partridge Family* in primetime.

So, I ignored The Monkees and dismissed them as SatAM pablum. I discovered later that *The Monkees* originally aired in primetime, but since it lasted only two seasons, I felt that it was a flash-in-the- pan phenomenon.

I became a Beatles fan in 1977 (thanks to an Eric Idle appearance on *Saturday Night Live!*) and started paying attention to groups that were contemporary to them, many of them were still around like The Kinks, The Hollies and The Bee Gees; and some were and are still around now like The Rolling Stones and The Beach Boys. The Monkees to me were still "that TV band," so I didn't equate them with these other rock stalwarts.

What brought me to starting to like The Monkees was Michael Nesmith. He's still my favorite Monkee. At the time (1981), I didn't know anything about Nesmith's solo record career, which was actually quite substantial. This success meant nothing to me. What peaked my interest was a little video sketch comedy and music variety show called *Elephant Parts*, released originally on home video in 1981. The show featured videos for a few songs like *Rio*, *Magic*, *Cruisin'* and *Silver Moon*, all of which came from Nesmith's various solo albums, and so I started seeking out his solo albums which was a little bit difficult to find as many of his albums were out of print at the time. Sadly, cut-out bins were the initial source.

Then in 1985, Nesmith expanded this one-time concept into a regular TV series that unfortunately only lasted a handful of episodes and quickly canceled. I was wanting more Nesmith and was in a used bookstore one day. In the store they had a small box with random LPs for 25¢ each. One of the albums was **MORE OF THE MONKEES**.

I had seen **MORE OF THE MONKEES** (along with **THE MONKEES, HEADQUAR-TERS** and **PISCES,...LTD.**) many, many times in thrift stores, but totally ignored them, such was my disdain for the group. I just flipped past them as well as the multiple copies of early Partridge Family LPs and that thrift store mainstay about President Kennedy – **THE FIRST FAMILY** to get to "the good stuff."

I decided to give **MORE** a shot. I gambled a quarter and figured that if I hated it, I would just turn it into the thrift shop to join the other copies. What happened instead was a quick conversion that turned me into a lifelong Monkees fan. I loved every track on the album. Every song is a gem with the possible exception of *The Day We Fall in Love*, which was and is the type of song typically on a Davy Jones solo album. I actually did already know *I'm a Believer, (I'm Not Your) Steppin' Stone, She* and *Mary, Mary* as I was a fan of oldies radio and these were played regularly on those stations.

After that album, I purchased **PISCES, AQUARIUS, CAPRICORN AND JONES, LTD.** for two reasons. I had heard *Peter Percival Patterson's Pet Pig Porky* on *The Dr. Demento Show*, and I was on a quest to get as many of the little gems that I could and also because I loved **MORE** so much. Well, **PISCES** *blew me away!* It's still one my favorite albums of all time, Monkees or otherwise.

So, from that point, I started to investigate The Monkees. When did they break up and why? Why hadn't they reunited? Would they ever play again together? I saw very basic articles stating that they four really were actors and have all gone their separate ways and that the four of them reuniting was even more unlikely than The Beatles reuniting, which meant not at all in this post-Lennon world.

This was all confirmed with Eric Lefcowitz's early Monkees tome *The Monkees Tale*. Though the original edition is hopelessly incomplete and dated today, at the time it was literally the *only* coverage of The Monkees apart from some TV books that said that the show ran from 1966-1968 on NBC and other basic facts like that.

That book told me exactly how many Monkees LPs there were. Most information at the time that wrote about The Monkees usually only spoke of the big four – the first four Monkees LPs that all went to #1 on the charts. The aforementioned **MORE** and **PISCES**, plus the first LP simply called **THE MONKEES** and the first LP recorded after their freedom and third overall, **HEADQUARTERS**. I was never as fond of these two as the first two I discussed, but they are still fine albums, nonetheless.

The Monkees Tale mentioned albums like **HEAD, INSTANT REPLAY, PRESENT** and **CHANGES**. What were those and why did they record and release them after the TV series went off the air? I thought The Monkees began and ended with the TV show and LPs (I did know about **THE BIRDS, THE BEES AND THE MONKEES** as I had seen it in the thrift shop once and knew it had *Daydream Believer* on it, but didn't own it yet.) There was more to this Monkees story than I originally thought. They even made albums, went on tours and did television appearances as a trio and a duo, and really outstayed their welcome after a flop theatrical movie and a failed TV special while the original TV series settled into the Saturday morning graveyard.

Why was this? Were these latter day projects really as bad as the charts and ratings and box office records reflected? Happily, in most cases, no! Some of these later projects have a creativity, cleverness and originality that were sometimes actually *missing* during The Monkees hit-making days.

I discovered that there was a Monkees fanzine called *Monkee Business Fanzine* in early 1986 and the very first issue I got said that Peter, Micky and Davy were reuniting for a one-off show at The Sheraton-Society Hill Hotel in Philadelphia, Pennsylvania. Rapture! I was so excited that the possibilities of three of the four Monkees were actually willing to sit in one room together was thrilling. The only thing I was annoyed with was that the reunion was to be in Pennsylvania and not in California (where I lived at the time). Fortunately, this one-time appearance blossomed into a full-blown US tour and then some...

And the rest...as they say...is history...

THE MONKEES AND ME
by Michael A. Ventrella

The frustrations of an eight-year-old. Here I was, heading to my Monday night Boy Scout meeting, knowing that I was missing not only *Rowan and Martin's Laugh-In*, but also that new show that came before it, featuring some silly musicians calling themselves *The Monkees*.

So I missed many of the original shows as a kid, catching a few when I was home sick or the meetings were cancelled. But those shows did give me one major life ambition: I was going to be in a rock band some day, where we all live in the same house and have wacky adventures. Isn't that how it worked?

I recall getting the *Daydream Believer* single and singing along with it many times, as well as trying to sing along with the flip side *Goin' Down* (what was Micky singing? It's too fast!). And then I'd get some of the albums used at various backyard sales, and even though they were scratched, it didn't mean much to me because all I had was a little mono record player with one tinny speaker anyway.

By the time *The Monkees* were on Saturday morning television, I was able to catch up with all the episodes I missed, but even then, I found myself more interested in the music than the show. And I still wanted to be in a rock band.

I had taken a few piano lessons when I was younger but didn't have the patience for learning how to read music. But I still loved music, so I began to teach myself to play guitar and piano, writing silly songs for myself. I would arrange the songs in a specific order and pretend they were on albums, drawing the covers myself as well.

By then it was the early 70s and I was starting high school. Boy Scouts ended when I had to make a choice between scouting and the high school's drama club, and the drama club had girls. (Easy decision, actually.) I had collected all of The Monkees albums — even **CHANGES** — and knew them inside and out. I could even do all the voices on the movie clip sections from the **HEAD** album, even though I had never seen the movie. (Remember, this was before video tapes or the internet.)

I of course knew of The Beatles, but at that time I didn't have any of their albums. Then I got **LET IT BE** — not one of their best — and played it endlessly, saying to myself, "Wow, these guys are better than The Monkees!" The Beatles then became my obsession for a while (and I guess they still are), but that doesn't mean I stopped loving The Monkees.

I had already started playing in bands with friends, writing our own songs, and I usually ended up as bassist for two reasons: First, no one else wanted to be the bassist, and second, I admired Paul McCartney and figured if it was good for him, it was good for me.

As life progressed and I went on to college, I organized more impressive bands, playing mostly top 40 hits for high school dances and the like. But then while in col-

lege, something amazing happened. I got together with some of my friends and we started an original band called The Naughty Bits. It was the very late 70s, the dawning of "new age" and "punk" music. We wrote our own songs, similar to the kind of music being done by Elvis Costello and Graham Parker, and got to be quite popular in our hometown of Richmond, Virginia. And the best part? We rented a house near campus, lived in the various rooms on the three floors, and practiced in the basement. It may not have been a beach house with a winding staircase, but it was as close as I'd ever get to being a Monkee. (And we even did a cover of *Steppin' Stone!*)

Life went on and I moved to Boston to go to law school, where I joined two other bands over the years (the most successful being *Agent 99*, named after another 60s TV show). We did an unusual cover of *Last Train to Clarksville*. We'd play it at normal speed but sing the verses in half-time, slowing it down with harmonies. The "oh no no no" part would be sung at regular speed, and then the "I don't know if I'm ever coming home" would be played at twice the normal speed. Try singing it that way in your head and you'll see what I mean — it really works.

I've followed The Monkees ever since, buying many (but not all) of the various solo projects. I saw Peter perform at a small club in Boston around 1982 or so, and got to pat him on the back as he walked to the stage. I saw Micky and Davy perform for free at the World Trade Center in Manhattan around 1995 or so, but I wasn't overly impressed with the Las Vegas-style show they put on. Much more impressive to me was the reunion tour with Mike, Micky and Peter they did around 2014, where the emphasis was on the music (and they even played most of the **HEAD** album, too). That's The Monkees I want to remember.

Micky has always been my favorite. Not only does he have the best singing voice, but I love all of the songs he wrote. I was always disappointed that he didn't continue writing and producing albums after he left The Monkees. It wasn't until years later that I found out he had indeed released some singles that went nowhere. I got to meet him at a Beatles convention, of all things, where he performed a few Beatles songs as well as Monkees songs, and signed autographs. I had him sign my copy of his book, and told him how much his music had meant to me. He didn't say anything, but smiled and held out his hand, and I shook it. In 2017, I went to one of his concerts and got one of his CDs autographed. Probably should have told him I was writing this book, but I didn't want to bug him...

Michael impressed me with his talent, but I've never much been into country music and some of his songs were just too Texas for me. I loved some of his *Elephant Parts* show, though. I made him laugh once on Facebook. He had posted that he was going to be officiating a wedding that weekend, and I wrote "Ah! Look, it's Michael blessing!" and he wrote back the standard "LOL." I was also floored when he friended me on Goodreads without any prompting from me. Maybe he had read that I was working on this book? (Hi, Michael!)

Peter is a great musician, and the more I learn about him the more impressed I am. I was thrilled to be sitting just a few feet away from him at a Monkees convention. I wanted so bad to ask him meaningful questions about music instead of the inane questions certain fans were giving him.

Davy was my least favorite. He was perfect for the TV show, but didn't add anything to the band. He was too Broadway and not enough rock and roll. In fact, the first time Davy had even heard The Beatles' music was when he just happened to be on *The Ed Sullivan Show* as part of the Broadway cast of *Oliver!* the same night as The Beatles' first appearance. He always saw The Monkees gig as an acting job, didn't care much for the music, and after they started having some control over their records, tended to bring in Broadway-like songs that didn't fit The Monkees sound at all.

I have to admit that I have never been one of the fanatics I see on The Monkees Facebook pages or at the one Monkees convention I attended. I don't have the TV shows memorized, nor do I go out of my way to watch them (although when I do see one, I usually say, "Hey, that's not bad.") Yes, they had some great music but there was also some really awful stuff in there as well. When I proposed this book to Mark, we agreed that we would present our views as we really feel and not produce a Monkees puff piece. We wanted to do a "fan's appreciation" as opposed to a learned treatise. And I hope we've accomplished that.

A BRIEF HISTORY OF THE MONKEES
By Mark Arnold

Much has been written about The Monkees from 1965-1971. To recap, Bob Rafelson and Bert Schneider had seen The Beatles in *A Hard Day's Night* and *Help!* and felt that a weekly TV series about a pop/rock band trying to make it would be a potential hit. At first, the real band called The Lovin' Spoonful was considered, but it was deemed that the series would probably be more successful if some real actors were involved.

In the meantime, Davy Jones was signed up for *The Monkees* even before a show was really created. Jones had a fairly successful career on the stage particularly as the Artful Dodger in *Oliver*. Coincidentally, it was Jones that appeared on the very same *Ed Sullivan Show* on February 9, 1964 that The Beatles made their very first live stateside appearance, so a tenuous connection to them was there from the very start, even though it was unintentional.

From there, Jones went on to record the very first LP of the four future Monkees, the eponymously titled **DAVID JONES**, released in 1965. **DAVID JONES** is a pleasant little album, but nothing remarkable. Most of the songs Jones recorded around that time were more of a show tunes type (read: sappy) than what The Monkees as a group would have recorded. This is due to Jones' stage upbringing. Jones would continue to sing showtune-type songs during and after The Monkees, but with The Monkees, Jones proved that he could do something much more rocking like *A Little*

MADNESS!!
AUDITIONS
Folk & Roll Musicians-Singers
for acting roles in new TV series.
Running parts for 4 insane boys, age 17-21
Want spirited Ben Frank's-types.

Have courage to work.

Must come down for interview.

CALL: HO. 6-5188

Bit Me, A Little Bit You, Valleri and *Daydream Believer*, all of which were Davy's biggest hits within the group.

Rafelson and Schneider had taken out the infamous *Variety* ad asking for "Ben Frank's types" which ran on September 8-10, 1965. The only Monkee truly hired from the "Madness!" ad was Michael Nesmith. Nesmith had some limited success with some singles released as far back as 1963, sometimes under the name of Michael Blessing.

The story goes that Nesmith brought his laundry with him to the audition for fear that it would get stolen. Also, he wore the wool hat that became a trademark for him on the first season of the TV show.

Peter Tork came through Stephen Stills, who answered the ad. Stills later found success as part of Buffalo Springfield and Crosby, Stills, Nash (and Young). Tork was similar to Stills in looks and talent and had better teeth.

Micky Dolenz did not come in through the *Variety* ad. As stated on the *Sunday Morning* show on May 29, 2016, Dolenz claimed, "I didn't go to the cattle call. I already had a series, you see." That series was *Circus Boy*, a show that ran from 1956-1958 and starred an 11-year-old Micky, then billed as Mickey Braddock.

The four grouped together after the requisite screen tests and a pilot for *The Monkees* was shot in November 1965, which becomes episode 10 of the resulting series. The first musical recordings occur on January 4, 1966 for Boyce and Hart's *(I'm Not Your) Steppin' Stone*, but not by The Monkees, rather Paul Revere and the Raiders. The Monkees recorded vocals for their version of this and other songs beginning in July 1966.

Filming of *The Monkees* TV series proper began in May 1966, and proceeded through two seasons and 58 episodes, when the show was mutually canceled. NBC considered a third season, but the actors themselves aren't too excited to resume a third series unless they could change the format, and instead decided to focus on their first feature film, eventually called *Head* and released in 1968.

In the meantime, records were also released that became hugely successful. The first single, *Last Train to Clarksville* was released on August 16, 1966, and proceeded to rise to #1. The first Monkees album simply called **THE MONKEES** was released on October 10 and also shot to #1.

This pattern was repeated throughout 1967 as **MORE OF THE MONKEES** (released January 9) **HEADQUARTERS** (released May 22) and **PISCES, AQUARIUS, CAPRICORN AND JONES, LTD.** (released November 6) all reached #1. The TV series did reasonably well and was renewed for a second season. Also, The Monkees had hit singles with *I'm a Believer* (#1, released on November 21, 1966); *A Little Bit Me, A Little Bit You* (#2, March); *Randy Scouse Git (Alternate Title)* (#2, released in UK only on June 16); *Pleasant Valley Sunday* (#3, July 10); and *Daydream Believer* (#1, October 25).

The Monkees' first tour began on September 1-11, 1966, as a quick promotion for the TV show with scant songs performed. It was more of a meet and greet type of affair in most cases. The first proper Monkees tour began on December 3, 1966 with a show in Honolulu, Hawaii. The tour continued as The Monkees were available through May 6, 1967, as they had to coordinate with filming and recording schedules. The tour continued from the US to the UK and back again from June 9, 1967 through August 27, 1967. It was during seven July shows of this leg that the Jimi Hendrix Experience opened for The Monkees. It was during this tour that the **LIVE 1967** recordings came from.

The Monkees did not tour the US in 1968 with the sole exception of one show in Salt Lake City, Utah for the purposes of recording *Circle Sky* for their movie *Head* on May 17. An entire show was performed. They did tour Australia and Japan from September 18 through October 8, 1968.

Season two of *The Monkees* ran from September 11, 1967 through March 25, 1968,

with reruns appearing throughout the summer, until the series was canceled. It returned in reruns on Saturday mornings on September 13, 1969, on CBS.

Only two albums were released during 1968: **THE BIRDS, THE BEES AND THE MONKEES** (#3, April 22) and **HEAD** (#45, December 1). Single releases in 1968 were *Valleri* (#3, March 2); *D.W. Washburn* (#19, June); and *Porpoise Song* (#62, October 5).

On November 27, 1968, Peter Tork tendered his resignation from the group. It was not be the last time he did this (see 2001). Apart from one-off appearances in 1970 and 1976, this was the last time Tork would be a Monkee until 1986. He resigned after completion of his footage shot for the *33 1/3 Revolutions Per Monkee* special televised on April 16, 1969.

As 1969 rolled in, The Monkees were now officially a trio. Their first photo shoot was in Las Vegas on December 7, 1968. During 1969, The Monkees made appearances on various TV shows including *Hollywood Squares*, *The Glen Campbell Goodtime Hour*, *Rowan and Martin's Laugh-In*, *The Tonight Show Starring Johnny Carson* and *The Johnny Cash Show*.

Mickey, Davy and Michael toured the US as The Monkees throughout 1969 from March 29 through December 6, even hitting Canada and Mexico in the process.

Albums released during 1969 included: **INSTANT REPLAY** (#32, February 15), **THE MONKEES' GREATEST HITS** (#89, June 9), **PRESENT** (#100, October 1) and **THE MONKEES' GOLDEN HITS** (released in late 1969 as a mail-order premium from Post cereals). Singles included *Tear Drop City* (#34, February 8); a double A-side: *Someday Man* (#81) and *Listen to the Band* (#47, both April 15); and *Good Clean Fun* (#82, September 6).

As stated earlier, the TV series resumed in Saturday morning reruns beginning on October 13, 1969, on CBS. The **GOLDEN HITS** compilation was the first record to promote this fact. As The Monkees recorded and released new songs, many of them were used as replacement songs on this run.

Nesmith stayed with The Monkees throughout 1969 and then, he too resigned and bought out his contract, beginning in November. He completed his obligations with a number of Kool-Aid ads shot at various intervals through April 14, 1970, for *The Monkees* series' Saturday morning reruns.

Now there were two. Micky and Davy soldiered on. They released **CHANGES**, an album that did not chart originally, in June 1970. The lone single from it, *Oh My My* dented the charts at #98 after its April 1970 release. They made a promotional film of the two riding motorcycles and did a brief tour from May 15 through June 13, 1970, and one final date with Peter Tork on November 21, 1970.

Micky and Davy ended up recording one last time as The Monkees on September 22, 1970 for a non-charting single of *Do it in the Name of Love* b/w *Lady Jane*. The record itself wasn't released until April 1971 on Bell Records, and except in some countries, wasn't released as a Monkees single, but instead like in the US as by "Mickey Dolenz & Davy Jones", with the "e" in Micky.

Going into 1971, Colgems released their final Monkees LP called **BARREL FULL OF MONKEES** in March, a two-volume compilation totally designed to attract the Saturday morning viewer. It didn't chart. On into 1972, Bell Records, the successor to Colgems, released **RE-FOCUS**, another compilation designed to tie in to *The Monkees* moving from CBS to ABC on Saturday mornings. Neither album charted, although technically **RE-FOCUS** did, when it was reissued by Arista Records in July 1976 as **THE MONKEES GREATEST HITS**, to cash in on the Dolenz, Jones, Boyce and Hart tour, where it charted at a reasonable #58.

With the possible exception of Michael Nesmith, none of The Monkees on their own garnered even a hint of the success the four members had as a group, as noble as those solo projects have been. Even The Beatles had albums of solo success that were equal to the levels of their group efforts: **BAND ON THE RUN** or **ALL THINGS MUST PASS** anyone?

After The Monkees dwindled from four to three to two, Jones recorded his second (and amazingly final) major album after the breakup in 1971. Released on Bell Records, the successor to The Monkees' Colgems label, **DAVY JONES** almost worked as a Monkees album excepting the fact that having Micky Dolenz vocals on a few tracks was sorely missed. Strangely, Jones' biggest post-Monkees success was with a song called *Girl*, which was never originally released on an album and that may have hurt the future of Jones' subsequent music career because it wasn't on the LP. The fact that the song lived on forever in *Brady Bunch* reruns reconfirmed the necessity of how important TV exposure always was important for songs to become hits.

Jones recorded a few more singles for Bell and MGM and one would think that these would have been compiled to make some sort of album, but they never have been. Jones was then quietly dropped from the label and removed from the latest teen magazines in favor of David Cassidy, Bobby Sherman and groups like The Tony DeFranco Family and The Bay City Rollers.

Jones did release a few more solo albums on minor labels and a couple live albums were released in Japan only, but overall, his success outside The Monkees was rather limited. Surprising, since Jones always maintained his looks, charm and figure, it seemed like he could have achieved more, but Hollywood is a talent gobbler and the public moved on.

More surprising than Davy's lack of post-Monkees success was that of Micky Dolenz. Since Dolenz sang on most of The Monkees' biggest hits, one would think that he would have been a shoo-in for a successful post-Monkees singing career provided that he surrounded himself with talented songwriters and musicians.

Strangely, apart from a few MGM and Romar singles, Dolenz didn't even bother releasing an album on his own and when he finally did in 1991, it was a children's album cheekily titled **MICKY DOLENZ PUTS YOU TO SLEEP**. That and 1994's follow-up **BROADWAY MICKY** were pleasant diversions and recommended listening for those who enjoy Dolenz's vocal stylings. They were somewhat puzzling considering that Dolenz could have kickstarted a rocking type of career circa 1972 or 1973 that never happened. Dolenz himself has gone on record that he was wandering in the wilderness during those years and this truly was a coffin nail in establishing himself as a viable solo artist.

Dolenz instead focused on his acting, performing many, many guest spots, but strangely no regular series roles, although he did try out for the role of Fonzie on *Happy Days* (1974-1984), but lost out to Henry Winkler. Micky had no other successes, unless one counted his Hanna-Barbera voiceover work for *The Funky Phantom* (1971-1973), *Butch Cassidy* (1973-1974), *Devlin* (1974-1976), *These Are the Days* (1974-1976) and *The Skatebirds* (1977-1978) and others. This direction was not surprising since he was the only Monkee to have a previous successful series *Circus Boy* (1956-1957). He also had a semi-successful directing career which ironically began with the final episode of *The Monkees* TV series.

Dolenz finally rebounded recording-wise and recorded two Monkees-worthy albums **KING FOR A DAY** (2010) and **REMEMBER** (2012). Assuming that the most-recent Monkees reunion tour was the last and there are no further group albums, Dolenz may be the only place to satisfy that Monkee craving if he continues to record albums of this quality.

Which brings us to the confusing career of Peter Tork. Tork was so dissatisfied with The Monkees experience that he was ready to quit the first time he was turned away from a recording session while holding a guitar, in 1966. One would think with two years of a TV show and recordings, Tork could have parlayed that into a music career, even as a session guitarist, but he ran out of money, didn't secure recording contracts and even landed in jail for a time.

His first non-Monkees release was a single cover of *(I'm Not Your) Steppin' Stone* in 1981 which went nowhere. He finally released his first solo album **STRANGER THINGS HAVE HAPPENED** in 1994. Its only bright spot was the song *Milkshake* as it featured guest appearances by Micky Dolenz and Michael Nesmith. Since it was almost a complete Monkees reunion, it is included within The Monkees discography discussion in this book. The rest of **STRANGER THINGS** uncovered a sad realization, Tork cannot sing — or to be kinder — cannot sing consistently well.

Tork has freely admitted on many Monkees tours that he didn't sing on most Monkees songs save for *Your Auntie Grizelda*, but it was disenchanting to discover that he really doesn't have the strongest voice. Besides *Grizelda*, Tork shined best on the latter day Monkees albums **POOL IT!** and **GOOD TIMES!**

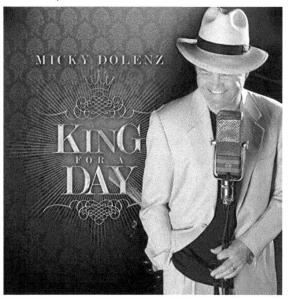

Also, Tork has recorded a number of bluegrass albums as part of the group Shoe Suede Blues. These, like many other Monkees solo albums, don't really sound like Monkees albums.

Finally, we come to the career of Michael Nesmith. Michael Nesmith was usually tagged as the sole dissenter from a reunion with good reason — as the inheritor of his mother's Liquid Paper fortune coupled with Nesmith's lengthy (if unspectacular, chartwise) solo career and his recent TV ventures, Nesmith had the least to prove and the least to gain from reuniting with his former co-stars. In fact, it could have been detrimental to his career. He had actually released nine studio albums, one live album and one greatest hits compilation during the 1970s and even had a minor hit in the US with a song called *Joanne* with his First National Band.

So, from 1971-1975, The Monkees were considered a thing of the past. The Saturday morning run of the TV series ran its course and by August 1973, it breathed its last on network TV. From 1966-1973, it had run on all three of the major networks: NBC from 1966-1968; CBS from 1969-1972; and ABC from 1972-1973, before it entered a new life in syndication.

It was at this point where the four Monkees met to discuss the possibilities of re-forming, even for a McDonald's commercial which was an item up for consideration. Nesmith pretty much vetoed any involvement in anything and Tork was almost as adamant, and surely didn't want to do the McDonald's commercial as he was a vegetarian, so Dolenz and Jones teamed up with Tommy Boyce and Bobby Hart, the writers of a good many of The Monkees' songs, and went out on tour.

The two Monkees who were in the final line-up in 1970, appeared on stage together as part of a short-lived group from July 4, 1975 through March 1977 called Dolenz, Jones, Boyce and Hart that spawned one studio and later one live album (both eponymously named). The tour was called *The Great Golden Hits of The Monkees Show*. Peter joined the group for the encore on July 4, 1976 at Disneyland for *Last Train to Clarksville* and *(Theme from) The Monkees*. This was the first time that these three took the stage since a one-off performance on November 21, 1970 at the Valley REC Center in Van Nuys, California.

The three also got together in late 1976 to record a Davy Jones Fan Club single called *Christmas is My Time of Year* (reviewed later in this book). Micky and Davy also toured together in 1977 (not billed as The Monkees) and performed and released an LP (albeit in Japan) of Harry Nilsson's **THE POINT** in September 1977. (Note: All of these projects occurred long before I became a fan and apart from the Christmas single, none of them are truly considered Monkees projects, just projects that happened to have two or three of the actors who formerly played Monkees on TV.)

From 1978 through 1985, the various ex-Monkees released infrequent records and separately toured Japan, but strangely were mostly under the radar. Arista released **MORE GREATEST HITS OF THE MONKEES** in 1982, followed by **MONKEES BUSINESS** in 1982 and **MONKEE FLIPS** in 1984, the latter two by Rhino Records, their first involvement with The Monkees.

Then, three events led to a 20th anniversary reunion tour that began on May 24 and ran through December 3, 1986. One was the fact that the music station MTV (which has its origins with Michael Nesmith and Popclips) was now rerunning the old TV series which hadn't been syndicated on TV very widely in recent years. Now it was once again being shown nationally to a very receptive audience. The second was *The Monkees Tale* book, as this was the first time a book really discussed The Monkees seriously. The third and possibly least cited reason was Michael Nesmith's *Elephant Parts* and *Television Parts* shows. So, in some strange coincidence, Michael Nesmith was the biggest proponent for two of the three reasons that The Monkees properly reunited for the first time in 15 years, and the fact that he remained elusive as a Monkee perpetuated the mythology.

That all changed during The Monkees concert on September 7, 1986 at The Greek Theatre in Los Angeles, where one Michael Nesmith sauntered onstage for the encore to play *Listen to the Band* and *Pleasant Valley Sunday* with the other three! The reunion was complete!

For now, this was a one-off deal as everyone would have to be content with this. (Note: I personally invested in a bootleg of this concert appearance as I felt like most others that this would be it — Michael's sole nod to his past.)

Fortunately, this was not the case as Nesmith appeared with the other Monkees on an MTV Christmas special aired on December 5, 1986 singing Christmas carols. Nesmith was disguised as Santa Claus, but right at the end, he pulled off his hair and beard to reveal that it was indeed he as Santa.

Also, on July 15, 1986, the very first episodes of *The Monkees* TV series was released to home video (Beta, VHS and 12" laserdisc). The complete series would not be fully released until 1995.

Unfortunately, after this MTV cut off the momentum of The Monkees and 1987 through 1989 were years of diminishing returns (similar to what had happened 20 years before!), by cutting back coverage of The Monkees and played their reruns with less frequency and eventually, not at all.

The Monkees (well at least Micky and Peter) had cut three new tracks for a new CD compilation released in 1986 on Arista Records called **THEN AND AND NOW...THE BEST OF THE MONKEES** and one of them (*That Was Then, This is Now*) was a respectable hit. Strangely, The Monkees also participated in blocking their momentum when they re-released *Daydream Believer* as the follow-up single instead of *Anytime, Anyplace, Anywhere*, a song which stood to become an even bigger hit than *That Was Then*. Due to Davy Jones' jealousy or animosity for not participating in these recordings, he actually left the stage while the other two performed any of these new songs and certainly didn't want any more of them released as singles. The seeds of the second break-up were sown. A live album of the 1986 tour appeared on vinyl and later on CD at Monkees shows; however the name "Monkees" does not appear officially as Micky, Davy and Peter had not secured the rights to use it on albums just yet.

Hey, hey it's the Monkees again when NICKELODEON premieres The Monkees, Monday, September 1 at 7:30 PM (ET). Catch their hilarious antics Monday through Saturday at 7:30 PM (ET).

The animated adaptation of Louisa May Alcott's LITTLE WOMEN, chronicles the lives of four sisters facing maturity, romance and hardship during the Civil War. This special delivery premieres Saturday, September 6 from 2:00–3:30 PM (ET) on NICKELODEON.

Rhino Records also saw fit to reissue all of the Colgems albums again, but only on vinyl. CDs for the later albums post-**PISCES** wouldn't happen until 1994. Arista did finally release the first four albums onto CD with no bonus tracks and inferior booklets in 1989. Amazingly, the first five Monkees albums recharted including the ninth album **CHANGES** from 1970 which finally broke into the charts for the first time and made it up to #152!

By 1987, the three were still on good enough terms to record **POOL IT!**, usually regarded as the worst platter ever released by the group. Songs like *Heart and Soul* have some merit; *She's Moving in With Rico*, not so much. There was a video documentary released by Rhino called *Heart and Soul* about the making of the album. It was later re-released with the **POOL IT!** reissue in 2012. A planned 1988 Christmas album follow-up never came to pass.

More exciting for fans from 1987 were the two archival releases by Rhino — **MISS-ING LINKS**, featuring a number of songs recorded by the group back in the 60s, but for whatever reasons remained unreleased. Some of these songs were actually better than some of the songs actually released by the group back then. The other was **LIVE 1967**, proving once and for all that at this early stage, The Monkees were a competent live touring band and not just a group of TV actors.

Two more **MISSING LINKS** compilations were to be released in the years that followed as well as the complete 1967 live recordings, which admittedly become a little redundant, since The Monkees performed the same few songs on stage during the course of that tour, not deviating even a little bit.

As if that weren't enough, in 1987, as a last gasp attempt by Columbia Pictures, a new group of actors were recruited to form The New Monkees. They lasted long enough to issue a single eponymous album with a single (*What I Want*) and a TV series that only lasted 13 episodes before hanging it up. The New Monkees reunited once in 2007, and if they continue to do so, maybe they will get a book of their own someday. Otherwise, enough about them, and back to the real deal. Incidentally, the original Monkees settled out of court for the use of their name.

The Monkees toured Australia in 1987 and 1988 and Europe and Japan in 1989 as well as the United States all of those years.

Before the reunion petered out in 1989, all four Monkees reunited a couple more times. First and foremost, after some pre-tour interviews, all four made a full-concert appearance at the Universal Ampitheatre in Los Angeles on July 9, 1989, where they performed 33 songs. Then, all four were present for the unveiling of The Monkees' star on the Hollywood sidewalk Walk of Fame on July 10, 1989, and by September 3rd with the final threesome Monkees concert, it was all over... for now.

All was dormant once again in Monkee-land and it seemed like the extended 20th anniversary tour would be the last gasp we would ever hear from any of these former Monkees as a group. But then in 1993, things began stirring up again. Micky and Davy appeared together in a TV commercial for Monsanto. This was short of miraculous as apparently Davy wasn't completely enamored with comments that Micky made in Micky's 1993 autobiography called *I'm a Believer*, but it wasn't enough to stop Davy and Micky from touring together as The Monkees starting on July 19, 1994.

Also in 1994 and 1995, Rhino Records released or re-released *all* of The Monkees albums to CD, along with additional bonus tracks not previously found on the three **MISSING LINKS** collections as they had finally secured all the rights for The Monkees from their previous label, Arista (which was the direct descendent of Colgems and Bell Records), as well as their famous guitar-shaped logo. This was because original Monkees creators Bert Schneider and Bob Rafelson won a lawsuit against Columbia Pictures that resulted in them gaining complete ownership of everything Monkees. Schneider and Rafelson quickly turned around and sold these new assets completely to Rhino Records. A wise choice.

Micky Dolenz and Michael Nesmith also joined Peter Tork on the track *Milkshake* for his very first solo album entitled **STRANGER THINGS HAVE HAPPENED**, released on 1994. This album also contained a studio version of *MGBGT* and Peter's versions of *Take a Giant Step*, (here called *Giant Step*) and *Gettin' In* from **POOL IT!**, and *Your Love Keeps Liftin' Me (Higher and Higher)* (here called *Higher and Higher*), which Peter also played on latter-day Monkees tours.

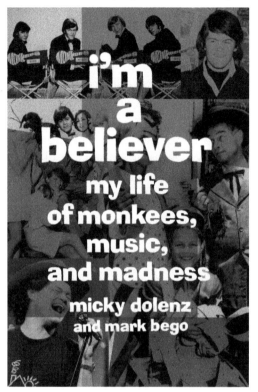

In 1995, Peter, Micky and Davy appeared with Ringo Starr in a Pizza Hut commercial for their new cheese crust pizza. Ringo shouts out, "Lads, the time has come…" to which everyone was hoping for a Beatles reunion (which ironically happened this year with the release of *The Beatles Anthology* TV documentary and album series), but which ended up with Ringo reunited with the three Monkees after saying, "…to eat our pizza crust first," and ended with "Wrong lads!" when he saw that it's The Monkees instead of Paul McCartney or George Harrison. Funny and clever. Critics said, "Well, this wouldn't work because you have two drummers with Micky and Ringo." Blah, blah, blah. It's funny, since Mike rarely appeared with The Monkees and well, you got it.

The three Monkees also made appearances in strange places including *A Very Brady Sequel* (1996), after Davy appeared alone in *The Brady Bunch Movie* (1995) and separately and together on *Boy Meets World* (singing *My Girl* and *Not Fade Away* of all things) on November 17, 1995 in an episode entitled "Rave On". Michael Nesmith was supposedly in attendance for this taping, but did not appear.

Michael *did* appear when all four were issued platinum records for their first five albums on January 5, 1995, at the Hard Rock Cafe in Hollywood, California.

Also, on October 17, 1995, the complete *Monkees* TV series was released for the first time to home video on VHS. Previously, only random episodes had been released to VHS and Beta since 1986. The series was also released piecemeal from the Columbia House Video Club.

All of these events led to the now inevitable 30th anniversary tour with Micky, Davy and Peter that kicked off on June 8, 1996. This anniversary went even further. All *four* Monkees participated in a brand new album recording called **JUSTUS**, released on October 15, 1996, with songs recorded June through August. Although the album was welcome, it was still somewhat disappointing that Nesmith's only lead vocal was on a remake of *Circle Sky* and re-recorded songs from other sources (*You and I* for example, wasn't a remake of a song done by The Monkees for **INSTANT REPLAY**; instead it was a remake of a song originally done for the 1976 **DOLENZ, JONES, BOYCE AND HART** album!).

The big deal at the time was that this was the first album made in the same way as **HEADQUARTERS**, meaning literally just them or "just us", however, if this was they best they could do completely on their own in 1996, they might be better just continuing with the oldies tours.

So tour they did. Peter rejoined Micky and Davy for the 1996 tour starting in March, while Michael remained in the studio to complete work on the new LP. Then, Mike finally did the impossible, he actually joined the other three not just for an encore, not for an entire show, but for an entire tour. Unfortunately for Americans, Michael rejoined The Monkees for a tour of the UK in 1997. However, prior to this Michael did perform for the others at one show on November 20, 1996 at Billboard Live! in Los Angeles.

To cap off this 30th anniversary and celebration of a new album, The Monkees made one more television episode — jokingly referred to as episode 781 as if they never stopped producing new episodes since 1968. It aired on February 17, 1997, on ABC called *Hey, Hey, It's The Monkees*. This was immediately preceded by a documentary that aired on January 22, 1997 called *Hey, Hey We're The Monkees*.

Disappointingly, Michael bowed out for the US leg of the 1997 tour and so the 1996 UK tour remained the final time all four Monkees toured together and on October 21, 1997, this reunion was done. This time, all four Monkees were very close to signing a deal with Rhino Records to do a brand new feature film for 1998, but Davy Jones was the sole holdout, demanding an impossibly high amount of money. It was supposed to be a million dollars to split among the four, but Davy wanted a million for himself.

On November 17, 1998, four episodes of *The Monkees* TV series were issued onto DVD in a package entitled *Our Favorite Episodes* with commentary by the four. This was the first Monkees DVD ever issued. The complete series would not be issued onto DVD until 2003.

Daydream Believers: The Monkees Story was aired on June 28, 2000. This time other actors portrayed The Monkees to tell their story, and if one obtains the DVD version, there are multiple commentary tracks by three of the real Monkees, but otherwise all was quiet about new Monkees projects until 2001. There was also a *VH1: Behind the Music* special on The Monkees this year and Rhino Handmade released **HEADQUARTERS SESSIONS** on September 21, 2000, featuring three CD's of unreleased material.

The 35th anniversary reunion was relatively short-lived, lasting one American tour from March 1, 2001 through August 24, 2001, when Peter handed in his resignation, citing the excessive partying ways of his fellow Monkees as the reason. He played through August 31, 2001. Micky and Davy carried on and continued the tour obligations of September 7 and 8, October 13 and December 1, and canceled the rest of the shows. Peter stayed long enough for the March 2001 Las Vegas shows to be recorded and released again as a live album without The Monkees name and sold at tours called **2001: LIVE IN LAS VEGAS!**

A recording of the final Peter show from August 31, 2001 surfaced officially on January 28, 2003 as **LIVE SUMMER TOUR**. There was also a DVD of this show released November 12, 2002, in abbreviated form. A massive letter-writing campaign concluded with a limited edition release of 1000 copies of the complete concert in 2004. Another live CD from this tour with a slightly different song lineup appeared as **EXTENDED VERSIONS** on September 29, 2003. This CD did feature The Monkees' name and logo.

Due to the rising popularity of the Internet and the infighting of the actual Monkees that seemed to have become permanent, Maggie McManus' *Monkee Business Fanzine* released their final issue with #101 in June 2002.

In that final issue the 2002 Micky-Davy tour was discussed. The UK portion of the 2001 tour was pushed back into 2002 due to the events of September 11, 2001, in New York. This tour went from January 11, 2002 from Canada to the UK and then back to the US, concluding on September 14, 2002. As with the previous year, a live CD sold at concerts only called **MONKEEMANIA 2002 LIVE IN TORONTO** featuring Micky and Davy. The shows no longer featured Peter or Michael songs (save for things like *Listen to the Band*) and instead showcased things like Davy's *Oliver Medley* and *Girl* from *The Brady Bunch*, which were both also performed during the 2001 tour and Peter's *Two-Part Invention in F*! Even *That Was Then, This is Now* was back in the set, and this time, Davy stayed on stage and sang along!

In 2003, *The Monkees* TV series was released to DVD in two little single season record-shaped boxes; season one on May 13; season two on November 18. The series was reissued in two single-season standard slipcase boxes on September 27, 2011. There were some bonus features like the 1969 *33 1/3 Revolutions Per Monkee* special and many commentaries added.

For the 40th anniversary in 2006, all was quiet on The Monkees front, and the celebration passed without note, excepting that the first four albums were reissued as two-disc sets with stereo and mono recordings and additional tracks from Rhino Records. Other new Monkees compilations continued to be released, sometimes with new unreleased tracks, and all three hit the road — separately — off and on from 2003 to 2010.

In 2010, Rhino Handmade started expanding their Monkees albums even further with the release of **THE BIRDS, THE BEES AND THE MONKEES DELUXE EDITION** containing three discs of released and unreleased materials as well as booklets and vinyl singles and other goodies. This was soon following over the next few years for expanded **DELUXE EDITIONS** of **HEAD, INSTANT REPLAY, PRESENT, LIVE 1967** and **THE MONKEES**. It's highly likely that the remaining Monkees albums will follow suit over the next few years. **HEADQUARTERS SESSIONS** even got an abbreviated

2012 vinyl release called **SELECTIONS FROM THE HEADQUARTERS SESSIONS**.

Cut back to 2011 and The Monkees' 45th anniversary. *Rolling Stone*, in its March 7, 2011 issue stated, "In 2009 Jones told the *National Enquirer* that he had no interest in a reunion, adding that he 'couldn't imagine sharing a stage with Micky Dolenz.'

"In a significant shift, Tork now takes full responsibility for the backstage problems on the 2001 tour. 'We were getting along pretty well until I had a meltdown,' he

says. 'I ticked the other guys off good and proper and it was a serious mistake on my part. I was not in charge of myself to the best of my ability — the way I hope I have become since. I really just behaved inappropriately, honestly. I apologized to them.'

"He now says alcohol played only a small role in the group's problems. 'I'm sure it played a part, but I cannot honestly say it was anything more than a very slight part,' he says. 'It could have been very, very minor. But the main thing was that I had a meltdown and I messed up.'"

So a new tour was undertaken with the three Monkees beginning May 12, 2011 in England and ending July 23, 2011, in the US. Plans were discussed for a 2012 tour when the untimely death of Davy Jones of heart failure occurred on February 29, 2012. (Note: I had seen Davy on February 11 and 12 at the Hollywood Autograph Show and had gotten his autograph. If someone had placed bets on which celebrity would not make it through the end of the month, I doubt that anyone there would have picked Davy Jones. *Mission: Impossible*'s Martin Landau, who was 83 at the time and looking not so well, is still with us as of this writing. Carla Laemmle, who was 101 at the time, died in 2014 at the age of 104. Both were at the show.)

Davy had started a solo tour, but his final show was on February 19, 2012. Micky and Peter held a moving tribute show on April 3. Micky began a solo tour on June 10, 2012 and also appeared at a later Hollywood Autograph Show than Davy that year. Then, the most unlikely thing happened.

The *other* three Monkees reformed and they went on the road together. The fact that Michael *finally* decided to go on a tour with Micky and Peter after all of these years and especially after the death of Davy, didn't sit well with everyone. It had been years since Michael toured even by himself in the US, so it was kind of sad that it took Davy's death for Michael to finally agree to perform with them again. It seemed that there must have been some sort of animosity between Michael and Davy, but Michael set the record straight and said there wasn't.

The Micky, Peter, Michael version of The Monkees ran from November 8 through December 2, 2012, and again from July 18 through August 15, 2013 and May 22 through June 7, 2014.

In March 2014, the three Monkees appeared at the American Pop Music Hall of Fame; different from the Rock and Roll Hall of Fame, where The Monkees are still severely neglected. After the 2014 tour which was also interspersed with solo Monkees shows, Michael once again called it quits.

The 2015 Monkees tour only had Micky and Peter and ran on and off from March 27 through September 6, 2015 in the US and the UK.

2016: The Monkees 50th Anniversary *and* a brand new Monkees album! **GOOD TIMES!** was released on May 26, 2016 to generally rave reviews and chart success, peaking at #14, the highest placement for a Monkees album since **THE BIRDS, THE BEES AND THE MONKEES** peaked at #3 in 1968. This time instead of composing all the songs themselves, The Monkees (including Michael) solicited songwriters from Weezer, Oasis and XTC among others to compose new material for them in the Monkee vein.

Nesmith contributed a new tune and even sang on a few, singing lead on three of them. Other songs were taken from the Monkee vaults that were only backing tracks with new vocals laid down and even Davy Jones was represented with the song *Love to Love* which did previously appear on **MISSING LINKS, VOLUME 3** minus some overdubs. Overall, it's generally considered to be a fine album and a great way to finish their career, should The Monkees decide not to release any more new albums. Michael did make a few interview appearances with Micky and Peter to promote the album, most notably on CBS's *Sunday Morning* on May 29, 2016.

The Monkees TV series was released to Blu-Ray on June 27, 2016. It's a limited edition of 10,000 with tons of bonus features including *Head* and *33 1/3 Revolutions Per Monkee*, but sadly no *Hey, Hey, It's The Monkees*.

Micky and Peter began yet another Monkees tour on February 18, 2016, and this time Michael did show up on a couple of occasions, most notably on June 1 in New York via Skype and in person on August 5 in Monterey, California and September 16 in Los Angeles at the Pantages Theatre. Michael has hinted strongly that the September 16th show would be his last with The Monkees. He didn't rule out future solo concerts, however.

Four additional tracks from the **GOOD TIMES!** sessions and released in various configurations including CD bonus tracks, a 7" single and in streaming form, were finally compiled together and released as a 10" Record Store Day vinyl called **GOOD TIMES PLUS**, on November 25, 2016.

The 2016 tour continued with Micky and Peter through November in the US, before they embarked on a tour of Australia and New Zealand in December. However, Mike once again Skyped in an appearance.

Asked when it will all truly stop, Peter said on *Sunday Morning*, "We'll tour until one of us drops, and then the other will go on as 'The Monkee'," but there were announcements that the final date of the Australian tour on December 16, would indeed be The Monkees' last.

As for 2017, Micky has indeed continued on as 'The Monkee' in concert, with Peter and Michael seemingly now retired from performing, although Mike is scheduled for some dates to promote his autobiography and new CD compilation. Peter has now joined Micky on the comic con autograph circuit, appearing at a number of Wizard World conventions, and at press time, the duo plan to do a tour of Greece.

THE MONKEES MUSIC

By Michael A. Ventrella

Music changed tremendously between 1966 and 1970. January 1966 began with *We Can Work it Out*. By 1967, The Beatles had given us **SGT. PEPPER**. Later in the year, *I Am The Walrus* expanded music even greater, and by the end of 1970, we were listening to *My Sweet Lord*.

The radio in 1970 sounded nothing like it did in 1966. There was no other time in musical history where music so drastically changed in such a short period of time.

And in the middle of all that were The Monkees.

That's why we decided to arrange this book in chronological order based on recording dates. Instead of a research book — an encyclopedia of songs — we would rather have you read this from start to finish. This way, you can see how the music changed, not only in response to what was happening elsewhere in the music world, but within The Monkees' own eras: The Boyce/Hart beginning, the Don Kirshner hits, the "we're a real band" rebellion, the "three solo artists sharing an album", the "we're just the singers", and the various reunions finally leading to **GOOD TIMES!** which tries to place us right back at the beginning again, full circle.

We'll also discuss the albums themselves in their proper times.

This organization is also important because many of The Monkees songs were released long after their recording dates — it's why *Tear Drop City* seems so out of place on the same album as *Shorty Blackwell*. Not all songs fit into this pattern, of course. If the song only had minor remixing years later, we still included it in the earlier time.

Many songs were also re-recorded over time. The version heard on the TV show may not be the one heard on the record. (And sometimes the TV show would speed up a song to make it fit into the show's time constraints!) When there is a conflict, we consider the songs on the twelve main albums as the "official" versions.

We include many songs that were never intended to be released but have seen the light of day through the **MISSING LINKS** albums and the other extended CD versions of various LPs. However, we'll also ignore some of them too. Some of those extras are just rehearsals, parts of songs, unfinished bits, and things that honestly you're not missing if you never hear. So please excuse us if we don't discuss extended CD track 17: "Micky burps into the microphone."

We also list significant other versions that were done of Monkees songs. We originally started to list as many as we could find, but then it got to the point where we were listing every garage band in America that had ever recorded *Steppin' Stone* and uploaded it to You Tube, so now we're just listing major cover versions that you might be interested in checking out.

My goal for this book is to discuss the songs as a musician and songwriter looks at them, paying attention to the structure of the song and the performance of it. That's the thing about music: Once you understand how it is made, you never look at it the same (or is it "hear it the same"?).

I don't know how to read music very well. I'm not going to discuss aoelian cadences or other technical words that someone with a Master's Degree in music would understand because I don't understand them either. This book is for people who just like music, even if we don't always know why we like it.

My wife is an artist. She has a Master's Degree in art. When we go to an art show or museum, I can appreciate works of art just fine but she sees things in the art I never notice. And it's the same when I listen to music — I notice and hear things she doesn't. So I hope to discuss some of that with this book.

Mark comes at this from a different direction than I do, and we disagree a lot on some of the songs; we hope that will make this a more fun read for you as well.

Our suggestion is to go to our web page and listen along to each song as you read about it. And if you can't find the song on our page, most of these songs can be found on YouTube.

By the way, you can also give *your* comments about the songs on the web page as well. (monkees.wordpress.com) We've included a few of the more interesting ones we've received here.

Finally, keep in mind the fact that neither Mark nor I claim to be Monkees experts. We're fans. We're fans who have done our research, but we're coming at this not as a historical book but as fans talking to other fans about the music. Keep in mind as well that some of the facts we present here are what we believe to be true, but you can always find someone who has a different opinion of what the facts are. As a criminal defense attorney, I am well aware that two people can experience something and have completely different memories of what happened, and when you're talking about The Monkees and all of the people involved and all the fans, some stories may not necessarily be true or may be completely exaggerated. Take *all* history you read with a skeptical eye.

DAVID PEEL of The Lower East Side (*The Pope Smokes Dope, Hippie from New York City, Have a Marijuana*) and good friend to John Lennon.

The Monkees ARE The Monkees FOREVER The Monkees AS A CLASSIC POP & TV BAND ... LONG LIVE The Monkees!!"

CHRONOLOGICAL SONGOGRAPHY BY LAST RECORDING DATE

(WITH SOME EXCEPTIONS AS NOTED).

**Special thanks to Rhino Records and Andrew Sanoval
for help in compiling this list.**

TAKE A GIANT STEP (Gerry Goffin/Carole King)
Monkee involvement: Vocals by Micky Dolenz
Recording dates: June 10, 1966; July 9, 1966
Highest chart position: uncharted single B-side
Original release date: August 16, 1966 from 7" single and **THE MONKEES**
Significant other versions: Taj Mahal

Mark: Fairly progressive sounding stuff for the very first song not recorded, but completed by The Monkees replete with such instruments as a harpsichord, glockenspiel and an oboe. This song was strong enough to be placed as the B-side of *Last Train to Clarksville*, but not strong enough to chart in its own right. Regardless, this song remains one of The Monkees' strongest songs ever, compositionally, lyrically, instrumentally and vocally. I've always liked that little "rattle" sound on every verse.

The Beatles hadn't even released **RE-VOLVER** yet. The Beach Boys had just released **PET SOUNDS** and The Rolling Stones had released **AFTERMATH** a couple months earlier, so sound experimentation and expansion was just beginning. The Beatles' **RUBBER SOUL** had come out at the tail end of 1965, with a few new instruments like sitars added to the mix, so instruments besides the standard guitars, bass and drums soon became the order of the day.

A great song and an excellent song to kickstart The Monkees' recording career, especially in light of the fact that the TV series was not to premiere for another two or three months.

A mono TV version of the song appears on **THE MONKEES SUPER DELUXE EDITION** (2014).

Michael: Starting off with a Goffin/King number is a good sign that maybe this will work out. And in fact, that is one of the reasons The Monkees music has lasted — they had the best writers available at the time, people who knew what made a good song.

Gerry Goffin and Carole King had been hit-makers for years before The Monkees. Carole had not yet gone on to record her own music yet (that would come with the 1970 huge best-seller **TAPESTRY**) but just look at some of the songs they had written previous to this one: *Some Kind of Wonderful, Halfway to Paradise, Chains, The Loco-Motion, Go Away Little Girl, Up On the Roof, Hey Girl, One Fine Day...* those are only a few of the hits they had written prior to *Take a Giant Step.*

What makes this an unusual start though is the feel of the song. The jangly guitar is accompanied by an eastern feel, with bells and an oboe. Not your traditional rock and roll pop song of the time.

You know what makes a good melody? Variations. Variations in the notes and the space between the notes. The timing of those notes. Too many songs tend to not vary much in their melodies, relying on the chords to progress the song along.

Now, I can hardly read music, but I think of a song like a graph. You don't have to read music to imagine each note like a point on the graph; the higher the note, the higher it is on the graph. The closer together the notes, the closer on the graph and so on. (This is indeed basically how music is written, but this helps me imagine it better in my mind.) If the notes don't vary much — if they don't rise and fall, if they're always at the same distance from each other — then the song probably becomes monotonous and boring. Variety is the key. (I'll come back to this later in this book when discussing other songs.) Listen to *Take a Giant Step* again and listen to the melody, imagining the notes on a graph and you'll see what I mean. It's what makes the song unique, memorable, and well-written.

The background vocals also provide a counter melody which was still fairly unusual for rock and roll songs at the time. Micky provides this at the later "Come with me..." parts and ends up harmonizing with himself. Very effective.

The lead goes nowhere, but what makes it work is the little tom-tom drum bit off to the side.

The song then smartly repeats the chorus and fades out rather than following the traditional song pattern of verse, verse, chorus, verse, chorus, lead, chorus, verse, chorus. Seriously, if you haven't noticed, 95% of all songs have that pattern — because it works — but knowing when and how to break that pattern is the sign of a good songsmith.

THIS JUST DOESN'T SEEM TO BE MY DAY (Tommy Boyce/Bobby Hart)
Monkee involvement: Vocals by Davy Jones
Recording dates: July 5, 1966; July 9, 1966
Original release date: October 10, 1966 from **THE MONKEES**

Michael: I think Boyce and Hart were listening to The Beatles' *I've Just Seen a Face* when they were writing this one. It had been released in America only a few months previous. The similarities are almost as amazing as the similarities between *Me Without You* and *Your Mother Should Know* (which comes later).

It's not a bad song, but nothing great to recommend it.

Mark: An ode to depression. Mike hits it on the head with this one. I won't repeat how similar sounding this song is to one of the Fabs', but The Monkees (or their writers) are guilty of sounding like other 60s pop songs many times over the years, which may or may not be a good thing. Personally, I think that it's a good thing. The Monkees had the "moon-june-spoon" of times past while their contemporaries were being progressive. The Monkees were progressive along with the best of them when musical progression was the order of the day.

What I will comment on again is on the instrumentation which this time includes a cello and gives the overall sound picture a deeper feel. That was the main goal of these early Monkees tunes: to sound as contemporary as they could. No small feat for an untested concept or show and it pays tribute to the many songwriters for The Monkees especially to Tommy Boyce and Bobby Hart who composed no less than six of the first album's twelve tunes and Tommy Boyce had a hand in writing a seventh with Steve Venet.

A mono TV version and the master backing track of the song appear on **THE MONKEES SUPER DELUXE EDITION** (2014).

SATURDAY'S CHILD (David Gates)
Monkee involvement: Vocals by Micky Dolenz
Recording dates: July 9, 1966
Original release date: October 10, 1966 from **THE MONKEES**
Significant other versions: Herman's Hermits, The Palace Guard

Mark: Although I am not totally fond of this song, I will admit that it is an earworm as it is highly catchy and I have found myself singing it during my leisure time, consarn it! It is now widely regarded as one of their best tracks, but I find it kind of limp, lyrically. One of those "let's mention every day of the week a la *Happy Days*" type of tracks. Granted this song predated that one, but I never really heard it until long after.

What strikes me as highly interesting is the guitar work which of course at this point was by studio musicians with Micky laying down vocals on top; a common practice for virtually every track created for the first two albums, until The Monkees demanded taking things over by their own hands. There is also a little bit more of those "Dave Clark Five" drum fills that are much more prominent on the theme song.

A mono TV version of the song appears on **THE MONKEES SUPER DELUXE EDITION** (2014).

Please note that songs with this title by The Walker Brothers and Hoyt Axton are not this song.

Michael: This was written by David Gates, who later went on to start the band Bread that had a bunch of hits in the 70s. In fact, at the time of this recording, he had already released a dozen or so singles on his own, none of which were hits. Davy later did a cover of Bread's *Look at Me* on his first and only post-Monkees solo album in 1971.

Saturday's Child starts off strong with a heavy guitar hook and lots of cymbal crashes. The hook continues on in the background till the chorus, where it disappears. By the second time it comes in, you feel like saying "Yes, I got it." I mean, it's not really that catchy or anything, is it?

The bridge ("Seven days of the week...") comes in strong, with a cymbal ride, but when the ride ends during the second half of the bridge, the energy of the song goes with it — it just seems empty in comparison. The lead afterwards isn't that great but I like the way the bass and drums pump it up in the second half of the lead.

Overall, not a bad song. Not one of their better, but certainly as good as many of the time.

LET'S DANCE ON (Tommy Boyce/Bobby Hart)
Monkee involvement: Vocals by Micky Dolenz. Backing vocals by Peter Tork.
Recording dates: June 10, 1966; July 5, 1966; July 9, 1966; July 16, 1966
Original release date: October 10, 1966 from **THE MONKEES**

Michael: What a terrible, slapped-together song. It's the kind of song I wrote when I was 14 — predictable and boring, and clearly rushed. I mean, they forgot to add a bass guitar to it even though they made room for the organ solo. Seriously, give me a break.

It sounds like a million other songs, and starts of with the same kind of feel as The Beatles' version of *Twist and Shout*. The only thing I like is the extra long pause after the lead.

The weakest song on the album, which is surprising as by the time the album came out, there were plenty of other songs they had recorded that could have replaced it.

Micky performed this live when I saw him in April of 2017 and it was much improved. For instance, there was a bass. Just goes to show that a good performance can make a bad song worth listening to.

Mark: Definitely the weakest song on the first album. This reeks of "made to order" on the level of "Write us a dance song". They should have swapped out this one for

All the King's Horses (see next entry) instead, but maybe the prevailing thought was that they should have at least one basic dance track in case the more "deeper" cuts with their oboes and glockenspiels and drug-inspired or Vietnam-inspired lyrics were too much to take for the average record buyer. They needn't have worried and *Let's Dance On* becomes a very disposable track indeed with banal lyrics and the very basics of rhythm. Highly forgettable.

The master backing track of the song appears on **THE MONKEES SUPER DELUXE EDITION** (2014).

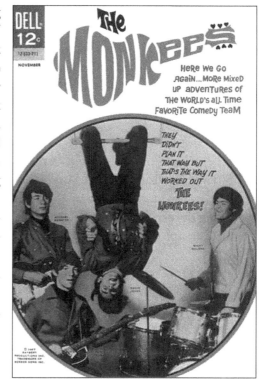

ALL THE KING'S HORSES (Michael Nesmith)
Monkee involvement: Lead vocals by Micky Dolenz; Backing vocals by Michael Nesmith, Peter Tork and Davy Jones.
Recording dates: June 25, 1966; July 16, 1966
Original release date: January 1990 from **MISSING LINKS, VOLUME 2**

Mark: Strangely, even though this song was used in the earliest Monkees' TV show episodes, it was left unreleased at least on record until the second **MISSING LINKS** collection. It appears on "The Spy Who Came in From the Cool" and "Don't Look a Gift Horse in the Mouth" episodes.

You would have thought that it would have found release on a B-side or album track somewhere along the way during the 1960s. Since that time, it has found a space on the 2006 and 2014 deluxe editions of **THE MONKEES**, an album where the song should have been all along.

Lyrically, it's one of Mr. Nesmith's most interesting tunes using nursery rhyme lyrics to describe his broken heart. It appeared on a few Monkees bootlegs before being properly released in 1990.

Michael: This should have been on the first album instead of *Let's Dance On*.

This is Mike's attempt to write a contemporary pop song, and fits in with the time, and you'd think the studio would prefer it to the more country-flavored songs of his they did include on the first album.

What I like is that all of The Monkees are singing on this instead of one Monkee and then backup singers who aren't even in the band. That makes this feel like a true

Monkees song. What I don't like is how everyone drops out except Micky (I think) singing backup on the very last line.

THE KIND OF GIRL I COULD LOVE (Michael Nesmith/Roger Atkins)
Monkee involvement: Vocals by Michael Nesmith. Backing vocals by Micky Dolenz, Davy Jones and Peter Tork. Steel guitar by Michael Nesmith.
Recording dates: June 25, 1966; July 16, 1966
Original release date: January 9, 1967 from **MORE OF THE MONKEES**

Mark: A song held over for the second album, probably due to the fact that there would be too many country-sounding songs on the first album. It's a strong Nesmith song, but once *Papa Gene's Blues* was recorded, this song was shelved.

An alternate mix where the backing vocals are stronger appears on **THE MONKEES DELUXE EDITION** (2006).

A mono TV version of the song appears on **THE MONKEES SUPER DELUXE EDITION** (2014).

Michael: Mike wrote this with Roger Atkins, who is probably best known for writing the Animals' *It's My Life* — he's not known so much for a song he wrote for the first album of a young pop star named David Jones.

Although the vocals sound country-inspired, the performance is basic 60s pop. "More cowbell!" Mike's steel guitar solo is perhaps the only nod to the country music he grew up with.

There really isn't a chorus, is there? It's just verse, verse, bridge, lead, verse. The bridge, as it is, is the best part of the song! I wish he had treated that like the chorus and repeated it. After all, the song doesn't even last two minutes.

SO GOES LOVE (Gerry Goffin/Carole King)
Monkee involvement: Vocals by Davy Jones
Recording dates: July 7, 1966; July 16, 1966
Original release date: July 1987 from **MISSING LINKS**
Significant other versions: The Turtles

Michael: With all the great writers submitting songs for The Monkees, why would they do a cover version? They also later did that with *Steppin' Stone*, but still, they didn't need to.

Goffin and King write good songs, but this one just puts me to sleep. I like how the acoustic guitar works. Davy's voice is just too loud during the bridge. But overall, this is just boring and forgettable. The Turtles' version had more energy and emotion, and this is really weak in comparison. I can see why The Monkees decided not to release this.

Mark: I really love The Turtles' version of this song and as a result, it is understandable why The Monkees decided to shelve this one. Not the worst thing they recorded by Goffin/King, it's just that The Turtles one was so good.

Strangely, their version just ended up as a bonus track on their **GOLDEN HITS** LP, even though it wasn't one — a golden hit, that is.

In regards to The Monkees' version, Davy does a passable job singing, but doesn't achieve the dreamy quality of Howard Kaylan's vocals.

The **MISSING LINKS** version also appears on **THE MONKEES DELUXE EDITION** (2006).

Alternate versions of the song appear on **THE MONKEES SUPER DELUXE EDITION** (2014).

I'LL BE TRUE TO YOU (Gerry Goffin/Russ Titelman)
Monkee involvement: Vocal by Davy Jones
Recording dates: July 9, 1966; July 13, 1966; July 16, 1966
Original release date: October 10, 1966 from **THE MONKEES**
Significant other versions: The Hollies

Mark: When The Hollies did this, the song was called *Yes, I Will*. In fact, they recorded two versions, one in mono and one in stereo. Regardless, it's a fine song sung well by Davy.

A stereo remix of the song appears on **THE MONKEES SUPER DELUXE EDITION** (2014).

Michael: Another cover where the original is better than The Monkees remake. Well, at least they weren't covering well-known hits. I mean, I never knew any of these songs were covers until many years later.

Once more, the Davy version is laid back and is missing the energy of the Hollies' take, even though the production values on The Monkees' version is better.

It's a wonderfully written song, I'll give it that. It's the performance that's lacking. The bridge should have kicked the song into high gear (like The Hollies' version) but that doesn't happen here. And the way Davy reads the third verse instead of singing it is a concept from the old days of rock and roll that had pretty much died by this time.

I WANNA BE FREE (Tommy Boyce/Bobby Hart)
Monkee involvement: Vocals by Davy Jones and Micky Dolenz.
Recording dates: July 19, 1966; July 24, 1966
Original release date: October 10, 1966 from **THE MONKEES**
Significant other versions: Jimmie Rodgers, The Lettermen, Tommy Boyce and
Bobby Hart, Andy Williams, Floyd Cramer

Mark: Yeah, yeah, it's one of those syrupy ballady type things that they typically gave
to Davy to sing, but strangely enough, this time it works. I'll tell you examples later
where it doesn't. Davy emotes to great effect the kind of teen angst necessary to sell
the song and he pulls it off well. The instrumental arrangement is very good as well. It
reminds me of The Rolling Stones' *As Tears Go By*, which I'm sure was intentional.

This song was not released as a single in the US, but was in some countries backed
with *You Just May Be the One*, which is probably the stronger song, but early Monkees
stuff pushed Davy and Micky far more up front than Michael and especially, Peter.

The fast version with Micky singing lead appears on **THE MONKEES DELUXE EDI-
TION** (2006). Micky does a decent job singing, but after hearing Davy all these years,
this is really a Davy song.

A mono TV version of the song and other various versions (seven to be exact)
appear on **THE MONKEES SUPER DELUXE EDITION** (2014). This TV version originally appeared on **MISSING LINKS, VOLUME 2** (1990).

Michael: As I said previously, Davy was my least favorite Monkee. For the most
part, he was given the heartthrob ballads to sing because he was the one all the girls
wanted (or at least that was the image the studio wanted). And Davy was perfect for
that role in the TV show, back in the days where rock and roll was just something
teenagers liked and no adult took seriously.

Davy fit wonderfully into that teeny-bopper mold. He was just not a good fit for a
rock and roll band. I mean, come on, look who did cover versions of this song. Andy
Williams? The Lettermen? Good rock and roll credentials there, fella.

Anyway, this is one of Davy's better songs. His performance here is very good. Of
all the ballads he did, this is one of the best.

Lyrics-wise, I can't say I identify with the singer, who is basically saying, "Hey, baby, I
want to be with you and have all the advantages of our relationship, but I'll be seeing
other girls too, know what I mean? Don't go thinking you mean anything to me." Not
exactly a love song here. It's the opposite of *I'll Be True To You*, recorded days earlier.

GONNA BUY ME A DOG (Tommy Boyce/Bobby Hart)
Monkee involvement: Vocals by Micky Dolenz and Davy Jones. Guitars by Peter Tork.

Recording dates: July 7, 1966; July 23, 1966; July 24, 1966
Original release date: October 10, 1966 from **THE MONKEES**
Significant other versions: Davy Jones

Mark: This was one of those songs I first heard on the old Dr. Demento radio show around 1973 and I really loved it for that reason. At that point, I was not a confirmed Monkees fan and really wanted more of their songs to be like this and *Peter Percival Patterson's Pet Pig Porky* — another Demento favorite. I didn't understand at the time why a musical group that had such a stupid TV show would try to be so serious on records. Hey, I was young. I was six at the time and as mentioned elsewhere, never really cared for the TV series when I was a kid and really didn't discover that The Monkees really put out some excellent songs until the 1980s. And yes, Davy refers to the July

1966 novelty song *They're Coming to Take Me Away, Ha-Haaa!* by Napoleon XIV on this record which was also a Dr. Demento favorite!

This is one of the few instances where Micky and Davy sang together or at least cracked wise together. A straight version of this exists with Davy only when he performed it on *The Farmer's Daughter* TV series. This 1965 version is much faster and shows that it's not that bad of a track. It's the lyrics that are abysmal.

The backing track of the song appears on **THE MONKEES DELUXE EDITION** (2006) and **THE MONKEES SUPER DELUXE EDITION** (2014). This version is heavier on the bass and appears to be a different take than the one used on the final released version.

Michael: You know, sometimes if you try too hard, it stops being funny.

The underlying song is obviously intended to be humorous, but it's just not that funny. Micky and Davy's comments are the only thing that saves it, but then it falls into the dilemma all similar comedy songs have: How many times can you listen to it? It's not funny the 15th time you hear it. (This is why Zappa's songs are good — they're funny *and* musically interesting, so even after the humor factor has worn off, the music still is worth hearing again.)

And when I first heard this as a kid, I thought, "Why aren't Mike and Peter saying anything? I mean, they must have been there playing their instruments, right?" This would have fit the image of the show better had they brought the other two in as well.

Musically, there's nothing here. It's all one chord during the verse, and only two notes. Duh duh duh duh DAH.

At the same time, we have to put this in context. This is a comedy song written for a comedy TV show. No one expected rock and roll songs to last fifty years. No one predicted that people would still be watching The Monkees TV show fifty years later. (Hell, network TV was not even 25 years old at the time The Monkees aired, and rock and roll music was only ten years old or so.) It was just a silly throwaway song meant to be fun for kids in a TV show aimed at teenagers.

The sad part is that at the same time, The Monkees were producing quality music that is still listenable fifty years later. (That's why we wrote this book!) This song doesn't fit that narrative.

LAST TRAIN TO CLARKSVILLE (Tommy Boyce/Bobby Hart)
Monkee involvement: Vocals by Micky Dolenz
Recording dates: July 25, 1966
Highest chart position: #1 single (1 week)
Original release date: August 16, 1966 from 7" single and **THE MONKEES**
Significant other versions: The Plastics, The Replacements, Zilch, Cassandra Wilson

Michael: Here's how you know The Monkees were going to be successful musically: This song hit #1 before the TV show was a hit. Now, admittedly, some of that was due to a promotional push, but it really is a good song that deserved to be a hit.

Songs with the guitar hook played in the lower register at the start of the song were popular at the time: Think of *Day Tripper* and *Paperback Writer*. The Monkees did this with *Saturday's Child*, *Pleasant Valley Sunday* and *Tear Drop City*. The hook is pretty damn simple but memorable.

Remember my comment about notes on a graph? Here's a good example. This song stays in the same chord up till the "oh no no no" part, but the melody is what propels it along.

Boyce and Hart also had some pretty good words, too, not just your normal love song. It's actually about a man going off to fight the Vietnam war wanting to see his girl one last time before they ship him off, because he doesn't know if he's ever coming home.

Mark: The Beatles' *Paperback Writer* inspired this, but so what? That was the point of the earliest Monkees records, to get on track with what the leaders in the music industry were doing, and they did it correctly! I wasn't around at the time, but I'm sure many quibbled about how derivative The Monkees were to The Beatles with this song, but apparently this was of minor concern as the song became a massive hit and was one of three #1 singles for the group.

I used to think that the lyrics were pretty dumb until I read what it was really about. I've since changed my mind

ASK FOR "THE MONKEES" LP ALBUM

and this is indeed one of their greatest songs! It was featured in more episodes of *The Monkees* (seven) than any other song!

Amusingly, The Monkees parodied this song as early as in the "Monkee Chow Mein" episode from season one where Micky and Peter sing it out of tune. And interestingly, there is a road sign in one of the videos that reads "Clarkesville"!

Fan Thoughts

In my rural hometown of Paris, Tennessee, we had one AM station in 1966. Its format was a mixture of farm reports, religious programs, country and vocal (Perry Como, Peggy Lee, etc.) songs and local news. However, in 1965 because of the British Invasion, the station devoted Saturday afternoon to rock and roll. They acquired Clarksville about a month before the television series went on the air and since the Clarksville mentioned in the song was only about 40 miles from Paris, the song got lots of play. In fact Clarksville was #1 on their top ten chart the week before the NBC debut. — Randall Buie

---

TOMORROW'S GONNA BE ANOTHER DAY (Tommy Boyce/Steve Venet)
Monkee involvement: Vocals by Micky Dolenz
Recording dates: July 23, 1966; July 26, 1966
Original release date: October 10, 1966 from **THE MONKEES**
Significant other versions: Dwight Yoakam, Floyd Cramer

Michael: This song starts off very similarly to *Last Train*, which means it shouldn't have been placed on the album right after it. It almost feels like a sequel or a coda that way.

The song progression is pretty predictable, but they break that up with the "tomorrow's gonna be, tomorrow's gonna be, tomorrow's gonna be another day" where all the instruments drop out except the percussion. This works, especially when the harmonies are added with a bit of echo.

Micky sings "Hey hey hey hey! I'm on my way!" in a way that should make Mick Jagger go "Wait a minute, I did that on *Satisfaction!*"

Mark: Great guitar kicks off a basically great song. With it, Micky shows off how versatile he is on The Monkees' first album by being able to shift effortless from a ballad to a pop hit to a harder rocking sound, which this is, especially for 1966. There are echoes of *Last Train to Clarksville*, which I am sure since Tommy Boyce was involved, intentional. Some interesting guitar and harmonica work appears in the middle section.

The backing track of the song appears on **THE MONKEES SUPER DELUXE EDITION** (2014).

(I'M NOT YOUR) STEPPIN' STONE (Tommy Boyce/Bobby Hart)
Monkee involvement: Vocals by Micky Dolenz
Recording dates: July 26, 1966
Highest chart position: #20 single B-side
Original release date: November 12, 1966 from 7" single and **MORE OF THE MONKEES**
Significant other versions: Paul Revere and the Raiders, Peter Tork, The Sex Pistols, Liverpool Five, Tom Petty and the Heartbreakers, Johnny Thunders, The Flies

Mark: A great, great song, especially for the whiny, droning guitar that is the song's signature sound. Methinks that it was a strong contender for an A-side, but ended up as the B-side to *I'm a Believer*. There are differences between the album and single versions.

Michael: I've never been much of a fan of this song. I'm not sure why; I can't really point to anything wrong with it. I even played it live with some of my bands.

It became a big hit but I'd be willing to bet that was mostly because it was the B side to *I'm a Believer*. Back then, the radio stations would often play both sides. I know, it's hard to believe, but top 40 DJs actually could decide what songs to play on their show instead of the songs being chosen by corporate owners who shy away from anything creative or new — but that's a topic for another book.

This is actually a cover of an old Paul Revere and the Raiders song that never went anywhere. I'm sure they would play it in concert after this and have people wondering why they were covering a Monkees song.

Lyrically, it's one of Boyce and Hart's best. It isn't your standard love song. It would be interesting to hear it sung by a woman who is complaining about being the "trophy wife."

SWEET YOUNG THING (Michael Nesmith/Gerry Goffin/Carole King)
Monkee involvement: Vocals by Michael Nesmith. Backing vocals by Peter Tork and Micky Dolenz. Guitars and bass by Peter Tork.
Recording dates: July 18, 1966; July 27, 1966
Original release date: October 10, 1966 from **THE MONKEES**
Significant other versions: Michael Nesmith

Michael: This is another song that demonstrates the great power of songwriting, and Mike has admitted that he learned a lot when he was writing this song with Goffin and King. Note once again that the chord changes are minimal — it's the melody that pushes this song forward.

The production gives it Nesmith's country rock feel, but the song doesn't need that. This could have been a generic rock and roll song, and had Micky been the singer, it would have a very different feel to it. (In fact, in their reunion concert tour in the mid 2010s, they did a very different version that I liked better, even though Mike still sang it.)

But let's talk a bit about Michael Nesmith's contribution to rock and roll — one that unfortunately, he doesn't get enough credit for. Back in those days, rock and roll and country music never mixed. Nesmith was the first to really say "Hey, we can take the best of both parts and make something new." Nothing on the radio sounded like this song or *Papa Gene's Blues*. He wasn't trying to copy The Beatles here like Boyce and Hart were — he wanted to make his own music his way.

Many rock historians overlook this contribution because, come on, this is The Monkees. They're not a real band. That kind of elitist attitude has kept Nesmith from getting the credit he deserves for not only creating this sound but also promoting it and making it mainstream.

At the same time, let's face it — if he wasn't in The Monkees and was doing this on his own, I will bet that no record label would have accepted this. "What the hell is that sound?" they'd say. "I can't sell that to the teenyboppers!" Nesmith was lucky enough to have a way for his sound to be heard by millions, and clearly it helped to shape the direction of music overall in a way many of his contemporaries could only dream about.

Mark: Nesmith teams up with Goffin/King to create this pleasant tune. Nothing really remarkable about it, but not too bad, either. Certainly better than *Let's Dance On*. The best part is the echo-stop before the chorus. Why Nesmith sings this with such a breathy voice i.e. "Sweet Young Thing-uh" is unknown to me.

Alternate versions of the song appear on **THE MONKEES SUPER DELUXE EDITION** (2014).

Mike also released it as an instrumental on his own **WICHITA TRAIN WHISTLE SINGS** (1968) album.

MARY, MARY (Michael Nesmith)
Monkee involvement: Vocals by Micky Dolenz. Guitar by Peter Tork.
Recording dates: July 25, 1966; July 27, 1966
Original release date: January 9, 1967 from **MORE OF THE MONKEES**
Significant other versions: The Butterfield Blues Band, Run-DMC

Fan Thoughts

I interviewed Micky back in the 1990s when I worked for a local music publication. He was in New York City, ready to visit with his friend, Paul McCartney, who was ready to premiere his "Oratorio" concert piece. Among other things, I brought up the fact that Run DMC's version of Mary Mary was moving up the Top 40. Micky didn't know anything about this, but his interest increased when I told him that if you listen closely, you could hear his voice on their recording and that they were "scratching" to his vocals. He told me he was going to look into this. I don't know if he ever did, but he honestly didn't know anything about it until I told him about the record. — Larry Lapka

---

Mark: Another great early Monkees song by Nesmith. Why this one was held back off the first album is anyone's guess. Perhaps it was a contender for their second single until *I'm a Believer* came along.

The backing track of the song appears on **THE MONKEES SUPER DELUXE EDITION** (2014).

Michael: I never quite understood the love for this song. It's pretty mediocre. There's no great hook and the melody just largely follows the chord changes. Think of how many songs follow that same pattern — lyrics start on one note, go up one note, back down to the original note, down one note, and then back up again to the starting note. It's like the most basic melody ever.

I think its inclusion on **MORE OF THE MONKEES** and its constant playing on the TV show made the difference, because I don't see why this would be preferred to so many better songs. I mean, it shows up on many of the greatest hits albums even though it was never a single or anything.

I also wonder why they let Peter play guitar on it but not Michael, who actually wrote the song.

OF YOU (Bill Chadwick/John Chadwick)
Monkee involvement: Vocals by Michael Nesmith. Backing vocals by Micky Dolenz.
Recording dates: July 25, 1966; July 27, 1966; July 22, 1969
Original release date: July 1987 from **MISSING LINKS**

Mark: An average sounding song that was originally planned for the second album. It is serviceable, but not remarkable, and so it remained on the shelf until 1987.

A mono mix version appears on the 2006 **MORE OF THE MONKEES DELUXE EDITION** CD. The backing track and a stereo remix of the song appear on **THE MONKEES SUPER DELUXE EDITION** (2014).

This song was also included on the **PRESENT DELUXE EDITION** (2013) as a November 1969 stereo mix and a 1969 mono mix.

Michael: A boring bit that was rightly rejected. Apparently, they tried to resurrect it by adding some extra vocals or something in 1969 but still decided not to put it out. There is a reason for that.

PAPA GENE'S BLUES (Michael Nesmith)
Monkee involvement: Vocals by Michael Nesmith. Backing vocals by Micky Dolenz. Guitar by Peter Tork.
Recording dates: July 7, 1966; July 17, 1966; July 30, 1966
Original release date: October 10, 1966 from **THE MONKEES**
Significant other versions: Michael Nesmith, Floyd Cramer

Mark: The first of many Nesmith tunes that don't include the song title in the lyrics. This apparently was the source of some confusion as early pressings of The Monkees' first LP called the song *Papa Jean's Blues*, supposedly as a play on blue jeans or something. Of course, it wasn't and so copies with this early error are worth a little bit more.

As far as the song goes, it's pretty basic stuff of the "I love you and you love me" variety, but things that stand out include Nesmith's amusing call to "Play magic fingers!" and indeed it is the very first Monkees song released to feature any instrumentation by The Monkees: guitar playing by one Peter Tork!

An alternate mix appears on **THE MONKEES DELUXE EDITION** (2006), which sounds the same as the final released version, but Nesmith also yells "Pick it, Luther!"

More alternate versions of the song appear on **THE MONKEES SUPER DELUXE EDITION** (2014).

Mike also released it as an instrumental on his own **WICHITA TRAIN WHISTLE SINGS** (1968) album.

A live version appears on Mike's **LIVE AT THE BRITT FESTIVAL** (1999).

Michael: Even this early on, Michael was giving songs titles that have nothing to do with the lyrics, and this would reach its peak by 1968 with nonsense titles like *Tapioca Tundra* and *Auntie's Municipal Court*.

Musically, the tune is quite catchy and Nesmith's variation on the melody is impressive. Notice how at the end of every line instead of a single syllable word, there is a double syllable so that it's not just single beats over and over again. And the rhyming scheme is also slightly unusual for a pop song of the time: A A B A A B, where the first two lines rhyme and the third line rhymes with the sixth.

And let's talk about the lyrics. Mike's lyrics are indeed far ahead of anything Boyce and Hart are writing, and are indeed comparable to Goffin/King's work.

Also: think about the "Pick it, Luther" bit. Here Michael is admitting, on the very first Monkees album, that they're not playing their own instruments. I'm not sure that was the wisest decision he could have made...

(THEME FROM) THE MONKEES (Tommy Boyce/Bobby Hart)
Monkee involvement: Vocals by Micky Dolenz.
Recording dates: 1965; July 5, 1966; July 9, 1966; August 6, 1966
Original release date: October 10, 1966 from **THE MONKEES**
Significant other versions: Floyd Cramer, Al Hirt, Ray Stevens

Michael: When I was a kid watching this show, I just thought all bands had theme songs. I'd pretend I had my own band and I knew the first thing I had to do was come up with a theme song.

This is a perfect theme song for the TV show. That opening thump set the mood, and then quietly and somewhat mysteriously "Here we come..." The chorus loudly kicks in and lets you know that something fun is going to happen.

The lyrics told the skeptical adults that while they were "the young generation" and they "had something to say" they were also "just trying to be friendly." See? Just because we have long hair doesn't mean you have anything to worry about!

The TV version is the best version because it kicks in and then modulates each chorus, building the excitement. The album version adds another verse and a completely forgettable lead that kind of slows everything down, but hey, I can understand the padding. You don't want to open the album with a song that only lasts one minute.

Mark: An excellent theme song for this or any TV show, produced at a time when theme songs were actually considered important and also told the story of what the show was about. This was most people's first exposure to The Monkees no matter when they saw it: on network TV, on Saturday mornings, in syndication, on home video or streaming or listening to the LP or CD. As a child, I loved this theme song when I saw this show on Saturday mornings, but I thought the show itself rather silly (still do), so I'd watch the opening, listen to the song, watch the crazy accompanying visuals, and then switch the station.

I also like the guitar strumming and the "Dave Clark Five" drum fills on this song and the cymbal use besides Dolenz very effective vocals, sung in his "dreamy" voice.

This song was not a single originally in the 1960s in the US. It was however, issued on many oldies-type singles and eventually was the B-side of the 1986 *That Was*

Then, This is Now reunion single. In other countries where this song actually was released as a single, *Mary, Mary* was usually touted as the B-side.

There is also an Italian sung version called *Tema Dei Monkees* that was originally released as a single there and later on an Australian compilation called **MONKEEMA-NIA** (1979). This version had a really clunky edit in the middle of it. Finally, Rhino issued it in the US on **MISSING LINKS, VOLUME 3** in a superior, corrected version. This is actually a different recording than the original theme, rather than just placing an Italian vocal over the original theme. A stereo remix of this appears on the **HEAD-QUARTERS DELUXE EDITION** (2007), which is probably the best sounding version of all, but ends abruptly.

Some thoughts about the TV version. On *The Monkees* second season, the backing visuals changed from the first season including some scenes that really concerned me as a child: One was of three of The Monkees pushing the fourth Monkee in a bed and also in a bathtub. The concern for me was of their safety in doing this in public in the middle of the street rather than deriving any humor out of it.

Other versions: On the 1994 Rhino CD reissue, an early version of the theme is included. The second recorded version also appeared on **THE MONKEES DELUXE EDITION** (2006), with a stronger vocal from Micky. This was ultimately rejected.

Though the standard shorter TV version of the theme song version first appeared on CD on **TELEVISION'S GREATEST HITS, VOLUME 2** (1986), it eventually did appear on a Monkees album on **MISSING LINKS, VOLUME 3** (1996) and **THE MON-KEES DELUXE EDITION** in 2006.

I LOVE YOU REALLY (Stu Phillips)
Monkee involvement: Vocals by Davy Jones
Recording dates: August 22, 1966
Original release date: May 13, 2003 from **THE MONKEES, SEASON ONE DVD**

Mark: Amazingly, with virtually everything by The Monkees being released, this song has not. It's not much of a song, really it's Davy kind of scat singing the words "Baby, I Love You, Really I Do" in various orders and in slightly different tempos and inflections. Micky gives all of these songs impossibly long and silly titles on the TV show (*Teardrops in the Playground, These Boots Are Made For Kicking, It's Been Lonesome in the Saddle Since My Horse Died*), but the songs all sound virtually the same. Incidentally, Stu Phillips composed all of those little instrumental background ditties for the TV show.

Michael: Not sure this is a real song. It's just a comedy bit from the TV show. Sure this should be mentioned in this book?

Mark: Ah, we should give Stu his due... at least he interviewed with me.

KELLOGG'S JINGLE (unknown)
Monkee involvement: Vocals by Micky Dolenz
Recording dates: 1966
Original release date: March 1996 from **MISSING LINKS, VOLUME 3**

Mark: There is no official recording date known for this little jingle, but since it appeared from the beginning as part of the TV show, it is easy to assume that it was recorded at the same time as the first album. The song was officially released as part of the **MISSING LINKS** series, and then later gained a spot on **THE MONKEES DELUXE EDITION** (2006) and the later **SUPER DELUXE EDITION** (2014), which both add the announcer tag.

As a song, it isn't much. Micky spells out the Kellogg's name and offers up the slogan with a little more of that "Dave Clark Five" drum fill and jangly guitar added. The writer for this is unknown. Stu Phillips said that he didn't write it, so it may have been written by a jingle writer at Leo Burnett (Kellogg's ad agency).

Michael: And now a word from our sponsor.

SHE (Tommy Boyce/Bobby Hart)
Monkee involvement: Vocals by Micky Dolenz. Backing vocals by Davy Jones and Peter Tork.
Recording dates: August 15, 1966; August 27, 1966
Original release date: January 9, 1967 from **MORE OF THE MONKEES**
Significant other versions: The Dickies

Mark: A strong opener to a very strong Monkees album — despite how The Monkees felt that they had no artistic control over their work, the powers-that-be certainly had their best interests at heart and definitely had an ear for what would make a good song and album. I enjoy **MORE OF THE MONKEES** much better than **HEADQUARTERS**, which is supposedly their masterpiece of independence and cooperation.

Michael: I never really liked this one. Like *Mary Mary*, I think that the only reason it ends up on so many greatest hits collections is because they played it to death on the show and it was on the **MORE OF THE MONKEES** album.

It kind of plods along, crams a bunch of words into a small space every now and then, and then continues its plod. It has a lot of different parts, none of which are specifically memorable.

I WON'T BE THE SAME WITHOUT HER (Gerry Goffin/Carole King)
Monkee involvement: Vocals by Michael Nesmith. Guitar by Peter Tork.
Recording dates: July 18, 1966; July 30, 1966; August 30, 1966
Original release date: February 15, 1969 from **INSTANT REPLAY**

Mark: The mono mix appears on **THE MONKEES DELUXE EDITION** (2006). This and more alternate versions of the song appear on **THE MONKEES SUPER DE-LUXE EDITION** (2014).

Of course, it ended up finally being used for **INSTANT REPLAY** (1969). Since Michael only had three leads on that album, including this one that was long in the can, one can easily see the disinterest he had in this project, when he just as easily could have premiered his recent *Listen to the Band* on the album. Michael would have much more interest in The Monkees following album in 1969 (**PRESENT**). I feel that his rekindling of interest at that point was his new master plan to make his exit after carving out the beginnings of a semi-successful solo recording career, instead of just abandoning things as he had done here.

Back to this song, it is definitely worthy of release. I'm sure it was passed over in the past in favor of Nesmith-penned originals. Nesmith sings this with much passion. I also love the bass, and since the song was not re-recorded in 1968 or 1969, Peter Tork's still plays guitar, marking his only appearance on **INSTANT REPLAY**.

The 1966 mono mix and the backing track appear on the **INSTANT REPLAY DE-LUXE EDITION** (2011). The backing track features some studio chatter.

Michael: Another great Goffin/King song. Can you tell I'm a fan of their work? Wish they had been hired to be in charge of The Monkees songs at the beginning instead of Boyce and Hart.

Anyway, this is a very catchy song that should have found an audience before **IN-STANT REPLAY**.

The bridge doesn't seem to belong to the same song, though — it's slightly jarring at first but then they repeat the little hook and jump into the chorus halfway through the bridge, which is perfect. Sometimes it's better not to completely finish a verse and cut to the chase, something too many bands and songwriters don't understand.

The guitarist on this, by the way, was a young Glen Campbell, who plays on many of the sessions for the first album, although often his takes weren't the ones ultimately used.

LADIES AID SOCIETY (Tommy Boyce/Bobby Hart)
Monkee involvement: Vocals by Davy Jones. Backing vocals by Micky Dolenz.
Recording dates: August 23, 1966; September 3, 1966; July 24, 1969

Original release date: October 1, 1969 from
PRESENT

Michael: When I was a kid, I thought this song was great because it was funny and was a deep social commentary. Now I realize that it's just embarrassingly bad — not really humorous at all and the kind of commentary that only seems deep to a kid. Why they resurrected it for **PRESENT** is beyond me. It should have stayed in the can.

Anyway, the song is about a group of little old ladies who "can't stop doing good" but is really about people who think anyone other than them needs to be criticized. You know, kind of like how the songwriter is treating the little old ladies.

Mark: A pretty lame tune by anyone's standards, but especially by The Monkees and Boyce and Hart. This one should have remained in the can until the **MISSING LINKS** series, and even then...

The original mono mix appears on the 2006 **MORE OF THE MONKEES DELUXE EDITION** CD. This has applause added and an extended fadeout.

This song was also included on the **PRESENT DELUXE EDITION** (2013) in a 1969 mono mix.

KICKING STONES a.k.a. **TEENY TINY GNOME** (Lynne Castle/Wayne Erwin)
Monkee involvement: Vocals by Micky Dolenz
Recording dates: August 23, 1966; August 27, 1966; September 3, 1966; July 24, 1969
Original release date: July 1987 from **MISSING LINKS**

Mark: This song is called *Kicking Stones* everywhere except when it was first released on **MISSING LINKS**, where it was called *Teeny Tiny Gnome*. The song has strange lyrics and a strange sound. I don't know what the percussion instrument is called after the chorus goes "doot da-doot da-doot da-doot da doot-doot-doot," but it sounds kind of like a boinging sound and it permeates throughout.

This song also appears on the 2006 **MORE OF THE MONKEES DELUXE EDITION** CD. This version has a longer fadeout than the **MISSING LINKS** version.

This song was also included on the **PRESENT DELUXE EDITION** (2013) as a 1969 stereo mix and a 1969 mono mix. They have the longer fadeout as well.

Michael: I always thought this was someone trying to copy David Bowie's awful *The Laughing Gnome* but it turns out this was recorded first. (Hey, you all know that David Bowie's real name was David Jones, right? And he changed it so he wouldn't be confused with our Davy?)

Anyway, there is a very good reason this was never released by The Monkees. The little hook at the start just isn't catchy enough for them to repeat it over and over at the start of each verse. Micky's voice is excellent as ever, and while there are clearly worse Monkees songs out there, I could do without ever hearing this one again. I give it some credit for at least not being another silly love song.

This terrible song, combined with *Ladies Aid Society*, supposedly made the TV producers question their choice of using Boyce & Hart as their musical directors, and Don Kirshner assumed a larger role after this.

And you have to ask — who are Lynne Castle and Wayne Erwin? Is this the only song they ever wrote? How embarrassing. Apparently Lynne was Boyce & Hart's hairdresser. I did a google search and found nothing on these two. Maybe they changed their names after they wrote this. I would have.

THE MONKEES
Original release date: October 10, 1966
Highest chart position: #1 (13 weeks) in 1966; #92 in 1986
Weeks on chart: 78 in 1966 - 1968; 24 in 1986 - 1987

(Theme From) The Monkees
Saturday's Child
I Wanna Be Free
Tomorrow's Gonna Be Another Day
Papa Gene's Blues
Take a Giant Step

Last Train to Clarksville
This Just Doesn't Seem to be My Day
Let's Dance On
I'll Be True to You
Sweet Young Thing
Gonna Buy Me a Dog

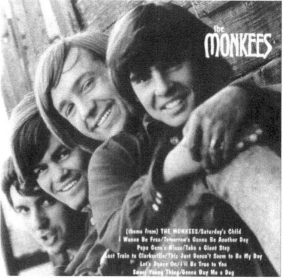

Michael: An impressive debut album. Yes, there is only one real hit on it, but it's the kind of album that many bands of the time (other than The Beatles) would be proud to have, with only a few songs that you want to skip over. And it could have been even better if they had replaced those skipping-over songs with some of the better ones they already had completed such as *I Won't Be The Same Without Her*.

The album stayed at the #1 position for 13 weeks and was only knocked off the top spot by the release of **MORE OF THE MONKEES**. It re-entered the charts in 1986 during the MTV showings.

Mark: I agree with Mike. Considering what *could* have been, this is very impressive. I have seen mock-ups out there where The Monkees concept was treated more like a TV Soundtrack to have been released on the Colpix label. Whether these mock-ups are real or not, the point remains that they could have gone *that* direction with the group: that this was just a soundtrack to a TV sitcom about a fictitious singing musical group, complete with sound bites of dialogue and the like. That they treated The Monkees as a bonafide pop group from day one and issued a proper *album* of finely crafted songs is a credit to the cleverness and creativity of the show's creators.

That being said, there are some weak areas of the album which we discussed on the separate songs, but as a 12-song longplayer, there couldn't have been a much stronger debut album from a virtually unknown group that was comprised of two actors and two singers hired to perform for a television series.

THE MONKEES SUPER DE-LUXE EDITION from 2014 contain elements and songs left off of the original album. There are a few bits that don't really qualify as songs contained on this edition including tracks with titles like *Monkees NBC Promo Spot*, *Monkees Radio Spot* and *Jokes*. Also, the complete **DAVID JONES** LP and single tracks from 1965 in both mono and stereo and six Michael Blessing songs from 1965 are included. While none of this really qualifies as Monkees material, the fact that it is now included as part of an official release, warrants its mention here.

THE MONKEES DELUXE EDITION (2006) only adds The Monkees *Radio Spot*. The spot features Mike, Micky and Davy (and barely Peter) promoting a KHJ TV Monkees contest.

YOUR AUNTIE GRIZELDA (Jack Keller/Diane Hilderbrand)
Monkee involvement: Vocals by Peter Tork
Recording dates: October 14, 1966
Original release date: January 9, 1967 from **MORE OF THE MONKEES**

Mark: This is one of those songs that I liked a lot better when I was younger and wanted The Monkees to do all novelty songs. As time has gone on and I've discovered The Monkees' other tunes, I've found that this one has become more annoying to me. I think Peter Tork found it more annoying as well, and when he sang it again live on the 1986 reunion tour, changed the "scat" part in the middle to phrases like "Hello? What happened to the guy with the hat? I used to watch you on television. I was only six years old." It is really one of the few Peter Tork lead vocals and his biggest song until the **HEAD** soundtrack.

Michael: I like this song, and it fits Peter's voice just fine. This is the **MORE OF THE MONKEES**' version of *Gonna Buy Me a Dog*, except that under all the silliness, there is actually a good song here.

The chord changes are simple and predictable, but at least the words aren't the same old love song you normally heard around this time. The musicians copy the fuzz bass from The Beatles' *Think For Yourself* and put it to good use here, and the tom drum beats at the end of every line are better fillers than any guitar lick would have had.

I agree I would have prefered an actual instrumental lead instead of Peter making noise, but hey, this was the comedy break for the album. I wonder how Peter felt about that. "Here, Peter, you're the most talented musician in the group. No, you can't play on this, but we'll let you sing on it because it's the throw-away song."

I saw Peter play live in a small club in Boston around 1982. His band started playing a slowish beat, and then he walked on stage and started singing a laid-back version of this (without the scat singing). It worked, and made me realize that it really wasn't that bad of a song.

It wasn't until a few years ago that I realized Peter was singing "Grizelda" as it faded out, but was mispronouncing it "Grizzle Dah."

I'M A BELIEVER (Neil Diamond)
Monkee involvement: Vocals by Micky Dolenz. Backing vocals by Davy Jones and Peter Tork.
Recording dates: October 15, 1966; October 23, 1966
Highest chart position: #1 single (7 weeks)
Original release date: November 12, 1966 from 7" single and **MORE OF THE MONKEES**
Significant other versions: Neil Diamond, The Four Tops, Smash Mouth, Robert Wyatt, The Fifth Estate, Weezer, Floyd Cramer, Shrek, Micky Dolenz

Mark: Neil Diamond's crowning achievement as a writer for The Monkees, although he did write another hit (*A Little Bit Me, A Little Bit You*) and other songs for The Monkees (*Love to Love*). An early version of the song appears as a bonus track on the 1994 CD version of **MORE** and the 2006 **MORE OF THE MONKEES DELUXE EDITION** CD.

Micky also sings this with Julie Driscoll in the 1969 *33 1/3 Revolutions Per Monkee* special, but this version has never been officially released to CD.

Of course, having it appear many years later in the movie *Shrek* rekindled the popularity of this song, certainly one of The Monkees' best. If you haven't heard this one, I'd be surprised if you're reading this book.

Michael: "Parents! Tell your kids that I sang this song before *Shrek*!" Micky would say years later in concert.

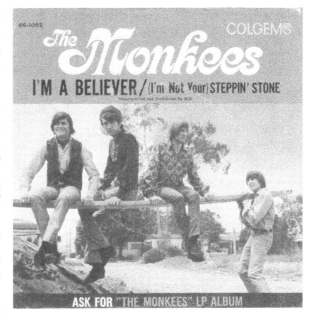

These days, when people think of The Monkees, it's usually one of the two Believer songs — "I'm a" or "Daydream." And it's easy to see why, because both are well written, well performed, and well sung. They deserve to be the songs people remember after all these years.

It starts off strong, like a hit song should, with a powerful organ followed by a simple guitar riff, and then jumps right into the tune itself. But like all hit songs, it's the powerful chorus that carries this along. A simple lead done with a fuzz box is all it needs to keep the energy going. And, let's face it, this just would not have worked as well without Micky's voice, as we can see by all of the lesser cover versions.

I like the meme that has been going around the internet recently based on this song: "I laughed at first when my girlfriend said she was leaving me because of my Monkees obsession. Then I saw her face."

A writer friend of mine (Keith DeCandido) has a band that does medieval versions of pop songs with funny lyrics. The band is called Boogie Knights and their version of this song is "And then I saw her face... and she's a medusa!"

LOOK OUT (HERE COMES TOMORROW) (Neil Diamond)
Monkee involvement: Vocals by Davy Jones. Backing vocals by Micky Dolenz and Peter Tork.
Recording dates: October 15, 1966; October 23, 1966
Original release date: January 9, 1967 from **MORE OF THE MONKEES**

Mark: Another great Neil Diamond tune tailor-made for The Monkees. The only part that gets a little sugary is when Davy does his spoken word pining for Mary and

Sondra, that even Davy makes fun of on later reunion tours by having Mary go off with Sondra, implying a lesbian relationship for the two. Otherwise, a fine fine tune.

An alternate version that is longer and includes narration by Peter Tork is included as a bonus track on the 1994 CD reissue of **MORE OF THE MONKEES** and this and the TV version appear on the 2006 **MORE OF THE MONKEES DELUXE EDITION** CD. The TV version sounds almost identical to the album version, but with a different organ instrumental break.

Michael: This is a great song. Well written, well performed, although I could do without the spoken word bit. I saw the group The Good Guys do a great cover of this one time, really rocking it up.

The version with Peter's narration is quite funny. It's slightly longer, with a lead where Peter does a voice over: "Ladies and Gentlemen, you are listening to the instrumental." After a few more seconds of listening, he says "Thank you. We hope you enjoyed it. And now, back to the song." Just in time for Davy to jump in with "Well, I see all kinds of sorrow..." After that chorus, it goes back to the opening riff for a few bars, and Peter comes back with, "Ladies and Gentlemen, this part of our record is here because if it weren't, the record would be seventeen seconds too short and we would have to do an interview at the end." (A bit of an insider joke of how they would pad the TV show if it came in under the time needed to fill.) And then finally, as the song is fading, he says, "Hi. This is me again, and this part is what we call 'the fade' where the record gets softer and softer and the disc jockey usually comes in and starts talking over it..."

But I'm glad they didn't use that version, because this really is a good song and shouldn't be used for comedy. Peter gets to do that on *Your Auntie Grizelda* this album anyway.

SOMETIME IN THE MORNING (Gerry Goffin/Carole King)
Monkee involvement: Vocals by Micky Dolenz. Backing vocals by Peter Tork and Davy Jones.
Recording dates: October 13, 1966; October 25, 1966
Original release date: January 9, 1967 from **MORE OF THE MONKEES**
Significant other versions: Micky Dolenz, Floyd Cramer

Michael: Another great Goffin/King song. You can't go wrong with talented songwriters like that. This was never a single, but appeared often on greatest hits collections, and deservedly so.

When we were kids, my sister and I used to sing "And you need no underwear this time!" Misheard lyrics at their best.

Micky later re-recorded it for his solo album **REMEMBER** — he didn't change too much, but the production values are much higher.

Mark: A great song sung with earnest, so much so that Micky's voice even cracks a bit on the high notes, somewhat surprising sing he usually achieved high notes with great ease. Micky uses his "dreamy" voice to great effect.

I DON'T THINK YOU KNOW ME (Gerry Goffin/Carole King)
Monkee involvement: Vocals by Michael Nesmith, Micky Dolenz and Peter Tork. Backing vocals by Davy Jones.
Recording dates: June 25, 1966; July 16, 1966; August 30, 1966; October 13, 1966; October 27, 1966
Original release date: July 1987 from **MISSING LINKS**

Mark: The **MISSING LINKS** liner notes mention that this song is the blueprint for Nesmith's *You Just May Be the One,* and that may explain why it was left in the can as The Monkees were starting to prefer their own compositions instead of those ones provided by outsiders. Mike takes lead vocals on this version, but the notes explain the first version had Peter singing lead. Regardless, it's a great song and now seems like a regular Monkees album standard, but it was never released in the 60s!

There's an alternate version sans Peter and Davy from June 25, 1966 that appears as a bonus track on the 1994 CD of **THE MONKEES,** with Micky singing lead. Why this song stayed in the can until 1987 is beyond belief. It certainly would have fit well on either of the first two Monkees albums and certainly was a better candidate for **INSTANT REPLAY** than some of the stuff that ended up on there. Perhaps it was Michael Nesmith who vetoed its release over the years, preferring to release songs he composed and sung rather than just sung.

A different Mike vocal version appears on **THE MONKEES DELUXE EDITION** (2006), which also contain more organ, more bass and more guitar, creating a much different overall sound. This CD also contains Micky's vocal version as well, which sounds like the **MISSING LINKS** version, but with Micky singing.

There's yet another version that ended up as a bonus track on the 1994 CD version of **MORE OF THE MONKEES** and the second recorded version appears on the 2006 **MORE OF THE MONKEES DELUXE EDITION** CD. This is the version that has Peter singing lead.

Michael: Another great Goffin/King song. Do you see a pattern here? Why so many of their songs ended up not being used is beyond me. They got their day later with *Pleasant Valley Sunday,* though.

As Mark points out, you can find this song sung by Micky, Mike and Peter. Pick your favorite! I'd like to know the story behind this. Did someone try it with each and then decide it just wasn't good enough to release at all?

Micky's version has the best vocals — I mean, come on, it's Micky. He still has a great voice in his 70s, and is one of the most underrated singers in rock and roll. Mike's version has the same backing track with his vocals, and his voice fits the song very well, too.

This version has that volume pedal lead sound that the George Harrison used in *I Need You*, and I dislike it just as much here as I do there. It also has a very noticeable mistake by the bass player at 1:22 that I can't unhear (being a bassist myself). Other than that, the song — while better than some Monkees songs that were released — just never really kicks in for me. It's like it's starting to build energy but never gets there.

The best performed version, in my opinion, was the one with Peter singing. It has a different backing track from the other two versions, with better energy and better backing vocals that are clearly the other Monkees instead of backing singers. I only could find this version in mono and the sound quality isn't as good as the Micky version. I wish they had released that version just to show that Peter could actually sing something other than a silly song like *Your Auntie Grizelda*, although admittedly, you can hear his voice crack in a few places so maybe that's why they didn't.

HOLD ON GIRL (Jack Keller/Ben Raleigh/ Billy Carr)
Monkee involvement: Vocals by Davy Jones. Backing vocals by Micky Dolenz.
Recording dates: September 10, 1966; September 24, 1966; October 14, 1966; October 23, 1966; October 27, 1966
Original release date: January 9, 1967 from **MORE OF THE MONKEES**

Michael: A pleasant little diversion, but quite forgettable. The harpsichord sound was popular at the time in the British music scene, probably copying the feel of The Beatles' *For No One*, which had come out a few months earlier. While *For No One* was on piano, not harpsichord, the feel is similar — a sort of classical feel in a "rock" song.

The drum sound at the very beginning is very clever but the heavy snare and handclaps on every beat is a bit much. It's like they wanted to have that classical feel and then said, "Nah. Too boring." And I can understand that. It does have some excitement, I get that. But when the song slows at the end while the claps continue at the same beat, it's very disconcerting.

The song is just the right length. Had it added a bridge or another verse, it would have started getting boring.

Mark: Another solid song on **MORE** with some good harpsichord and excellent vocals by Davy with the help of Micky.

The first recorded version appears on **MISSING LINKS, VOLUME 2** (1990), and on the 2006 **MORE OF THE MONKEES DELUXE EDITION** CD called *Hold on Girl (Help is on Its Way)*. It's slower with much more prominent harpsichord.

LAUGH (Hank Medress/Phil Margo/Mitch Margo/Jay Siegal)
Monkee involvement: Vocals by Davy Jones
Recording dates: October 28, 1966
Original release date: January 9, 1967 from **MORE OF THE MONKEES**

Mark: One of the weaker songs on the second album mainly because Davy doesn't seem to sing with any particular enthusiasm.

Michael: How could it take so many people to write such a weak song? Seriously, what a dumb song. It's like they took the Charlie Chaplin classic song *Smile* and just rearranged the words a bit, then stuck it on a boring, instantly forgettable tune. Skip this one.

TEARS OF JOY (unknown)
Monkee involvement: Electric 12-string guitar by Michael Nesmith
Recording dates: October 26, 1966; October 30, 1966; October 31, 1966

Mark: A completely unreleased song to date (actually a demo), listed only because it may someday be eventually included in a **MORE OF THE MONKEES SUPER DELUXE EDITION**.

Michael: Neither of us can really comment on this, because it doesn't seem to be available anywhere so we haven't heard it.

APPLES, PEACHES, BANANAS AND PEARS (Tommy Boyce/Bobby Hart)
Monkee involvement: Vocals by Micky Dolenz
Recording dates: October 28, 1966; October 30, 1966; October 31, 1966; July 24, 1969
Original release date: July 1987 from **MISSING LINKS**

Mark: It was a happy day for me in 1987 when Rhino saw fit to start releasing tracks held in the vaults that were only mentioned by name in Ed Finn and T. Bone's *Monkees Scrapbook*. They got most of them correct, but did miss a few, but by 1996, virtually everything listed was released. This song kicked off the first collection and I love it, with a great *Clarksville/Tear Drop City* vibe. It is, admittedly quite corny, lyric-wise, so I'm sure that's why it stayed in the can for so long, but man, is it catchy. It says the song was intended for The Monkees' second album in the **MISSING LINKS**' liner notes.

This song also appears on the 2006 **MORE OF THE MONKEES DELUXE EDITION** CD. Sandoval's *Monkees Day by Day* says there was a recording date of July 24, 1969 in the back of the book, but no other mention is made within the book or elsewhere about this session, so October 31, 1966 is assumed to be the real final recording date, despite it not being officially released until 1987.

In any case, it was probably shelved because of the simplistic and silly *Gonna Buy Me a Dog* type lyrics as The Monkees were starting to assert their authority about the quality of songs offered to them. The tune's not that bad, however.

This song was also included on the **PRESENT DELUXE EDITION** (2013) in a 1969 mono mix.

Michael: I remember hearing this on the TV show when I was younger and thinking "What is this? This isn't on any of the albums." And while it is not one of their better songs, it's certainly better than *Laugh*. (Of course, that's not saying much...) Still, talk about your weak lyrics. "I'll give you apples, peaches, bananas and pears." No thanks, guy, I can go down to the store and get them myself easily enough.

Like Mark, I'm not sure why there is a 1969 recording date in there when it first appeared on the TV show before that date. (Or did it? Maybe it only appeared in the reruns.)

TEAR DROP CITY (Tommy Boyce/Bobby Hart)
Monkee involvement: Vocals by Micky Dolenz
Recording dates: October 26, 1966; October 30, 1966; October 31, 1966; November 6, 1966; January 13, 1969
Highest chart position: #56 single
Original release date: from 7" single and **INSTANT REPLAY**

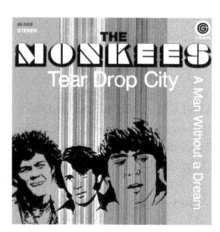

Mark: Can I say here that I *love* the guitar riff on this song?

An early mix version appears on the 2006 **MORE OF THE MONKEES DELUXE EDITION** CD. This version sounds markedly slower than the ultimately recorded and released version.

There are the inevitable comparisons to *Last Train to Clarksville*, but I still feel that this song stands on its own fairly well, but I wouldn't have released it as a single due to its similarity because it was now 1969 and not 1966. About the only group that could get away with releasing such an old song and have a hit with it in 1969 was The Zombies with *Time of the Season* (recorded in 1967 and released *after* The Zombies broke up!). I do love the guitar sound on the track, though.

The mono promo single mix appears on the **INSTANT REPLAY DELUXE EDITION** (2011).

Michael: This would have fit in just fine on **MORE OF THE MONKEES** but it really sounded dated by the time it was finally released on **INSTANT REPLAY**. I think the 1969 recording date was simply when they took the original song and sped it up.

It's not a bad little ditty, but nothing special. I don't share Mark's love for the riff — it's just the chord being played string by string. You don't even have to move your left hand at all.

Why they thought it might be a hit in 1969 is beyond me, and it didn't even make the top 40.

LOOKING FOR THE GOOD TIMES (Tommy Boyce/Bobby Hart)
Monkee involvement: Vocals by Davy Jones
Recording dates: October 26, 1966; October 30, 1966; November 6, 1966; November 12, 1966; July 24, 1969
Original release date: October 1, 1969 from **PRESENT**

Michael: Like *Tear Drop City*, this is a song that would have fit in just fine on an album in 1966 but wasn't released for another three years — and the period between 1966 and 1969 gave us a huge shift in music unlike any other. So it's out of place on **PRESENT**. (Apparently the 1969 recording was to add horns, which helped a bit to make it not sound so 1966ish.)

Not to say that it's a bad song — it isn't. It's the kind of tune that might have even been a hit single a few years earlier. The words are nothing special, but hey, they can't all be *Pleasant Valley Sunday*.

Mark: This and *Ladies Aid Society* are the two nods by The Monkees to do an **INSTANT REPLAY**-like song recycling on **PRESENT**. Perhaps Davy was having a little writer's block by the time of the **PRESENT** sessions or was having second thoughts about the whole Monkees thing, similar to how Mike was for **INSTANT REPLAY**.

Regardless, this is a strong, upbeat tune and probably could have been a single release had it been released earlier or if The Monkees' fortunes were stronger in 1969. It was wise that they stuck with Nesmith for the second half of 1969 for their single releases rather than continue to rely on older material like they did with *Tear Drop City*.

This song was also included on the **PRESENT DELUXE EDITION** (2013) in a mono version.

THE DAY WE FALL IN LOVE (Sandy Linzer/Denny Randell)
Monkee involvement: Vocals by Davy Jones
Recording dates: October 28, 1966; November 23, 1966
Original release date: January 9, 1967 from **MORE OF THE MONKEES**

Mark: This song probably gets my vote as the worst song on an otherwise great album, even surpassing *Your Auntie Grizelda*, which was a novelty song, so it gets off the hook. This was done in Davy's "dreamy" voice, but was kind of spoken more than actually sung and the entire effect comes off as extremely gooey.

Then, the arrangement takes it one step further by emphasizing the rather insistent violins. Syrup at its worst.

Michael: This is the worst Monkees song ever (from the original 12 albums). Cringeworthy. Hardly a song at all, just Davy talking. Appealing to 12 year old girls in 1966 and nobody else.

I can just imagine Mike and Peter pulling their hair out when they discovered this song on the album. And seriously, this is where the whole problem with Kirshner was — he was interested in product. He really didn't care about quality, he just wanted to sell records. That's what he was hired to do, after all, and he did deliver, but at what cost? Sales don't always have anything to do with quality. Kirshner went on to do music for The Archies after The Monkees kicked him out, and *Sugar Sugar* outsold almost every Monkees song ever. Doesn't make it any good.

You know what the real test of quality is? Time. If people are still listening to your music 50 years later, that's a good sign that the music is good. You know what they're specifically not listening to 50 years later? *The Goddamn Day We Fall in Love*. Oh, and *Sugar Sugar*.

WHEN LOVE COMES KNOCKIN' (AT YOUR DOOR) (Neil Sedaka/Carole Boyer)
Monkee involvement: Vocals by Davy Jones
Recording dates: November 23, 1966
Original release date: January 9, 1967 from **MORE OF THE MONKEES**

Mark: A nice pleasant tune heartily sung by Davy Jones with great gusto. This is Neil Sedaka and Carole Boyer's (later Carole Boyer Sager) first issued song for The Monkees and it's a winner.

Michael: If you played this for me and asked me to guess who had written it, I would have immediately answered "Neil Sedaka." His style is pretty consistent! You can just hear his voice singing this, can't you?

DEAN FRIEDMAN (*Ariel, Well Well Said the Rocking Chair*)

The first 45 single I ever bought with my own money — a pocket full of change from my newspaper delivery route — was The Monkees' debut single *Last Train to Clarksville*. I was 11 years old and had been playing guitar since I was nine, so knew more than a few chords. I slowed the speed down to 33 1/3, trying to figure out the iconic, jangly, opening guitar lick. It's got all the elements of a great pop record — an attention grabbing guitar intro, an infectious hook, relaying a passionate tale of yearning and angst. I know the song's writers, Tommy Boyce and Bobby Hart, readily acknowledge it being strongly influenced by The Beatles' previous hit *Paperback Writer*, but with all due respect to Lennon and McCartney — the greatest pop songwriters of all time — I've always felt, that in this instance, at least, *Last Train to Clarksville* was the better song, musically and lyrically. My favorite line: "We'll have time for coffee flavored kisses and a bit of conversation." I mean, seriously! To an 11 year old pre-teen in the 1960s, on the verge of adolescence, the vivid image that phrase conjured up was just short of pornographic.

I had the pleasure of opening for Peter Tork, at a small music venue in New Jersey, the Record Collector, a few years back. He was a gentleman and performed a mostly blues set with authenticity and sincerity, while graciously throwing in the occasional Monkees hit to delight his audience. When we met, briefly, during the soundcheck, he was a little bit taken aback when my wife, a zoologist, specializing in primatology, introduced him to our 40 year old capuchin monkey, Amelia. I suppose he had a reflex regarding the inevitable Monkees puns he must have endured throughout his career; but in this case there was no pun intended — it was simply a matter of my wife, Alison, insisting on bringing Amelia with her, wherever she went.

This is a really great pop song. The words are simple but eh, most songs were back in those days.

I like the way the melody isn't predictable. So many songs have four lines for a verse where the melody is basically repeated four times, then it goes to a chorus and back to another verse where the melody is repeated four times and so on. Not this song.

"When love comes knockin' at your door / Just open up and let him in." Typical start to a song, but usually in a basic rock and roll song, the next two lines would repeat the same melody. We don't do that here.

"It's gonna be a magic carpet ride / So little girl now don't you run and hide." Completely different.

Now, for the next line, it looks like we're going to repeat the first two again, because "I know that you've been hurt before" matches the opening. But then the second part is completely new again: "So don't you be afraid no more."

We're really building up to an exciting chorus here: "Throw off the chains that bind and leave the past behind" — and then it resolves without a chorus at all: "When love comes knocking at your door."

Now we repeat the process by first doing the old trick that always works: changing the key — by rising up a bit, it increases the excitement. But then Sedaka adds something new — a second Davy vocal, double-tracked, giving a counter melody behind the original one! "I know that you're afraid of loving me..." This counter melody fills in between the original lyrics and never steps over them. It's getting two songs in one!

Then, instead of just repeating the complete lyrics, "You'll see a rainbow every day / the sun will shine in every way" replaces the "I know that you've been hurt before" line from the first verse.

But wait! There's more! Instead of just repeating the melody of the first verse completely, it changes again. Instead of resolving after the line "Throw off the chains that bind and leave the past behind" it adds the line "No need to worry any more" before "When love comes knocking at your door."

Then there are a few back and forths and it ends, in under two minutes, never allowing itself to be boring.

Now that's a well-written song. It's not necessarily one of their best, but I admire the way it was arranged and put together.

MORE OF THE MONKEES
Original release date: January 9, 1967
Highest chart position: #1 (18 weeks) in 1967; #96 in 1986-1987
Weeks on chart: 70 in 1967-1968; 26 in 1987-1988

She
When Love Comes Knockin' (at your Door)
Mary Mary
Hold On Girl
Your Auntie Grizelda
(I'm Not Your) Steppin' Stone

Look Out (Here Comes Tomorrow)
The Kind of Girl I Could Love
The Day We Fall in Love
Sometime in the Morning
Laugh
I'm a Believer

Michael: Look at this. Another album in only three months. Surprise!

Most surprised by this were The Monkees themselves, who had no idea that a new album was coming out. For one thing, there was a cover picture of them they didn't like, wearing JC Penney's clothes they hated and looking down and sort of distorted as if they're trying to copy **RUBBER SOUL**. But worse were the liner notes on the back written by Don Kirshner that praised himself greatly while thanking everybody involved except, of course, The Monkees.

It was Kirshner's comments as much as anything that helped fuel the ridicu-

lous complaints that The Monkees weren't a "real band" and didn't play their own instruments — which was mostly true, but come on, this was a TV show. The main problem, I think, is that they used their real names. Had they been "Freddy Handsome, played by David Jones" then maybe no one would have thought anything of it. But apparently in the 60s people thought The Monkees really had wacky adventures, worrying about how they could pay their bills while living in a nice beach house and with a fancy car. (Oh, and having #1 records.)

The "real name" problem also made it difficult for people to see the difference between their TV characters and the real person. While Mike, Davy and Micky were played as exaggerated versions of themselves, Peter had to play "the stupid one" which was not like him at all. Micky later complained about how hard it was to find an acting job after being typecast as that character, and wondered himself if it would have been better to have taken on a fake name on the show. (After all, he didn't play "Micky Dolenz" on *Circus Boy*, did he?) But anyway, on to the album...

Mike Nesmith was the one who was mostly insulted by Kirshner and this album, and you can see why. Davy and Micky get five songs each. Mike only gets to sing one, the same as Peter, and Peter's not really one of the three lead singers in this band. In some ways, that makes this feel less like a real Monkees album to me, even though there are some really good songs on here.

We're not going to discuss the history much here — after all, there are plenty of books that already do that. But this is important to recognize because soon after this is where The Monkees' music entered the second phase: Where the band actually gets a say in what they record, actually play on the records, and become as much of a real 60s band as many others that also used session musicians to supplement their own work.

Like **THE MONKEES**, this album reappeared on the charts during the MTV reunion thing. How many other bands do you know whose albums reappear after twenty years and then make the top 100? Maybe the songs really were good.

Mark: Despite what the members of The Monkees thought of this, the second album of The Monkees is definitely one of their finest works. I even prefer it over **HEAD-QUARTERS**. While I see the point as to why The Monkees wanted to wrestle away creative control of their songs and albums from Don Kirshner, there is no denying that Kirshner definitely had an ear for what made a hit song, especially since Kirshner was able to make The Archies a hit group a year later. I feel that if The Monkees had been allowed to produce and record their own material from the beginning, we wouldn't be talking about them now, so they needed Kirshner's guidance, at least at the start.

I agree with both Mikes that the front cover photo is awful. In fact, I can firmly say that the weakest spot on *all* of The Monkees' albums are their cover images. **HEADQUARTERS** features a fun shot, but appearing at the same time as The Beatles' **SGT. PEPPER** album shows how far off the mark cover image wise they were. I would have to say that **HEAD** featured the best album cover for The Monkees – and they weren't even on it! There were better photos reserved for the group's singles.

As a side note, and in response to co-author Michael's comments about the actors of The Monkees using their own names (yes yes, I know that Micky's real first name is George and Peter's real last name is Thorkelson), but it got me to thinking. How many people in film history actually made a career of performing in films or television under their own names? Other than classic film comedians like The Three Stooges and Laurel & Hardy, virtually everyone changes their names for acting. Even Abbott & Costello didn't use their real names in films, which was always confusing to me. Costello was known for screaming, "Hey, Abbott!" on radio and TV, yet in films like *Abbott and Costello Meet Frankenstein*, they portray Chic and Wilbur. And Bob Newhart became Bob Hartley. But I really digress.

In conclusion, if one was to pick up one or two of the original Monkees albums after getting into a comprehensive greatest hits collection, **MORE OF THE MONKEES** would be one I would suggest to get next, then **PISCES**. Then, probably **THE MONKEES** and **HEADQUARTERS** (despite my misgivings about it). After that, you're on your own.

SHE'S SO FAR OUT SHE'S IN (Baker Knight)
Monkee involvement: Electric 12-string guitar by Michael Nesmith. Bass by Peter Tork. Drums by Micky Dolenz. Maracas by Davy Jones.
Recording dates: January 16, 1967
Original release date: September 21, 2000 from **HEADQUARTERS SESSIONS**

Mark: This instrumental rehearsal seems to have had potential, but it's difficult to tell. It also seems like the backing track of a later Monkees song with a different name. In any case, there was never a final, released version of this, but it does show all four Monkees playing competently.

Michael: I'm not sure if this was ever meant to be considered as a release and may have just been a recording made while they were rehearsing for their live show, where it was performed — probably because it's such a simple, easy song to learn and play. There is a live version you can find on YouTube, played at the Coliseum in Phoenix, Arizona a week after this session (January 21, 1967) with Mike singing although the quality is so bad you can hardly tell.

In any event, this is a predictable rock song with no surprises and a terrible title, so I'm glad they never finished recording this.

BLACK AND BLUE (Neil Diamond/Jerry Leiber/Mike Stoller)
Monkee involvement: none
Recording dates: January 26, 1967

EVE OF MY SORROW (Jeff Barry/Joey Levine/Jerry Leiber/Mike Stoller)
Monkee involvement: none
Recording dates: January 26, 1967

THE LOVE YOU GOT INSIDE (Jeff Barry/Andy Kim/Jerry Leiber/Mike Stoller)
Monkee involvement: none
Recording dates: January 26, 1967

POOR LITTLE ME (Jeff Barry/Andy Kim)
Monkee involvement: none
Recording dates: January 26, 1967

I WANNA BE YOUR PUPPY DOG (Denny Randell/Sandy Linzer)
Monkee involvement: none
Recording dates: January 22, 1967; January 27, 1967

LOVE IS ON THE WAY (Denny Rendell/Sandy Linzer)
Monkee involvement: none
Recording dates: January 22, 1967; January 27, 1967; January 28, 1967; October 3, 1969

SUGAR MAN (Denny Randell/Sandy Linzer)
Monkee involvement: none
Recording dates: January 22, 1967; January 27, 1967; January 28, 1967; October 3, 1969

Mark: All of the above seven songs' backing tracks were recorded on the same couple of days in January 1967 by Jeff Barry in hopes that they would later receive vocals by The Monkees. They are listed here for completeness, but the authors have not heard these backing tracks. They may be released someday as part of a **MORE OF THE MONKEES SUPER DELUXE EDITION**, which to date has not been compiled, or if The Monkees choose to record vocals over these tracks for some future follow up to **GOOD TIMES!**, that is a possibility.

Michael: If it's Jeff Barry and Andy Kim song choices, I can do without hearing these.

I DIDN'T KNOW YOU HAD IT IN YOU SALLY, YOU'RE A REAL BALL OF FIRE
(Denny Randell/Sandy Linzer)
Monkee involvement: Vocals by Micky Dolenz
Recording dates: January 22, 1967; January 28, 1967; September 15, 1969; October 3, 1969
Original release date: September 21, 2000 from 7" single issued with pre-orders from **HEADQUARTERS SESSIONS**.

Mark: An attempt was made on October 3, 1969 to finish the previous seven plus this one off, but only this one got completed with a Micky Dolenz vocal and is the only one of these songs to actually be released...barely. It was on a 7" single issued with pre-orders for **HEADQUARTERS SESSIONS**.

Michael: This song would have been in the list above with the Jeff Barry sessions, as it was recorded at the same time without any involvement from The Monkees. It has only seen the light of day because a few years later, Micky added a vocal.

This is a *Magnolia Simms* kind of song (or maybe *D.W. Washburn*) where they're trying to sound like an old 1920s ditty, with references to flappers and everything. It's actually not a bad little song, and at just over two minutes, it ends before it gets boring.

ALL OF YOUR TOYS (Bill Martin)
Monkee involvement: Lead vocals by Micky Dolenz; Backing vocals by Davy Jones, Michael Nesmith and Peter Tork; Drums by Micky Dolenz; Electric 12-string guitar by Michael Nesmith; Harpsichord by Peter Tork; Tambourine by Davy Jones.
Recording dates: January 16, 1967; January 19, 1967; January 23, 1967; January 24, 1967; January 30, 1967; January 31, 1967
Original release date: July 1987 from **MISSING LINKS**

Mark: Hands down, the best tune on the first **MISSING LINKS** collection. At the time in 1987, I felt that Rhino should have released this as a 7" single to promote the album. I felt that it would have gotten tons of airplay and would have propelled **MISSING LINKS** to a charting position, but probably the reformed Monkees vetoed this in favor of the inferior new material released on **POOL IT!**

There is a lengthy tale elsewhere about how this song was supposed to be considered for The Monkees' third single release, but because it wasn't in Screen Gems copyrights, it was passed over and not released for 20 years! Regardless, it is one of The Monkees' finest tunes and it is a shame that it remained on the shelf for so long and isn't even highly regarded now, unless you are a Monkees aficionado, like us. For those wondering if those **MISSING LINKS** collections are worth getting, this is a fine example as to why, especially the first set of which this song is from.

Overall, it's a nice, joyful, bouncy song with a staccato harpsichord and great harmony vocals by the boys — one of their best together. It's also a very nice production with an ending build up that must be heard to be appreciated.

Another slightly inferior version with an alternate mix appears as a bonus track on the 1995 Rhino CD reissue of **HEADQUARTERS** and a stereo remix appears on the **HEADQUARTERS DELUXE EDITION** (2007), which has a very crisp, clear sound. There is also an early mono mix which sounds a lot like the **MISSING LINKS** version.

On **HEADQUARTERS SESSIONS** (2000), there are 10 takes of the song, plus the rehearsal and the backing track of the song. Amusingly, since the majority of these takes are instrumentals, sometimes Peter's harpsichord takes on a Vic Mizzy *Addams Family* feel. Probably subconscious rather than intentional. The mono master shows that this song was originally intended for the **HEADQUARTERS** album, but was left off for the reasons already stated.

The boys finally played it live on their 2011 tour!

Michael: This was the first real song that The Monkees played as a real group. And it's a good song, played adequately enough.

I never liked the lead, where they all sing "ahh" instead of playing an instrument. For one thing, they were way too loud. (Some of the remixes in the various editions fix that.) It slows the song down for me and drains out all the energy of it.

But this would have been a great addition to **HEADQUARTERS.**

YOU CAN'T TIE A MUSTANG DOWN
(Jeff Barry)
Monkee involvement: Vocals by Davy Jones
Recording dates: January 21, 1967; February 4, 1967; August 15, 1969
Original release date: July 29, 1997 from **DAYDREAM BELIEVER AND OTHER HITS** and later on **HEADQUARTERS DELUXE EDITION** (2007).

Michael: Another song left over from the Jeff Barry/Andy Kim sessions before The Monkees took over with **HEADQUARTERS.** It's a poorly recorded song with predictable chords and a very obnoxious organ that sounds like it escaped from a Doors session (their first album having just been released weeks before this was recorded).

Mark: This is an okay song, nothing special, but it would have been fine if it was released on **HEADQUARTERS**. For some reason, it was passed over even for the **MISSING LINKS** series. The song was recorded in 1967, but Davy didn't lay vocals on it until 1969.

IF I EVER LEARNED TO PLAY THE VIOLIN (Artie Resnick/Joey Levine)
Monkee involvement: Vocals by Davy Jones
Recording dates: January 26, 1967; February 4, 1967
Original release date: October 29, 1996 from **HEY HEY WE'RE THE MONKEES** CD-Rom game. First CD appearance on **HEADQUARTERS DELUXE EDITION** (2007).

Mark: Truly a throwaway song, which is seriously why it wasn't ever released back in the 60s. The only saving grace of it now is that with the death of Davy Jones, any unreleased Jones vocals have taken on a somewhat bittersweet and nostalgic tone.

It was barely released when it was (if that makes sense). Story goes, Rhino was re-leasing some budget-line Monkees greatest hits compilations in the mid-1990s. This time there was a selling point to get longtime fans to plop down some more money by adding one more unreleased song. This was after the successful **MISSING LINKS** series and the 1994-1995 CD reissue series with bonus tracks, so pickings were slim. *Ceiling in my Room* and *You Can't Tie a Mustang Down* (also both with Jones vocals) made the cut on the first two compilations, but when it was time to do the third compilation, Rhino discovered that the added new track was not really encouraging sales. And so it was buried, literally, inside The Monkees' CD-ROM game (which I have never bought, much less seen). Later, it was more properly released on **HEAD-QUARTERS DELUXE EDITION** (2007), but now in the days of YouTube, one can just punch it up and listen easily, despite it not being Jones' best moment.

Michael: I can't hear this song without thinking of the scene in *Head* where Davy plays the violin to Annette Funicello.

And my God, how the lyrics were dated immediately. Awful, awful stuff. "If I learned to the play the violin / and I traded my old guitar in / would your parents still object / and would I earn their respect? / I would even go and cut my hair / though my friends would point and say I'm square / I'd give up my beat ways / Take up more discrete ways..." Okay, that's enough, I can't listen to any more. You can thank me for saving you from having to check this out.

LOVE TO LOVE (Neil Diamond)
Monkee involvement: Vocals by Davy Jones. Backing vocals by Peter Tork and Micky Dolenz.

Recording dates: January 21, 1967; February 4, 1967; February 5, 1967; August 5, 1969; February 2016

Original release date: First release on the Australian **MONKEEMANIA** album (1979); First US album release on **MONKEE BUSINESS** (1982); First CD release from **MISSING LINKS, VOLUME 3** (1996). Version with new backing vocals from **GOOD TIMES!** (2016).

Mark: While it was nice to finally have a version with backing vocals by Peter and Micky produced for **GOOD TIMES!** in 2016, this song really belongs back with the **HEADQUARTERS** sessions. In fact, a stereo remix of it appears on the **HEADQUARTERS DELUXE EDITION** (2007). It's a good song, but somehow just always kind of slipped through the cracks over the years, even appearing on the TV show way back when, but passed over for *A Little Bit Me, A Little Bit You*, another Diamond composition. Davy's vocals were laid down in 1969 and Peter and Micky's in 2016.

The **MISSING LINKS** version was the first time the song appeared in true stereo and is listed as a previously unreleased alternate mix.

Michael: I remember back in the late 70s buying **MONKEEMANIA** that had this song and *Steam Engine* on it, and both sounded terrible. They seemed like good songs underneath the production, but if I recall correctly, they were in mono and muddy. I was frustrated that I had spent all that money just for two songs I didn't have that weren't that good.

We included this here at this time in the book because that's when Davy recorded it and, as Mark pointed out, it even was heard on the TV show at the time. It was later cleaned up, and some overdubs were added for the **GOOD TIMES!** album, where it sounds great. It's not one of Neil Diamond's best, but it's a good song, and it was wonderful to hear Davy's voice on that reunion album at least once.

A LITTLE BIT ME, A LITTLE BIT YOU (Neil Diamond)
Monkee involvement: Vocals by Davy Jones
Recording dates: January 21, 1967; February 4, 1967; February 6, 1967; February 8, 1967
Highest chart position: #2 single
Original release date: March 8, 1967 from 7" single. First album appearance **THE MONKEES GREATEST HITS** (1969); First CD appearance on **THEN AND NOW...THE BEST OF THE MONKEES** (1986).
Significant other versions: The Specials

Michael: Kirshner had Davy come in and record a bunch of songs without the involvement of any of the other Monkees, and this was *after* Mike had complained about **MORE OF THE MONKEES** and even after they had started doing their own music with *All of Your Toys*. It was almost as if Kirshner was saying "Screw you, I'm the boss, and I'm going to rub your faces in it."

> ### Fan Thoughts
>
> A Little Bit Me, A Little Bit You *was the A-side of the first record I ever bought with my own money. I was nine years old in 1966, and took my money to the local Kress store in my old neighborhood, Rochdale Village, South Jamaica, Queens, New York. The store kept the singles in a glass cabinet behind the checkout in its record section, so you had to ask the cashier to get if for you. I did just that, went home, played the record, and have since gone on to purchase thousands of records, with my own money, of course. And yes, I still have the exact record that I purchased all those years ago in my collection, and yes, it still plays pretty well!*
> — Larry Lapka

Davy, of course, didn't care about those "Monkees aren't a real band" stories, because he only thought of himself as an actor and wasn't really a rock and roll guy anyway. He was just doing his job. So he showed up and recorded this, *99 Pounds, If I Learned to Play the Violin, Love to Love,* and the first version of *She Hangs Out.*

Kirshner then released *A Little Bit Me, A Little Bit You* as a single, backed with the first version of *She Hangs Out* (Davy on both sides of the single, no other Monkees

involved) without letting anyone else know, and that's what led to the huge fight that eventually got him fired. The single got pulled but the DJs had already been playing it, so it was re-released with the B-side *The Girl I Knew Somewhere,* written by Mike, with the participation of all of The Monkees. *She Hangs Out* would later be re-recorded for **PISCES**.

I can see why they didn't want to put it on **HEADQUARTERS** since it wasn't a group effort, and that's one thing they bragged about in the liner notes of **HEADQUARTERS**. *The Girl I Knew Somewhere* would have fit perfectly on that album, though.

In any event, this is a pretty good song. I can see why Kirshner wanted to follow up the huge success of *I'm a Believer* with another Neil Diamond song, but on the other hand, Diamond's style is so distinctive that I think it would have been better to get a different feel for the follow-up.

There is more than one version of this, and the stereo mix with the beat heavy in front is the best. It was a hit, but sold nowhere near the numbers for *I'm a Believer.* In fact, it only got as high as #2 on the charts which, after the #1 hits of *Last Train to Clarksville* and *I'm a Believer,* had to be disappointing.

Mark: Another great tune from the prolific Neil Diamond, the composer of *I'm a Believer,* with great guitar and bass, and the first Monkees single without a Micky

Dolenz lead vocal. The single version has a few extra "Oh girls" from Davy during the instrumental break.

Why this was left off of **HEADQUARTERS** is anyone's guess, but it probably would have been on the album if Kirshner stuck around, and eluded album inclusion until 1969. It just missed being The Monkees' third number one (although it did go to #1 on *Cashbox's* list), beaten by *Somethin' Stupid* by Nancy and Frank Sinatra of all things.

A stereo remix appears on **HEADQUARTERS DELUXE EDITION** (2007). The separation is far greater than the standard mono single version, and is perhaps the best-sounding version of the song.

99 POUNDS (Jeff Barry)
Monkee involvement: Vocals by Davy Jones
Recording dates: January 21, 1967; February 4, 1967; February 6, 1967; February 8, 1967
Original release date: June 1970 from **CHANGES**

Mark: It is kind of interesting that when Micky and Davy did decide to go through the archives, that this song was chosen for inclusion on **CHANGES**. I realize that they couldn't choose any Mike or Peter songs, which might have been confusing to listeners, but surely there were better songs still left in the can that they could have used. Even *Love to Love*, which finally received a proper non-compilation release on **GOOD TIMES!** and also has a Davy vocal would have been better than this, or even recording another new song. Heck, they could have even thrown on the excellent *Someday Man*, which was only a single B-side at this point, in place of this.

The one saving grace is that there is a nice thrashing guitar sound throughout and Davy seems to be into with his tiger growl while singing.

A stereo remix version appeared on **HEADQUARTERS DELUXE EDITION** (2007).
Michael: This is another one of those from the Jeff Barry sessions that sat around for years before finally being issued on **CHANGES** where it sounded completely out of place because of the recording styles of three years earlier.

I'm sure the reason they included it instead of *Love to Love* or some other song is because **CHANGES** is essentially a Jeff Barry album with vocals by Micky and Davy, and Jeff wanted the royalties from *99 Pounds*.

Anyway, it's a pretty typical rock song that has plenty of energy but apparently was only mixed into mono, which makes it much less powerful than it could be.

UNTIL IT'S TIME FOR YOU TO GO (Buffy Sainte-Marie)
Monkee involvement: Vocals by Michael Nesmith and Davy Jones. Acoustic guitar by Michael Nesmith.

Recording dates: 1967
Original release date: September 21, 2000 from **HEADQUARTERS SESSIONS**
Significant other versions: Buffy Sainte-Marie

Michael: This is where we're starting to get into the **HEADQUARTERS** sessions, where The Monkees actually got control over their music and played most of the instruments. There have been a lot of releases of rehearsals and half-written songs that, honestly, aren't worth your time. Unlike some of the great songs that were recorded for the TV show but never used, these were never meant to see the light of day, and rightly so.

This is pleasant song, originally performed by Buffy Sainte-Marie, so I can see why The Monkees didn't record it. They didn't need cover songs. I think Michael was just playing around in the studio and I doubt they ever intended to record this as a group. Still, it's a nice way to appreciate Mike's fine voice.

Mark: This song is a demo only, with the rest of The Monkees razzing Michael Blessing! In any case, Nesmith sings it in a very heartfelt way, but it really doesn't seem like a Monkees type of track. In fact, it seems like something Peter would actually sing. And, truth be told, Michael did release a pre-Monkees version as a Michael Blessing single that was eventually re-released on **THE MONKEES SUPER DELUXE EDITION** (2014).

FEVER (unknown)
Monkee involvement: Piano by Peter Tork. Drums by Micky Dolenz. Tambourine by Davy Jones.
Recording dates: 1967
Original release date: September 21, 2000 from **HEADQUARTERS SESSIONS**

Michael: Nothing to hear here folks, move along. Just another jam done while practicing, never meant to see the light of day. Peter basically plays one note on the piano like it's a percussion instrument, Micky beats the drums, and the only one who does something interesting is Chip Douglas on bass.

Mark: Yet another instrumental jam featuring adequate playing by the group. Nothing special.

THE GIRL I KNEW SOMEWHERE (Michael Nesmith)
Monkee involvement: Vocals by Michael Nesmith and Micky Dolenz. Backing vocals by Davy Jones and Peter Tork. Electric and acoustic 12-string guitar by Michael Nesmith. Acoustic guitar, harpsichord by Peter Tork. Drums by Micky Dolenz. Tambourine by Davy Jones.

PETER NOONE (Herman's Hermits: *Mrs. Brown You've Got a Lovely Daughter*)

I love a lot of The Monkees records and I play them often for pleasure.

We cheered The Monkees on! There was no competition in the music business. Every popular act was unique. None of us were like each other: Beatles, Stones, Who, Kinks, Herman's Hermits, Zombies ... see any competition?

As above average British grammar school educated twerps, we did not need to be reminded that being the flavor of the month/year/season was also applicable to ourselves.

Davy was a great entertainer who I believe was stifled in The Monkees. He was quite simply one of my generation's greatest comedians, and had he not been in The Monkees, he would have been a huge solo star someday. Every time I saw Davy I felt a surge of joy! He was a very talented actor. Watch him on *My Two Dads*. Very, very clever.

One time I was singing *Mrs. Brown, You've Got a Lovely Daughter* live onstage, when Davy walked on dressed as Mrs. Brown and hit me with a very heavy purse and said, "Leave my daughter alone!" Show stopping moment. He looked hot, too.

I was sad that he had some deep resentments about the other Monkees, but I have similar issues and so do the Stones and Genesis. I think that just makes Davy more likeable.

He let me do the "are you standing in a hole" routine and often had the greatest comeback lines on a level that was brilliance!

Davy and I did *Today's the Day* [in 1998, but released it in 2011] in a garage in West Hollywood. It was produced by Calvin Hayes, who was Mickie Most's son. Davy and I both chose the same accent which proves we were separated at birth somewhere in Manchester or had the same British influences. Listen to *What Are We Going To Do?* to hear his Herman accent.

We also did *Phineas and Ferb* and once again from a different city and time zone we chose a Cockney rebel.

Micky Dolenz is a fascinating man and I enjoy every minute I spend with him. His voice is closing in on Paul McCartney, which is not usual. Most singers lose something at whatever age Micky thinks he is.

I did not enjoy singing *Daydream Believer* with David Cassidy. I sing it every day in my own show and it is listed as one of my top 10 recordings of all time. I don't think Cassidy's musicians knew how to approach the song and give it the attention it needs to present it for what it is...magic....

[In 2016, **AN EVENING WITH PETER NOONE & MICKY DOLENZ** was released.] I was offered a job to do a series of interviews. My list was Eric Burdon, Roger Daltrey, Micky Dolenz and Eric Clapton. Micky was first because he is so interesting and doesn't only talk about The Monkees.

I don't know the other two very well at all so I haven't a clue who they are personally. I think I did a concert at Pepperdine with Peter Tork. He was playing

Continued on page 70

PETER NOONE *Continued from page 69*
in a band called Shoe Suede Blues, and I enjoyed his concert immensely. I only see him on those "Who is Still Alive?" type TV shows and I am always happy to be on those and I hope to see him a lot over the next 50 years.

Did The Monkees impact me? The Monkees had an impact on my older sister! I am but a fan of their music and their recordings are all in my collection of things I like. They impacted my record collection!

Recording dates: January 16, 1967; January 24, 1967; January 30, 1967; January 31, 1967; February 23, 1967
Highest chart position: #39 single B-side
Original release date: March 8, 1967 from 7" single B-side. First LP appearance on **MORE GREATEST HITS OF THE MONKEES** (1982). First CD appearance on **THEN AND NOW…THE BEST OF THE MONKEES** (1986).

Mark: The single B-side is a classic. Again, like its A-side (*A Little Bit Me, A Little Bit You*), its omission from the final **HEADQUARTERS** line-up is somewhat of a mystery. The bonus track alternate version from the 1995 Rhino CD reissue is quite weak, so it is good in this case that they took another stab at it. It is now a Monkees greatest hits compilation mainstay.

About the song: Once again they use the *Paperback Writer* bass riff to great effect here and Peter Tork's harpsichord is a standout. Micky takes on the lead vocals (with Mike in the background) for the popular single version that eluded album inclusion until 1982.

On **HEADQUARTERS SESSIONS** (2000), there are 16 takes of the song, plus multiple tracking and overdub sessions of two different versions of the song. The mono master shows that this song was originally intended for the **HEADQUARTERS** album.

The second recorded version, stereo remix and the second recorded version, alternate mono remix appear on **HEADQUARTERS DELUXE EDITION** (2007). The vocals are noticeably different because they're by Michael. Otherwise, it basically sounds the same. The single version, stereo remix and the mono single mix sounds like the standard released version with Micky's vocals intact, but with a much longer fadeout.

Michael: I wish this had been the single instead of *A Little Bit Me, A Little Bit You.* It's a much better song. However, Kirshner had already released *A Little Bit Me, A Little Bit You* and it had been getting radio airplay so it was too late to pull it.

Michael's melody is memorable and not predictable (like *Mary Mary* was) and I really like the way it goes into a minor key for the start of the bridge (Some way, some how...). Peter's keyboard lead on this really excellent and helps push the song forward, proving that hey, these guys can be as good in the studio as many other 60s bands at the time were. This never really got the attention it deserved, and somehow never made the greatest hits albums for some time, even though it belonged there. After all, it really did make the top 40 (admittedly as a B-side, because they did that in those days).

SHE'LL BE THERE (Coco Dolenz/Micky Dolenz)
Monkee involvement: Vocals by Micky Dolenz. Guitar by Micky Dolenz.
Recording dates: February 1967
Original release date: March 1996 from **MISSING LINKS, VOLUME 3**

Michael: I wish Micky had written more songs. I really enjoy all of his works. This one is very nice but nothing special, although Coco's harmonies help the song quite a bit. If recorded with a full band, instead of just the acoustic guitar, it could have been a hit.

There's one point of the song (around the 1:24 mark) that sounds way too much like Peter, Paul and Mary's *I Dig Rock and Roll Music.* Then I looked it up and found out that *I Dig Rock and Roll Music* was released a month after this was recorded. Go figure.

Mark: This demo version of this song that was recorded at the same time as the demo for *Midnight Train* was later released on **HEADQUARTERS SESSIONS** (2000), which almost sounds like The Everly Brothers due to Micky's and sister Coco's vocals. This version also appears on the **HEADQUARTERS DELUXE EDITION** (2007) as an acoustic duet.

MR. WEBSTER (Tommy Boyce/Bobby Hart)
Monkee involvement: Vocals by Micky Dolenz. Backing vocals by Davy Jones. Guitar by Micky Dolenz. Tambourine by Davy Jones. Steel guitar by Michael Nesmith. Piano by Peter Tork.
Recording dates: September 10, 1966; September 24, 1966; February 24, 1967
Original release date: May 22, 1967 from **HEADQUARTERS**

Mark: The first recorded version appears on **MISSING LINKS, VOLUME 2** (1990) and on the 2006 **MORE OF THE MONKEES DELUXE EDITION** CD. It features more harpsichord, violin and flute and almost sounds like a Jefferson Airplane outtake.

This is one of the few cases where the **HEADQUARTERS** version is better with sufficient echo added to Micky's vocals to make them suitably chilling and effective. Nice steel guitar by Mr. Nesmith as well. The song ends kind of abruptly, though.

Tracking session take 28 appears on **HEADQUARTERS SESSIONS** (2000).

Michael: I always loved this song. The abrupt ending of the song matches the ending of each verse and, given the story of the song (about a bank teller who steals from the bank) it fits.

The **HEADQUARTERS** version is much better than the original version, which was slower, dirge-like, and clumsy. It was clearly trying to sound medieval or something. I could see it being performed at a Renaissance Faire instrumentally. It's frankly boring.

ZILCH (Michael Nesmith/Peter Tork/Micky Dolenz/Davy Jones)
Monkee involvement: Vocals by Michael Nesmith, Peter Tork, Micky Dolenz and Davy Jones.
Recording dates: March 1967
Original release date: May 22, 1967 from **HEADQUARTERS**

Mark: Along with *Band 6*, the worst part of **HEADQUARTERS**. It's fun to hear...once. It has its fans. The isolated tracks by each Monkee appear on **HEADQUARTERS SESSIONS** (2000) and *that* is more interesting to hear, IMHO.

Michael: I agree with Mark — this is fun to listen to once, or maybe once every few years. The Monkees had a bit too much to smoke that afternoon, I think. Fortunately, like *Band 6*, they didn't consider this a "real song" to take the place of something else, so it's kind of like an extra treat.

Peter starts with "Mr. Dobalina, Mr. Bob Dobalina" which was apparently something he had heard in an airport intercom. Davy then adds "China Clipper Calling Alameda" which is from the movie *China Clipper*. I have no idea why he picked that. Micky adds "Never mind the furthermore, the plea is self-defense" which is a line from the play *Oklahoma!* And finally Mike adds, "It is of my opinion that the people are intending" which doesn't seem to come from anywhere in particular and may have just been Mike trying to sound like a politician. The more they try to keep it going, the more they mess up, and then there is a splice where they try again, faster, and it all ends up in gibberish, until Micky is saying "Hobber reeber sabosoben hobba seeba snick" — which then ends up as the first line of the next song on the album, *No Time*.

In 1991, a rapper named "Del the Funky Homosapien" took Peter's "Mr. Dobalina, Mr. Bob Dobalina" and used it as the basis for a really good rap song called *Mista Dobalina*. Check it out!

They Might Be Giants later incorporated the line "Never mind the furthermore, the plea is self-defense" into their song *Memo to Human Resources*. Not sure if they got it from *Zilch* or *Oklahoma*...

PETER GUNN'S GUN (Henry Mancini)
Monkee involvement: Steel guitar by Michael Nesmith. Piano by Peter Tork. Drums by Micky Dolenz. Tambourine by Davy Jones.
Recording dates: March 1967
Original release date: January 24, 1995 from **HEADQUARTERS** bonus track
Significant other versions: Henry Mancini

Mark: Forgettable instrumental version of Henry Mancini's *Peter Gunn Theme*. Interesting at best; cringe-inducing at worst, since The Monkees' playing is subpar. It also appears on **HEADQUARTERS SESSIONS** (2000) and **HEADQUARTERS DELUXE EDITION** (2007).

Michael: Meh. More noodling in the studio, never meant to be released, never meant to be heard.

BAND 6 (Micky Dolenz/Peter Tork/Michael Nesmith/Davy Jones)
Monkee involvement: Steel guitar by Michael Nesmith; Electric guitar by Peter Tork; Drums by Micky Dolenz.
Recording dates: March 2, 1967
Original release date: May 22, 1967 from **HEADQUARTERS**

Mark: **HEADQUARTERS'** novelty song, and what a waste. There must have been something... anything...better than this! Where's Don Kirshner when you need him?

A stereo master appears on **HEADQUARTERS SESSIONS** (2000).

Michael: Yes, I'm so glad they put the stereo master on **HEADQUARTERS SESSIONS**. If there is one thing Monkees fans have been demanding all these years, it was the stereo master of *Band 6*.

Garage bands usually don't let people hear their rehearsals. For some reason, The Monkees decided that was a good thing. Why? Were they trying to say, "See? We really are playing these instruments!" Why would anyone want to hear this? I mean, come on, this sounds like the bands I was in when I was 15.

The good thing is that they didn't count this as a real song. The Monkees albums always have six songs a side, but for **HEADQUARTERS**, they didn't count this or *Zilch*.

MEMPHIS TENNESSEE (Chuck Berry)
Monkee involvement: Electric 12-string guitar by Michael Nesmith. Electric six-string guitar by Peter Tork. Tambourine by Davy Jones. Drums by Micky Dolenz.
Recording dates: March 7, 1967
Original release date: September 21, 2000 from **HEADQUARTERS SESSIONS**
Significant other versions: Chuck Berry, The Beatles

Mark: The Monkees perform a competent instrumental version of Chuck Berry's *Memphis*, probably never intended for release, just rehearsal.

TWELVE-STRING IMPROVISATION (unknown)
Monkee involvement: Electric 12-string guitar by Michael Nesmith. Electric six-string guitar by Peter Tork. Tambourine by Davy Jones. Drums by Micky Dolenz.
Recording dates: March 7, 1967
Original release date: September 21, 2000 from **HEADQUARTERS SESSIONS**

Mark: More noodling around by The Monkees similar to how they did on *Where Has it All Gone?* This is honestly what makes **HEADQUARTERS SESSIONS** tedious listening for me. Honestly, The Monkees are competent players, nothing more, at this point in their career, like any other up-and-coming garage band.

There is also a **SESSIONS** track called *Six-String Improvisation*. As you can imagine, the results are very similar.

Michael: Yeah, you'll forgive me if I don't comment on all of the studio noodling.

WHERE HAS IT ALL GONE? (Michael Nesmith)
Monkee involvement: Electric 12-string guitar by Michael Nesmith. Electric six-string guitar by Peter Tork. Tambourine by Davy Jones. Drums by Micky Dolenz.
Recording dates: March 7, 1967

Original release date: September 21, 2000 from **HEADQUARTERS SESSIONS**

Mark: Kind of an instrumental improvisation...nothing much more, but yes, The Monkees are playing their own instruments! Two versions appear on the album.

RANDY SCOUSE GIT a.k.a.
ALTERNATE TITLE (Micky Dolenz)
Monkee involvement: Vocals by Micky Dolenz. Backing vocals by Davy Jones and Peter Tork. Drums and tympani by Micky Dolenz. Electric guitar by Michael Nesmith. Piano and organ by Peter Tork.
Recording dates: March 2, 1967; March 4, 1967; March 8, 1967
Original release date: May 22, 1967 from **HEADQUARTERS**
Significant other versions: Micky Dolenz, Bad Manners, The Orwells

Michael: Absolutely one of my favorite Monkees songs. I was always depressed that Micky didn't write more for The Monkees because his songs always were my favorites (sorry Nesmith fans!). In the 1970s, I remember constantly looking for a Micky solo album that I knew was coming with all the great songs he could write.

When I saw them perform this live a few years ago in the reunion concert after Davy died, Micky was handed a colorful tablecloth to wear to match the poncho he had on in the original video.

The lyrics are about his trip to England, where he met his future wife ("Wondergirl"), Cass Elliot ("The girl in yellow dress") and The Beatles ("Four kings of EMI"). He had watched a TV show where someone was called a randy scouse git, and he didn't realize that it was not the kind of thing you would say on a TV show for teenyboppers. He just liked the phrase. Besides being the kind of phrase that should not be said in polite company, "randy scouse git" was so associated with the British TV show that RCA (who distributed The Monkees albums in England) demanded an alternate title from Micky. So Micky renamed it *Alternate Title* for them.

I rewatched *Monty Python and the Holy Grail* recently and jumped when I thought I heard Eric Idle (as Sir Robin) call someone a "randy scouse git" — It's in the scene with the killer rabbit and everyone is talking at once. However, when I checked the script online, I see that the actual line was "mangy Scot git." Given how much of a music fan Eric Idle is (after all, just look at The Rutles), I wonder if this was his wink and nod to Micky Dolenz.

This was a hit single in the UK, and should have been a single in the US too. Back in those days, pop bands would churn out albums every six months or so and a new single every two or three months (depending on how well the single performed). By the time **HEADQUARTERS** was released, *A Little Bit Me, A Little Bit You* had already fallen off the chart and eight weeks went by before *Pleasant Valley Sunday* was released. That's two months; more than enough time for *Randy Scouse Git* to go up and down the chart. It's a shame we'll never know how well it would have performed, and as such, **HEADQUARTERS** contains no hit singles at all.

On the **GOOD TIMES!** extra songs, Micky sings a bit of this on *Love's What I Want*. Wonder if that was his idea or writer Andy Partridge's idea.

Micky also did a slower version on his solo album **REMEMBER** that is very good and has a completely different feel to it.

Mark: I have always had mixed feelings about this song. While it is in the general Monkees' vein, it always has struck me as an incomplete song and am actually surprised it was a big hit in the UK, but considering the time of its release, almost anything The Monkees put out in 1967 would have probably been a hit.

As stated, it was released in the UK under the title *Alternate Title* since *Randy Scouse Git* basically means "Horny Liverpudlian Jerk". Of course, this all presaged the punk movement by a decade so that a group like The Sex Pistols could have released such a song with that title with no issue.

I will agree with Mike that it has become a stage favorite since the mid-80s, and in that capacity, I think it works much better than in the studio. I especially like it when Micky really gets into it by pounding the kettle drum and shouting, "The colors, the colors!" near the end, to which (traditionally) Davy and Peter have to snap him out of it.

Incidentally, for those interested, the B-side of the UK single was *Forget That Girl*.

HEADQUARTERS SESSIONS (2000) includes a track called *Setting Up the Studio for Randy Scouse Git*, plus a tracking session composite, an alternate version, an alternate mix with an unused tag vocal and the backing track.

The **HEADQUARTERS DELUXE EDITION** (2007) has an alternate version with significantly different vocals and drumming.

YOU TOLD ME (Michael Nesmith)
Monkee involvement: Vocals by Michael Nesmith. Backing vocals by Micky Dolenz, Peter Tork and Davy Jones. Electric 12-string guitar by Michael Nesmith. Banjo by Peter Tork. Tambourine by Davy Jones. Zither and drums by Micky Dolenz.
Recording dates: March 3, 1967; March 9, 1967
Original release date: May 22, 1967 from **HEADQUARTERS**
Significant other versions: Michael Nesmith

Mark: After a sloppy count-in, **HEADQUARTERS** starts off with a strong Nesmith song which could have been a better single choice than *Randy Scouse Git* (which wasn't even a single in the US). The backing track and a version with a rough lead vocal appear on **HEADQUARTERS SESSIONS** (2000).

A live version from May 17, 1968 appears on the **HEAD DELUXE EDITION** (2010).

Mike also released it as an instrumental on his own **WICHITA TRAIN WHISTLE SINGS** (1968) album.

Michael: I think the count-in at the beginning where they're all shouting "one two three four" may have been inspired by **REVOLVER**'s *Taxman* intro. And if you listen closely, you can hear the *Taxman* bass line in the background.

This is one of Mike's strongest songs, and I think it's really important to note that they chose this to start off **HEADQUARTERS**, as if to say to Kirshner, "Hey look, Mike is one of the lead singers in this band, you know." I think they also wanted to establish their own sound, too, because you have to admit, there was no one in popular music at the time that sounded like Mike's country-rock. Peter even plays banjo on this song! Banjo, on a rock song getting played on the radio!

I like this song a lot, and especially like the way the vocals overlap near the end.

FORGET THAT GIRL (Douglas Farthing Hatlelid)
Monkee involvement: Vocals by Davy Jones. Backing vocals by Micky Dolenz and Peter Tork. Maracas by Davy Jones. Electric 12-string guitar by Michael Nesmith. Electric piano by Peter Tork. Drums by Micky Dolenz.
Recording dates: March 7, 1967; March 8, 1967; March 10, 1967; March 11, 1967
Original release date: May 22, 1967 from **HEADQUARTERS**

Michael: Forget that tune!

No, in all seriousness, it's not a bad song, written by their producer Chip Douglas.

Chip, by the way, used to be in The Turtles and helped produce their huge hit *Happy Together.* He left The Turtles after Mike asked him to produce *All of Your Toys* and then later this album. Chip plays bass on **HEADQUARTERS** and **PISCES** (which he also produced) and I think his bass playing needs to be acknowledged as very important in the feeling of the songs. He did a great job at that and at producing. (He later went on to produce The Turtles' best album **THE BATTLE OF THE BANDS**.)

I am surprised we didn't hear more from Chip over the years, given his talent. He later worked with The Monkees on his song *Steam Engine*, and did a Christmas song for a reunion single with Micky, Peter and Davy that was co-written with Turtles leader Howard Kaylan, but there doesn't seem to be much else on his resume.

Mark: A decent, if somewhat forgettable song, despite the title which is about the only memorable part, since additional lyrics are pretty sparse. The swooping "ooh, ahh" vocals also save it from complete obscurity, somewhat.

HEADQUARTERS SESSIONS (2000) has a rehearsal, the backing track, rough backing vocals and a rejected overdub session vocal.

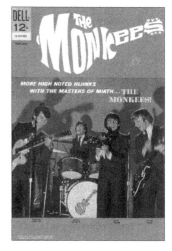

EAST VIRGINIA (Traditional)
Monkee involvement: Vocals by Peter Tork. Backing vocals by Micky Dolenz. Banjo by Peter Tork.
Recording dates: March 11, 1967
Original release date: September 21, 2000 from
HEADQUARTERS SESSIONS

Mark: Also known as *I Was Born in East Virginia*. Once again, it's a tune very atypical of The Monkees, but it's very well sung with sparse banjo playing by Peter.

MICKY IN CARLSBAD CAVERNS (Micky Dolenz)
Monkee involvement: Vocals by Micky Dolenz.
Recording dates: March 14, 1967
Original release date: September 21, 2000 from **HEADQUARTERS SESSIONS**

Mark: Really not a song at all, but rather Micky having fun with the echo chamber. Fun for him...not for us... It leads to Micky's earliest recorded version of *Pillow Time*.

YOU JUST MAY BE THE ONE (Michael Nesmith)
Monkee involvement: Vocals by Michael Nesmith. Backing vocals by Peter Tork, Davy Jones and Micky Dolenz. Electric 12-string guitar and acoustic guitar by Michael Nesmith. Bass by Peter Tork. Tambourine by Davy Jones. Drums by Micky Dolenz.
Recording dates: July 18, 1966; July 27, 1966; March 2, 1967; March 16, 1967
Original release date: May 22, 1967 from **HEADQUARTERS**
Significant other versions: Michael Nesmith

Michael: Who the heck is Nimbus? "Oh Nimbus / have someone..." Misheard lyrics at their best.
Speaking of best, this is one of Michael's best — short and to the point and catchy all the way through. That rough start with the unusual beat even works. I mean, listen to it. Most rock songs are in 4/4 timing, meaning you can count 1, 2, 3, 4 along with it. Here, at the beginning, you have to count to 5 for a few beats. "All men must..." Then it kicks into the 4/4 time signature.

Mark: The one who really benefitted most from The Monkees' newfound freedom was Michael Nesmith, as he contributed some of his strongest songs of his career and on this album at this time. This is one of them. A mono TV version of the song appears on **MISSING LINKS, VOLUME 2** (1990), and on **THE MONKEES DELUXE EDITION** (2006) and **THE MONKEES SUPER DELUXE EDITION** (2014). It sounds about the same as the final released version.

The tracking session and backing track both appear on **HEADQUARTERS SESSIONS** (2000).

A live version from May 17, 1968 appears on the **HEAD DELUXE EDITION** (2010).

Mike also released it as an instrumental on his own **WICHITA TRAIN WHISTLE SINGS** (1968) album.

MASKING TAPE (unknown)
Monkee involvement: Electric 12-string guitar by Michael Nesmith. Electric six-string guitar by Peter Tork. Tambourine by Davy Jones. Drums by Micky Dolenz.
Recording dates: March 16, 1967
Original release date: September 21, 2000 from **HEADQUARTERS SESSIONS**

Mark: More studio chatter listed as a song that eventually evolves into yet another instrumental jam. Boy, there are a lot of these.

Michael: Yeah, I have very little to say about these non-songs like *Band 6*. I'm a huge Beatles fan, and I don't even like listening to *their* rehearsals. It's like reading the first draft of a novel, I guess — interesting for historical reasons but unless you're doing research like that, a waste of time. I didn't even want to list all these in the book, but Mark is more of a completist than I am.

TWO-PART INVENTION IN F-MAJOR (Johann Sebastian Bach)
Monkee involvement: Piano, harpsichord and organ by Peter Tork.
Recording dates: March 17, 1967
Original release date: September 21, 2000 from **HEADQUARTERS SESSIONS**
Significant other versions: J.S. Bach

Mark: Peter performs an informal version of this famous Baroque piece in the studio during the **HEADQUARTERS** sessions.

A live version was performed at the May 17, 1968 concert in Salt Lake City that resulted in the *Circle Sky* footage for **HEAD**.

Tork has performed this live many times since and a live version was officially released on **2001: LIVE FROM LAS VEGAS!**

BUTCH PATRICK (Eddie Munster on *The Munsters*; Mark on *Lidsville*; Milo in *The Phantom Tollbooth*)

Any fond memories or any memories of working with The Monkees on their Christmas episode?

Well, yeah, you've got to remember that this is 1968 and I'm a 14-year-old kid spending a week with the hottest group and the hottest TV show at that particular point in time, that was really a dream come true for me. In addition, I consider it to be one of the best episodes they ever did — not so much because I was in it — but because of the way they broke down the fourth wall at the end of it. They sang the a capella *Riu Chiu* and then they invited all the cast and the crew and the assistants to be on camera and introduce them to the country. It really kind of showed how light-hearted and how much fun that set was to be around.

I was just a kid. I had my week with The Monkees and then went on to other things, but then I saw them over the years as I became an adult and I ran across them quite often and I'm still friends with them. I saw Davy right before he passed. I always had a good time. He called me the little chap, even though I was taller than he was by that time! Peter and Micky I am pretty close with. I see them quite often and Mike, I've met a couple times.

Just put them in the Hall of Fame — geez, c'mon guys!

BLUES (unknown)
Monkee involvement: Vocals by Micky Dolenz. Drums by Micky Dolenz. 12-string guitar and steel guitar by Michael Nesmith. Piano by Peter Tork.
Recording dates: March 17, 1967
Original release date: September 21, 2000 from **HEADQUARTERS SESSIONS**

Mark: Nothing much to say about this except the most briefest of instrumental jams ends the second disc of **HEADQUARTERS SESSIONS**.

BANJO JAM (unknown)
Monkee involvement: Banjo by Peter Tork. Guitar by Michael Nesmith. Drums by Micky Dolenz.
Recording dates: March 17, 1967
Original release date: September 21, 2000 from **HEADQUARTERS SESSIONS**

Mark: Only an excerpt appears on record showing off Peter's respectable banjo playing skills, but yes, it is another jam session.

CRIPPLE CREEK (Traditional)
Monkee involvement: Vocals by Peter Tork. Banjo by Peter Tork. Drums by Micky Dolenz.
Recording dates: March 17, 1967
Original release date: September 21, 2000 from **HEADQUARTERS SESSIONS**

Mark: Tork performed this song for his solo spot during The Monkees 1967 tour and his live version was eventually released in 1987 on the **LIVE 1967** album. The studio version is the one attempted above.

I'LL SPEND MY LIFE WITH YOU (Tommy Boyce/Bobby Hart)
Monkee involvement: Vocals by Micky Dolenz. Backing vocals by Peter Tork. Electric six-string guitar by Micky Dolenz. Steel guitar by Michael Nesmith. Acoustic 12-string guitar by Peter Tork. Tambourine by Davy Jones.
Recording dates: October 26, 1966; November 12, 1966; March 4, 1967; March 5, 1967; March 9, 1967; March 10, 1967; March 11, 1967; March 18, 1967
Original release date: May 22, 1967 from **HEADQUARTERS**

Mark: The first recorded version appears as a bonus track on the 1994 CD version of **MORE OF THE MONKEES** and the 2006 **MORE OF THE**

MONKEES DELUXE EDITION CD. That version only contains Micky vocals over session musicians and is a slower tempo. Apparently, The Monkees thought highly enough of it to re-record it here for **HEADQUARTERS**.

I actually prefer the non-**HEADQUARTERS** versions as the **HEADQUARTERS** version seems a little lightweight. It needs some punching up. I think I know what The Monkees were striving for, but they missed the mark, especially with the tinkly piano music break and Micky's somewhat weak vocals.

The backing track appears on **HEADQUARTERS SESSIONS** (2000).

Michael: This has Mike's style all over it even though it's a Boyce/Hart song. The acoustic guitar and steel guitar make a difference. It's not a bad song, but it was never one I paid much attention to. I agree with Mark that the piano break doesn't help. The song needed to get some energy somewhere in there and it never achieved it.

The version recorded months earlier is better, without much Monkees involvement except Micky's vocals. I see why they wanted to re-record it for **HEADQUARTERS**, but they lost all the energy from the first version, which also includes harmonies (from non-Monkees) the whole way through.

CANTATA AND FUGUE IN C&W (Michael Nesmith)
Monkee involvement: Electric six-string guitar by Michael Nesmith. Piano by Peter Tork. Drums by Micky Dolenz.
Recording dates: March 18, 1967
Original release date: September 21, 2000 from **HEADQUARTERS SESSIONS**
Significant other versions: Michael Nesmith

Mark: This Nesmith demo was inserted as part of Micky's demo for *Randy Scouse Git*. Nesmith would not release a proper version of this instrumental until his 1972 album **AND THE HITS JUST KEEP ON COMIN'**.

I CAN'T GET HER OFF OF MY MIND (Tommy Boyce/Bobby Hart)
Monkee involvement: Vocals by Davy Jones
Recording dates: July 25, 1966; March 17, 1967; March 19, 1967
Original release date: May 22, 1967 from **HEADQUARTERS**

Michael: Another Davy vaudevillian-type of song that could have been written by Nilsson. It's like the prequel to *Cuddly Toy*, complete with rinky-tink piano. This is the kind of song Herman's Hermits would have loved to record and probably even have a hit with it.

By the way, Davy never sings "I can't get her off my mind" anywhere in this version, and instead sings "I don't think I'll ever get her off of my mind." And if you listen to the earlier version where he does sing "I can't get her off of my mind" you can see why — "Can't" is dragged out as if it had three syllables and it just doesn't work. This earlier version has some things to recommend it, but the lead is really boring. I actually like the **HEADQUARTERS** version better. It seems to capture that sound they're going for.

Mark: An early version (July 25, 1966) appears as a bonus track on the 1994 CD of **THE MONKEES**. This version is much slower in pace and lighter in feeling, kind of like a song from the 1920s and has a prominent marimba and zither. This version also appears on **THE MONKEES DELUXE EDITION** (2006).

The actual released version on **HEADQUARTERS** is fine, but as in many cases with the **HEADQUARTERS** versions, I prefer the versions made under Don Kirshner's supervision. Sorry, guys.

The backing track appears on **HEADQUARTERS SESSIONS** (2000).

DON'T BE CRUEL (Otis Blackwell/Elvis Presley)
Monkee involvement: Piano by Peter Tork. Drums by Micky Dolenz.
Recording dates: March 19, 1967
Original release date: September 21, 2000 from **HEADQUARTERS SESSIONS**
Significant other versions: Elvis Presley, Ringo Starr, Cheap Trick

Mark: Another instrumental jam featuring the Elvis classic, kind of sloppily played by the group.

JERICHO (Traditional)
Monkee involvement: Vocals by Peter Tork and Micky Dolenz.
Recording dates: March 11, 1967; March 22, 1967
Original release date: January 24, 1995 from **HEADQUARTERS** bonus track

Mark: Silly nonsense from the **HEADQUARTERS** sessions. If it weren't for completeness' sake and the fact that this was released, it coulda/shoulda/woulda stayed in the can. Lots of time-wasting going on during the **HEADQUARTERS** sessions. The drugs have taken effect.

A longer version appears on **HEADQUARTERS SESSIONS** (2000) and on the **HEADQUARTERS DELUXE EDITION** (2007), where it's labeled as *Studio Dialogue*.

Michael: This is why **HEADQUARTERS** took so long to record. They spent a lot of time goofing off and doing nonproductive things. On the other hand, they had just spent the busiest year of their lives — recording a TV show, making albums, performing live, doing promotional tours — I guess they needed this!

SHADES OF GRAY (Barry Mann/Cynthia Weil)
Monkee involvement: Vocals by Davy Jones and Peter Tork. Backing vocals by Micky Dolenz. Maracas and tambourine by Davy Jones. Piano by Peter Tork. Drums by Micky Dolenz. Steel guitar by Michael Nesmith.
Recording dates: March 16, 1967; March 22, 1967
Original release date: May 22, 1967 from **HEADQUARTERS**
Significant other versions: Sons of Champlain

Michael: An excellent song that appears on many greatest hits collections, and rightly so. Peter's voice fits well here, and I'm glad they brought in some session musicians to fill the song.

Let's once again give Peter credit for some great keyboard work. His little piano solo at the start really sets the feel for the song that a simple playing of the chords would not do. I also really like how the harmonies on the chorus aren't there for the first time and kick in for the later ones to help build it. It was also a good idea not to do a third verse, because it would have dragged the song out too long. As it was, this was the longest Monkees song at the time — almost three and a half minutes! (That would be a short song by the standards of today.)

Mark: Probably Peter Tork's strongest vocals, sung alternately with much earnestness with Davy Jones and great backing vocals by Micky. One of the high points of the **HEADQUARTERS** album and of The Monkees' career. If only there were more like these on **HEADQUARTERS**.

The backing track appears on **HEADQUARTERS SESSIONS** (2000).

EARLY MORNING BLUES AND GREENS (Jack Keller/Diane Hilderbrand)
Monkee involvement: Vocals by Davy Jones. Backing vocals by Peter Tork. Maracas by Davy Jones. Electric 12-string guitar by Michael Nesmith. Electric piano and organ by Peter Tork. Drums by Micky Dolenz.
Recording dates: March 22, 1967
Original release date: May 22, 1967 from **HEADQUARTERS**

Mark: The Monkees get trippy...with Davy on vocals, no less! It is actually a high point of **HEADQUARTERS** outside of Nesmith's songs.

The backing track appears on **HEADQUARTERS SESSIONS** (2000).

Michael: I never considered this trippy — I'd save that description for *Daily Nightly*. This feels like a kind of smoky jazz number you'd hear in a dimly lit nightclub with a guy in a tuxedo with the tie undone standing in a spotlight singing while holding a gin and tonic. At least until the lead comes in with its echoey organ and that drum that sounds like it was recorded in the back of a cave.

Anyway, I very much like this song. The lyrics aren't your typical love song, it has its own sound and feel apart from any other Monkees song, and once again Peter's keyboard playing makes the song.

FOR PETE'S SAKE (Peter Tork/Joseph Richards)
Monkee involvement: Vocals by Micky Dolenz. Backing vocals by Davy Jones and Peter Tork. Tambourine by Davy Jones. Electric 12-string guitar by Michael Nesmith. Electric guitar by Peter Tork. Drums by Micky Dolenz.
Recording dates: March 23, 1967; March 25, 1967
Original release date: May 22, 1967 from **HEADQUARTERS**

Michael: This is an excellent tune — not sure if Peter worked on the music or the lyrics or both with Joseph Richards, though.

It's pretty simple and short though if you look at it. Four lines, and then it jumps into a chorus of sorts and then that's it — it repeats it and fades out. That's a good thing — sometimes short and simple is best. It also allowed this to be edited to a minute to use as the closing title for the second season of the show.

The problem is with the lyrics — nothing wrong with peace, love and understanding but you know, say something about it that is a bit more meaningful than "We were born to love one another / this is something we all need." And come on, "In this loving time" doesn't really rhyme with "we will make the world a-shine." And a-shine isn't a word, anyway. Shine was short a syllable, so you couldn't think of a two syllable word that rhymes with "time"? Ah well, it was the 60s, don't let The Man tell you how to write lyrics and all.

Mind you, the lyrics I wrote when I was Peter's age weren't much better...

Mark: Another strong song from **HEADQUARTERS**. Another one that could have been a hit single. As it was, it became the closing theme for the second and final season of The Monkees' TV show. Peter was such a strong composer in those days, one wonders why he wasn't more prolific.

The backing track appears on **HEADQUARTERS SESSIONS** (2000).

NO TIME (Hank Cicalo)
Monkee involvement: Vocals by Micky Dolenz. Backing vocals by Davy Jones. Electric 12-string guitar by Michael Nesmith. Piano by Peter Tork. Drums by Micky Dolenz. Tambourine by Davy Jones.
Recording dates: March 17, 1967; March 20, 1967; March 22, 1967; March 28, 1967
Original release date: May 22, 1967 from **HEADQUARTERS**

Mark: A hard-rocking tune especially for The Monkees, sung with great gusto by Micky. Despite for all it has going for it, it really is not a favorite of mine. The best part is the "Scooby Snack" gibberish lyrics at the beginning. Otherwise, for me, it ranks at about the level of *Let's Dance On* from the first album.

A tracking session composite of two different versions, the backing track and a master take with backing vocals appear on **HEADQUARTERS SESSIONS** (2000).

Michael: A basic standard three chord garage band song. It's Chuck Berry with new words. Completely predictable and forgettable.

All four Monkees threw it together and wrote it, but then gave the writing credit to their sound engineer Hank Cicalo to thank him, knowing the royalties would get him more money than his engineering gig gave him.

For years I was trying to figure out what Micky was saying at the start of the song, and then I realized he was simply repeating the nonsense he had fallen into at the end of *Zilch*, where he mumbles "Hober reeber sabasoben hobaseeba snick."

One of the things that really bugs me is Davy's percussion playing. Once you notice that, you can't not hear it. It's random, following no pattern. Percussion needs to follow some sort of pattern! You can't just hit the tambourine on the 1 and 3 and then decided to shake it for a few bars and then start hitting it on the 2 and 4 and so on. Listen around 1:30 where Davy apparently gets tired of hitting the tambourine so much so he just stops for a beat and then slows down. It then gets worse from there. Makes me cringe.

SUNNY GIRLFRIEND (Michael Nesmith)
Monkee involvement: Vocals by Michael Nesmith. Backing vocals by Micky Dolenz and Davy Jones. Electric 12-string and acoustic guitar by Michael Nesmith. Electric six-string by Peter Tork. Drums by Micky Dolenz. Maracas from Davy Jones.
Recording dates: February 23, 1967; April 18, 1967
Original release date: May 22, 1967 from **HEADQUARTERS**

Michael: Another great Nesmith tune. You know what really pushes this song and makes it work? The bass once again, played by Chip Douglas. Listen to it and try to ignore the bass and you'll see there's not a lot to the performance.

But even without the bass, it's well written. Well sung, and well performed. A Monkees classic.

Mark: Nesmith continues his winning streak on **HEADQUARTERS** with another classic, once again in the country rock vein. Micky and Davy's backing vocals add to the mix greatly.

2000's **HEADQUARTERS SESSIONS** includes an acoustic remix of the master vocal and a tracking session take with the master vocal.

A live version from May 17, 1968 appears on the **HEAD DELUXE EDITION** (2010). This version is preceded by an alternate version of *War Chant*.

I DON'T KNOW YET (unknown, but possibly Micky Dolenz)
Monkee involvement: Drums by Micky Dolenz.
Recording dates: April 24, 1967

Mark: This unreleased rock 'n' roll song by Micky, strangely remains so, since the **HEADQUARTERS SESSIONS** box should have cobbled all of this stuff together.

Michael: Who wrote this? I don't know yet.

HEADQUARTERS
Original release date: May 22, 1967
Highest chart position: #1 in 1967; #121 in 1986
Weeks on chart: 51 in 1967-1968; 17 in 1986

You Told Me
I'll Spend My Life With You
Forget that Girl
Band 6
You Just May Be The One
Shades of Gray
I Can't Get Her Off My Mind

For Pete's Sake
Mr. Webster

COM-103

Sunny Girlfriend
Zilch
No Time
Early Morning Blues and Greens
Randy Scouse Git

Mark: This album is a favorite among The Monkees and Monkees' fans alike. It is not, by my opinion. I feel that it fell short of the mark similar to how **JUSTUS** did in 1996. Like it or not, I feel that The Monkees thrive better with a little help from their friends than totally left to their own devices. The **HEADQUARTERS** sessions were lengthy with many songs attempted, but not fully recorded and are at best mediocre and directionless rather than truly productive or experimental. In fact, instrumentation is downright sloppy sometimes as evidenced by many of the sessions' outtakes and even by stuff that made it onto the final album. Most of the best of this ended up on the resulting album, but I feel that the album would have been *much* stronger with the inclusion of the *A Little Bit Me, A Little Bit You / The Girl I Knew Somewhere* single in place of *Band 6* and *Zilch*, both of which showcase examples of how weak a lot of these recordings were and are. What seems to be drug-induced creativity at the time now seems to be a lot of excessive self-indulgence when listening to the entire **HEADQUARTERS SESSIONS** (2000) experience.

So, is there anything to recommend with **HEADQUARTERS**? Yes, lots of stuff. This album is the beginning of Michael Nesmith's reign as a recording artist. He has three top tunes on this album and are easily the best of an uneven selection. Runners up include *Shades of Gray, Early Morning Blues and Greens* and *For Pete's Sake.* The rest are honestly pretty dispensable, but most of it is better than some later stuff The Monkees would do. To quote another record reviewer, "Hindsight displays its charms." Ultimately in this case, the parts are better than the sum of its whole.

Note: Certain versions of this album contain a back cover photo where three of the four Monkees (Davy excluded) sport beards. I feel that this photo is preferable to the cover photo actually used.

Michael: I will disagree with Mark here in a few ways (and agree in a few others). I think **HEADQUARTERS** is a fine album, better than the first two. I agree that it would have been better if they had allowed in more session musicians (like they did with **PISCES**, their best album).

It was a very important album for The Monkees themselves. They needed to make this album to prove to the world they could. Once they got that out of their system, they went into a sort of hybrid area where they brought in session musicians a lot more (which is good) but still had a ton of control over the songs.

This is an album that is listenable all the way through. There aren't any bad songs on this album like there were on the first two. No *Let's Dance On* or *The Day We Fall in Love* here. Yes, I could skip *No Time* but it's not unlistenable. Then again, there's *Band 6,* which isn't really a song.

Band 6 and *Zilch* were extras, and I don't think they could have replaced these with other songs. Every Monkees album has six songs per side, and *Band 6* and *Zilch* made

7 so they don't really count toward the total. I can see why The Monkees didn't want *A Little Bit Me, A Little Bit You* on the album because they didn't play on it, but *The Girl I Knew Somewhere* would have fit perfectly and is an excellent song.

This reached #1 easily but only stayed at #1 for one week because of the release of a little album called **SGT. PEPPER'S LONELY HEARTS CLUB BAND.** **HEADQUARTERS** was knocked down to #2 where it stayed for 11 more weeks with **SGT. PEPPER** at #1. In 1986, it once more made the charts, reaching #121.

PLEASANT VALLEY SUNDAY (Gerry Goffin/Carole King)
Monkee involvement: Vocals by Micky Dolenz. Backing vocals by Michael Nesmith, Davy Jones and Peter Tork. Guitar by Micky Dolenz. Electric guitar by Michael Nesmith. Piano by Peter Tork.
Recording dates: June 10, 1967; June 11, 1967; June 13, 1967
Highest chart position: #3 single
Original release date: July 10, 1967 from 7" single and **PISCES, AQUARIUS, CAPRICORN AND JONES, LTD.**
Significant other versions: Carole King

Mark: It's the *Friends* theme...whoops! Seriously, this is one of the greatest songs ever done by The Monkees. I love the lyrics, the singing, the guitar work, the piano... Everything about this song is perfect! Truly the peak of the 1960s Monkees songography.

Michael: This would definitely make my top three favorite Monkees songs. Tremendously catchy, interesting words, and have I mentioned Goffin/King before? Like I said earlier, it's the melody that matters. The verse stays on one chord, but that's just fine, because the tune is so catchy.

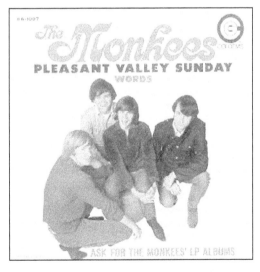

In some ways, it is a protest song — which was popular at the time — about the conformity of suburbia and how life can be boring in it. I saw a documentary on Carole King where she said she wrote this after moving away from the city and meeting all the housewives who couldn't deal with her as a working mother, even though her "work" was writing songs. "Mothers complain about how hard life is and the kids just don't understand." The "Pleasant Valley" refers to an area near West Orange, New Jersey, right outside of New York City where she lived. When I moved to the Poconos, I was thrilled to discover a Pleasant Valley near me, but I suppose it's a pretty common name...

It's the first Monkees single to last longer than three minutes, and the last part of it is just a repeat of the opening lick over and over and then reverbed so heavily as to make it all one befuddled mess, but it works and was something new and exciting. Andy Partridge admits he copied the reverb-heavy ending of *Pleasant Valley Sunday* for XTC's *Great Fire* many years later.

I often point to this song when I talk to other people about The Monkees actually playing their own instruments. "You know that's Mike playing the lead hook at the beginning of the song, right?"

WORDS (Tommy Boyce/Bobby Hart)
Monkee involvement: Vocals by Micky Dolenz. Backing vocals by Peter Tork, Davy Jones and Michael Nesmith. Organ by Peter Tork. Electric guitar and percussion by Michael Nesmith. Percussion by Davy Jones.
Recording dates: August 15, 1966; August 27, 1966; June 14, 1967; June 15, 1967
Highest chart position: #11 single B-side
Original release date: July 10, 1967 from 7" single and **PISCES, AQUARIUS, CAPRICORN AND JONES, LTD.**
Significant other versions: The Leaves

Michael: One of Boyce/Hart's best songs, and this version is much better than the original one heard on TV. A lot more power and feeling behind it. And another song about a bad relationship to match *Steppin' Stone*.

It starts off kind of dreamy, with Davy playing (of all things) wind chimes that are mixed much too loud. Peter gives an echoey counterpart to Micky's lead singing that works very well — for this song, I think his voice fits better than Davy or Mike's very distinctive voices would have fit.

Pay attention to how important Chip Douglas' bass is in this song and how it really pushes the beat along. Without it, the song would be half as good.

This was actually released a year earlier by a group called The Leaves but it's quite sloppier and doesn't have that progressive bass line that pushes it along. Then again, The Monkees had done it on their TV show before that, so I guess the Leaves version is technically the cover.

Mark: Another great song from the great **PISCES** album. Certainly, this features Peter's best vocals and of course, Micky is great again with his voice alternating from dreamy to emphatic.

The first recorded version appears on **MISSING LINKS, VOLUME 2** (1990), and again on the 2006 **MORE OF THE MONKEES DELUXE EDITION** CD, which is basically the version heard on the TV show with more pronounced bass and a flute instrumental and a little backwards masking.

INSTRUMENTAL (unknown)
Monkee involvement: Acoustic guitar by Michael Nesmith. Organ by Peter Tork.
Recording dates: June 1967

YOURS UNTIL TOMORROW (Gerry Goffin/Carole King)
Monkee involvement: Electric guitar by Michael Nesmith. Bass by Peter Tork.
Recording dates: June 22, 1967

I'VE GOT RHYTHM (Eddie Hoh)
Monkee involvement: none
Recording dates: June 22, 1967

SIXTY-NINE (Eddie Hoh)
Monkee involvement: none
Recording dates: June 22, 1967

THE BELLS OF RHYMNEY (Idris Davies/Pete Seeger)
Monkee involvement: Vocals by Peter Tork. Acoustic guitar by Peter Tork.
Recording dates: June 22, 1967

JAM (Michael Nesmith)
Monkee involvement: Guitar by Michael Nesmith
Recording dates: August 23, 1967

Mark: Another group of six songs that were recorded on the same day (except the last one) in hopes that they would later receive vocals by The Monkees (except *Bells* does have Tork vocals). They are listed here for completeness, but the authors have not heard these tracks. They may be released someday as part of a **PISCES, AQUARIUS, CAPRICORN AND JONES, LTD. SUPER DELUXE EDITION**, which to date has not been compiled, or if The Monkees choose to record vocals over these tracks for some future follow up to **GOOD TIMES!**, that is a possibility.

YOU CAN'T JUDGE A BOOK BY ITS COVER (Willie Dixon)
Monkee involvement: Vocals by Michael Nesmith. Harmonica and maracas by Michael Nesmith.
Recording dates: January 21, 1967; August 12, 1967; August 25, 1967; August 26, 1967
Original release date: March 1, 1987 on **LIVE 1967**

GONNA BUILD A MOUNTAIN (Leslie Bricusse/Anthony Newley)
Monkee involvement: Vocals by Davy Jones.
Recording dates: January 21, 1967; August 12, 1967; August 25, 1967; August 26, 1967; August 27, 1967
Original release date: March 1, 1987 on **LIVE 1967**

I GOT A WOMAN (Ray Charles)
Monkee involvement: Vocals by Micky Dolenz.
Recording dates: January 21, 1967; August 25, 1967; August 26, 1967; August 27, 1967
Original release date: May 18, 2001 from **SUMMER 1967: THE COMPLETE LIVE RECORDINGS**

Mark: These three songs, plus *Cripple Creek* for Peter (which was also attempted as a studio recording and listed elsewhere for that reason), comprise the songs utilized by the individual Monkees for their solo sets during the 1967 tour. Footage of each Monkee performing their solo song is shown in "The Monkees On Tour" episode of the TV series that closes out season one. Interestingly, Davy sings *I Wanna Be Free* for the cameras during his solo set on the episode, probably due to music rights issues for *Gonna Build a Mountain.*

It's an interesting episode as DVD commentaries by Peter and Mike indicate, since The Monkees TV show was supposed to be about the comedic adventures of an unsuccessful pop group, yet this episode shows The Monkees as being wildly successful and somewhat serious (if you don't count the parts where Davy is chasing a goose and Micky becomes a robotic autographer).

That said, none of these songs saw official release until Rhino decided to finally put out a live album and CD of the 1967 tour in 1987. *I Got a Woman* didn't see official release until 2001 when Rhino released ALL of the 1967 concert recordings in a limited edition box set. The rest of the songs performed on this tour were all standard Monkees hits that had studio versions and so do not warrant a special mention here.

CUDDLY TOY (Harry Nilsson)
Monkee involvement: Vocals by Davy Jones. Backing vocals by Micky Dolenz and Peter Tork. Tambourine by Davy Jones. Drums by Micky Dolenz. Piano, electric piano by Peter Tork. Acoustic guitar by Michael Nesmith.
Recording dates: April 26, 1967; September 5, 1967
Original release date: November 6, 1967 from **PISCES, AQUARIUS, CAPRICORN AND JONES, LTD.**
Significant other versions: Harry Nilsson

Mark: A classic Nilsson song earnestly sung by Davy. Nilsson also does a great version. Harry Nilsson's songs always seemed to be tailor-made for The Monkees even more than Boyce & Hart or Goffin/King. Small wonder that Davy and Micky performed and released an LP of Nilsson's **THE POINT** in 1977, and Dolenz also did a tribute album to Nilsson with **REMEMBER** in 2012. Love that echoey ending which fades into *Words* on the album.

An alternate mix was included on the **PISCES, AQUARIUS, CAPRICORN AND JONES, LTD. DELUXE EDITION** (2007). It sounds almost exactly like the originally released version with a much longer fadeout since it doesn't segue into *Words*.

Peter claims on one of his *Season Two* commentaries of *The Monkees*, that this song was the last time that Micky actually played drums on a Monkees track until the **JUSTUS** sessions in 1996, although that honor may go to Micky's own *Mommy and Daddy*. Regardless, after this session, Micky only did a handful of sessions where he played the drums until 1996, and he may have indeed recorded them before this session.

In actuality, if you want to *see* Micky play the drums one last time with The Monkees as a foursome before their 1986 reunion, one needs to look no further than the version of *Listen to the Band* recorded in late 1968 for the 33 1/3 *Revolutions Per Monkee* special, which is indeed the last time the foursome played live in the 1960s. Micky confirms this on the DVD commentary.

Michael: One of my favorite Davy songs. It fits his voice and personality perfectly.

As noted above, this was written by Nilsson, who at that time had only one album out and had not made much of a name for himself. Nilsson's version this song appeared on his own **PANDEMONIUM SHADOW SHOW** album, which came out a month after **PISCES**.

Let's take a moment to once again congratulate Peter on his wonderful keyboard playing, which really makes this song.

My old band would play this sometimes just for a laugh, and I loved doing Micky's harmonies. They're almost like a new song, because they're not just the next note up like most harmonies are.

Fan Thoughts

I was born after The Monkees had already gone their separate ways, but their music has been a part of my life forever. Every day in third grade, before school started, I would make a beeline to the classroom record player and listen to this song. I didn't realize then that this was from The Monkees, but when the 20th anniversary rolled around, I fell head over heels for them and their music. I was obsessed with watching the TV show ... 3 times each day, 3 different channels, same episode. I never tire of listening to their music, and I never will. They are a part of me, now and forever. — Marie Bingaman

---

DAYDREAM BELIEVER (John Stewart)
Monkee involvement: Vocals by Davy Jones. Backing vocals by Micky Dolenz. Piano by Peter Tork. Electric guitar by Michael Nesmith.
Recording dates: June 14, 1967; August 9, 1967; September 5, 1967
Highest chart position: #1 single (4 weeks); #79 single (1986 remix version)
Original release date: October 25, 1967 from 7" single and later on **THE BIRDS, THE BEES AND THE MONKEES.**

Significant other versions: Susan Boyle, The Four Tops, Anne Murray, Shonen Knife, John Stewart

Michael: Even though this was recorded during the **PISCES** sessions, it wasn't released until later and instead ended up on **THE BIRDS, THE BEES AND THE MONKEES**. I guess they thought *Pleasant Valley Sunday* had a better chance to be a hit. Or maybe they just didn't want to do another Davy single right after *A Little Bit Me, A Little Bit You*. In any event, when finally released, this outsold *Pleasant Valley Sunday* by a huge amount and became The Monkees' second biggest hit, after *I'm a Believer*.

So The Monkees' two biggest hits had "believer" in their title. Go figure. I can't even think of another hit song that has "believer" in its title. (Although I'm reminded of how the Hollies followed their hit *Bus Stop* with *Stop Stop Stop*...)

This starts off with that catchy piano jingle from Peter. Try to imagine the song without it — with just a lone piano playing the chord or something. Just wouldn't be the same, would it?

The song is so well produced, starting off simple and quiet and building bit by bit until you reach the catchy chorus. Come on, who doesn't automatically sing along when this plays? The chorus plays once and then we're back to a quieter verse two, with strings adding a counter melody, then a powerful chorus again, which is repeated but with a slightly different melody for the second time. Then a very short instrumental and back to the chorus again, over and over. The choice not to do a third verse was the correct one, as that would have dragged the song out much longer than needed. Instead, we have a perfect pop song coming in at around three minutes (which was still kind of the limit in those days until The Beatles broke all the rules a year later with *Hey Jude*).

Mark: Some say that this is the last great Monkees tune, and the last time all four Monkees appeared on the same recording. This is actually incorrect on both counts as there were many songs recorded in the next few months that are great and also feature all four Monkees. Regardless, this is still a darn good tune and as such, became The Monkees third and deservedly final #1 record. A nice understated recording which works in its favor.

Please note that songwriter John Stewart (1939-2008) is not the same Jon Stewart who hosted *The Daily Show* from 1999-2015.

Also, for those interested, what Davy says at the beginning of this is, "What number is this, Chip?" referring to Chip Douglas, who was in the control booth. I always thought he said, "What number is this, chaps?", referring to the other Monkees using an English word. Not so.

For completists, seek out the 1986 remixed single version of *Daydream Believer* featuring a heavier 1980s drum sound added and doesn't have the "What number is this, Chip?" opening and is slightly faster. This version was not included on all copies of the **THEN AND NOW...THE BEST OF THE MONKEES** collection.

SALESMAN (Craig Smith)
Monkee involvement: Vocals by Michael Nesmith. Backing vocals by Micky Dolenz and Davy Jones. Electric guitar and shaker by Michael Nesmith. Acoustic guitar by Peter Tork.
Recording dates: June 14, 1967; July 15, 1967; September 5, 1967
Original release date: November 6, 1967 from **PISCES, AQUARIUS, CAPRICORN AND JONES, LTD.**

> **Fan Thoughts**
>
> *This song is doubly special to me. Mike told me in 1997 that The Monkees chose to do this song because it sounded like something The Sir Douglas Quintet would do. I got to tell Doug this shortly before he died, and he was so-o-o pleased and proud to find out! And I got to tell Mike in 2001 how pleased Doug had been; he was so-o-o proud to hear that!* — Ken Lieck

Mark: One of The Monkees more psychedelic songs, strangely discussing a typically mundane subject — sales — which comes off greatly. A wonderful way to kick off The Monkees fourth album. I like the backing "high" vocals and Nesmith's vocals are the best yet. His improvement since the first album is marked.

I also like the hissing snake sounds on the "s" on "salesman". S-s-s-s-slimy.

An alternate mix was added to the 1995 Rhino CD reissue.

An alternate stereo mix and an alternate mono mix were included on the **PISCES, AQUARIUS, CAPRICORN AND JONES, LTD. DELUXE EDITION** (2007). The alternate stereo mix includes some spoken dialogue by Davy at the beginning and more echo on the vocals, plus Nesmith's spoken word part and a few extra "salesmans" uttered near the end of the song that were removed before final release. The alternate mono mix loses Davy's spoken dialogue and the extra "salesmans", but keeps Nesmith's spoken word part.

Michael: I always thought this song was about drugs, not just "sales." I mean, maybe that was the original intent with comments about copper pans and whatever, but then when you get to the bridge and they start singing "There goes salesman and he's sailing high again / He's sailing so high..." The salesman is a pusher, no? "Short life span..."

Anyway, no matter what it's about, it's not a bad song. Note how The Monkees have now had Mike sing the lead song off two albums in a row.

WHAT AM I DOING HANGIN' 'ROUND? (Travis Lewis/Boomer Clarke)
Monkee involvement: Vocals by Michael Nesmith. Backing vocals by Davy Jones and Micky Dolenz. Electric guitar by Michael Nesmith.
Recording dates: June 20, 1967; September 5, 1967
Original release date: November 6, 1967 from **PISCES, AQUARIUS, CAPRICORN AND JONES, LTD.**

Michael: One of Nesmith's best, even though he didn't write it. It was written by the guys behind the 60s rock group The Lewis and Clarke Expedition whose names were — this is an amazing coincidence — Lewis and Clarke.

This winds up on a lot of greatest hits collections and was performed on the TV show more than once.

This is also where pop songs are getting longer. There are no songs on the first two albums reaching three minutes, and that was normal for all bands at the time — or at least all pop bands that do singles. There were certainly more "alternative" bands playing long solos and longer pieces at the time, but rarely from the "pop" bands. The Beatles then had two songs lasting more than five minutes on **SGT. PEPPER**. The Monkees, by this point, only had two songs lasting more than three minutes: *Shades of Gray* and *Pleasant Valley Sunday* (*Daydream Believer* not having yet been released). On **PISCES**, however, we get this song and *Star Collector* which comes in more than four and half minutes long! (The **DELUXE EDITION** also includes the four-and-a-half minute *Goin' Down* as well as the five minute version of *Star Collector*.)

This song also gets notice for having too many apostrophes. Especially when I've also seen it written as *What Am I Doin' Hangin' 'Round?* I've had editors for my novels that would come at me with a knife if I wrote that.

Mark: Another Nesmith vocal and another Nesmith classic, strangely *not* written by Nesmith. I always thought it was until writing this book. I figured that a lyric like "loudmouth Yankee" was totally Nesmith, but that may have been what attracted him to sing this.

An alternate mix was included on the **PISCES, AQUARIUS, CAPRICORN AND JONES, LTD. DELUXE EDITION** (2007), that sounds almost identical to the final released version except at the very tail end.

SHE HANGS OUT (Jeff Barry/Ellie Greenwich)
Monkee involvement: Vocals by Davy Jones. Backing vocals by Micky Dolenz. Electric guitar by Michael Nesmith. Organ by Peter Tork.
Recording dates: January 21, 1967; February 4, 1967; February 6, 1967; February 10, 1967; June 21, 1967; July 3, 1967; August 9, 1967; September 5, 1967; September 23, 1967
Original release date: November 6, 1967 from **PISCES, AQUARIUS, CAPRICORN AND JONES, LTD.**

Mark: There are a couple different versions of this song. I much prefer the final released version on the **PISCES** album than the February 1967 version that was originally scheduled to be the single B-side of *A Little Bit Me, A Little Bit You*, which was eventually released on **MISSING LINKS, VOLUME 3** (1996) and later on the **HEADQUARTERS DELUXE EDITION** (2007), in both stereo remix (with a longer fadeout) and mono single mix. The final released version is more meaty with strong brass and soulful vocals by Davy — some of his strongest ever.

An alternate stereo mix was included on the **PISCES, AQUARIUS, CAPRICORN AND JONES, LTD. DELUXE EDITION** (2007). This wasn't as meaty as the final version, but similar to that version than the original version, except that it has a much longer fadeout.

Michael: This version is much better than the original one recorded by Kirshner. Davy's vocals are wonderful here, and the horns help push the song into high gear. Stylistically, there's not a lot to the music — fairly predictable chords and tune, but the performance makes it work.

HARD TO BELIEVE (Davy Jones/Kim Capli/Eddie Brick/Charlie Rockett)
Monkee involvement: Vocals by Davy Jones.

Recording dates: August 23, 1967; September 5, 1967; September 8, 1967; September 9, 1967; September 15, 1967; September 23, 1967
Original release date: November 6, 1967 from **PISCES, AQUARIUS, CAPRICORN AND JONES, LTD.**

Michael: Oh look, a third Monkees song with "Believe" in the title.

This song sounds like the kind of thing Burt Bacharach would write, and then you'd hear it in some 60s movie directed by an old guy who thinks Bachrach is "hip." The muted horns and strings would fit right in. And that's why I don't like this song very much; it's well written and everything, but if you take Davy's vocals out of it, and I said "This is a Monkees song," you'd probably say that was "hard to believe." (See what I did there?)

Mind you, it's done very well. There's a key change between the two verses that works, the ending "I love you / I need you / I do love you" is a great climax, and then it continues on and fades out effectively. I just don't like this kind of music very much. And given that this is never listed on anyone's favorite Monkees tunes — despite it being on what is arguably their best album — tells me that my opinion is not unique.

Mark: *Hard to Believe* is a nice song, nothing spectacular, but nice. The violins do get to be a bit much at times. Still it's a great track from a great album, but could possibly be considered the weakest track of the bunch. I still like it and Davy pours his heart and soul into it. Does that make sense? Just look what we're comparing it to on the rest of the album.

LOVE IS ONLY SLEEPING (Barry Mann/Cynthia Weil)
Monkee involvement: Vocals by Michael Nesmith. Backing vocals by Micky Dolenz and Davy Jones. Electric guitar by Michael Nesmith. Organ by Peter Tork. Tambourine by Davy Jones.
Recording dates: June 19, 1967; July 10, 1967; September 5, 1967; September 7, 1967; September 23, 1967; October 1, 1967
Original release date: November 6, 1967 from **PISCES, AQUARIUS, CAPRICORN AND JONES, LTD.**

Mark: I love the guitar work on this and the vocals, organ, and heck, even the tambourine. Good for you, Davy! Nesmith again commands with some of his best singing ever. This song was not originally planned to be on the **PISCES** album, but wisdom prevailed and this excellent tune bumped *Special Announcement* and *Goin' Down* from the final line-up. In fact, this song was supposed to be a single backed with *Daydream Believer.*

An alternate mix was added to the 1995 Rhino CD reissue. This mix was also included on the **PISCES, AQUARIUS, CAPRICORN AND JONES, LTD. DELUXE EDITION** (2007) and has a much longer fadeout with some studio chatter at the end.

Michael: This is a fine song, but why anyone would consider this as a single is beyond me, especially if the B-side was the far superior *Daydream Believer.* There are better contenders on this album. This isn't even the best Nesmith-sung song on the album — that would be either *What Am I Doing Hangin' 'Round* or *The Door into Summer*.

This song starts out with a weird off-kilter hook that puts the song into 7/8 time or something (I'm not sure, I can't read music). Seriously, try counting the beats. Most rock songs are 4/4 — you can count 1, 2, 3, 4 along to it. For the start of this song, you have to count 1, 2, 3, 4, 5, 6, 7 and then do it again a few times before you get into the 1, 2, 3, 4. As they'd say on *American Bandstand*, "You can't dance to it."

That's not a bad thing, but that's not a hit single in the 60s.

RIU CHIU (Traditional)
Monkee involvement: Vocals by Micky Dolenz, Davy Jones, Michael Nesmith and Peter Tork.
Recording dates: August 24, 1967; September 7, 1967; October 3, 1967
Original release date: January 1990 from
MISSING LINKS, VOLUME 2

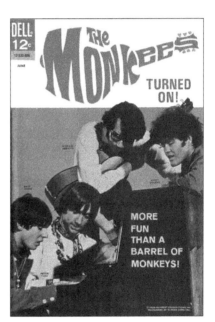

Mark: A song that first appeared on *The Monkees* TV episode called "The Christmas Show" featuring Butch "Eddie Munster" Patrick, featuring some of the best Monkees harmonizing ever recorded. An alternate studio version was finally released in 1990 as part of Rhino's **MISSING LINKS** series, which is the superior recording.

The TV version was included on the **PISCES, AQUARIUS, CAPRICORN AND JONES, LTD. DELUXE EDITION** (2007). It still has the excellent harmonies of the **MISSING LINKS** version, but sounds quite flat in comparison.

Michael: Hey, look, these guys really can sing! A very well arranged version of this old song, but I'm glad they never put it on one of their traditional albums.

THE DOOR INTO SUMMER (Bill Martin/Chip Douglas)
Monkee involvement: Vocals by Michael Nesmith. Backing vocals by Micky Dolenz. Drums by Micky Dolenz. Keyboards by Peter Tork.
Recording dates: May 29, 1967; June 22, 1967; August 23, 1967; August 24, 1967; September 5, 1967; September 7, 1967; October 3, 1967; October 4, 1967
Original release date: November 6, 1967 from **PISCES, AQUARIUS, CAPRICORN AND JONES, LTD.**

Michael: This is my favorite of the Mike songs on the album. A well written song, with great vocals and even good drum work by Micky. Once again, Peter's keyboards add a lot to the backing and isn't just a simple playing of the chords. Micky's harmonies on the second chorus build the song well, and then instead of a lead and another verse, we just repeat the chorus again, which is good — it would have dragged the song out had we done another verse. Mike and Micky then overlap their vocals as it fades. Excellent!

Lyrics aren't your typical rock song, too. This was co-written by Chip Douglas and Bill Martin. Martin went on to write many songs for others in the future, the most famous probably being *Saturday Night* by The Bay City Rollers.

Mark: Wow! So many good Nesmith vocals on this album! No wonder Nesmith is my favorite Monkee. This is another excellent example. An alternate mix was added to the 1995 Rhino CD reissue. Also, Peter's keyboards are a great subtle touch.

A 2007 remastered alternate mix was included on the **PISCES, AQUARIUS, CAPRICORN AND JONES, LTD. DELUXE EDITION** (2007) which makes the tinkly piano much more prominent in the mix and a longer fadeout.

PETER PERCIVAL PATTERSON'S PET PIG PORKY (Peter Tork)
Monkee involvement: Vocals by Peter Tork.
Recording dates: June 10, 1967; October 4, 1967
Original release date: November 6, 1967 from **PISCES, AQUARIUS, CAPRICORN AND JONES, LTD.**

Mark: More silliness from The Monkees, but for some reason, this one isn't as annoying as *Zilch* is. I know *Zilch* has its defenders, but I'd rather listen to *Ditty Diego* (from **HEAD**). Peter meanwhile was another Dr. Demento favorite and an interesting vocal diversion by Mr. Tork, who rarely saw a lead vocal otherwise and pops his "p's" for comedic effect. Nowadays, I can't listen to this without thinking of *Pleasant Valley Sunday* — the track that follows this one on the album — playing next.

Michael: I don't have a problem with them putting a few silly things on the album, and this stops just before it get tiring. The fact that they jump right into *Pleasant Valley Sunday* helps.

DAILY NIGHTLY (Michael Nesmith)
Monkee involvement: Vocals by Micky Dolenz. Moog synthesizer by Micky Dolenz. Electric guitar by Michael Nesmith. Organ by Peter Tork.
Recording dates: June 19, 1967; September 5, 1967; October 4, 1967
Original release date: November 6, 1967 from **PISCES, AQUARIUS, CAPRICORN AND JONES, LTD.**

Mark: A great, great song. Interesting about the **PISCES** album is that Mike has four lead vocals for songs he did not write and then we come to the first song on the album that he did write, and he doesn't sing lead! A great early use of the Moog synthesizer by Micky which at the time was still in its experimental sound stages. At the time, the audio taped sounds had to be cut and spliced together in order to make any sort of recognizable tune. Otherwise, it was just random noises like those heard on George Harrison's **ELECTRONIC SOUND** album. An alternate mix was added to the 1995 Rhino CD reissue.

The Monkees never played this live until 2012 and when they did, Micky had to read Nesmith's lyrics from a book while onstage, due to their complexity.

An alternate mix was included on the **PISCES, AQUARIUS, CAPRICORN AND JONES, LTD. DELUXE EDITION** (2007). This mix eliminates the Moog.

Michael: This was always a Monkees' fans favorite based on polls and surveys I've seen. It never appeared on greatest hits albums or anything, which is a shame. It's an excellent song, and one of Mike's best written even if it doesn't mean anything.

Notice how the tune changes slightly between verses — very effective. Micky's not singing the exact same notes on the second verse as he did on the first verse. There's not really a chorus to speak of, but there is a bridge between verse two and verse three. Micky's voice is muted in a way that The Monkees used (and abused) later on **THE BIRDS, THE BEES AND THE MONKEES**.

Once again, Chip Douglas' bass pushes the song along well, and is really an important part of the feel of the song. Peter keeps the organ simple, which is good. Any fancy doodling would definitely distract here.

When Mike and Micky performed this live in their recent tours, they'd have this routine where Micky would bug Mike for forgetting to bring the Moog and Mike would say "Don't worry about it, I got it covered." They'd then perform the song and whenever it would get to one of the parts where the Moog would make a weird noise, Mike would walk to the microphone and make the silly noise with his mouth.

I'm pretty sure the "Micky reading the lyrics from a book" was part of the comedy routine. I mean, come on, Micky is an actor who is used to memorizing dialog. He's done Broadway plays. I'm sure he could learn a few verses of an old song easily enough.

GOIN' DOWN (Diane Hilderbrand/Peter Tork/Michael Nesmith/Micky Dolenz/Davy Jones)
Monkee involvement: Vocals by Micky Dolenz. Electric guitars by Michael Nesmith and Peter Tork.
Recording dates: June 21, 1967; July 5, 1967; September 15, 1967; September 23, 1967; October 3, 1967; October 4, 1967
Highest chart position: #104 single B-side

Fan Thoughts

Garden State Park, Cherry Hill, NJ, August 11, 1989. The Monkees gave two shows that day, an afternoon and evening. However, it was an outdoor venue with spots given to whoever got there first, so we arrived when the park opened that day. We got our spots front and center and settled down to wait. In the rain. The stage was under cover, but we were not. In no time we were soaked. But we stayed. When Micky sang Goin' Down, he burst out laughing when he got to the line "when they find me in the morning wet and drowned." And after the song in the second show, he yelled, "I can't believe they're standing in the rain!" Die hards, we were. — Kerry Gans

Original release date: October 25, 1967 from 7" single. First album appearance on **MONKEE BUSINESS** (1983); First CD appearance on **THEN AND NOW...THE BEST OF THE MONKEES** (1986).

Mark: Please don't take this the wrong way, but I always felt that Micky spoke the gayest "sock it to me" at beginning of this song. After that, Micky blows it out of the water with a powerful and soulful vocal rendition in his best James Brown style. The musicianship is also top-notch. This was relegated to the B-side of *Daydream Believer* originally, but deserved much better exposure, and eluded album inclusion until 1983. It did, however, make at least three separate appearances on the TV series.

In fact, it originally was supposed to be included on the **PISCES** album. At least it was on the B-side of a #1 single so all a fan would have to do was flip the record order. An alternate mix was added to the 1995 Rhino CD reissue of **PISCES**.

A stereo mix and the mono single version were included on the **PISCES, AQUARIUS, CAPRICORN AND JONES, LTD. DELUXE EDITION** (2007). They basically sound identical.

A 7" single featuring the TV mono mix was included with the Blu-ray version of *The Monkees* TV Series, released in 2016.

Michael: "Sock it to me," of course, was a catchphrase from *Rowan and Martin's Laugh-In* which came on directly after *The Monkees*. Micky saying it really was a bad thing, as it dates the song too much, in the same way the "sock it to me" bits do to Aretha Franklin's *Respect* — although I guess most people who aren't my age would have no idea where that came from.

This apparently was mostly a jam with Mike, Peter, and the backing musicians led by arranger Shorty Rogers, who gives it that big-band/jazz feel. The musicians understand dynamics — having the song get quieter and louder, more exciting and less so, and as such it never gets boring. I never get tired of hearing this song.

The song has two parts — At 1:30 or so, it switches to a two-chord split and never goes back. Think about that — it's just two chords over and over again for the majority of the song, and that's just fine because good musicians can make all the difference.

I'm not sure who gets credit for the music. All four Monkees and Diane Hildebrand wrote the lyrics about a man who throws himself into the river to kill himself after a bad relationship, and then decides to live again as he "flows on down to New Orleans."

DON'T CALL ON ME (Michael Nesmith/John London)
Monkee involvement: Vocals by Michael Nesmith. Spoken chatter by Micky Dolenz and Davy Jones. Electric guitar by Michael Nesmith. Organ by Peter Tork.
Recording dates: June 20, 1967; July 7, 1967; September 5, 1967; October 9, 1967
Original release date: November 6, 1967 from **PISCES, AQUARIUS, CAPRICORN AND JONES, LTD.**
Significant other versions: Michael Nesmith

Michael: I think Micky's introduction at the start of the song was meant to set the scene for this kind of song, which seems to fit into that same feel as *Early Morning Blues and Greens*. A lounge band in a smoky nightclub would play this song, not a rock and roll band. Still, Mike's vocals are excellent here, and he shows that he isn't just some country crooner.

This is an old song of Mike's — he had originally performed it back in his folkie days.

This song also uses the words "little girl" — which was common at the time — but seems kind of creepy now. More on this later.

Mark: Mike's fifth and final vocal on the **PISCES** album and he sang it in a dreamy type voice that is usually a Micky specialty. Personally, if I was Mike, I would have given this one to Micky and kept *Daily Nightly* for myself, but maybe Mike was a bit self-conscious with it. The track starts off sounding a party with Micky speaking an amusing introduction about the song asking a musical question, which this doesn't.

Mike also released it as an instrumental on his own **WICHITA TRAIN WHISTLE SINGS** (1968) album.

SPECIAL ANNOUNCEMENT (unknown)
Monkee involvement: Vocals by Peter Tork
Recording dates: October 9, 1967
Original release date: January 1995 from **PISCES, AQUARIUS, CAPRICORN AND JONES, LTD.** bonus track

Mark: Not a song at all, but a spoken word announcement by Peter testing various sound frequencies in a way best designed to annoy most dogs and even some people. I guess it's nice they finally released this in 1995, but I would have opted for another alternate mix song than this, despite the fact that this was originally slotted to open the **PISCES** album.

This was also included on the **PISCES, AQUARIUS, CAPRICORN AND JONES, LTD. DELUXE EDITION** (2007).

Michael: This is kind of funny and makes fun of those weird albums that came out in those days where people would listen to sound effects and stuff to test out their new stereo systems, since stereo was still an unusual thing at the time. The whole joke is that it eventually tests frequencies that only dogs can hear, ha ha. I can imagine you laughing right now.

Anyway, fortunately, Peter came up with *Peter Percival Patterson's Pet Pig Porky* and that got onto the album instead.

STAR COLLECTOR (Gerry Goffin/Carole King)
Monkee involvement: Vocals by Micky Dolenz and Davy Jones. Electric guitar by Michael Nesmith. Organ by Peter Tork.
Recording dates: June 22, 1967; July 6, 1967; October 4, 1967; October 16, 1967
Original release date: November 6, 1967 from **PISCES, AQUARIUS, CAPRICORN AND JONES, LTD.**

Michael: Hello! (Pickle)

Micky starts this one off with his "hello" and then it kicks into high gear, using the Moog for only the second time on a pop record. Micky sings backup here, and as the jam goes on and on at the end, he insists on saying "bye bye" in the background since he also said "hello." That makes this an appropriate album closer.

The Moog lead is quite good, never boring, and works quite well

to give us what was, at the time, the longest Monkees song, lasting over four and a half minutes. On the album, however, they had it listed as lasting 3:30 — still the longest Monkees song for the time — but when I was younger, making cassette tapes of my favorite Monkees songs, it caused me no end of troubles. The tape would run out of space even though I had done all my math correctly to make sure I could fit as many songs as possible. It never occurred to me that the album was wrong — I blamed the tape manufacturers.

There is an even longer version available on the **DELUXE EDITION** but you can see why they edited it down, because it drags in parts.

Since it was written by Goffin and King, you know it's going to be good, and heart-throb Davy was the perfect one to sing about groupies. "She only aims to please the young celebrities" but "How can I love her when I just don't respect her?"

Which brings up an interesting point. Davy's songs on this album seem to have a theme — *Cuddly Toy*, *She Hangs Out* and *Star Collector* are all about women who the singer doesn't seem to have a lot of respect for, to put it mildly. And they're all three written by different people, too. Hmm.

Mark: An early ode to groupies, usually not a subject of songs of this vintage, as our pop stars were supposed to be cute and virginal and wholesome, not decadent and having Roman orgies. Some of Peter's best organ playing and Nesmith's best guitar playing accompany this. A silly but fun opening and also some crazy psychedelic music add to the fun.

An alternate stereo mix and an alternate mix were included on the **PISCES, AQUARIUS, CAPRICORN AND JONES, LTD. DELUXE EDITION** (2007). The alternate stereo mix has a longer instrumental break and a longer fadeout with much stranger sounds at the end. The alternate mix sounds closer to the released version, but has a longer fadeout as well, but not a longer instrumental break.

A 7" single featuring the TV mono mix was included with the Blu-ray version of *The Monkees* TV Series, released in 2016.

PISCES, AQUARIUS, CAPRICORN AND JONES, LTD.

Original release date: November 6, 1967
Highest chart position: #1 (5 weeks) in 1967; #124 in 1986
Weeks on chart: 46 in 1967-1968; 17 in 1986

Salesman
She Hangs Out
The Door into Summer
Love is Only Sleeping
Cuddly Toy
Words

Hard to Believe
What Am I Doing Hangin' 'Round?
Peter Percival Patterson's Pet Pig Porky
Pleasant Valley Sunday
Daily Nightly
Don't Call on Me
Star Collector

Michael: What a change from **MORE OF THE MONKEES**, where Mike only got to sing one song. Here, he has five, the most on any album (although he only wrote two, one of which Micky sings). In fact, of the first four songs on the album, Mike sings three of them! Davy has four on the album and Micky, usually the lead singer, only has three. In fact, you don't even hear him singing lead until the end of side one, and even then he's sharing vocals with Peter.

This is my favorite Monkees album — not a bad song in it. (**HEAD** would probably be my favorite but it's hard for me to consider it a real album when it only has six songs). Imagine how much better this would be had they replaced *Hard to Believe* with *Daydream Believer*, which was the #1 song at the time this was released. And then I would also replace *Don't Call on Me* with *Goin' Down*. That would have been a great way to close side one. I also don't like putting two Mike songs back to back (*Door Into Summer* and *Love is Only Sleeping*). Here's what my perfect **PISCES** would be if I had been choosing the songs back then:

Salesman
She Hangs Out
The Door into Summer
Cuddly Toy
Words
Goin' Down

Daydream Believer
What Am I Doing Hangin' 'Round?
Peter Percival Patterson's Pet Pig Porky
Pleasant Valley Sunday
Daily Nightly
Love is Only Sleeping
Star Collector

However, I understand why they didn't put *Daydream Believer* on the album, because they wanted to save it for a single. After all, many Monkees fans at the time wouldn't go out and buy a single that was already on the album...

Mark: This is my favorite Monkees album. Despite the silliness of *Peter Percival* and the slight weakness of *Hard to Believe*, this is one solid album and deservedly #1 with an almost double-sided #1 single hit with *Pleasant Valley Sunday / Words*. Every track is a winner and since Michael is my favorite Monkee, I have no problem with the fact that he has five lead vocals, as author Mike has mentioned above. The Monkees would not achieve this level of album consistency again until **GOOD TIMES!**

HAWAIIAN SONG (Micky Dolenz)
Monkee involvement: Vocals by Micky Dolenz. Sleigh bells by Micky Dolenz.
Recording dates: September 7, 1967

CROW ON THE CRADLE (Sydney Carter)
Monkee involvement: Vocals by Peter Tork. Acoustic guitar by Peter Tork.
Recording dates: November 12, 1967

THE DOLPHINS (Fred Neil)
Monkee involvement: Vocals by Peter Tork. Acoustic guitar by Peter Tork.
Recording dates: November 12, 1967

UNKNOWN #1 (unknown)
Monkee involvement: Acoustic guitar by Peter Tork
Recording dates: November 12, 1967

THE WATER IS WIDE (Traditional)
Monkee involvement: Vocals by Peter Tork. Acoustic guitar by Peter Tork.
Recording dates: November 12, 1967

Mark: A third group of five songs that were recorded on the same day (except *Hawaiian Song*). This time, all but one have vocals and it is unknown why none of them have been officially released. They are listed here for completeness, but the authors have not heard these tracks. They may be released someday as part of a **PISCES, AQUARIUS, CAPRICORN AND JONES, LTD. SUPER DELUXE EDITION,** which to date has not been compiled, or if The Monkees choose to release these tracks for some future follow up to **GOOD TIMES!**

Apparently, *Hawaiian Song* isn't much, just Micky chanting along with sleigh bells. The rest is part of a lengthy Peter Tork session that really only resulted in *Lady's Baby*, and even that wasn't released until the **MISSING LINKS** collections, and the version released wasn't even from this session.

CEILING IN MY ROOM (Davy Jones/Dom DeMieri/Bobby Dick)
Monkee involvement: Vocals by Davy Jones

Recording dates: November 14, 1967
Original release date: July 29, 1997 from **I'M A BELIEVER AND OTHER HITS** and later on **THE BIRDS, THE BEES AND THE MONKEES DELUXE EDITION.**

Mark: This is one of those songs that was mysteriously held back from the **MISSING LINKS** series. It's not one of their best songs, but I would have much preferred this included with the series than some of the songs that were. The best version is the one released on the **I'M A BELIEVER** budget-line disc. *Monkee Business Fanzine* reported that the master tapes had gone missing which is why it was held back until later, but I have my doubts. It seems like Rhino always leaves a few odds and ends in the vault, so they can always have a goodly supply of "never before released" tracks for future compilations such as this.

A 1967 stereo mix and a 1967 mono mix appear on **THE BIRDS, THE BEES AND THE MONKEES DELUXE EDITION** (2010). The stereo version is noticeably double-tracked to where Davy has made no attempt to be in sync with his own vocal. The mono mix is identical to the **I'M A BELIEVER** version.

Michael: Another slow Davy song that sounds like it came from some obscure sixties off-Broadway musical, because that's the kind of music he listened to, I guess. The lyrics are introspective about being a millionaire pop star, the theme of which Davy will approach again with *You and I* from **INSTANT REPLAY.**

This is really forgettable and is the start of the era where Davy is bringing songs to The Monkees that don't sound at all like Monkees songs. Mike will also soon start producing songs that are very country-inspired and don't sound like Monkees songs, too, so by the time we get to **PRESENT**, it feels like there are three different performing artists just sharing an album instead of a cohesive album from one artist.

MAGNOLIA SIMMS (Michael Nesmith/Charlie Rockett)
Monkee involvement: Vocals by Michael Nesmith. Guitar by Michael Nesmith.
Recording dates: December 2, 1967
Original release date: April 22, 1968 from **THE BIRDS, THE BEES AND THE MONKEES**
Significant other versions: First National Band

Michael: In 1966, The New Vaudeville Band released a hit single called *Winchester Cathedral* which tried to recapture the sound of the 1920s, before microphones were used, with the lead singer going through a megaphone. The quality was hurt by this and gave the singer a nasally sound.

Nesmith decided to do his own version and take it one step further. He added the scratchy sound inherent to old records but then did the song in mono and only coming out of one speaker. (Later versions mixed that to the center but kept the mono sound.)

Note that this predates The Beatles' *Honey Pie*, which also used the scratchy record and megaphone-sound for the line "Now she's hit the big time."

Not a bad song, but I think it goes on way too long, even when taking into consideration the skipping bit. I wonder how many people rushed to their turntable to fix the record the first time they heard that.

Mark: A very, very odd track, but at least Nesmith mentions the title character in the song's lyrics. As with the end of **HEAD**, where the film burns up and melts in the film gate, this song is replete with a needle drop, pops, skips, and scratches inherent in old 78 RPM records. The effect is achieved with much finesse. I love it at the end where the song really skips and goes back to an earlier part of the record to finish out correctly...almost. Surprises await you until the very end.

An acoustic version and a stereo remix appear on **THE BIRDS, THE BEES AND THE MONKEES DELUXE EDITION** (2010). The stereo remix features Nesmith's vocal effect, but none of the other special effects. The stereo remix has more prominent drums and similar percussive effects, but again doesn't have the other special effects, except Michael's coughing at the end.

WHO WILL BUY? (Lionel Bart)
Monkee involvement: Electric guitar by Peter Tork
Recording dates: December 3, 1967
Significant other versions: Davy Jones

Mark: Peter attempts 26 takes of this *Oliver!* song usually associated with Davy Jones, and even those are fragmented, so a releasable take by Peter probably doesn't exist. There were also attempts at *(I Prithee) Do Not Ask For Love*, *Two-Part Invention in F-Major* and *You Can't Judge a Book By the Cover*, all attempted elsewhere. Peter has many of these unproductive lengthy sessions at this time, probably because of his frustration over the whole Monkee thing as well as that he has the freedom to utilize this lengthy session time.

Micky, Davy and Mike also indulged in their session time with differing results. Micky was more like Peter by working one song to death, which Davy and Mike tended to complete multiple recordings at their various sessions.

Davy finally released his version of *Who Will Buy?* with The Monkees as part of his solo spot called *Oliver Medley* on **2001: LIVE FROM LAS VEGAS!** See that entry.

Michael: What the hell was Peter thinking? Seriously? Did he really expect to release this? Was he trying to show Davy that he could sing *Oliver!* songs too? Admittedly, he used to sing this in his pre-Monkees days playing the clubs in Greenwich Village, but still... This really doesn't belong on any Monkees album.

VALLERI (Tommy Boyce/Bobby Hart)
Monkee involvement: Vocals by Davy Jones
Recording dates: August 6, 1966; August 27, 1966; December 26, 1967; December 28, 1967
Highest chart position: #3 single
Original release date: March 2, 1968 from 7" single and **THE BIRDS, THE BEES AND THE MONKEES**

Mark: I love, love, love this song and its brass. I also love the flamenco guitar even if Nesmith really isn't playing it. The version I love best is the fade-out version from this album rather than the abrupt cold ending.

A first recorded version appears on the 2006 **MORE OF THE MONKEES DELUXE EDITION** CD. This is one is basically the version heard on the TV show, which originally appeared on **MISSING LINKS, VOLUME 2** (1990). It's a little more lax than the punched-up single version.

Michael: I don't share in the love for this simple little song. In fact, Michael Nesmith is reported to have said that this was the worst song ever. I don't think I'd go that far. The performance is pretty good, and the horns improve the song tremendously from the earlier version done for the TV show, but the words are simple and the tune basically consists of the hook and then two lines, repeated in various ways.

This song fits much better in 1966 when it was first recorded, before the show even debuted. They redid it here and added horns, and it is a better version but it still sounds dated, since music had changed so much in that short period of time.

This was their last hit single, released at the tail end of the TV show before the summer repeats kicked in.

THE STORY OF ROCK AND ROLL (Harry Nilsson)
Monkee involvement: Electric 12-string guitar by Michael Nesmith. Piano by Peter Tork. Drums by Micky Dolenz. Percussion by Davy Jones.
Recording dates: March 18, 1967; March 19, 1967; April 21, 1967; January 10, 1968
Original release date: September 21, 2000 from **HEADQUARTERS SESSIONS**
Significant other versions: The Turtles

Mark: If you want to know how this could have sounded, please check out The Turtles version. As it stands, The Monkees only accomplished two different instrumental versions.

Michael: Not one of Nilsson's best. I don't even like The Turtles' version that much.

MR. RICHLAND'S FAVORITE SONG (Harry Nilsson)
Monkee involvement: Electric guitar by Michael Nesmith
Recording dates: January 11, 1968

LANCE'S (Lance Wakely)
Monkee involvement: Bass by Peter Tork
Recording dates: January 14, 1968

TITLE (unknown)
Monkee involvement: Conga by Micky Dolenz
Recording dates: January 18, 1968

JUST ANOTHER DREAM (unknown)
Monkee involvement: Vocals by Peter Tork. Piano by Peter Tork.
Recording dates: January 24, 1968

MY SONG IN #7 (Peter Tork)
Monkee involvement: Guitar by Peter Tork
Recording dates: January 24, 1968

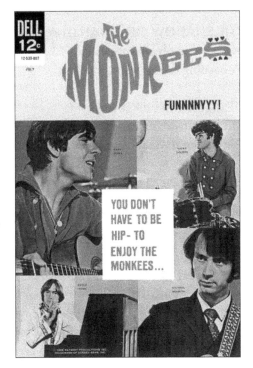

PINBALL MACHINE (unknown)
Monkee involvement: Michael Nesmith
Recording dates: January 24, 1968

NO TITLE (Michael Nesmith)
Monkee involvement: Organ by Michael Nesmith
Recording dates: January 23, 1968; January 25, 1968

EMPIRE (Michael Nesmith)
Monkee involvement: Electric guitar by Michael Nesmith
Recording dates: January 25, 1968

SEASONS (Michael Nesmith)
Monkee involvement: Acoustic guitar by Michael Nesmith
Recording dates: February 2, 1968

IMPACK (Michael Nesmith)
Monkee involvement: none
Recording dates: February 17, 1968

UNTITLED (unknown)
Monkee involvement: Acoustic guitar by Peter Tork
Recording dates: June 22, 1967; February 9, 1968; February 18, 1968

THE SHADOW OF A MAN (Helen Miller/Howard Greenfield)
Monkee involvement: none
Recording dates: March 9, 1968

DEAR MARM (unknown)
Monkee involvement: none
Recording dates: February 16, 1968; April 2, 1968

Mark: These 13 tracks were various songs attempted at different sessions from January through March 1968 which ultimately resulted in **THE BIRDS, THE BEES AND THE MONKEES** album with some songs held over for **INSTANT REPLAY**. Many of the finished unreleased songs finally saw release as part of the **MISSING LINKS** series and later as bonus tracks on **THE BIRDS, THE BEES AND THE MONKEES DELUXE EDITION** (2010).

Most of these 13 tracks are either fragments, rehearsals, jams, instrumentals or lost! Since **BIRDS...BEES** is not as highly a sought-after period in Monkees history, it is doubtful a **BIRDS, BEES AND MONKEES SESSIONS** will arise out of all this. However, since there still has not been a **PISCES DELUXE EDITION**, what exists here could be thrown on there. Time will tell, but in reading about the various tracks in Sandoval's *Day by Day*, we're probably not missing all that much.

Michael: I would have loved to have heard Davy try Nilsson's *Mr. Richland's Favorite Song*, which is a much better song than Nilsson's *Daddy's Song*, which was eventually recorded for **HEAD**.

WHILE I CRY (Michael Nesmith)
Monkee involvement: Vocals by Michael Nesmith. Guitar by Michael Nesmith.
Recording dates: January 14, 1968; January 15, 1968
Original release date: February 15, 1969 from **INSTANT REPLAY**
Significant other versions: Michael Nesmith

Michael: Years ago, I did a blog post with the top ten greatest Monkees songs you've probably never heard, and this was one of them. A really wonderful song.

In case you're wondering, the others on that list were (in no particular order) *Porpoise Song*, *The Girl I Knew Somewhere*, *Shorty Blackwell*, *Goin' Down*, *Daily Nightly*, *Star Collector*, *Long Title: Do I Have to Do This All Over Again*, and *Auntie's Municipal Court* (with *Randy Scouse Git* as a contender because maybe enough people had heard that one before).

Anyway, look at how well this song is arranged. It starts pleasantly enough with acoustic guitar which is then doubled by an electric guitar. Mike starts singing. At this point, the notes are fairly monotone but the changing progression of the music in the background makes up for that. Then there's a bit of a chorus of sorts, and instead of going back to the verse, it has a big harmony part. And now there's a bridge that is completely different but fits perfectly — it's quite catching and could be a song in itself but instead it's perfect for building the song. Another run-through of mostly instrumental, and then finally it's on to the second verse, and then it slows and ends, without ever repeating the "chorus" or bridge again. Perfect. Well written and well performed.

I'm not much for Mike's country music in general but this is one of his best. I'm sorry it seems to have been lost somewhere, because I rarely hear anyone put this on their favorites list.

Mark: A 1968 mono mix and an alternate mono mix appear on **THE BIRDS, THE BEES AND THE MONKEES DELUXE EDITION** (2010). These versions are more acoustic than the final released version.

As with *Don't Wait For Me*, this song was far more country-sounding than what was being released by The Monkees prior to Peter Tork's exit and is probably one reason why it was shelved by The Monkees until afterwards and The Monkees were clamoring for something by Nesmith to add to the **INSTANT REPLAY** album, since he provided absolutely no new contributions to the project. It's pretty good country, not great, but pretty good.

The UK mono mix appears on the **INSTANT REPLAY DELUXE EDITION** (2011), which is subtly different than the 1968 mono mix. Very subtle. Like non-existent subtle.

Mike also released it as an instrumental on his own **WICHITA TRAIN WHISTLE SINGS** (1968) album. Here it is called *While I Cried*.

AUNTIE'S MUNICIPAL COURT (Michael Nesmith/Keith Allison)
Monkee involvement: Lead vocal by Micky Dolenz. Backing vocals by Michael Nesmith.
Recording dates: January 6, 1968; January 15, 1968; January 16, 1968
Original release date: April 22, 1968 from **THE BIRDS, THE BEES AND THE MONKEES**

Mark: Is this Michael's sequel to *Your Auntie Grizelda*? It's a typical Nesmith song where the title doesn't fit in with the lyrics, which are very cryptic. Micky sings here in a very nice way. Nice guitar picking throughout and Harry Nilsson plays keyboards!

There's an "owee-owee-owee-owee" sound near the end that's quite a lot like The Beatles' *Tell Me What You See*.

A version sung by Mike appears on **THE BIRDS, THE BEES AND THE MONKEES DELUXE EDITION** (2010). It's very nice. I don't know why he gave it to Micky to sing. Micky still sings lead a little bit near the end on this version.

Michael: I think Michael recorded this first and then had Micky overdub his voice, so it's basically two of them singing the exact same notes but with Micky more prominent.

This is a favorite. There's not a lot to it — the chord changes are pretty predictable — but there sure are a lot of guitars in there, and it works. Instead of merely duplicating each other, they play off each other quite well and build a very full sound. The performance of this piece makes it special.

I remember when I was a kid, the album I had featured Micky at the end singing "herewegoagain herewegoagain herewegoagain" over and over as it faded out. More recent versions don't fade out as quickly and you can hear Micky saying it, like an announcer, with more and more echo added until all your hear is his voice.

MERRY GO ROUND (Peter Tork/Diane Hilderbrand)
Monkee involvement: Vocals by Peter Tork. Acoustic guitar, piano, bass by Peter Tork.
Recording dates: December 17, 1967; January 20, 1968; January 22, 1968; January 31, 1968
Original release date: March 1996 from **MISSING LINKS, VOLUME 3**

Mark: **MISSING LINKS** was pretty much scraping the bottom of the barrel at this point as this song really isn't very good, nor is it complete. It's sung out of tune and the instrumentation is with awkward minor chords, although that seems to be the intention here.

A 1968 mono mix and version one and three appear on **THE BIRDS, THE BEES AND THE MONKEES DELUXE EDITION** (2010). This mono version really is not a good version. It's absolutely cacophonous. Version one is pretty, but sparse, instrumentally. Version three is very similar to version one.

Michael: Peter was trying to be weird. But that doesn't mean it's good. Given that the only instruments are Peter overdubbing, this seems more like a demo than a real attempt to make a song. It's not too listenable, but underneath it all, there is something there. Seriously, I could see this being done by a good band. It almost sounds like the kind of thing XTC could do well.

WAR GAMES (Davy Jones/Steve Pitts)
Monkee involvement: Vocals by Davy Jones. Acoustic guitar by Michael Nesmith.

Recording dates: January 23, 1968; February 6, 1968; February 8, 1968
Original release date: July 1987 from **MISSING LINKS**

Michael: Davy and Steve Pitts got together and wrote some songs around this time, none of which are especially good. I am assuming Davy wrote the lyrics, but who knows? They all sound like off-Broadway rejects to me. I mean, I *like* Broadway music (well, I like *good* Broadway music) but that's not why I listen to The Monkees.

It's not especially catchy, but the lyrics are actually not bad for a 1960s protest song, about politicians who send kids to war without putting themselves into any harm: "Did you buy your tickets for the war game? / Aren't you glad that you're sitting in the back? / For the game is deadly heavy for the players / Aren't you glad it's a spectator sport? / You don't have to play the game if you don't want to / You can sit at home and hear it on the news / They will show you colored pictures of the killings ...."

Mark: Davy's attempt to do something a little more meaty that Micky did to greater effect later on with *Zor and Zam* or *Mommy and Daddy*. It's not that bad, but it's not that memorable or has much of an impact, either.

Version one and two appear on **THE BIRDS, THE BEES AND THE MONKEES DELUXE EDITION** (2010). Version one sounds completely different other than the vocals, more like a protest song with Davy singing harshly against an acoustic guitar, some organ and drums. Version two is identical to the **MISSING LINKS** version.

The 1968 mono mix appears on the **INSTANT REPLAY DELUXE EDITION** (2011). The tempo is slower on this version and Davy's vocals almost seem lethargic.

CHANGES (Davy Jones/Steve Pitts)
Monkee involvement: Vocals by Davy Jones
Recording dates: February 6, 1968; February 8, 1968
Original release date: January 1990 from **MISSING LINKS, VOLUME 2**

Michael: A weird little song where Davy sings "We always stay the same" a lot. It's really... um... bad. I mean, it's not *The Day We Fall in Love* bad, but it just rambles on and on with horns whizzing all over the place and a drummer who thinks the song is better the more times he hits the snare. It just... goes nowhere, and sounds like maybe Tom Jones should be singing it or something.

Mark: Why wasn't this released on **CHANGES** in 1970? Perhaps, we'll never know.

A 2009 mix appears on **THE BIRDS, THE BEES AND THE MONKEES DELUXE EDITION** (2010) that sounds almost the same as the **MISSING LINKS** version.

The 1968 mono mix appears on the **INSTANT REPLAY DELUXE EDITION** (2011). It's more meaty on the brass and that rattling piece of percussion that I can't remember the name of.

THE GIRL I LEFT BEHIND ME (Neil Sedaka/Carole Bayer)
Monkee involvement: Vocals by Davy Jones
Recording dates: November 23, 1966; October 31, 1967; November 7, 1967; November 21, 1967; February 6, 1968; February 9, 1968
Original release date: February 15, 1969 from **INSTANT REPLAY**

Mark: The **INSTANT REPLAY** version wasn't recorded until February 6, 1968. Not a bad song; not a great song. Kinda sappy, kinda ok. Davy sings it reasonably well. It has a bit more prominent guitar than other versions.

A previously unissued early version was released as a bonus track from **THE BIRDS, THE BEES AND THE MONKEES** reissue from 1994. That version is quite dreary compared to the final version.

A 1967 stereo mix, a 1967 mono mix and a third recorded version appear on **THE BIRDS, THE BEES AND THE MONKEES DELUXE EDITION** (2010). The violin, drums and chimes are much more prominent in these versions, but they are the same tempo as the final released version. There is also a longer fadeout where Davy just kind of keeps singing long after he was supposed to and the instrumentation really goes on much longer than normal. The third recorded version has some vocal mistakes!

Michael: The Monkees are getting more control over their own music, and instead of working as a band like they did for **HEADQUARTERS**, they're each going their own way, with their own backing musicians, and making The Monkees more of a showcase for individuals than as a group. And of course, that's kind of understandable. These guys would have never gotten together to form a band if it wasn't for the TV show — they all are just too different.

Mike is writing more and more country songs and not even trying to do a "country/rock" mix that he created; Davy just wants to sing show tunes; Peter is writing hippie love songs and old folk songs; and Micky is just being Micky — his music still kind of fits into what The Monkees sound was originally like better than the others.

And we can see exactly what kind of music each of them really liked. What we get from Davy are a pile of sappy easy listening ballads that any rock band would be embarrassed to have on their album. Mind you, I like Davy's voice — he's great on *Daydream Believer* and *Star Collector* and *She Hangs Out...* songs other people with better taste in music pick out for him. But when he gets to choose his own songs to sing, it's clear that he doesn't belong in a rock band at all — he just wants to be back on Broadway.

But onto *The Girl I Left Behind Me*. As much as I liked Neil Sedaka's previous Monkees contribution *When Love Comes Knockin' at Your Door*, this one is just another of the sappy Davy songs I don't like much. He sings it quite well, but this could have been performed on the Lawrence Welk show without a change.

SEEGER'S THEME (Pete Seeger)
Monkee involvement: Acoustic guitar and electric guitar by Peter Tork.
Recording dates: January 30, 1967; November 12, 1967; January 14, 1968; January 20, 1968; January 22, 1968; February 10, 1968
Original release date: January 1990 from **MISSING LINKS, VOLUME 2**

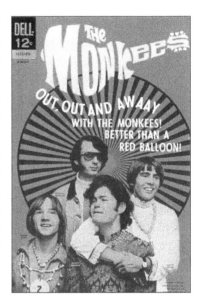

Mark: So many versions of this. Where to begin? It's a sprightly instrumental, but it's amazing that it was recorded so many times. The **MISSING LINKS** version is probably the best.

An early demo version of the song (January 30, 1967) was finally released on **HEADQUARTERS SESSIONS** (2000).

An acoustic version, an alternate version and an electric version appear on **THE BIRDS, THE BEES AND THE MONKEES DELUXE EDITION** (2010). The acoustic version is shorter than the others. The alternate version is much faster than the others. The electric version has a barely audible electric guitar in the background.

Michael: And here's Peter doing his folk thing. I don't think they ever really planned on releasing this, but hey, Peter can indeed play.

P.O. BOX 9847 (Tommy Boyce/Bobby Hart)
Monkee involvement: Vocals by Micky Dolenz.
Recording dates: December 26, 1967; February 10, 1968
Original release date: April 22, 1968 from **THE BIRDS, THE BEES AND THE MONKEES**
Significant other versions: Boyce & Hart

Michael: This is actually a pretty clever song, lyrically. The singer is composing the kind of ad that used to appear in newspapers before Tinder came along, where someone is looking for love. He first tries one version, rips it up, tries a second one, throws that one away, and then tries a third, and is still unhappy describing himself to possible romantic interests.

It's the instruments that don't seem to work. The heavy drums and weird violins distract instead of emphasize the song.

Boyce & Hart's own version isn't any better. Heavy on the drums and bass, it kind of plods along but adds an out-of tune heavy guitar and a very dated weird organ solo that jumps in for a few bars and then mysteriously ends without any resolution. I much prefer The Monkees' version.

It's a well-written song that suffers from a bad performance. At this point, The Monkees have not only gone on to do their own thing but they've actually started producing the songs themselves as well — which may be one of the reasons the quality starts to go down around here. If Chip Douglas was still in charge, **THE BIRDS, THE BEES AND THE MONKEES** may have been a much better record, and a bigger hit.

Mark: Boyce and Hart's attempt to do The Beatles' *Paperback Writer* or Elvis Presley's *Return to Sender* or something. I am curious as to what Rafelson's contribution was. His name is listed in Sandoval's *Day by Day* as a writer, but nowhere else.

There is another unissued alternate mix that was added as a bonus track to the 1994 Rhino CD reissue of **THE BIRDS, THE BEES AND THE MONKEES**. I don't care for the instrumental backing as much on this version.

An alternate 1968 stereo mix appears on **THE BIRDS, THE BEES AND THE MONKEES DELUXE EDITION** (2010), but this sounds almost like the standard version with a few more electronic buzzes.

TEAR THE TOP OFF MY HEAD (Peter Tork)
Monkee involvement: Vocals by Peter Tork. Acoustic guitar and bass by Peter Tork.
Recording dates: June 22, 1967; February 5, 1968; February 6, 1968; February 8, 1968; February 12, 1968
Original release date: March 1996 from **MISSING LINKS, VOLUME 3**

Mark: Strangely, as the liner notes state, the master tapes were missing when compiling the third **MISSING LINKS** collection, so the song had to be lifted from a bootleg called **MONKEESHINES**. It's a strange track, too, with bizarre lyrics and an awkward beat, but I like it.

A version sung by Micky appears on **THE BIRDS, THE BEES AND THE MONKEES DELUXE EDITION** (2010). There is also another version on this CD sung by Peter that sounds like the **MISSING LINKS** version, but on helium, with stranger vocals.

Micky and Peter are seen and heard singing an impromptu version of this song in the "Hitting the High Seas" episode of the TV series.

Michael: Peter can't decide if he wants to do a country song, a sixties hippie rocker, or a comedy song with funny voices so he does them all, changing from one to the other within seconds of each other. It's a mess.

See, this is why you need a producer. Seriously, it is always hard to look at your own work objectively. Very few musicians are good at producing themselves. Even Prince, who produced all his own music, often would fill his albums with stuff that was only interesting to him. The Beatles solo albums that use producers are (mostly) better than the ones they self-produced.

As a writer of fiction, I've dealt with editors who saw things in my work I missed completely, and gave suggestions that made the story so much better. Having a professional edit and produce your work is very important.

So here's another wish that Chip Douglas had come back.

COME ON IN (Jo Mapes)
Monkee involvement: Vocals by Peter Tork. Electric piano, guitar, bass by Peter Tork. Drums by Micky Dolenz. Guitar by Michael Nesmith.
Recording dates: May 1, 1967; February 8, 1968; February 9, 1968; February 11, 1968; February 12, 1968; February 13, 1968
Original release date: January 1990 from **MISSING LINKS, VOLUME 2**

Mark: One of the better Tork vocals adorn this song that seems to be one more typically suited to and sung by Nesmith, although Nesmith does play a nice guitar throughout.

A 1968 mono mix appears on **THE BIRDS, THE BEES AND THE MONKEES DE-LUXE EDITION** (2010). This version is really, really draggy on the chorus. It almost sounds as if Peter was fighting sleep until the verses.

Michael: This was written by the folkie hero Jo Mapes, but I don't know if this is a cover version or if she gave it to Peter to do it as a song for The Monkees. Given the lyrics, which I think would fit better for a female singer, I tend to believe it was just something Peter wanted to cover.

While the harmonies are good, this sounds like a typical garage band performance, because this is one of the last performances by the group (well, without Davy but he didn't add much except vocals anyway). Certainly the quality wasn't good enough for a Monkees album.

I'M GONNA TRY (Davy Jones/Steve Pitts)
Monkee involvement: Vocals by Davy Jones
Recording dates: February 15, 1968; February 17, 1968
Original release date: September 20, 1994 as a bonus track from **THE BIRDS, THE BEES AND THE MONKEES** reissue

Michael: You only have to hear the sappy strings in the first two seconds to say "Oh, it's another Davy song." Yep, another song he wrote with Steve Pitts, and if there's one thing I can say about these songs, it's that they really are the Pitts'.

Mark: It's another nice pleasant song co-written by Davy that didn't make the final cut for **BIRDS AND BEES**. It might have made it, but The Monkees wisely chose *Dream World* and *The Poster* instead. Surprisingly, it stayed in the can even after the **MISSING LINKS** series.

This also appears on **THE BIRDS, THE BEES AND THE MONKEES DELUXE EDITION** (2010).

THE PARTY (Davy Jones/Steve Pitts)
Monkee involvement: Vocals by Davy Jones
Recording dates: February 15, 1968; February 17, 1968
Original release date: July 1987 from **MISSING LINKS**

Mark: **MISSING LINKS** lists this as simply *Party*. It sounds similar to *The Poster* in places, which might have been the reason it was thrown in the vaults. You can hear the marimba a little more prominently in this version.

A 2009 mix appears on **THE BIRDS, THE BEES AND THE MONKEES DELUXE EDITION** (2010), which sounds very similar to the **MISSING LINKS** version except it has a much longer fadeout.

The 1968 mono mix appears on the **INSTANT REPLAY DELUXE EDITION** (2011). This also has a much longer fadeout.

Michael: In case you don't get that Davy "might just fall in love with you" don't worry, he'll repeat it a dozen more times, and then in case you're wondering "with who?" He ends the song repeating "with you" about eight times over and over again with no variation.

If you took all these Jones/Pitts songs and ran them one after another, you'd barely be able to tell where one ended and the next one begins. Or maybe that's just me falling asleep to them.

Who is Steve Pitts anyway? My google search only turned up these songs written with Davy (as well as another Steve Pitts who produced rap albums in the 90s — don't think it's the same guy). With all of the great songwriters at their disposal, why did Davy choose Pitts?

Maybe they were trying to corner the lucrative "elevator music" market.

SHAKE 'EM UP AND LET 'EM ROLL (Jerry Leiber/Mike Stoller)
Monkee involvement: Vocals by Micky Dolenz
Recording dates: February 24, 1968
Original release date: March 1996 from **MISSING LINKS, VOLUME 3**

Mark: This bouncy track was released as simply *Shake 'Em Up* on **MISSING LINKS**, and has a somewhat clunky ending.

An alternate vocal version appears on **THE BIRDS, THE BEES AND THE MONKEES DELUXE EDITION** (2010). On this version, Micky sings with a slight Southern accent.

Michael: Leiber and Stoller are well known songwriters of the rock and roll era: *Hound Dog, Jailhouse Rock, Kansas City, Yakkety Yak...* the list goes on and on, and includes this one. Why Micky decided to do this as a cover is beyond me, and the

STU PHILLIPS (Monkees TV series composer)

Bert Schneider hired me mainly because I had been a successful record producer and would have an understanding of both areas of music: Composing the background score and the songs. (I never did have anything to do with the songs as that was all handled in New York by Donnie Kirshner.) I did however, record David in one song and did the recording of another silly song that the group did at the end of one of the episodes.

Technically, I was paid and worked for Screen Gems. I had nothing to do with Kirshner or NBC. I did, however, take my orders from Bert & Bob.

Hard to say what composing for The Monkees did for my career. I was still working as a record producer for Epic Records and doing some independent films while I was writing The Monkees' music. Certainly didn't hurt my career.

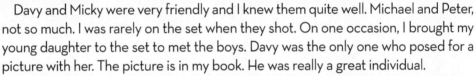

Davy and Micky were very friendly and I knew them quite well. Michael and Peter, not so much. I was rarely on the set when they shot. On one occasion, I brought my young daughter to the set to met the boys. Davy was the only one who posed for a picture with her. The picture is in my book. He was really a great individual.

Had not Michael been so greedy (he wanted to direct and write), The Monkees show might have gone on quite a bit longer. If you mean would it still be a hit TV show, I would think not. If you are asking me if their records would be hits... then I would say it's very possible, since several of their hits are classics and still being played, and are a part of the pop musical history of this country — and the rest of the world.

I feel that I was part of a "happening" that took place in the 1960s, and it will always be relevant. It was something special and I was proud to be a part of it.

fact that he speaks the lyrics more than singing them kind of ruins the fun for me. It's like he's saying "I don't take my job entertaining you very seriously, I'm just having fun" which is not a bad thing for a song they never intended to release, but then he does the same thing to *D.W. Washburn* later (another Leiber/Stoller song, by the way — maybe Micky just doesn't like them).

Then again, this was probably never meant to be released and was just a studio jam.

DON'T SAY NOTHIN' BAD (ABOUT MY BABY) (Gerry Goffin/Carole King)
Monkee involvement: Vocals by Micky Dolenz
Recording dates: February 24, 1968

Original release date: February 20, 2010 from **THE BIRDS, THE BEES AND THE MONKEES DELUXE EDITION**

Mark: Micky does a reasonable, but not outstanding take on the old Cookies song. If it was tightened up with a few more takes, it might have been a stronger contender for release. As it stands, it resembles a warm-up rehearsal.

Michael: Another old rock and roll remake from Micky that I don't think was ever intended to be released. It only has a guitar, bass and drums — no lead guitar or anything else. I think they're just jamming around, especially given that the song doesn't really end but just kind of peters out.

WE WERE MADE FOR EACH OTHER (Carole Bayer/George Fischoff)
Monkee involvement: Vocals by Davy Jones
Recording dates: November 4, 1967; February 6, 1968; February 7, 1968; February 8, 1968; March 13, 1968
Original release date: April 22, 1968 from **THE BIRDS, THE BEES AND THE MONKEES**

Mark: Unlike *Dream World*, this song shows a little bit too much strings. This song sounds like a typical early Monkees song, while *Dream World* feels much more advanced. Small wonder as this song was recorded earlier.

A version with an alternate backing track appears on **THE BIRDS, THE BEES AND THE MONKEES DELUXE EDITION** (2010). You really notice the banjo a lot more on this version.

Michael: Another sappy Jones song with too many strings. The best thing about this song is that it's really short.

I think it's been forty years since I last heard this, because once I started recording my albums onto cassette tape so the records wouldn't get worse with pops and scratches, I would leave off stuff like this. However, I had to listen to this in order to write this book — but *you* don't have to.

TAPIOCA TUNDRA (Michael Nesmith)
Monkee involvement: Vocals by Michael Nesmith. Percussion and electric guitar by Michael Nesmith.
Recording dates: November 11, 1967; March 13, 1968
Highest chart position: #34 single B-side
Original release date: March 2, 1968 from 7" single and **THE BIRDS, THE BEES AND THE MONKEES**
Significant other versions: Michael Nesmith

Michael: Ah, now we get to some good stuff.

I remember playing this for a friend when we were about 12 years old, and during the whistling beginning, he said "I hate this song! Why do you like it?" and then it finally kicked in and he nodded his head and enjoyed it.

So I wonder if it would have gotten more airplay had Mike left that introduction off. I can imagine DJs sticking that on, listening for a few seconds, and then saying "Nope!" It might have also done better if it had a title people could remember with the song. I re-

call when Talking Heads' single *Life During Wartime* was released with an added parenthesis: "(This ain't no party, this ain't no disco)". If they had cut the first 28 seconds of *Tapioca Tundra* for the single and subtitled it *(Now It's Part of You)*, I'll bet it would have done better on the charts. I mean, seriously, it's a far better song than the A-side *Valleri*.

This is another example of the importance of a good tune not needing a complicated arrangement. Lyrically, I have no idea what it (or the title) mean, but it's certainly catchy! When I was a kid, I was convinced he was saying "It makes Brooks Wright standing more at ease" and I'd wonder who this Brooks Wright fella was. (The real lyrics are "Midnight looks right standing more at ease" which makes the same amount of sense.)

And it's well performed, too. Electric guitar on the left, acoustic on the right, lots of extra percussion (more cowbell!) and energy! Makes me want to dance.

This marked the first time that Mike sang lead on a single (although it's the second time one of his songs was the B-side, after *The Girl I Knew Somewhere*).

I really like Mike's songs on **THE BIRDS, THE BEES AND THE MONKEES**. I think they're some of his best.

Mark: Another strange Nesmith song with a crazy title that has nothing to do with the lyrics, but it is so great! Nesmith turns on the echo chamber so that it sounds like he's singing it from the bottom of a well, and then he jumps off a cliff at the end. Nice acoustic guitar complements everything.

A 1967 alternate stereo mix and an acoustic version appear on **THE BIRDS, THE BEES AND THE MONKEES DELUXE EDITION** (2010). I can't tell any differences with the alternate stereo mix from the standard mix. The acoustic version gives the song an entirely different feel that does not resemble psychedelicized tone of the final release.

Mike also released it as an instrumental on his own **WICHITA TRAIN WHISTLE SINGS** (1968) album.

He also performed it live in 2016 as they way he felt it should have been done…in a more acoustic way.

WRITING WRONGS (Michael Nesmith)
Monkee involvement: Vocals by Michael Nesmith. Piano, electric guitar and organ by Michael Nesmith.
Recording dates: December 3, 1967; March 13, 1968
Original release date: April 22, 1968 from **THE BIRDS, THE BEES AND THE MONKEES**

Mark: Nesmith again! He was certainly on a hot streak! And again, he sounds like he's recording from the bottom of a well. Intense organ permeates throughout. The first line always reminds me of the first line of *Tear Drop City*. The middle instrumental section has always ranked up there as the best of what the 60s has to offer, sounding like something The Doors could have done.

Michael: This song has to grow on you, because that long middle instrumental break can scare away listeners expecting happy teenybopper pop songs. That middle kind of reminds me of the sort of music you'd hear in the background of a 60s movie about hippies smoking pot at a party while the lights and colors dance around them. You know, like certain scenes from this crazy hippie movie called *Head*...

I do like this song a lot, though, although I think I would have cut the middle bit earlier. Near the end of it where he just pounds the chord over and over again feels like he's saying "Okay everyone, stop HERE! Oh, you missed it. Okay, then stop HERE! Missed it again. We'll get it this time..."

I always thought that was Peter playing the keyboards but I've recently learned it was Mike, which kind of explains why it's not that complicated. I imagine a Peter solo would have been quite different.

> ### Fan Thoughts
>
> *This song is from my perspective Mike Nesmith's foray into jazz specifically free or modal jazz. The piano melody is very melancholy and dark but very attention grabbing. The organ is very abrasive which gives the song its menacing tone. The instrumental section is very menacing and the minor key makes the song sound like a horror movie. The instrumental break is interesting; each soloist will pick a phrase and repeat and expand on it in striking ways. This is simple but effective and shows off Nesmith's talent in understanding modal concepts. The lyrics seem to be about the apocalypse and a prophet warning everyone about their impending death. The lyrics are cryptic which means anyone can interpret them differently. The theme seems to be ignorance of the common people or the end of our times which is a theme that runs through the song. One of my favorite Monkees songs. – Michael Chantiri*

As Mark points out, The Monkees producing themselves sure did seem to like that "bottom of the well" echo sound on this album. Even Davy uses it on *Dream World*. It does get tiring after a while.

ZOR AND ZAM (Bill Chadwick/John Chadwick)
Monkee involvement: Vocals by Micky Dolenz. Percussion by Micky Dolenz.
Recording dates: January 7, 1968; January 13, 1968; January 18, 1968; February 14, 1968; February 17, 1968; March 13, 1968
Original release date: April 22, 1968 from **THE BIRDS, THE BEES AND THE MONKEES**

Michael: A quite clever little song that I really like, and a very good way to end an album.

I recall seeing posters in the 60s saying "What if they gave a war and nobody came?" and I wonder if the poster came first or this song...

The TV version is inferior, as Mark says, and if you watch the episode where it was played, it doesn't fit at all. This is not the kind of song that should be playing in the background while The Monkees run around doing silly things like the TV show always had them do. Then again, have you seen that episode (which was written and directed by Micky?). It's all about this strange alien plant that produces this smoke that makes everyone go silly... Perhaps being under the influence of that alien plant may have hurt Micky's judgment.

Anyway, this was the last song on the last album released while the TV show was still on, and it was a good song to go out on. Like Davy's earlier *War Games*, this one has that military snare giving us the proper feeling, but what makes this song work better is the way the music builds. First verse is just drums, then the guitar comes in, and then horns, and finally it's pounding in your ears with the noise of war, only to fade out until just the booming of a kettle drum is left (kind of a sequel to *Randy Scouse Git*'s kettle drum echoing off at the end of **HEADQUAR-TERS** — Why don't you hate who I hate, kill who I kill to be free?)

Mark: Dolenz attempts to do Grace Slick and succeeds quite well. Listen to this and then listen to Jefferson Airplane's *Lather* and let me know who you think does the better job.

The TV version appears on **MISSING LINKS, VOLUME 3** (1996) and on **THE BIRDS, THE BEES AND THE MONKEES DELUXE EDITION** (2010). The sound of this version is much thinner than the final released version, so it was wise that it was rerecorded for the album.

ALVIN (Nick Thorkelson)
Monkee involvement: Vocals by Peter Tork
Recording dates: January 20, 1968; March 13, 1968
Original release date: September 20, 1994 as a bonus track from **THE BIRDS, THE BEES AND THE MONKEES** reissue

Mark: This is kind of a redux of *Seeger's Theme* by Peter. Too short to say much more about it. This version also appears on **THE BIRDS, THE BEES AND THE MONKEES DELUXE EDITION** (2010), as well as a 1968 mono mix and an alternate take where Peter flubs a line.

Michael: It's an a capella bit from Peter that only lasts about twenty seconds. I think Peter felt that the only way he could get his voice on the albums was to do silly things like *Zilch, Peter Percival Patterson's Pet Pig Porky,* or this. And I guess he was right — with the exception of his keyboard playing on *Daydream Believer* (which was recorded before the **PISCES** album), Peter appears nowhere on **THE BIRDS, THE BEES AND THE MONKEES**. I mean, come on, they could have stuck this on there somewhere.

DREAM WORLD (Davy Jones/Steve Pitts)
Monkee involvement: Vocals by Davy Jones
Recording dates: February 6, 1968; February 8, 1968; March 13, 1968
Original release date: April 22, 1968 from **THE BIRDS, THE BEES AND THE MONKEES**

Michael: The Jones/Pitts team does a good job here. This one is listenable, although it would have been better without all the strings and horns. Underneath all that, it's not a bad song. The chorus kicks in nicely with "Why don't you come out of your dream world / It's not real" but then it plods and Davy kind of says the next lines in bits that make it seem like he's stuttering or something: "It's not (pause) the way (pause) it seems (pause) to be!" That would have worked better with more words filling the pauses, and would have matched the rest of the chorus much better.

While that "singing from the bottom of a well" sound (as Mark puts it) works well on some of Mike's songs, it really doesn't fit here, and isn't exactly the best way to start off an album.

Mark: A nice and pleasant way of opening the album with Davy Jones taking his turn on the dreamy type vocals that Micky usually does. The strings and the brass are very nice and not overbearing as they are sometimes in some Monkees songs, rendering them too syrupy.

As an aside, I always thought that the long gone California theme park Marine World should have used this song for an ad: "Why don't come out to Marine World? It's so real! Why don't you come into Marine World? Come with me!"

THE POSTER (Davy Jones/Steve Pitts)
Monkee involvement: Vocals by Davy Jones
Recording dates: February 15, 1968; February 17, 1968; March 13, 1968
Original release date: April 22, 1968 from **THE BIRDS, THE BEES AND THE MONKEES**

Mark: Davy's version of *Being for the Benefit of Mr. Kite*. Nice calliope sounds make this a very pleasant listening experience. I will say here that Davy is very underrated as a songwriter. Granted, he wrote very few songs completely by himself, but many of his collaborations are absolutely marvelous!

Michael: And here's where Mark and I will disagree again! "Absolutely marvelous" aren't words I'd use to describe any of the Jones/Pitts songs.

I'll agree that of the Jones/Pitts songs, this is one of the better ones, but that's not saying much. The reason may be because they weren't trying to write a sappy love song but instead decided to copy *Mr. Kite*. I mean, come on, it's practically the same theme. John Lennon wrote *Kite* while reading a poster about a circus. Davy does the exact same thing here six months later, while **SGT. PEPPER** is still on the charts! Doesn't really help dispel the "Monkees are just trying to copy The Beatles" talk.

I'LL BE BACK UPON MY FEET (Sandy Linzer/Denny Randell)
Monkee involvement: Vocals by Micky Dolenz. Electric guitar by Michael Nesmith.
Recording dates: October 28, 1966; August 23, 1967; March 9, 1968; March 13, 1968; March 14, 1968
Original release date: April 22, 1968 from **THE BIRDS, THE BEES AND THE MONKEES**

Michael: This is a catchy little number and I'm glad they resurrected it and gave it new life. Those earlier recording dates listed above were for an version that was used on the TV show; the version on **THE BIRDS, THE BEES AND THE MONKEES** was re-recorded from scratch.

It starts off with someone making gorilla noises (gorillas aren't monkeys!) which is kind of cool. The horns add a lot, especially when they kick in quietly during the second verse adding an extra layer in the background. I also like how, after the instrumental break, there is a small harmony on the word "down."

A very good song that should get greater attention from Monkees fans!

Mark: The Monkees start a trend that they have continued to the present day: that is, going through the archives and either adding to or rerecording an older song. This is one of those cases. In this case, I do prefer this rerecording precisely for the Tijuana Brass-type horns that were added.

The first recorded version appears on the 2006 **MORE OF THE MONKEES DE-LUXE EDITION** CD, which also appeared on the TV show and on **MISSING LINKS, VOLUME 2** (1990). This 1966 version lacks the distinctive brass of the later released album version and has a cold ending.

LADY'S BABY (Peter Tork)
Monkee involvement: Vocals by Peter Tork. Acoustic guitar, bass, harpsichord and clavinet by Peter Tork.
Recording dates: November 12, 1967; December 1, 1967; December 3, 1967; December 17, 1967; December 21, 1967; January 14, 1968; January 19, 1968; January 24, 1968; January 25, 1968; February 2, 1968; February 7, 1968; March 13, 1968; March 17, 1968
Original release date: July 1987 from **MISSING LINKS**

Mark: Peter had marathon sessions with this one that lasted over four months, and still remained unreleased, similar to George Harrison with his *Not Guilty* for **THE BEATLES** (White Album). After all the attempts, there seems to be a little missing something to help push it over the edge, and the entire effort comes off as somewhat lackluster. It's a shame considering how much effort was put into it.

The version released in 1994 as a bonus track from **THE BIRDS, THE BEES AND THE MONKEES** reissue includes more baby sounds.

A 1968 stereo mix, a 1968 mono mix and an acoustic version appear on **THE BIRDS, THE BEES AND THE MONKEES DELUXE EDITION** (2010), and an alternate acoustic version appears on a 7" vinyl single included with this set. The stereo mix has a "wobbly" vocal effect that has Peter's vocals wavering between the left and right speaker for much of the song. The mono mix is the baby sounds version. The acoustic version has more banjo and guitar than the one from **MISSING LINKS.**

Michael: This is a lazy bluesy song from Peter, but like *Tear the Top Off My Head,* he changes tempo more than once and tries to do a bit too much in one song. It's only two and a half minutes long but it feels longer... I guess it's not a bad song, but it sure doesn't sound like a Monkees' song.

LAUREL AND HARDY (Jan Berry/Roger Christian)
Monkee involvement: Vocals by Davy Jones.
Recording dates: 1966-1968

Original release date: February 20, 2010 from **THE BIRDS, THE BEES AND THE MONKEES DELUXE EDITION**
Significant other versions: Jan & Dean

Mark: This song has a lengthy genesis and story that is better told elsewhere, but to sum up, Jan Berry of Jan & Dean suffered a near-fatal auto accident on April 12, 1966. He was working on and later continued to work on a new Jan & Dean album that was to be called **CARNIVAL OF SOUND**, which was supposed to be released in 1968, but instead was shelved until November 19, 2009.

Jan & Dean did release their version of *Laurel and Hardy* as the B-side of *I Know My Mind* in June 1968, but for some reason Davy Jones was recruited by the duo to record his vocals on the track. This version also remained unreleased until February 2010. It technically is not a Monkees track, but since it now has been released in official capacity on a Monkees album, it is included here.

It's actually a really good track. It's a shame that it was kind of sitting in limbo for so long and then when it was finally released, it was put on this **DELUXE EDITION**, where a casual Monkees fan would probably never hear it. A little bit of Laurel & Hardy's *Cuckoo Song* theme is included as part of the instrumental.

Fortunately, there is YouTube and it is highly recommended listening.

Michael: I think Jan and Dean were trying to copy Brian Wilson, who was making songs by mixing many different parts together to make something new, as with *Good Vibrations* and *Heroes and Villains*. It doesn't work as well here. I mean, I love the idea of doing a song about Laurel and Hardy, and I certainly don't dislike songs that are quite complicated and have many parts, but it has to flow properly and feel right (like *You Never Give Me Your Money* does, or, for a more pertinent example, *Shorty Blackwell*.)

Anyway, this is certainly worth listening to, but I also agree that it wasn't good enough to release.

THE BIRDS, THE BEES AND THE MONKEES
Original release date: April 22, 1968
Highest chart position: #3 (4 weeks) in 1968; #148 in 1986
Weeks on chart: 39 in 1968-1969; 11 in 1986

Dream World
Auntie's Municipal Court
We Were Made for Each Other
Tapioca Tundra
Daydream Believer
Writing Wrongs

I'll Be Back Upon My Feet
The Poster

PO Box 9847
Magnolia Simms
Valleri
Zor and Zam

Michael: When I was a young kid and didn't know any better, I remember seeing this album in the store and thinking "I don't want to get this album because it has other groups on it as well." I knew there was a band called The Byrds, and I figured there must have been a band called The Bees, so clearly this was an album that had songs from all three of those bands together. (Hey, I *said* I was young.)

This is the first Monkees album that didn't reach #1, only getting up to #3. Partially I think it was due to the fact that by the time it came out, the TV show was almost at its end and interest had dropped a bit — but also because, well, it's just not as "pop" of an album as the previous two, though it has its charms. It isn't trying to be a teeny-bopper album. The songs have more maturity and take more risks than usual. This is one of the reasons I like it a lot, but that's not necessarily what sells. After all, a year or so after this and what outsells everyone? The freakin' Archies. (By the way, the albums that kept this from reaching #1 were both from Simon & Garfunkel: **BOOKENDS** and the soundtrack to **THE GRADUATE**. *Mrs. Robinson* was a huge hit at the time — and the song was, too. Nyuk nyuk.)

One sad note, as I pointed out earlier: With the exception of his piano playing on *Daydream Believer* — which was recorded back during the **PISCES** sessions — Peter appears nowhere on this album. That had to hurt. Then again, I guess they made it up to him with **HEAD**, where he writes two songs out of the six and sings lead on one...

This is where The Monkees began not being "The Monkees" and instead became three (or four) separate musical acts sharing a record. While all four could be found all over every song on **HEADQUARTERS**, there were much fewer group efforts on **PISCES** (including *Daydream Believer* which was recorded at the same time), and on this album, the only new song that has more than one Monkee on it is *Auntie's Municipal Court* (once Micky overdubbed his vocals over Mike's).

Mike and Davy trade lead vocals on the first side, and Micky has none. By side two, Micky gets three songs, Mike has one and Davy has two, giving us a grand total of Davy: 5, Mike: 4, Micky: 3, Peter: 0. This is unusual, as Micky usually has the most. Then again, he was underrepresented on **PISCES**, too.

In fact, if we look back at all the songs released up to this time, Micky sang 26 songs, Davy sang 23, Mike sang 14, and Peter 3 (when you include *Words* and *Shades of Gray*, where he shared vocals with others).

Mark: One wonders if this album would have done as well without the inclusion of *Daydream Believer* and *Valleri*, since the whole Monkees thing was starting to wind down — this album being released at the very end of *The Monkees* second and final TV season.

This is very much a Davy and Mike album with Davy getting all the pop hits in there, while Mike is frankly being wildly experimental, moreso here than on any Monkees album.

Micky shows up a couple times as well and the entire effort hangs together amazingly well considering the kind of the patchwork quilt of an album that it is. The cover image of various photos and other assorted trinkets kind of is a tip off to the variety of sounds contained herein.

Michael is right that it's not as "pop" of an album, but I never really thought about it that way. I first heard this album around 1987 while in college and at the time was a huge fan of psychedelic and progressive sounds. This album fit the bill nicely, especially with *Magnolia Simms* and *Tapioca Tundra*.

THE BIRDS, THE BEES AND THE MONKEES DELUXE EDITION (2010) includes a *Teen Radio Spot* and an *Adult Stereo 8 Spot* which contain brief snippets of old and new Monkees tunes and some dialogue by Davy.

D.W. WASHBURN (Jerry Leiber/Mike Stoller)
Monkee involvement: Vocals by Micky Dolenz
Recording dates: February 17, 1968; March 1, 1968; April 3, 1968; April 23, 1968
Highest chart position: #19 single
Original release date: June 8, 1968 from 7" single. First album appearance on **MONKEE BUSINESS** (1983); First CD appearance on **THEN AND NOW...THE BEST OF THE MONKEES** (1986).
Significant other versions: The Coasters

Mark: This song falls into the "What were they thinking?" category. **THE BIRDS, THE BEES AND THE MONKEES** was saved from failure by the inclusion of *Daydream Believer* and *Valleri*, and this was the first song The Monkees recorded and released after that album, that was supposed to be the crucial, "Can they do it beyond the TV series and without the TV series' help?" Although this song isn't too bad, it is truly a lousy choice for such an important follow-up single, and would have been better utilized as an album track. Even *It's Nice to Be With You*, the single's B-side, would have been a better selection than this for that all-important placeholder to appease fans waiting for new Monkees material between the end of the TV series and the upcoming *Head* motion picture. It is here where The Monkees saga starts to go disastrously wrong, as The Monkees really were a lousy judge of their own best material sometimes. It, unlike its similar non-album B-side, eluded album inclusion until 1983.

A 1968 stereo mix and a mono single mix and an alternate mix with bass vocal appear on **THE BIRDS, THE BEES AND THE MONKEES DELUXE EDITION** (2010). The stereo mix really separates the vocals much better than the mono version. The alternate mix with bass vocal has a second vocalist parroting Micky's singing in the background. Otherwise, it's the same take and mix as the standard mix.

Michael: The main problem I have with this song is Micky's singing. During the part where Micky sings "If you can only make it from your hands to your knees, I know you can make it to your feet" he sort of talk-sings it in a way that one might do when one thinks, "This song sucks and I'm just going to make fun of it by being silly." He also goes into a weird falsetto as it's fading that is just as annoying, which is sad since this is not a bad song underneath it all. When I saw him perform live in April of 2017, he sang it normally and it was much improved.

It's certainly well written, and not a typical silly love song. Notice how there is a basic first verse then it goes into what I guess is a chorus ("Can't you hear the bugle call?") and when that ends, instead of going for a second verse, it does a bridge of sorts ("Up, up, come on get up") before going back to a second verse. That second verse then has a change near the end, leading to the repeating bits as it fades out. This is good writing, because instead of just repeating a verse and chorus over and over again, we keep getting new stuff that keeps us interested.

This was written by rock and roll songwriting heroes Leiber & Stoller, and had been released as a B-side from the Coasters just a few months earlier. I have no idea whose idea this was to make Micky record a version (since none of the other Monkees were involved) or why someone thought this would be a good song to release as a single.

IT'S NICE TO BE WITH YOU (Jerry Goldstein)
Monkee involvement: Vocals by Davy Jones
Recording dates: February 6, 1968; February 7, 1968; February 8, 1968; March 14, 1968; April 25, 1968
Highest chart position: #51 single B-side
Original release date: June 8, 1968 from 7" single. First album release on **MONKEE BUSINESS** (1982). First CD release on **LISTEN TO THE BAND** (1991).

Mark: As I said above, this would have made for a better song selection than *D.W. Washburn* for that critical single to be released while fans were biding their time waiting for the next Monkees project, which is in this case was *Head*. As it charted as high as #51 on its own, it proves that the song did have some merit, or at least proved that there was still some momentum left in The Monkees phenomenon. It avoided album appearance all the way until 1982.

A 1968 stereo mix and the mono single mix appear on **THE BIRDS, THE BEES AND THE MONKEES DELUXE EDITION** (2010). The stereo and mono versions are almost identical, but the instruments are more spread out along the sound spectrum on the stereo version as to be expected.

Michael: I'm not certain that this would have done any better than *D.W. Washburn*. It's just another sappy Davy song that fits better in an elevator than on rock and roll radio.

It's not that badly written but it's a lullaby of a song, isn't it? Instantly forgettable.

LOOK DOWN (Carole King/Toni Stern)
Monkee involvement: Vocals by Davy Jones
Recording dates: March 14, 1968; March 15, 1968; April 6, 1968; April 25, 1968
Original release date: March 1996 from **MISSING LINKS, VOLUME 3**

Michael: This is a Motown-inspired song with the fancy horns and come on, this is The Wrecking Crew doing the backing. (And if you don't know who they are, check them out — they're the session musicians on most of the Motown songs as well as a few other Monkees songs). This should have been the single instead of *D.W. Washburn* or *It's Nice to Be With You.*

Have I mentioned that I really like Carole King's songwriting? Oh, right, only every time a Carole King song was performed by The Monkees! While this is not one of her best, it's certainly worth listening to. It's a shame it wasn't released until many years later.

Mark: A jazzy uptempo song with lots of brass and Davy really belts it out. Co-composer Carole King actually provides backing vocals. It would have been a nice addition to **PRESENT**, but alas it was left in the proverbial can awaiting rediscovery.

The same track and a backing track version appear on the **INSTANT REPLAY DE-LUXE EDITION** (2011).

SMILE (Davy Jones)
Monkee involvement: Vocals by Davy Jones
Recording dates: May 10, 1968
Original release date: January 1995 from **INSTANT REPLAY** bonus track

Michael: Apparently Davy wrote this himself, so maybe I shouldn't be blaming Steve Pitts for the sappy music. It's not bad, but nothing special. Hearing Davy turn smile into two syllables doesn't work though: "Smiiiii — yull."

Mark: This is not the famous Charlie Chaplin-penned song, but rather a nice song written and sung by Davy. Other than that, it's nothing terribly special. Somehow it was overlooked through the three **MISSING LINKS** compilations, being finally released as a bonus track in 1995. It also ends sort of abruptly, giving the impression that this was an abandoned demo.

This version plus the 1968 mono mix and the backing track appear on the **INSTANT REPLAY DELUXE EDITION** (2011).

THAT'S WHAT IT'S LIKE LOVING YOU (Davy Jones/Steve Pitts)
Monkee involvement: none
Recording dates: May 10, 1968
Original release date: November 21, 2011 from **INSTANT REPLAY DELUXE EDITION**

Mark: Interesting instrumental that Davy wrote. It's a shame that Davy never got around to laying down a vocal for this.

Michael: ZZzzzzzzzzzzz.

BO DIDDLEY (Elias McDaniel)
Monkee involvement: Vocals by Micky Dolenz. Drums by Micky Dolenz. Electric guitar by Michael Nesmith. Bass by Peter Tork. Maracas, organ and tambourine by Davy Jones.
Recording dates: May 17, 1968

REHEARSAL JAM (unknown)
Monkee involvement: Electric guitar by Michael Nesmith. Bass by Peter Tork. Maracas by Davy Jones. Drums by Micky Dolenz.
Recording dates: May 17, 1968

Mark: For the purposes of the *Head* film, a concert was held in Salt Lake City on this date in order to get a good live take of *Circle Sky*. The Monkees also performed the above songs at that concert as well as live versions of *You Just May Be the One*, *Sunny Girlfriend*, *Cuddly Toy*, *Two-Part Invention in F-Major*, *Last Train to Clarksville*, *I Wanna Be Free*, *Forget That Girl*, *The Girl I Knew Somewhere*, *You Told Me* and *Mary, Mary*. Originally, only the live version of take 3 of *Circle Sky* has been officially released, both in the film and on the 1994 Rhino CD reissue of *Head*, but four more songs (*You Just May Be the One*, *Sunny Girlfriend*, *You Told Me* plus a different take of *Circle Sky*) were finally released on the **HEAD DELUXE EDITION** (2010), including the eight-minute *"Introduction to Live Show" (recorded in Salt Lake City: May 17, 1968).*

The full concert may eventually be released someday, but it is a haphazard affair as there are multiple takes of many songs including 10 alone for *Circle Sky* and a couple rehearsal jams and there are sound quality issues. Andrew Sandoval in his *Day by Day* book claims, "Despite the group turning in some decent renditions of such rarely performed numbers as *You Told Me* and *Cuddly Toy*, today's tapes are very poorly engineered. Most of the vocals are barely audible. Because of this, take 3 of *Circle Sky*, which is to be used as the basis for the film version, will be given a newly recorded vocal by Michael on May 21st."

HOW INSENSITIVE (Antonio Carlos Jobim/Vincius DeMoraes/Norman Gimbel)
Monkee involvement: Vocals by Michael Nesmith. Guitars by Michael Nesmith.
Recording dates: May 31, 1968
Original release date: March 1996 from **MISSING LINKS, VOLUME 3**

Michael: Michael takes a 1963 Portuguese bossa nova song that had been translated into English and does a country version of it. The English version had already previously been recorded by Perry Como, Frank Sinatra, Peggy Lee, Doris Day — you get the idea. Not exactly a rock and roll standard. Then again, Mike's is probably the first (and maybe the only) country music version.

It's doubtful this was ever intended to be released.

Mark: Another Nesmith-sung country song, and not his strongest, that sounds strangely out of tune, but that was probably the intention. This version also appears on the **INSTANT REPLAY DELUXE EDITION** (2011).

SHORTY BLACKWELL (Micky Dolenz)
Monkee involvement: Vocals by Micky Dolenz. Piano by Micky Dolenz.
Recording dates: January 19, 1968; February 4, 1968; February 15, 1968; April 9, 1968; April 30, 1968; May 2, 1968; June 7, 1968
Original release date: February 15, 1969 from **INSTANT REPLAY**

Mark: The closest thing to a novelty song on **INSTANT REPLAY**. It's Micky's attempt at some sort of epic build song. Even Micky claimed it was "my feeble attempt at something to do with **SGT. PEPPER**." My dislike of it stems from the too prominent backing vocals from Micky's sister Coco, and the inanity of the lyrics about his cat. Micky should have saved it for a solo project as it really has no place on a Monkees release.

A rehearsal version appears on **THE BIRDS, THE BEES AND THE MONKEES DELUXE EDITION** (2010) with many errors. Micky's sister Coco also sings.

An alternate stereo mix appears on the **INSTANT REPLAY DELUXE EDITION** (2011).

Michael: This is one of my favorite Monkees tracks. It's creative and never boring, and Micky does a very good job of making all the various parts of this work together.

It starts with a trumpet fanfare, announcing the song like you'd introduce the King, and then Micky calls to his cat. "Shorty Blackwell, be friends with me." It's light and simple with just a piano at first and then the bass and horns come in slowly along with a harmony vocal, but it's still light. Then it becomes ominous. Low horns in the background, switch to a minor key, and Micky sings "He built a house upon a hill / Ask him if he's happy and then give him a pill / He's going mad / He bought another car today..." Is Micky's cat answering, and talking about Micky himself, unhappy in his rich house with all his cars and drugs? Or, as some have suggested, is this a reference to Mike Nesmith, who had recently purchased a house upon a hill?

We then get the "he's going mad" section which is appropriately mad, with vocals overlapping, frenzied horns in the background, and that kettle drum Micky loves pounding back and forth, until things calm down and we get back to the verse again, only this time there's an echoing voice in the background and that kettle drum keeping the beat, building on the previous verses.

We then switch to a new section ("Black and shiny / now you've finally / gotten everything you wanted...") which is tense... it builds like the questions Micky is asking himself about fame ("And you're taunted by the power / that you really don't want any more"). After another run-through which includes a wonderful harmony that runs down the scale in opposition to the monotone, we slow down as Shorty

Blackwell is busy licking his paws ("polishing my shoes") and not paying any attention to Micky's pleas.

So we calm down to a short piano solo played by Micky which is quite simple — the left hand simply plays the chords note by note while the right plays the melody without harmony. This part could have used some backing or perhaps a professional pianist to make it a bit more interesting (there was this guy named Peter Tork who was available...). It also shifts to a 3/4 waltz time. (If you're counting, you go 1, 2, 3, instead of the standard rock beat of 1, 2, 3, 4) I remember when I first got **INSTANT REPLAY**, this solo was mixed to one side which really made it sound empty. Later versions mixed it to the middle.

After one run-through, Micky comes in with a harmony that is kind of unnerving and the horns come back in to make a scary sort of warped carnival feel. This then ends and we come back to the verse again, but this time it's heralded in by trumpets announcing the second coming or something. Micky sings this time instead of his cat. "I'm feeling very bad today / Another girl came by to say / I can't think of a word / to tell you what I've heard / I've been away..."

And then just when you think it's over, Micky switches to 5/4 timing — something never done in rock and roll — as it fades out with more harmonies, making this the longest Monkees song at almost six minutes.

Is it rock and roll? Definitely not. But it's also far from boring, and it's one of my favorites.

CAN YOU DIG IT? (Peter Tork)
Monkee involvement: Vocals by Micky Dolenz. Guitar by Peter Tork.
Recording dates: June 22, 1967; January 28, 1968; January 29, 1968; January 30, 1968; January 31, 1968; February 1, 1968; February 3, 1968; March 8, 1968; August 1, 1968
Original release date: December 1, 1968 from **HEAD**

Michael: After recording a bunch of songs that weren't good enough to be released, Peter finally hits a homerun with this one. An eastern-inspired hippie number that, while not very deep or complex, really makes it because of the excellent performance. Peter was right to let Micky sing this one, and the way the song builds at the end before quitting and coming to a stop is very effective.

You have to admit, some of The Monkees' best songs were from the *Head* film. It's a shame it didn't do better.

Mark: Another great *Head* song, sung by Micky in his dreamy voice. One of Peter's best songs. Peter really went out of his way to come up with some great material for his swan song before bowing out of The Monkees. Yes, I know that Peter also appeared on the 33 1/3 TV special, but that was more of an afterthought after the failure of *Head*. These were Peter's finest moments with the group.

An early demo version of the song (June 22, 1967) was finally released on **HEAD-QUARTERS SESSIONS** (2000).

An alternate mix was first issued on the 1994 CD reissue of **HEAD**. It is longer instrumentally and contains a different vocal take than the final version.

The mono mix and the mono movie mix appear on **HEAD DELUXE EDITION** (2010). They sound virtually identically to the stereo mix except the mono movie mix has a longer guitar instrumental break. There is also a version with Peter singing lead, but it's easy to see why Peter gave the vocal chores over to Micky as his singing is vastly superior. There is also a stereo rough mix of this version which emphasizes the bass.

CIRCLE SKY Version 1 (Michael Nesmith)
Monkee involvement: Vocals by Michael Nesmith. Guitar, organ and percussion by Michael Nesmith.
Recording dates: December 9, 1967; December 17, 1967; January 6, 1968; January 8, 1968; May 17, 1968; May 21, 1968; August 1, 1968
Original release date: December 1, 1968 from **HEAD**
Significant other versions: Does version 2 count?

Mark: A great, great song and sorry Mike N., the best version is this 1968 studio version. It was remade (Why?) for 1996's **JUSTUS** and there was a live version that was used in the *Head* movie, but the original studio version still remains superior.

The live version from May 21, 1968 first appeared on CD on **MISSING LINKS, VOLUME 2** (1990), and then as a bonus track on the 1994 **HEAD** reissue. A different performance from this live concert from May 17, 1968 appears on the **HEAD DELUXE EDITION** (2010).

An alternate studio mix with more percussion and no feedback at the end appears on **MISSING LINKS, VOLUME 3** (1996). This version originally appeared on vinyl on **MONKEE FLIPS** (1984).

The mono mix appears on **HEAD DELUXE EDITION**, which sounds virtually identical to the stereo mix. The alternate mono mix buries Nesmith's vocals more into the mix, with more prominent organ and guitar. An alternate stereo mix sounds identical to the released studio version.

This song was also included on the **PRESENT DELUXE EDITION** (2013) as a "new" 1969 stereo and a 1969 "new" mono mix. There are some lyric alterations.

Michael: I, too, prefer the studio version to the live version. While the live version has the advantage of really being played by all four Monkees, I think that's also why it isn't as good. The bass in the original version slides around and has a lot of energy, while Peter's bassline, while interesting, I think distracts from the song. The studio version also has a second guitar that adds depth. The one thing the live version has over the studio version is that Mike's voice is louder, and it's a bit too buried on the album version.

Mike admits he wrote this to be a simple song that The Monkees could play live easily — one guitar, no lead.

DADDY'S SONG (Harry Nilsson)
Monkee involvement: Vocals by Davy Jones and Michael Nesmith. Acoustic and electric guitar by Michael Nesmith.
Recording dates: January 10, 1968; January 16, 1968; January 19, 1968; March 1, 1968; March 23, 1968; April 4, 1968; April 25, 1968; August 1, 1968
Original release date: December 1, 1968 from **HEAD**
Significant other versions: Harry Nilsson

Mark: Davy's showcase in *Head*, and he sings and performs it excellently. The movie version with dancer/singer Toni Basil with their alternating black/white outfits must be seen to be fully appreciated. As usual, Harry Nilsson contributes a song which is perfect for The Monkees' vibe.

A version sung by Mike was added to the 1994 CD reissue of **HEAD**. This version sounds like *Magnolia Simms* in that Nesmith's voice was altered to sound like it was a 1920s type of recording. Once *Daddy's Song* was to become a showcase for Davy in the film, Mike's vocals were abandoned. This version also appears on the **HEAD DELUXE EDITION** (2010).

The mono mix appears on the **HEAD DELUXE EDITION** (2010). This version is identical to the stereo mix, except that there is a long pause near the end of the song. The mono movie mix includes Davy's spoken word part near the end which does not appear in any other version. There is also a remix with slow verse version that has more prominent backing vocals by Mike and also a majorly different spoken word near the end by Davy accompanied by slight piano.

Michael: Nilsson songs work great for Davy and he always gives them justice. Definitely one of his better songs.

The remix version with the slow verse is the one shown in the film, but I'm glad they didn't use that for the record because it just brings the song to a screeching halt. It works well in the movie though, and is kind of a cliche that is used on Broadway all the time. I wonder if the producers of the film were actually making fun of Davy with this bit.

And yes, the Toni Basil who danced with Davy in *Head* is the same Toni Basil who had a hit a dozen or so years later with *Mickey* ("Oh Mickey you're so fine / You're so fine you blow my mind / Hey Mickey!") which is definitely not a song about our Micky.

LONG TITLE: DO I HAVE TO DO THIS ALL OVER AGAIN? (Peter Tork)
Monkee involvement: Vocals by Peter Tork. Backing vocals by Davy Jones. Electric guitar by Peter Tork.
Recording dates: January 14, 1968; January 20, 1968; January 22, 1968; January 25, 1968; January 26, 1968; January 27, 1968; January 28, 1968; February 1, 1968; February 3, 1968; February 4, 1968; February 10, 1968; February 12, 1968; February 14, 1968; February 15, 1968; August 1, 1968
Original release date: December 1, 1968 from **HEAD**

Michael: A 1960s rocker, perfect for the party scene in the film, and Peter's voice works just fine in it. I appreciate the writing in this song. Look at how it's structured: After a loud opening, the verse comes in and then it cuts to an instrumental break which is different from the opening bit. On to the second verse and the same instrumental break but then it veers off, does a few interesting beats back and forth a few times, then cuts to something new for a few bars and then on to the third verse. And then on to the fade before it gets boring. And listen to that bass! Try to imagine the song without that catchy bass pushing it along.

A very underrated Monkees song.

Mark: A very rocking tune for The Monkees that sounds like it could have come straight from the Jefferson Airplane songbook. This is some of Peter's strongest singing and playing on record.

An alternate mix appears on **THE BIRDS, THE BEES AND THE MONKEES DELUXE EDITION** (2010), which sounds about the same as the released version, but Davy's backing vocals are more pronounced.

The mono mix appears on the **HEAD DELUXE EDITION** (2010) and it sounds exactly like the stereo mix. A rough mix acetate sounds close to the final released version, but Peter sings with it with much more intensity. An alternate stereo version also sounds exactly like the standard stereo mix except Davy's backing vocals are more prominent in the mix.

PORPOISE SONG (Gerry Goffin/Carole King)
Monkee involvement: Vocals by Micky Dolenz. Backing vocals by Davy Jones.
Recording dates: February 26, 1968; February 28, 1968; February 29, 1968; April 3, 1968; August 1, 1968
Highest chart position: #62 single
Original release date: October 5, 1968 from 7" single and **HEAD**
Signficant Significant other versions: Bongwater, The Church, Trouble, The Grapes of Wrath, And You Will Know Us By the Trail of Dead, Lollipop Train, Django Django, The Polyphonic Spree

Mark: One of the best songs ever recorded by The Monkees and one of the best ever written by the Goffin/King team. Why it stalled on the charts at #62 is a bit of a mystery as this should have been a massive hit regardless of what one thought of The Monkees or their movie *Head* at this point. Like The Beach Boys, by late 1968, The Monkees couldn't catch a break despite releasing some of their best material. This song shows a great progression and maturity from the old *Clarksville* days and one wonders where The Monkees would have gone had this song

been a big hit. A longer ending was tacked on the Rhino reissue.

An alternate stereo mix appears on **HEAD DELUXE EDITION** (2010), which features this longer ending. The mono single mix also appears on this collection. The rough mono mix also features a rougher vocal that is not as endearing as the released version. I suspect that Micky was still figuring out how to sing this on this recording.

The **HEAD DELUXE EDITION** also includes a 7" vinyl single featuring the instrumental version of the song.

Michael: Oh, look, it's a Carole King song – do you think I'm going to like it? (Insert smiley face)

Absolutely one of the best Monkees songs, with great psychedelica. It's only two verses long, no real chorus or lead or bridge, but that's just fine – it doesn't need any of those things.

Micky said once that he thinks Carole King wrote this song specifically for him. As the former child star of the TV show *Circus Boy*, he could relate to the lyrics "Riding the backs of giraffes for laughs is all right for a while." But the lyrics also reference "a life of style" and say that "an overdub has no choice / an image cannot rejoice" which might also refer to The Monkees.

The album version fades in as the sirens and other noises fade out from the intro, which makes the start of the song very exciting in a way the single version (which has none of that) misses. On the album, the song ends suddenly and goes right into *Ditty Diego*, but the single version has a long fade out with some sound effects and bells and other things that frankly muddy it up too much, but I like it better. My favorite **HEAD** release was the one where they mixed the two versions, with all the soundtrack bits at the start and then the long fade-out at the end.

This also has the most cover versions I could find on YouTube since the early days of The Monkees. Just goes to show what a great song this is. My favorite is the version by And You Shall Know Us By The Trail of Dead.

Note the recording dates here – the first tracks were laid down in February of 1968 but this wasn't finished until August. I wonder what was done at the subsequent sessions, and more importantly, I wonder what would have happened if they had said, "What a great song! Let's use it in the movie, but release it earlier than that!" Had this come out in, say, May, after *Valleri* but before *D.W. Washburn*, while The Monkees reruns were still on TV, I'll bet it would have sold much better.

Seeing Micky sing this in concert while he's in his 70s was amazing. He still hit all the high notes and his voice was just as beautiful as when he was younger. Such a talent.

AS WE GO ALONG (Carole King/Toni Stern)
Monkee involvement: Vocals by Micky Dolenz
Recording dates: May 30, 1968; July 31, 1968; August 1, 1968
Highest chart position: #106 single B-side
Original release date: October 5, 1968 from 7" single and **HEAD**

Michael: Two Carole King songs on one album! This beautiful song gave Micky trouble because of the timing of it. Most of the song is in 5/4 which is not that easy to sing along to, but Mike had used 5/4 timing for the start of *You Just May Be The One* and oh, yes, Micky did it with the fade-out for *Shorty Blackwell* so he shouldn't complain!

Anyway, all teasing aside, try counting along. You have to count to 5 for a few bars at the start, and then you have to go to 3/4 for the most of it and revert back to 5/4 when the verse comes back in and during the fade. All with beautiful acoustic guitars played by Neil Young, Ry Cooder, and Carole King herself!

But it's very well produced. The acoustic guitars are pleasant, the flute in the background isn't too prominent, and Micky's voice is beautiful in this. This should have been the second single from the album instead of the B-side to *Porpoise Song* — maybe it would have been more successful than *Porpoise Song*, which was a bit weird for the radio at the time. I mean, even The Beatles couldn't hit the top 40 with *I Am The Walrus*...

Mark: Micky's singing here as well as on *Porpoise Song* and *Can You Dig it?* are some of his finest. All of The Monkees really tried hard with *Head*, only for it to be such a box office disappointment. It must have been extraordinarily painful for the group, who probably finally felt vindicated and validated for their efforts, only to have it all come crashing down.

The mono mix appears on **HEAD DELUXE EDITION** (2010), which sounds just like the standard stereo mix. An alternate stereo mix has a longer lead-in and fade-out.

The **HEAD DELUXE EDITION** also includes a 7" vinyl single featuring the instrumental version of the song.

DITTY DIEGO (Jack Nicholson/Bob Rafelson)
Monkee involvement: Vocals by Micky Dolenz, Michael Nesmith, Davy Jones and Peter Tork.
Recording dates: July 25, 1968; July 16, 1968; August 1, 1968; August 3, 1968
Original release date: December 1, 1968 from **HEAD**

Michael: A cute little non-song introducing the theme of the film. "Hey hey we are The Monkees / You know we love to please / A manufactured image / With no philosophies."

Mark: Another spoken word chant along the lines of *Zilch* from **HEADQUARTERS**, but unlike *Zilch* which is basically nonsense, the group makes a concerted effort through actor Jack Nicholson's words to describe their plight of be a manufactured group and the consequences of that fact. The varying speeds of their spoken dialogue adds to the hilarity.

The song is often referred to as *Ditty Diego - War Chant*, but the *War Chant* part is actually dialogue from the film which was recorded live on May 17, 1968. An alternate version of *War Chant* appears on the **HEAD DELUXE EDITION** (2010).

An alternate version of *Ditty Diego* appears as a bonus track on the 1994 CD reissue of **HEAD**. In this version, each individual Monkee recited their lines in a much more exaggerated way. If one listens closely, you can hear the voice of Jack Nicholson giving directions during the recordings.

In the end, on the final version, a straight reading was recorded and used and the exaggerations came from speeding up or slowing down the tapes of the recitations, rather than The Monkees changing the pitches and tones of their voices.

The mono mix appears on **HEAD DELUXE EDITION** (2010). This version is more jumpy in the reading, but at the same time straighter. An alternate version has more tinkly piano in the background and the voices sped up faster and much more inflection by the boys.

For masochists, there is a complete 23 minute session version also included. Bob Rafelson and Jack Nicholson are heard throughout.

HAPPY BIRTHDAY TO YOU (Mildred Hill/Patty Smith Hill)
Monkee involvement: Vocals by Micky Dolenz, Davy Jones and Peter Tork.
Recording dates: August 3, 1968
Original release date: November 15, 1994 from **HEAD** bonus track

Mark: They sound more like the monks instead of The Monkees here, then the chanting transitions into a semi-sarcastic version of the birthday standard. The group is apparently singing to Mike, despite the fact that his birthday is on December 30.

An alternate stereo mix that essentially sounds the same is included on the **HEAD DELUXE EDITION** (2010).

Michael: In the movie *Head*, this is sung by the three to Mike and then it cuts to a typical 60s party with *Long Title: Do I Have To Do This All Over Again*, at the conclusion of which Mike says that he hates birthday parties, "and I'll tell you something else — the same thing goes for Christmas!"

There was a court case recently that proved that the two Hill sisters didn't write this song, so they shouldn't get credit any more! Ironically, this was recorded on my birthday, so I hereby get to pretend they were singing to me.

HEAD

Original release date: December 1, 1968
Highest chart position: #45
Weeks on chart: 15

Opening Ceremony
Porpoise Song (Theme from "Head")
Ditty Diego War Chant
Circle Sky
Supplicio
Can You Dig It?
Gravy

Superstitious
As We Go Along
Dandruff?
Daddy's Song
Poll
Long Title: Do I Have to Do This All Over Again?
Swami Plus Strings

Michael: I admit that this may be my favorite Monkees album because there isn't one song I want to skip. I even like the Jack Nicholson-edited lines from the movie that come between each song to pad the album so you don't notice that there are only six songs here. The entire album is only about 28 minutes long. **THE BEATLES** (White Album) had been released a month earlier, had four sides, and each one was almost 25 minutes in itself... (I wonder how much the **HEAD** album cover was inspired by the White Album...)

If they had cut all the extra padding and not repeated *Porpoise Song* at the end (*Swami Plus Strings*) they could have put all the new songs on side one and then filled side two with non-movie songs that had only appeared on singles previously or were otherwise available (you know, like The Beatles did with **MAGICAL MYSTERY TOUR** the previous year). I'm sure it would have sold much better, instead of only reaching #45.

I suggest the following for side two:

A Little Bit Me, A Little Bit You
While I Cry
D.W. Washburn
The Girl I Knew Somewhere
It's Nice to Be With You
Goin' Down

With the exception of *While I Cry*, these had all been released on singles by this time but never on an album. Not that it matters. Can't go back in time. Just fun speculating.

Like **THE BIRDS, THE BEES, AND THE MONKEES**, and the entire film *Head*, the group tried to move away from their teenybopper image and they sincerely wanted to be respected by the real music elite. It didn't work. Instead, they further alienated their original fans and the "serious" musicians refused to even give them a chance. This is a shame because there's some excellent music here that, if released under a fake name, would have been embraced by the music critics of the time.

It's also interesting to note that soon after this, Peter quit, even though he had two songs on this album, more than even Mike.

Mark: Since *Opening Ceremony, Ditty Diego - War Chant, Supplicio, Gravy, Superstitious, Dandruff?, Poll and Swami Plus Strings, Etc.* are really just bits of dialogue from the movie, we haven't listed them as separate entries elsewhere. Admittedly, it is a bit short weight and I do like Michael's idea of them doing a **MAGICAL MYSTERY TOUR** compilation to get all those missing tracks, some of which were *still* not compiled onto an album until well into the 1980s!

As for what was released, this is still a marvelous album with some of the best, most consistent tunes ever released by the group.

The 1994 Rhino CD reissue adds a *Head Radio Spot*, which is not included in the regular listings as it just contains snippets of songs and dialogue from the film and the album and no new music.

On the **HEAD DELUXE EDITION** (2010), this track was retitled *Head Promo: Coming Soon*. Other promos featuring unnamed announcers are included and bears the names of *Head Promo Questions and Answers, Head Promo: It's This and That* and *Head Promo: Now Playing*. There is also an alternate stereo mix of *Swami Plus Strings* which sounds exactly like the released version.

Another feature is the eight-minute *"Introduction to Live Show" (recorded in Salt Lake City: May 17, 1968)* plus the live show itself which resulted in the *Circle Sky* footage and song for the film.

A third disc of the **DELUXE EDITION** features a *Head Open-End Radio Special Interview Platter with Davy Jones*, which features a 20-minute 1968 interview with Davy, plus excerpts from the six *Head* songs.

Peter always seemed to be extraordinarily frustrated despite the fact that everyone did just about everything to accommodate the man back in the day. They finally let him play; they put his composition on the closing credits of the second season; they used his name to comedic effect on the opening credits of the second season, drawing more attention to him; they had episodes in the second season focusing on him; they allowed him to have marathon recording sessions; they allowed him to break from his "dummy" character in *Head*; he composed two of the six tunes on the soundtrack, yet Peter was always extremely dissatisfied. I don't think he really came to terms with it all until he got fired in 2001.

ST. MATTHEW (Michael Nesmith)
Monkee involvement: Vocals by Michael Nesmith. Acoustic guitar and electric guitar by Michael Nesmith.
Recording dates: December 2, 1967; February 8, 1968; June 2, 1968; June 12, 1968; August 5, 1968; August 21, 1968
Original release date: January 1990 from **MISSING LINKS, VOLUME 2**

Mark: This Nesmith original, similar to Peter's *Lady's Baby*, was recorded multiple times over many sessions and still remained unreleased, largely in favor of Nesmith's *Listen to the Band*, which was the superior tune.

An acoustic version appears on a 7" vinyl single included with the **THE BIRDS, THE BEES AND THE MONKEES DELUXE EDITION** (2010). This is a very nice version and it is upsetting that it is not available on CD, but it is on YouTube.

The previously unreleased alternate mix from the 1995 **INSTANT REPLAY** CD issue adds more vocal effects on Mike's singing to no great effect. The **MISSING LINKS** version is preferable.

The **MISSING LINKS** version and an alternate vocal version appears on the **INSTANT REPLAY DELUXE EDITION** (2011).

Michael: Mike has completely abandoned trying to write rock songs by this time, and has moved into his country phase, which will reach its peak when he breaks away to form The First National Band a year or so later.

Anyway, it's not a bad song but we're deep into the era of Monkees becoming completely separate individuals who just happen to share albums every six months or so.

PROPINQUITY (I'VE JUST BEGUN TO CARE) (Michael Nesmith)
Monkee involvement: Vocals by Michael Nesmith
Recording dates: May 28, 1968; August 21, 1968
Original release date: March 1996 from **MISSING LINKS, VOLUME 3**
Significant other versions: The First National Band, Michael Nesmith

Michael: Another country song, complete with that ubiquitous slide guitar that is apparently a requirement for country music in the sixties. The lyrics are pretty good, but the music is quite forgettable honestly, especially because we know Mike is capable of so much more.

I can see why they never released this as The Monkees — I can imagine the record company saying, "Look, we're letting you have lots of control over your albums these days, but seriously, not this. This doesn't sound like The Monkees at all."

Mark: The first take from May 28, 1968 appears on the **MISSING LINKS** collection and is another straight country song from Michael.

An early demo version appears on **THE MONKEES DELUXE EDITION** (2006). There are a few different lyrics on this version.

A mono mix appears on the **INSTANT REPLAY DELUXE EDITION** (2011), which sounds completely different from the other versions with a slower tempo and a different vocal take and a more prominent steel guitar. There is also a 1968 stereo mix on this collection.

Michael finally rerecorded and released his own solo version on **NEVADA FIGHTER** (1971).

Michael performs a live solo version on **LIVE AT THE PALAIS** (1978) and again on **LIVE AT THE BRITT FESTIVAL** (1999).

HOLLYWOOD (Michael Nesmith)
Monkee involvement: Vocals by Michael Nesmith. Guitar by Michael Nesmith.
Recording dates: May 29, 1968; May 31, 1968; June 2, 1968; August 21, 1968
Original release date: March 1996 from **MISSING LINKS, VOLUME 3**
Significant other versions: First National Band

Mark: Michael's disdain for the Hollywood life shines through on this song, which sounds like *Don't Wait for Me* or *Good Clean Fun* with different lyrics. Apparently, the song was around as far back as the **HEADQUARTERS** sessions, but no recordings have emerged from this era.

The **MISSING LINKS** version and the 1968 mono mix appear on the **INSTANT REPLAY DELUXE EDITION** (2011).

This song was also included on the **PRESENT DELUXE EDITION** (2013) as a stereo mix.

As with many, many Nesmith songs of this time, he rerecorded and released this song on his first solo album with The First National Band, **MAGNETIC SOUTH** (1970).

Michael: An even more countrified song, adding the constant fiddle to the ubiquitous slide guitar. As usual, Mike's lyrics are interesting but there's not much to this song.

GOOD CLEAN FUN (Michael Nesmith)
Monkee involvement: Vocals by Michael Nesmith
Recording dates: June 1, 1968; August 21, 1968
Highest chart position: #82 single
Original release date: September, 6, 1969 from 7" single and **PRESENT**

Michael: While this song uses both the constant fiddle to the ubiquitous slide guitar, it's a high-energy song that has a very nice opening and a chorus that does not feel countrified at all absent the instruments performing it. In other words, unlike *Hollywood* and *Propinquity*, you could perform this with a traditional rock band and it would work.

This was left off of the next album coming up (**INSTANT REPLAY**) but later made its appearance on **PRESENT** and then was released as a single as well. I have a feeling the record company decided on the songs for **INSTANT REPLAY** but then later gave up and let the three remaining Monkees pick the songs for **PRESENT**. They then released a single with this Mike-written song on side one and a Micky-written song on side two (*Mommy and Daddy*).

Mark: The first single off of **PRESENT** and a very self-assured, straight country tune which seems out of place on a Monkees album unless you consider what was going on in the music industry at the time. The Byrds and Bob Dylan among others were releasing country albums and country rock was becoming a regular thing. This fact alone was enough for Nesmith to reviving his long-dormant solo career, this time as a country artist, but the seeds were first planted in The Monkees.

Once again, Nesmith uses a title that is not mentioned in the lyrics and really has nothing to do with the song in general.

The mono mix appears on the **INSTANT REPLAY DELUXE EDITION** (2011).

The alternate mix with extra percussion was released as the A-side of a vinyl single included in the **PRESENT DELUXE EDITION** (2013).

YOU AND I (Davy Jones/Bill Chadwick)
Monkee involvement: Vocals by Davy Jones
Recording dates: May 10, 1968; June 19, 1968; June 21, 1968; September 10, 1968; September 11, 1968; September 20, 1968
Original release date: February 15, 1969 from **INSTANT REPLAY**

Mark: This is not the *You and I* that appeared on **DOLENZ, JONES, BOYCE AND HART** (1976) and remade by The Monkees for **JUSTUS** (1996). This song has nothing in common with the latter and is a much more intense song. It's still kind of forgettable now, however. The Neil Young guitar is what saves it...almost.

The 1968 mono mix and the backing track appear on the **INSTANT REPLAY DELUXE EDITION** (2011). There is also a 1968 rough mix which sounds exactly as described. The organ is much more pronounced and as a result, much more piercing on this version.

The backing track appears on the **INSTANT REPLAY DELUXE EDITION** (2011).

Michael: The best Davy-written song, with a strong melody and introspective and prognostic lyrics ("In a year or maybe two / We'll be gone and someone new will take our place / There'll be another song / Another voice / Another pretty face"). Powerful and catchy, and I like the way it switches to 3/4 timing at the end of each verse which instead of slowing it down, punches it up. It deserves more attention than it has gotten.

NINE TIMES BLUE (Michael Nesmith)
Monkee involvement: Vocals by Michael Nesmith and Davy Jones. Acoustic guitar by Michael Nesmith.
Recording dates: February 2, 1968; February 8, 1968; April 5, 1968; August 21, 1968; October 29, 1968
Original release date: July 1987 from **MISSING LINKS**
Significant other versions: Michael Nesmith, First National Band

Mark: The Monkees performed a version of this on *The Johnny Cash Show* in 1969, but it eluded release on **INSTANT REPLAY** or **PRESENT**. Mike released it as an instrumental on its own on his **WICHITA TRAIN WHISTLE SINGS** (1968) and again with vocals on **MAGNETIC SOUTH** (1970).

A demo version appears on the 1995 Rhino CD reissue of **HEADQUARTERS** that sounds exactly like what it is — a demo. This also appears on **HEADQUARTERS SESSIONS** (2000) and on the **HEADQUARTERS DELUXE EDITION** (2007).

Version two with Davy's vocal and version two with Mike's vocal appear on **THE BIRDS, THE BEES AND THE MONKEES DELUXE EDITION** (2010). Davy's vocal version is quite cool and would have been a deserving release had Mike not reappropriated for his own solo records. Mike's vocals here have a lighter touch than the **MISSING LINKS** version.

The **MISSING LINKS** version plus the backing track and the mono mix appear on the **INSTANT REPLAY DELUXE EDITION** (2011).

Michael: Another very country song from Mike with a very catchy melody — one of Mike's best, actually — but once again not very Monkees sounding. The Davy version is a bit better and it's interesting to see how he handles it differently.

The version Mike did for his **WICHITA TRAIN WHISTLE SINGS** album is almost unrecognizable as the same song at first, with a strong organ doing the chords — sounds more like *A Whiter Shade of Pale* than anything written by Nesmith.

I remember buying the **WICHITA TRAIN WHISTLE** album when I was young — I think it was in the discount rack at 99 cents — and while I didn't like it much, I had fun trying to recognize the songs. *Tapioca Tundra* is almost as weird as the original, but overall that album sounds like a lost movie soundtrack except it's not recorded very well. It's like they put one microphone out in the middle of the auditorium and that was it.

THE CRIPPLED LION (Michael Nesmith)
Monkee involvement: Vocals by Michael Nesmith
Recording dates: May 29, 1968; August 21, 1968; October 29, 1968
Original release date: January 1990 from **MISSING LINKS, VOLUME 2**
Significant other versions: First National Band, Michael Nesmith

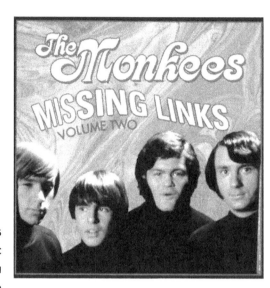

Michael: After a while, all these songs sound alike. Same basic feel — acoustic guitar, drums, bass and slide guitar. You could almost mix these together into one song and not be able to tell where one ends and the other begins.

Mind you, when taken individually, they're fine songs, but after a while, you say "Give me something that sounds different, will you?"

Mark: This country-sounding song has a mono mix that appears on the **INSTANT REPLAY DELUXE EDITION** (2011). It is slower in pace with a different vocal take than the **MISSING LINKS** version. There is also a 1968 stereo mix that appears on this collection.

This song was also included on the **PRESENT DELUXE EDITION** (2013) as a November 1969 stereo mix. There is a little cricket sound on this version.

Nesmith rerecorded it for his **MAGNETIC SOUTH** album in 1970 with a slightly faster tempo.

Michael performs a live solo version for **LIVE AT THE PALAIS** (1978), which was finally released as a bonus track on the 2004 CD reissue.

DON'T WAIT FOR ME (Michael Nesmith)
Monkee involvement: Vocals by Michael Nesmith
Recording dates: May 29, 1968; August 21, 1968; October 29, 1968
Original release date: February 15, 1969 from **INSTANT REPLAY**

Mark: As stated elsewhere, Mike's disinterest in anything Monkees after Peter Tork's exit in late in 1968 is evidenced by Mike's lack of new contribution to **INSTANT REPLAY**. This is his most recent recording for the project, completed before Peter left. It's a nice, wistful tune at least.

It was probably left unreleased prior to this time as it is truly country, with no pretenses of sounding anything like rock and roll or folk music.

The 1968 mono mix and an alternate 1968 stereo mix appear on the **INSTANT REPLAY DELUXE EDITION** (2011).

Michael: The one country song that made **INSTANT REPLAY** was this one, but I'm not sure why Mike picked this one over any of the others, especially since *Nine Times Blue* is much better. It does have some interesting chord changes and bits that make it stand out from the others but... well, I guess I'm just not into this kind of music. If you are, this is certainly well performed, well sung, and well written. Doesn't do anything for me, though.

I GO APE (Neil Sedaka/Howard Greenfield)
Monkee involvement: Vocals by Micky Dolenz
Recording dates: November 11, 1968
Original release date: April 14, 1969 on *33 1/3 Revolutions Per Monkee* TV special: first CD appearance on November 21, 2011 from **INSTANT REPLAY DELUXE EDITION**
Significant other versions: Neil Sedaka

Michael: See, they're The Monkees, so they're singing "I go ape"? Get it? Get it?

This is an old standard, originally performed by Neil Sedaka back in 1959. A rock and roll romp with a yakkety sax — but Micky sings this in the same way he did *D.W. Washburn* so it doesn't quite work.

We're getting into the sessions for the *33 1/3 Revolutions Per Monkee* special now. This is The Monkees' version of *Magical Mystery Tour* where the band is given control over the content and produce a messy TV special. Some of the music is good, and it's nice to see the guest stars, but this special is more dated than *Head*... and has the same theme, which is "We know we're manufactured, but we really want to be taken seriously as musicians and singers." They began work on this special before the *Head* movie was released, so they had no idea that the film would bomb — maybe they would have done something different with the TV special otherwise.

The special bombed too and it didn't help matters that it was scheduled opposite the Oscar ceremony — in the days where you couldn't record shows to watch them later.

Overall, the music for the special really wasn't good enough to release on a record, so I'm glad they never did one. And if you ever watch the special, you'll find yourself fast-forwarding through most of it. Yes, it's really that bad, sadly.

Mark: The backing track and the 1968 mono soundtrack master appears on the **INSTANT REPLAY DELUXE EDITION** (2011). An acetate version appears as the A-side of a vinyl single included in the package (an acetate version of *I Prithee* being the B-side). This version includes a short introduction not included on any other version.

It's not too bad, but it's kind of stupid, too, especially when viewed as part of the *33 1/3 Revolutions Per Monkee* special, where The Monkees appear in monkey costumes. "I don't believe it," one of the other characters says. I agree. Micky surprisingly comes off okay, but when Peter, Mike and Davy are seen prancing around singing "ugga chooka", it is easy to see why Peter turned in his resignation at this point.

WIND UP MAN (Bill Dorsey)
Monkee involvement: Vocals by Michael Nesmith, Peter Tork, Davy Jones and Micky Dolenz.
Recording dates: November 11, 1968
Original release date: April 14, 1969 on *33 1/3 Revolutions Per Monkee* TV special: first CD appearance on November 21, 2011 from **INSTANT REPLAY DELUXE EDITION**

Mark: The backing track appears on the **INSTANT REPLAY DELUXE EDITION** (2011), but strangely no mono soundtrack version, which features the boys singing repetitious lyrics in a somewhat monotone way on the *33 1/3 Revolutions Per Monkee* special, but their costumes are cool.

Michael: This song is quite insulting, actually. I know The Monkees were trying to kill their image as teenybopper singers, but lyrics like this don't do it:

I'm a wind up man
∙Programmed to be entertaining
Turn the key
I'm a fully automatic
Wind up man
Invented by the teeny bopper
Turn me on
And I will sing a song about a
Wind up man
Can you hear me laughing at you?

Yeah, thanks for laughing at me, guys. How dare I be entertained by you before. I must have been really stupid.

The song itself is meant to sound robotic, I get that, with no harmonies whatsoever and a staccato sort of singing — but it goes on much too long (and it's only a minute and a half).

NAKED PERSIMMON (Michael Nesmith)
Monkee involvement: Vocals by Michael Nesmith
Recording dates: November 12, 1968
Original release date: April 14, 1969 on *33 1/3 Revolutions Per Monkee* TV special: first CD appearance on November 21, 2011 from **INSTANT REPLAY DELUXE EDITION**

Michael: This is an interesting experiment. On the show, Mike sings with himself in a dual screen, with the Mike on the left dressed like a traditional country singer on the left and Mike in a suit on the right rapping out the rock song. Then they mix together and the country singer takes over. I really like Mike's rapper version better and wish it was a complete song.

This really doesn't work. It's a schizophrenic song. I mean I understand what he was trying to do, and I guess it works for a TV show, but it's not much of a song.

Looks like Mike's back to using nonsense titles again!

Mark: The backing track and the 1968 mono soundtrack appear on the **INSTANT REPLAY DELUXE EDITION** (2011).

Though Mike had good intentions, his duet with himself on *33 1/3 Revolutions Per Monkee* comes off as chaotic and confusing and generally not very good. Without the visuals, it comes across a bit better, but not much.

(I PRITHEE) DO NOT ASK FOR LOVE (Michael Martin Murphey)
Monkee involvement: Vocals by Micky Dolenz and Peter Tork. Acoustic guitar by Peter Tork. Electric guitar by Peter Tork.
Recording dates: July 25, 1966; October 18, 1966; December 3, 1967; November 12, 1968; November 17, 1968
Original release date: April 14, 1969 on *33 1/3 Revolutions Per Monkee* TV special: first CD appearance in January 1990 from **MISSING LINKS, VOLUME 2**
Significant other versions: Micky Dolenz

Michael: This is weird — a song sung in old English ("Thou Makest Me Free..."), which includes the traditional harpsichord, but otherwise sounds nothing like an actual medieval song. It doesn't really work. But apparently The Monkees wanted very badly to make it work, and tried it many times.

Micky's version seems to be the earliest one, and his vocal is fine.

Then there's a version with Davy singing, but it appears to have the same backing as the first version.

Peter then does a version that is slower and really plods along.

And then finally, there's Peter's version from *33 1/3 Revolutions Per Monkee* which has a kind of eastern *Can You Dig It* feel.

And then, as if that wasn't enough, Micky did a fifth version on his solo album **RE-MEMBER**. This one is kind of amazing, because it's a completely *a capella* version with Micky singing all the parts, and it sounds like a hundred monks in the background. This is the best version (although not technically a Monkees song).

Mark: This song is listed as *Do Not Ask For Love* on **MISSING LINKS**. No *Prithee*.

This Micky-sung ballad also appears on the 2006 **MORE OF THE MONKEES DE-LUXE EDITION** CD. A rehearsal and a stereo remix with Davy's vocals appears on **THE MONKEES DELUXE EDITION** (2006) and **THE MONKEES SUPER DELUXE EDITION** (2014).

The second recorded version appears on **THE BIRDS, THE BEES AND THE MON-KEES DELUXE EDITION** (2010). It's much slower and sounds like a demo or rehearsal.

The 1968 backing track appears on the **INSTANT REPLAY DELUXE EDITION** (2011). An acetate version appears as the B-side of a vinyl single included in the package. *I Go Ape (Acetate Version)* is the A-side.

The 1968 mono soundtrack master (also on **DELUXE**) which appears in the *33 1/3 Revolutions Per Monkee* special is the best version of this song, sung well by Peter with a sitar, and is a highlight of an otherwise dismal special.

STRING FOR MY KITE (Bill Dorsey)
Monkee involvement: Vocals by Davy Jones
Recording dates: November 11, 1968; November 18, 1968
Original release date: April 14, 1969 on *33 1/3 Revolutions Per Monkee* TV special: first CD appearance on November 21, 2011 from **INSTANT REPLAY DELUXE EDITION**

Mark: Two versions of the backing track appear on the **INSTANT REPLAY DE-LUXE EDITION** (2011), but strangely enough, not the mono soundtrack master from the *33 1/3 Revolutions Per Monkee* special. It's an average sounding song with nothing much remarkable to say about it. Dull.

I guess I should mention here that The Monkees' 50s medley that includes *At The Hop*, *Shake a Tail Feather*, *Little Darlin'*, and *Peppermint Twist*, backed up by Jerry Lee Lewis, Little Richard, Fats Domino, We Three, and The Clara Ward Singers has also not been released to CD, nor has Peter's performance of *Solfeggietto* by C.P.E. Bach.

Michael: More of Davy's "Broadway rock" — forgettable like most of the others.

DARWIN (Bill Dorsey)
Monkee involvement: Vocals by Davy Jones, Micky Dolenz, Peter Tork and Michael Nesmith.
Recording dates: November 18, 1968
Original release date: April 14, 1969 on *33 1/3 Revolutions Per Monkee* TV special: first CD appearance on November 21, 2011 from **INSTANT REPLAY DELUXE EDITION**

Mark: The backing track and the 1968 mono soundtrack master appears on the **INSTANT REPLAY DELUXE EDITION** (2011). Direct from the *33 1/3 Revolutions Per Monkee* special, the less said about this, the better.

Michael: This was never meant to be a song to be released; it's clearly just a TV bit, lasting about thirty seconds. It's basically a fanfare with vocals.

For some reason, this was never covered by any other musical artists. That was a joke.

GOLDIE LOCKS SOMETIME (Bill Dorsey)
Monkee involvement: Vocals by Davy Jones
Recording dates: November 18, 1968
Original release date: April 14, 1969 on *33 1/3 Revolutions Per Monkee* TV special: first CD appearance on November 21, 2011 from **INSTANT REPLAY DELUXE EDITION**

Michael: Davy once again shows how he doesn't really fit into The Monkees music. It's actually not a bad song. It has a slowed-down chorus which of drags down the energy of the song. But it's a kiddie song about fairy tale people, and on the show, Davy sings, dresses and dances like a small toy, with an oversized set to make it even more child-like.

The Monkees start off *33 1/3* singing about how everyone needs to take them seriously as real musicians and how they're not for teenyboppers and then when Davy gets his segment of the show, he does a bit appealing only to teenyboppers. That's why I insist that Davy was the least-Monkee Monkee. He just wanted to be an entertainer and had no desire to be taken seriously as a musician or a rock-and-roller.

Mark: The backing track and the 1968 mono soundtrack master appear on the **INSTANT REPLAY DELUXE EDITION** (2011).

One of Davy's showcases in *33 1/3 Revolutions Per Monkee* is not bad, but it also comes across as quite cloying, but better than most of the garbage on the special.

CALIFORNIA, HERE IT COMES (Buddy DeSylva/Al Jolson/Joseph Meyer)
Monkee involvement: Vocals by Peter Tork. Banjo by Peter Tork.
Recording dates: December 17, 1968
Original release date: April 14, 1969 on *33 1/3 Revolutions Per Monkee* TV special: first CD appearance on October 26, 2010 from **HEAD DELUXE EDITION**

Mark: Straight from the soundtrack of *33 1/3 Revolutions Per Monkee* comes a bizarre version of *California, Here I Come* sung by Peter that originally appeared on the show's closing credits. There is nothing much to recommend it.

THROUGH THE LOOKING GLASS (Tommy Boyce/Bobby Hart/Red Baldwin)
Monkee involvement: Vocals by Micky Dolenz
Recording dates: September 10, 1966; September 24, 1966; December 30, 1967; December 20, 1968; December 28, 1968
Original release date: February 15, 1969 from **INSTANT REPLAY**

Mark: Another Monkees song with a very lengthy genesis. I really prefer the ultimate version that appeared on **INSTANT REPLAY** with its heavier brass backing with violins and tinkly piano. This remake was first recorded on the December 30, 1967 date.

The previously unissued alternate mix dates released on the 1995 **INSTANT REPLAY** CD issue is from the September 10, 1966. It's not as meaty as the final released version with a very sparse instrumental break that is supplemented by a single plucking bass.

Another alternate version from September 10, 1966 appears on **MISSING LINKS, VOLUME 3** (1996), which is similar to the other alternate mix, but it definitely a different take with more "howling" vocals, and is heavy on drums and piano.

The first recorded version appears on the 2006 **MORE OF THE MONKEES DELUXE EDITION** CD. This version is a little bit faster than the final released version and has none of the brass of the later version and more kettle drum.

A 1968 stereo mix appears on **THE BIRDS, THE BEES AND THE MONKEES DELUXE EDITION** (2010). This version is very sparse on instrumentation in comparison to what was finally released on **INSTANT REPLAY,** but otherwise sounds very similar vocally and on the piano.

The backing track appears on the **INSTANT REPLAY DELUXE EDITION** (2011). There is also a 1968 mono mix on this collection. The vocals sound a bit different on this version.

An interesting one also on the **DELUXE** collection is the fuzz guitar version mono mix, where it sounds like Jimi Hendrix stopped by the sessions. Although a clever idea, I don't think it really works.

Michael: The first version is guitar-based and has a good feel, but the slowed-down version is much better, with the horns adding the energy lost by slowing it down. One of Boyce/Hart's better songs, with a catchy melody and interesting words. Even though this also has its origins years earlier, this probably would have been a better choice for a single than the more dated-sounding *Tear Drop City*.

DON'T LISTEN TO LINDA (Tommy Boyce/Bobby Hart)
Monkee involvement: Vocals by Davy Jones
Recording dates: October 28, 1966; November 6, 1966; December 31, 1967; December 20, 1968; December 28, 1968
Original release date: February 15, 1969 from **INSTANT REPLAY**

Michael: Don't listen to this song.

OK, sorry, that was an easy insult. In all seriousness, this kind of plods along. It's an old song that was never deemed to be good enough to release until **INSTANT REPLAY**, which appears to be an album that was rushed out after **HEAD** bombed. ("Quick! We need twelve songs for an album! What do we have lying around?")

Mark: An early version appears as a bonus track on the 1994 CD version of **MORE OF THE MONKEES** sung by Micky. The first recorded version with Davy on vocals and faster tempo and a clarinet appears on the **MORE OF THE MONKEES DELUXE EDITION** (2006).

A 1968 mono mix appears on **THE BIRDS, THE BEES AND THE MONKEES DELUXE EDITION** (2010) that sounds essentially the same as the final released version.

That said, I have never really cared for this song and it's amazing that Davy and company seemingly tried so hard to create a releasable version of this track with recordings lasting a little over two years. The **INSTANT REPLAY** version was first recorded on December 31, 1967. Davy almost shedding a tear at the end doesn't help.

A 1968 mono mix and the backing track appear on the **INSTANT REPLAY DELUXE EDITION** (2011). The backing tracks is comprised of multiple takes and studio chatter.

ME WITHOUT YOU (Tommy Boyce/Bobby Hart)
Monkee involvement: Vocals by Davy Jones
Recording dates: December 26, 1967; February 3, 1968; December 20, 1968; December 28, 1968
Original release date: February 15, 1969 from **INSTANT REPLAY**

Mark: Sounds like The Beatles' *Your Mother Should Know*. That's it.

A 1968 stereo mix and a 1967 mono mix appear on **THE BIRDS, THE BEES AND THE MONKEES DELUXE EDITION** (2010). These versions mix the organ up more prominently and give it a slightly more psychedelic feel than what was finally released on **INSTANT REPLAY**.

The previously unissued alternate mix from the 1995 **INSTANT REPLAY** CD issue has some "bop shop a lula" backing vocals and is less bombastic than the final released version. A calliope and an electric fuzz guitar are also more prominent. This version also appeared on the **INSTANT REPLAY DELUXE EDITION** (2011) and renamed fuzz guitar version mono mix and was in mono...obviously. There was also an alternate stereo mix included in this collection.

Michael: This was first recorded about a month after *Your Mother Should Know* was released. Make of that what you will. Mind you, the verses are different enough, but when you can practically sing The Beatles' song during the chorus, that's bad.

The fuzz guitar version sounds exactly like someone took a song at random added an unnecessary and annoying noise in the background. It reminds me of when I was young and practiced guitar by playing along with records. Good thing they decided not to release that.

It's a Nilsson-like song with a *Cuddly Toy* sort of feel, which is perfect for Davy to sing, and he does a great job, but why listen to the rip-off when *Your Mother Should Know* is available?

LISTEN TO THE BAND (Michael Nesmith)
Monkee involvement: Vocals by Michael Nesmith. Electric guitar by Michael Nesmith.
Recording dates: June 1, 1968; June 2, 1968; October 29, 1968; December 9, 1968; December 28, 1968
Highest chart position: #63 single
Original release date: April 26, 1969 from 7" single and **PRESENT**
Significant other versions: First National Band, Michael Nesmith

Michael: One of Mike's best songs, very well written and very exciting.

Mike still has the country slide guitar in the background, but absent that, it doesn't sound like a country song at all, and I think it would be better without it.

What bugs me about this song is the production. This should be big and fill the room, and instead it's mixed almost entirely mono, which tends to make everything flat.

The song is too short, too — it ends after about a minute and a half, and then it's like Mike said, "Hey, we need more" so he had it fade back in again. I remember hearing this on the radio once when I was young and having the DJ start to talk at that point and then stop when he realized the song was coming back in. When I was a DJ at my college station, one thing we were told to always avoid is "dead air" so I wonder if that silence in the middle of the song kept many DJs from playing it, which must have hurt sales.

In fact, the first time I ever heard this song was when I was young and I bought the double-album collection called **A BARREL FULL OF MONKEES**. The song was placed at the end of one of the sides, and I picked up the needle before the song was over, and then immediately realized that there was more. That impressed my juvenile mind as being something really clever. (I had not yet experienced songs like *Strawberry Fields Forever* or *Helter Skelter* that fade out and come back in.)

Listen to the Band was released as the B-side to *Someday Man* originally. When *Someday Man* bombed, they flipped the record over and started promoting this instead, and it charted higher than *Someday Man* (although still would be considered a flop).

Mark: A great song! Strangely, this song had a very long gestation, considering what a classic it is for The Monkees. It is a fantastic track and certainly deserved a much higher chart placing than #63.

Also, just as strange is Mike leaving this in the can and off of the **INSTANT REPLAY** album, where it might have had a much greater impact than *Tear Drop City* as a single. Even here, there was some debate about its merits, as *Someday Man* was sometimes touted as the A-side.

In any case, as mentioned under the *Cuddly Toy* comments, the version that appeared on the 1969 *33 1/3 Revolutions Per Monkee* special was the last time the foursome played together until 1986. Ironically, when Michael Nesmith sauntered onstage in 1986 at the Greek Theatre in Los Angeles on September 7, 1986, *this* was the song they played (and also *Pleasant Valley Sunday*).

An earlier, simpler version is included as a bonus track on the 1994 CD issue of **PRESENT**. It is not as effective and now sounds like a work in progress.

The mono single mix version also appears on the **PRESENT DELUXE EDITION** (2013) as well as the LP version true mono mix and an alternate stereo mix which has no brass.

The First National Band version appears on **LOOSE SALUTE** (1970).

Michael performs a live solo version for **LIVE AT THE PALAIS** (1978), which was finally released as a bonus track on the 2004 CD reissue.

JUST A GAME (Micky Dolenz)
Monkee involvement: Vocals by Micky Dolenz. Electric six-string guitar by Micky Dolenz. Percussion by Peter Tork and Davy Jones.
Recording dates: March 28, 1967; April 9, 1968; June 7, 1968; June 13, 1968; December 28, 1968; January 10, 1969
Original release date: February 15, 1969 from **INSTANT REPLAY**

Michael: A very short jazzy song from Micky, totally unlike anything he had written before. Musically, it's the same verse over and over with different words each time. It builds very nicely, with strings and other instruments slowly adding to the excitement, and then it just kind of ends before it gets as big and powerful as it should have gotten, and it slowly fades.

Although Peter and Davy are said to do percussion, I don't hear it.

Mark: An instrumental demo was attempted on March 28, 1967 and this version was included on **HEADQUARTERS SESSIONS** (2000).

Micky re-recorded this in 1968, possibly and probably to remove Peter Tork's contributions to the song since he was no longer in the group by the time this song was first officially released.

It's not a bad track, but the arrangement kind of borders on schmaltz. The negative influence **SGT. PEPPER** had on a lot of recordings: i.e. just slap on a bunch of instruments and it'll sound better.

The alternate vocal mono mix and the backing track appear on the **INSTANT REPLAY DELUXE EDITION** (2011). I prefer the alternate vocals to the actual released version as Micky sang them with more passion. Strangely, on the instrumental version, of which there are two takes, it was introduced as *French Song*.

CARLISLE WHEELING (Michael Nesmith)
Monkee involvement: Vocals by Michael Nesmith. Acoustic guitar, organ, percussion by Michael Nesmith.
Recording dates: November 4, 1967; April 5, 1968; April 11, 1968; May 31, 1968; August 21, 1968; October 29, 1968; January 10, 1969
Original release date: July 1987 from **MISSING LINKS**
Significant other versions: Michael Nesmith, First National Band

Mark: Mike rerecorded this song as *Conversations* for his **LOOSE SALUTE** album from 1970, but **MISSING LINKS** released it under its original name. It's a pleasant enough country sounding song, but it wasn't and isn't as strong as the other songs The Monkees were releasing at the time.

A 1967 stereo mix and a 1968 mono mix appear on **THE BIRDS, THE BEES AND THE MONKEES DELUXE EDITION**

(2010). These early versions aren't as full as the **MISSING LINKS** version, with a little too much organ.

An alternate version appears as a bonus track on the 1995 CD issue of **INSTANT REPLAY**. It sounds about the same as the other versions with some vocal differences.

An alternate stereo mix and the backing track appear on the **INSTANT REPLAY DELUXE EDITION** (2011). There is also an alternate vocal 1969 mono mix, which to me is not preferable to the other vocal versions.

This song was also included on the **PRESENT DELUXE EDITION** (2013) as a November 1969 stereo mix.

Michael also released an instrumental version under its original name on his **WICHITA TRAIN WHISTLE SINGS** (1968) album.

Michael: I like Mike's version on **LOOSE SALUTE** much better, recorded a year or so later, and the title *Conversations* is a great improvement over *Carlisle Wheeling*. It's really one of my favorite of this era's Mike songs. Interesting melody, and the long stops at the end of each verse on the **LOOSE SALUTE** version add to the tension of the song. Very much inspired by *Mr. Webster*, I believe.

Who or what is "Carlisle Wheeling"? There's a town called Carlisle in Pennsylvania and then Wheeling in West Virginia — did Mike write this in those two places? Here's another clue for you all: On the back of **THE BIRDS, THE BEES AND THE MONKEES**, on his picture, Mike signed it "Love, Carlisle Wheeling."

ROSEMARIE (Micky Dolenz)
Monkee involvement: Vocals by Micky Dolenz. Acoustic guitars by Micky Dolenz and Peter Tork.
Recording dates: February 19, 1968; February 28, 1968; March 1, 1968; March 13, 1968; March 14, 1968; June 7, 1968; June 13, 1968; December 18, 1968; January 10, 1969
Original release date: July 1987 from **MISSING LINKS**

Michael: Not one of Micky's best. I like the horns and production just fine, and there's plenty of energy, but somehow it never seems to come together into a full satisfying whole. There's some clever bits in there, but when it's over, you don't remember much about it except Micky saying "Rosemarie" over and over again in a monotone.

Mark: Sometimes this song is listed as *Rosemarie* and sometimes as *Rose Marie*. For convenience and consistency sake, *Rosemarie* will be used in all cases as it was when first released on **MISSING LINKS**.

A 1968 stereo mix and a 1968 mono mix appear on **THE BIRDS, THE BEES AND THE MONKEES DELUXE EDITION** (2010). These versions seem to drown out Micky's passionate vocals with the brass and other instruments mixed up way too high. The **MISSING LINKS** version is much more preferable and is a highlight of that collection.

A previously unissued early version appeared on the 1995 CD issue of **INSTANT REPLAY**. Although it doesn't say in the booklet, it does sound like Micky's sister, Coco is singing on this version. Lyrics aren't complete as there's a lot of scat-type singing on this version and it isn't as intense as the **MISSING LINKS** version. It's also not a complete take as it fades out prematurely.

The 1969 mono mix appears on the **INSTANT REPLAY DELUXE EDITION** (2011). The bass is very prominent in this version, but otherwise is identical to the unissued early version, but with more howling vocals. There is also an alternate stereo mix on this collection with some slightly different lyrics.

This song was also included on **PRESENT DELUXE EDITION** (2013) as a November 1969 stereo mix.

A MAN WITHOUT A DREAM (Gerry Goffin/Carole King)
Monkee involvement: Vocals by Davy Jones. Acoustic guitar and piano by Peter Tork.
Recording dates: May 8, 1967; June 22, 1967; August 14, 1967; September 15, 1967; March 9. 1968; November 7, 1968; January 4, 1969; January 10, 1969; January 11, 1969; January 13, 1969
Highest chart position: uncharted single B-side
Original release date: February 8, 1969 from 7" single and **INSTANT REPLAY**

Mark: As with many other **INSTANT REPLAY** tracks, this song had a lengthy genesis and multiple re-recordings. The version that ended up on the album was first recorded on November 7, 1968. This version is more brassy than earlier versions and sounds like Herb Alpert and the Tijuana Brass or Chicago at times. It's a very powerful song sung with much earnestness by Davy.

The mono promo mix appears on the **INSTANT REPLAY DELUXE EDITION** (2011). The double-tracked vocals sound a bit different on this version. The backing track and alternate vocal versions (both sans brass) also appear on this collection.

Michael: Underneath this Burt Bacharach-style production, there's not a bad song. Oh, it's Carole King — should have realized. Perfectly suited for the elevator of your choice. It's good to actually see a second Monkee participating, though.

SOMEDAY MAN (Roger Nichols/Paul Williams)
Monkee involvement: Vocals by Davy Jones
Recording dates: November 7, 1968; January 4, 1969; January 10, 1969; January 11, 1969; January 13, 1969
Highest chart position: #81 single B-side

Original release date: April 26, 1969 from 7" single. First album appearance from **MONKEE BUSINESS** (1982). First CD appearance from **INSTANT REPLAY** bonus track (1995).

Michael: This is an interesting track, well written. There are basically three parts: The verses which zoom along, then it slows down for the chorus, and then there's a third feel for a few lines. It repeats this twice and then repeats the chorus for a fade before it gets boring. It all fits together fine and works.

My complaint, once again, is the easy-listening way Davy likes his songs produced. This easily could be another Broadway song.

This is co-written by Paul Williams, who went on to write hit songs like *We've Only Just Begun* and *An Old Fashioned Love Song* (covered by Micky on his **REMEMBER** album), and of course Kermit's *The Rainbow Connection*.

This was released as a single and only lasted two weeks on the chart.

Mark: A great track. In fact, even though we have listed it as a B-side, it was also an A-side for a time. Since it was coupled with *Listen to the Band*, I would call it a double A-side, honestly. It charted reasonably, but this single should have been a knockout best-seller, but the mighty had fallen by April 1969. *33 1/3 Revolutions Per Monkee* had aired on April 14th, which did nothing to help the potential of this single as the TV special was dreadful with the *Listen to the Band* performance devolving into chaos unlike the single version. This song wasn't performed at all, which I feel was a major mistake.

The Monkees' fortunes would continue to sink during 1969, despite undertaking a major concert tour and Peter out (and Mike out) by 1970. Ha ha.

The standard single version, the 1968 mono mix, the backing track and an alternate mix all appear on the **INSTANT REPLAY DELUXE EDITION** (2011). The alternate mix sounds like a different vocal and instrumental take. It is also incomplete.

MY SHARE OF THE SIDEWALK (Michael Nesmith)
Monkee involvement: Vocals by Davy Jones and Michael Nesmith. Piano and guitar by Michael Nesmith.
Recording dates: January 9, 1968; January 19, 1968; March 13, 1968; January 22, 1969; January 31, 1969
Original release date: July 1987 from **MISSING LINKS**

Mark: A little Herb Alpert and the Tijuana Brass and some Burt Bacharach influence throughout, in this tune surprisingly penned by Nesmith, as it doesn't sound like a typical composition from him.

A 1968 stereo mix, a 1968 mono mix and Mike's vocal version appear on **THE BIRDS, THE BEES AND THE MONKEES DELUXE EDITION** (2010). The stereo and mono mixes sound essentially the same as the **MISSING LINKS** version. Mike's version is interesting, but he really can't get the high notes as well as Davy. His version is also sans brass.

Version two with mono backing tracks appears on the **INSTANT REPLAY DELUXE EDITION** (2011). A marimba, violins and a slide guitar are more prominent on this version and doesn't seem to be the backing track used on the final version, unless these instruments were all buried in the mix.

Michael: This sure doesn't sound like a Mike song! Maybe he wrote it specifically to appeal to Davy.

The Davy version is once more overly-produced with horns that make it clear that this is not a rock and roll song and should never even be considered one. Like *Someday Man*, it has a kind of staccato verse that then shifts tempo for the chorus, which makes it interesting to listen to just for the complexity of the thing.

But geez, try counting this song out. I could hardly keep up. It goes from 5/4 to 7/4 and then there's some 4/4 bits and then I gave up. It slows down to a 3/4 beat at one point as well. Maybe if I had studied music instead of being mostly self-taught, I could explain it better. For all I know, some of the timing is 7/5 or 9/32 or something. The most complicated Monkees song ever. There's a version where Mike and Davy share vocals and they're often off by a beat or so because hey, this is tough.

ALL THE GREY HAIRED MEN (Jack Keller/Bob Russell)
Monkee involvement: none
Recording dates: March 9, 1968; January 31, 1969
Original release date: November 21, 2011 from **INSTANT REPLAY DELUXE EDITION**
Significant other versions: The Lettermen

Mark: This is a mono backing track. It has potential, but sounds like it developed from *You Just May Be the One*.

Michael: I'm curious as to what the history of this is. Apparently someone recorded a backing track for them to sing, and no one wanted to. And I can see why.

This song was later recorded by that heavy rock and roll group The Lettermen. That was sarcasm.

INSTANT REPLAY

Original release date: February 15, 1969
Highest chart position: #32
Weeks on chart: 15

Through the Looking Glass
Don't Listen to Linda
I Won't Be the Same Without Her
Just a Game
Me Without You
Don't Wait for Me

You and I
While I Cry
Tear Drop City
The Girl I Left Behind Me
A Man Without a Dream
Shorty Blackwell

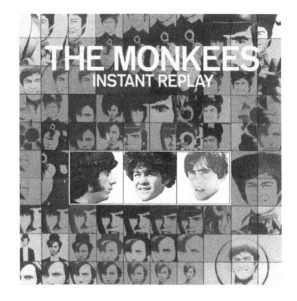

Mark: **INSTANT REPLAY** is an interesting album for a number of reasons. It is the first "serious" Monkees album. There's no *Zilch*. There's no *Gonna Buy Me a Dog*. There's no *Auntie Grizelda* or *Ditty Diego* or *Peter Percival Patterson's Pet Pig Porky*. The closest they come to a silly song is *Shorty Blackwell*, which is more bizarre than funny.

Another reason is this is the first Monkees album that really starts delving into the archives. This may have been a cost-cutting measure, but also a practical one. At least half of the album's twelve tracks date back to 1966-1967, however, many of these were re-recorded especially for this release. This was probably done to update their sound for 1969, but more likely to replace any Peter Tork instrumentations or vocals, since he now had officially left the group, despite the fact that the *33 1/3 Revolutions Per Monkee* special with Peter had yet to air at the time of this album's release.

As a whole, this album is pretty solid considering its haphazard construction. Even the album cover is quite nice except for the three Monkees photos at center bottom. Rhino noticed this and replaced these lame photos with better ones for their 1994 CD reissue.

Strangely, as a threesome, The Monkees weren't any more diplomatic as Micky gets four lead vocals, while Davy gets five, and Mike just gets three.

Also just as strangely, none of the songs on this collection ever appeared on The Monkees' TV series, either in first-run or in reruns.

In fact, Mike's vocals on his three tracks were all completed prior to mid-1968 with one track (*I Won't Be the Same Without Her*) completed in 1966, such was his disinterest in staying in The Monkees at this point after Peter left. Mike would go on to rekindle his interest in The Monkees during the course of 1969 with a tour and especially on their next album **PRESENT**. This was solely to be self-serving and to establish his own solo career before making his final exit in early 1970.

One final thought. Although I like *Tear Drop City*, I've always felt that *Through the Looking Glass* might have been a better choice for leadoff single. At least they didn't ruin the album by including the months-old *D.W. Washburn* on there. As such, **INSTANT REPLAY** becomes an interesting placeholder in The Monkees canon; not a great album, but not that bad, either. Certainly better than the *33 1/3 Revolutions Per Monkee* special airing a couple months after this release.

Michael: This feels like a patched-together album, which it really is. As I said previously, I think Colgems wanted to get an album out fast before The Monkees faded away completely, and only ten weeks after **HEAD** was released, they grabbed a bunch of unreleased songs, finished them quickly, and stuck them on vinyl — sort of a **MISSING LINKS** before there was a **MISSING LINKS**.

That doesn't make it a bad album. Some of these are very good. It's just that some sound really dated and don't fit well with the others. Music had changed tremendously from the time many of these were recorded.

However, since this is not a planned album in the sense that most albums are but instead a collection of random songs, Colgems should have capitalized on it. If I were putting together this album, I would have included *D.W. Washburn* and *A Little Bit Me, A Little Bit You*, and *Goin' Down* and other songs that had only appeared on mono singles before this. That would have helped sales quite a bit. Previous albums had included songs that everyone had already heard either on the radio or on the TV show. Instead, potential buyers looked at **INSTANT REPLAY** and saw a bunch of songs they'd never heard of before.

This seems to be a theme here, huh? How the record label didn't do a good job of picking the best songs or promoting the band after the first year or so. On the other hand, this coincides with The Monkees having more control over the music, so maybe the blame belongs with them. They were quite successful when they let the professional experts run things. (Then again, the "experts" also made them put out some terrible stuff, too.)

IF I EVER GET TO SAGINAW AGAIN (Jack Keller/Bob Russell)
Monkee involvement: Vocals by Michael Nesmith
Recording dates: March 9, 1968; January 31, 1969; March 6, 1969; March 7, 1969
Original release date: January 1990 from **MISSING LINKS, VOLUME 2**

Mark: Apparently, Davy also tried lead vocals on this song, but this version remains unreleased. The **MISSING LINKS** version plus the mono backing track version appear on the **INSTANT REPLAY DELUXE EDITION** (2011). It's not a bad song, but as usual, was passed over for Michael Nesmith originals.

Michael: This is a pretty good song, but I can understand why Mike would rather release his own country songs than do a cover. I don't really have much to say about it — after a while, some of Mike's country songs (and Davy's Broadway songs for that matter) just kind of seem to be so similar that they blend together and later, I can't recall one from the other.

KOOL-AID JINGLE (unknown)
Monkee involvement: Vocals by Micky Dolenz, Michael Nesmith and Davy Jones.
Recording dates: 1969
Original release date: August 2013 from **PRESENT DELUXE EDITION**

Mark: This song is also known as *Kool-Aid Spot*. It was created for the Saturday morning reruns of *The Monkees* TV series. This two-minute version was never used in its entirety for the ads.

Michael: "The money's in, we're made of tin, we're here to give you more."

OPENING NIGHT (Charlie Smalls)
Monkee involvement: Vocals by Davy Jones
Recording dates: May 1, 1969
Original release date: August 2013 from **PRESENT DELUXE EDITION**

Michael: This is the kind of song the leading man sings while standing in a spotlight in the late second act, just before the big climactic scene that ends the play.

I'm getting tired of reviewing Davy's Broadway songs, actually. If you really like this kind of stuff, there's plenty of it out there, but you probably aren't a Monkees fan because of songs like this.

Mark: Davy sings this rather well, but the song itself is rather pedestrian and slow. Some brassy sounds help, but not much, making it sound kind of like 1990s Chicago or something else similarly cheesy like a lame song from someone's Vegas act.

EVERYBODY LOVES A NUT (with Johnny Cash) (Jack Clement)
Monkee involvement: Vocals by Micky Dolenz, Davy Jones and Michael Nesmith.
Recording dates: May 6, 1969
Original release date: July 19, 1969 aired on *The Johnny Cash Show*
Significant other versions: Johnny Cash

Mark: Though The Monkees performed this Cash original with him on his variety series, it has never been officially released, though the performance can be viewed easily on YouTube.

Michael: The only version of this is a bad mono recording from TV, with Johnny Cash performing with Mike, Davy and Micky. This is really ridiculous and frankly embarrassing. Johnny Cash plays guitar, and the three Monkees tell dumb stories that would fit better on *Hee Haw* and then they all sing a quick chorus of *Everybody Loves a Nut*. It looks mostly improvised, and I'm not entirely convinced that The Monkees enjoyed this.

I'M A MAN (Barry Mann/Cynthia Weil)
Monkee involvement: none
Recording dates: October 10, 1967; November 4, 1967; August 21, 1968; May 12, 1969
Original release date: February 20, 2010 from **THE BIRDS, THE BEES AND THE MONKEES DELUXE EDITION**

Mark: This is just a backing track that has Beach Boys overtones — *Good Vibrations*, in particular. It is performed reasonably well, but without any vocals, it is hard to tell if this would have been a great track. Crossing fingers that Micky, Mike or Peter see fit to add some vocals before too long.

Michael: Another song The Monkees decided to never record. They're not playing any of the instruments, and there are no vocals so this is more of a Monkees wannabe song.

TODAY (Chip Douglas)
Monkee involvement: none
Recording dates: May 12, 1969

WINDY DAY AT KITTY HAWK (Bill Martin)
Monkee involvement: unknown
Recording dates: May 12, 1969

Mark: Two unreleased tracks from a Chip Douglas session that had different fates. *Today* was intended for Davy to record vocals at some later date, but alas this never happened, and *Windy Day* actually went missing, but apparently there were no vocals recorded for this song, either.

Michael: Guess *Windy Day at Kitty Hawk* wasn't the Wright song for The Monkees to sing. Get it? Wright song? Because... I'll show myself out.

OKLAHOMA BACKROOM DANCER (Michael Martin Murphy)
Monkee involvement: Vocals by Michael Nesmith
Recording dates: May 27, 1969
Original release date: October 1, 1969 from **PRESENT**

Michael: She's the best thing since soap! This is a very enjoyable song, with a great piano solo that always brings to mind one of those old westerns where the dancing girls are on stage while the hero grabs a milk and then is confronted by a trio of mangy-looking guys in black hats who haven't shaved in weeks...

Mark: Although this sounds like a Nesmith-penned original, it isn't. That's one thing about Michael Nesmith; when he does a cover, he really makes it his own, similar to how Nesmith made Murphy's *What Am I Doing Hangin' 'Round* his own.

CALICO GIRLFRIEND (Michael Nesmith)
Monkee involvement: Vocals by Michael Nesmith
Recording dates: May 29, 1969
Original release date: November 15, 1994 as a bonus track from **PRESENT** reissue
Cover version: First National Band, Michael Nesmith

Mark: This song is actually titled *Calico Girlfriend Samba* on the **PRESENT** reissue. This was recorded before Michael re-re-corded it for his own **MAGNETIC SOUTH** (1970) album. The **MAGNETIC SOUTH** version is superior, but it's nice in this case to hear what is actually a demo, and what could have been a fantastic Monkees track had Michael continued with the group on recordings into 1970.

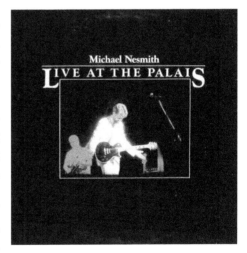

This song also appears on the **PRESENT DELUXE EDITION** (2013), but it is a different take than the *Samba* version, because Nesmith improvises some of the lyrics and the take is incomplete.

Michael performs a live solo version on **LIVE AT THE PALAIS** (1978).

Michael: An interesting feel that reminds me of Mike's later *Tengo Amore* from his album **LOOSE SALUTE**. I don't think this song ever got past the practice stage, given how Mike talks about going back to Rhode Island at the end. I mean, seriously, who talks about going to Rhode Island? How do you rhyme anything with that?

THANK YOU MY FRIEND (Michael Nesmith)
Monkee involvement: none
Recording dates: May 29, 1969
Original release date: August 2013 from **PRESENT DELUXE EDITION**

Mark: A pleasant sounding backing track (called take 4) of guitar, drums and piano, but nothing more. As far as I can tell, Nesmith never went back to this either with The Monkees or with The First National Band.

MY STORYBOOK OF YOU (Tommy Boyce/Bobby Hart)
Monkee involvement: Vocals by Davy Jones
Recording dates: May 30, 1969; May 31, 1969
Original release date: July 1987 from **MISSING LINKS**

Michael: If you don't already know what I think of these Davy songs by now, just go back and read my other song descriptions.

Mark: **MISSING LINKS** lists this as simply *Storybook of You*. It's all right, but it just kind of plods along and has some random brass mixed way in the background. A little too melancholy for my tastes.

This song was also included on the **PRESENT DELUXE EDITION** (2013) as Tommy and Bobby's stereo mix. This version has a longer fade-out and more brass. There is also a "new" 1969 stereo mix and a mono version included on this set.

SUZANNA SOMETIME a.k.a. **LOVE BANDIT** (Tommy Boyce/Bobby Hart)
Monkee involvement: none
Recording dates: May 30, 1969; May 31, 1969

Mark: A song recorded at the same session as *My Storybook of You* above, but no Monkees vocals exist for this, only Bobby Hart's guide vocal.

Michael: You'll forgive me if I don't comment on all these unfinished bits, instrumentals, and songs that have no Monkees involvement at all. I'm glad they're listed here for completeness, though.

THIRTEEN IS NOT OUR LUCKY NUMBER (Michael Nesmith/Michael Cohen)
Monkee involvement: Acoustic guitar by Michael Nesmith.
Recording dates: October 15, 1965, May 28, 1969, June 2, 1969
Original release date: August 2013 from **PRESENT DELUXE EDITION**
Significant other versions: Michael Nesmith, First National Band

Mark: Mike brought out an old tune to try out for The Monkees that predates The Monkees. It was performed here only as a backing track left in the can. Mike worked on it again post-Monkees for The First National Band, but didn't release that version, either. The music itself has somewhat jarring chord and tempo changes.

Michael: This one starts out quite interesting, with a very prominent bass but with predictable chords. And then it repeats. There are a few stops and starts, and then the song finally kicks in, ignoring what has come before and is pretty much a bass solo song! Seriously, what the hey?

Would have liked to have heard a finished version with vocals.

NEVER TELL A WOMAN YES (Michael Nesmith)
Monkee involvement: Vocals by Michael Nesmith. Acoustic guitar by Michael Nesmith.
Recording dates: June 2, 1969
Original release date: October 1, 1969 from **PRESENT**

Mark: Mike returns with this upbeat, honky tonk-type tune, as this is really his only new song written for **PRESENT** as both *Good Clean Fun* and *Listen to the Band* were recorded some time before. *Oklahoma Backroom Dancer*, recorded around this same time, also features Nesmith vocals, but he didn't write it.

Michael: This has the same kind of feeling as *Oklahoma Backroom Dancer*, and is quite successful. It's a story song, which you don't get much in rock and roll. This is very well produced and performed, and Mike sings it and tells it at the same time, which works wonderfully. One of the highlights of **PRESENT**.

OMEGA (Michael Nesmith)
Monkee involvement: Acoustic guitar by Michael Nesmith
Recording dates: June 2, 1969
Original release date: August 2013 from **PRESENT DELUXE EDITION**

Mark: This upbeat semi-jazzy instrumental is similar in vein to *A Bus That Never Comes*, minus marimba. It could have been from a long lost Charlie Brown special.

DOWN THE HIGHWAY (Carole King/Toni Stern)
Monkee involvement: Vocals by Michael Nesmith
Recording dates: June 5, 1969
Original release date: January 1990 from **MISSING LINKS, VOLUME 2**

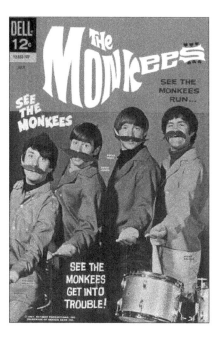

Michael: This is a fairly simple song that Mike sings well. What is disappointing to me is that it's a Carole King song, and well, it's just not up to the standards we've come to expect from her. The words are just fine, but the music is pedestrian. It plods along, no high points or low points, and then just fades out.

Mark: This song was issued under the title *Michigan Blackhawk* in error, which is a rather strange error since "down the highway" is sung in the first line of the song. It's an upbeat, country-influenced song totally suited for Nesmith.

The actual *Michigan Blackhawk* was finally released on the **PRESENT DELUXE EDITION** (2013).

Down the Highway was also included on the **PRESENT DELUXE EDITION** (2013) with the correct title as a November 1969 stereo mix.

GOOD AFTERNOON (unknown)
Monkee involvement: none
Recording dates: June 5, 1969
Original release date: August 2013 from **PRESENT DELUXE EDITION**

Mark: This is a jazzy instrumental featuring piano and drums and is labeled as take 14. It's rather nice, but it's difficult to tell what the final song would have sounded like if lyrics were added.

LONDON BRIDGE (Michael Nesmith)
Monkee involvement: none
Recording dates: June 6, 1969
Original release date: August 2013 from **PRESENT DELUXE EDITION**

Mark: A sparse instrumental mainly featuring a beating drum and other assorted sound effects before finally getting into some sort of tune that just plods along. It is listed as a backing track, take 4, and sounds like an outtake from The Beach Boys' **PET SOUNDS**.

A BUS THAT NEVER COMES (Jack Keller/Bob Russell)
Monkee involvement: none
Recording dates: June 6, 1969
Original release date: August 2013 from **PRESENT DELUXE EDITION**

Mark: This lively instrumental for this sounds like something from Herb Alpert and the Tijuana Brass or from the soundtrack of some lightweight 1960s movie.

ANGEL BAND (William Bradbury/Reverend J. Hascal)
Monkee involvement: Vocals by Michael Nesmith
Recording dates: June 9, 1969
Original release date: March 1996 from **MISSING LINKS, VOLUME 3**

Michael: This is just as boring as most church music is. It has that 60s feel to it — 1860, that is, when it was written. Why Mike thought he should do a version is beyond me.
Mark: This song was also included on **PRESENT DELUXE EDITION** (2013) as a November 1969 stereo mix. It's a different-sounding old time Gospel song, sung with much conviction by Michael, and is a most unlikely Monkees or Nesmith song as you could probably get.

TILL THEN (Eddie Seiler/Guy Ward/Sol Marcus)
Monkee involvement: Vocals by Michael Nesmith
Recording dates: June 9, 1969
Original release date: August 2013 from **PRESENT DELUXE EDITION**

Mark: An instrumental vaguely reminiscent of *Tumbling Tumbleweeds*, but with much laughter added in the background for unknown reasons. It is a backing track, take 2.

YOU'RE SO GOOD (Robert Stone)
Monkee involvement: Vocals by Micky Dolenz
Recording dates: May 27, 1969; June 26, 1969
Original release date: March 1996 from **MISSING LINKS, VOLUME 3**

Mark: Micky belts out this song with such passion, it's kind of surprising it didn't get release on **PRESENT** or **CHANGES**, as it is superior to most of the tracks actually released at the time. According to the liner notes of **MISSING LINKS, VOLUME 3**, Nesmith produced.

An alternate mix of this song also appears on the **PRESENT DELUXE EDITION** (2013), which sounds more grungy.

Michael: This is not to be confused with the later *You're So Good to Me*. Micky sings this very well, but there's not much to this song, and the melody is pretty much just one note while the chords move around behind it. It sounds like the Tamla songs that were popular on the radio at the time. The Temptations would probably do a very good version of this.

LITTLE RED RIDER (Michael Nesmith)
Monkee involvement: Vocals by Michael Nesmith
Recording dates: May 28, 1969; June 17, 1969; June 26, 1969
Original release date: March 1996 from **MISSING LINKS, VOLUME 3**
Significant other versions: First National Band

Mark: This song was rerecorded and ended up being Mike's first post-Monkees single when he joined The First National Band and was released on **MAGNETIC SOUTH** (1970). This first single flopped, but Nesmith's follow up *Joanne* became a major hit, a song apparently never tried with The Monkees.

Strangely, even though The First National Band was supposed to be a country out-fit, this first song (at least in The Monkees' version) is much more electric and rocking than the majority of what Michael was doing at the time with the group. The **MISSING LINKS** version ends abruptly.

An acoustic version appears on **THE BIRDS, THE BEES AND THE MONKEES DELUXE EDITION** (2010). This one is very nice, just Mike and an acoustic guitar with a somewhat slower tempo than the other known versions.

An alternate mix of this song also appears on the **PRESENT DELUXE EDITION** (2013), which has more brass.

Michael: This is a lot more rocking than the version Mike eventually released. Like most of the stuff The Monkees were recording around this time, there's a lot of emphasis on horns. It's like they got a bunch of musicians on contract and wanted to use the hell out of them.

I don't like the way the bass runs all over the place. I love a good fill every now and then but when the bass is constantly moving all over the place, it's distracting.

The problem with this song is that for all the energy the musicians are trying to provide, it never quite makes it. Not sure why, but it just seems to be there, never quite bringing it up from just a practice session. Even the most simple song can become great by an energetic performance. Just look at some of the rock and roll standards The Beatles played …

LYNN HARPER (Michael Nesmith)
Monkee involvement: none
Recording dates: May 29, 1969; June 26, 1969
Original release date: August 2013 from **PRESENT DELUXE EDITION**

Mark: Like *Good Afternoon*, this jazzy brassy song sounds kind of like 1990s Chicago and only exists as an instrumental. Although Michael wrote it, he apparently never got around to recording vocals for it.

LITTLE TOMMY BLUES (unknown)
Monkee involvement: none
Recording dates: June 10, 1969; June 26 1969
Original release date: August 2013 from **PRESENT DELUXE EDITION**

Mark: A slow blues instrumental that sounds like something The Rolling Stones could have done. It is listed as backing track, take 5.

SOME OF SHELLY'S BLUES (Michael Nesmith)
Monkee involvement: Vocals by Michael Nesmith
Recording dates: May 29, 1968; June 2, 1968; August 21, 1968; June 27, 1969
Original release date: January 1990 from **MISSING LINKS, VOLUME 2**
Significant other versions: Michael Nesmith, The Stone Poneys, The Nitty Gritty Dirt Band

Michael: Another unabashed country song that doesn't even try to be rock and roll. Underneath it all is a good tune and a good melody, one of Mike's better ones.

The Nitty Gritty Dirt Band's version is much better, heavy on the banjo but with great harmonies and a lot more energy.

Mark: The 1968 stereo mix and the 1968 mono mix appears on the **INSTANT RE-PLAY DELUXE EDITION** (2011). It has a slower tempo than the **MISSING LINKS** version. It is a very country sounding song with fiddle, harmonica and steel guitar.

Nesmith rerecorded and released his own solo version for **PRETTY MUCH YOUR OWN STANDARD RANCH STASH** (1973), which has a slightly faster tempo.

Michael performs a live solo version on **LIVE AT THE PALAIS** (1978) and again on **LIVE AT THE BRITT FESTIVAL** (1999).

HOW CAN I TELL YOU (Davy Jones/Bill Chadwick)
Monkee involvement: Vocals by Davy Jones
Recording dates: June 27, 1969
Original release date: August 2013 from **PRESENT DELUXE EDITION**

Mark: A not half-bad track with Davy singing with a piano and light drums. Why this remained in the can so long is a bit of a mystery. It sounds like something Michael Buble would do today. I actually would have prefered this to be Davy's showcase on **GOOD TIMES!** since *Love to Love* already had been previously released.

Michael: Another slow Davy ballad that my grandfather would have liked. Davy sings it wonderfully. You know, Perry Como sings well, too, but I don't want to listen to his songs, either.

The title reminds me of a song my friend Steve Sain and I wrote when we were 13 or so, called *How Can I Tell You I Love You (When I Hate Your Guts)*.

WE'LL BE BACK IN A MINUTE (Micky Dolenz)
Monkee involvement: Vocals by Micky Dolenz. Acoustic guitar by Micky Dolenz.
Recording dates: July 1, 1969
Original release date: March 1996 from **MISSING LINKS, VOLUME 3**

Michael: This is actually quite good! It's perfect for what it is — fast and exciting little bumper for the show. And you have to admire a song that is catchy, lasts less than thirty seconds, and contains kazoos.

Mark: A handy little tune created to announce the station breaks when *The Monkees* TV series arrived on Saturday mornings. It's nice that they got Micky to sing *and* compose this little ditty, because they really didn't have to.

A slower version also included on **MISSING LINKS** and referred to as #2, also appears on the **PRESENT DELUXE EDITION** (2013), where it referred to as take 4. A faster version listed as take 18 is similar to the **MISSING LINKS** version. Then, there is a version three which is even faster.

PENNY MUSIC (Michael Leonard/Bobby Weinstein)
Monkee involvement: Vocals by Davy Jones
Recording dates: May 1, 1969; July 11, 1969
Original release date: March 1996 from **MISSING LINKS, VOLUME 3**

Mark: MISSING LINKS states that this bouncy song was recorded to be one of the new tracks to be added to the Saturday morning run of The Monkees TV series, but ended up being rejected. It's quite nice, however, Davy and this song comes across like Jack Wild on *H.R. Pufnstuf*. Very bubblegum.

This song was also included on the **PRESENT DELUXE EDITION** (2013) in a TV mono mix version.

Michael: This is a pretty good song and unlike most of Davy's works at the time, doesn't put me to sleep. It has that Nilsson-like feel that Davy does so well. "Any requests? I'll play them for a penny and not a penny less!" I would have preferred this to any of the other songs Davy put on **PRESENT**.

Can I say here how depressing it is that for a very short period, The Monkees were a really good band (from about **HEADQUARTERS** through **HEAD**) with a true band sound, but now, with a few exceptions, they're just three guys who show up in the studio and sing other people's songs that are vastly different from each other? **INSTANT REPLAY** and **PRESENT** don't feel like the work of a band at all, but of three separate performers who just happen to be sharing vinyl. It's depressing, really, because when the four of them worked together in a studio at the same time with a good producer, they gave us wonderful music.

THE GOOD EARTH (Ben Nisbet)
Monkee involvement: Vocals by Davy Jones
Recording dates: July 21, 1969
Original release date: November 15, 1994 from **PRESENT** bonus track

GENE CORNISH (The Young Rascals: *Groovin', People Got to be Free, How Can I Be Sure***)**

I thought The Monkees were cute kids and made some good records thanks to Don Kirshner. We didn't take them very seriously as far as a band was concerned. They were more of a television phenomena. They sold a hell of a lot of records, so you've got to give them credit for that.

Their fans were a little younger than our fans. They had their niche.

When The Rascals first started, we were friends of Neil Diamond and he hadn't yet had a hit record. And he brought us some of those songs that he gave to The Monkees. But they just weren't our kind of stuff. They were a little too poppy for us. And look what happened — Neil Diamond! He had hits with The Monkees before he had hits for himself.

At one point when the show had been on a while, they wanted to get more credibility in the rock and roll world and they came up with an idea for a five minute segment at the end of the show where they would interview different rock people. I think they did an interview with a couple of the guys from Buffalo Springfield and Frank Zappa. Dino Danelli and I joined Davy and we did a segment that was never aired unfortunately. Davy was just a sweetheart.

It's a shame that Mike Nesmith never joined the band [on reunion tours] when Davy was alive. It could have made a lot of fans happy. That's the problem with bands, you know? All bands. My band The Rascals. Rolling Stones — they fight, they fight, they get back together and tour. Now Mike Nesmith is retiring. From what? Give me a break.

I went to see The Monkees a few months ago and there was an advertisement that Mike Nesmith was going to be there. Well, he wasn't. A lot of people felt cheated by that. All power to Micky and Peter, they're great guys and great talents and I wish them well.

Do they deserve to be in the Rock and Roll Hall of Fame? I won't make that call. There are a couple of acts in there that I don't feel belong in there. If anyone makes the Hall of Fame, God bless them. People like Tommy James deserve to be in there a long time ago. Because of Jann Wenner and his crowd in California — You know, it took The Rascals eight times to get in there. It took The Lovin' Spoonful nine times. Billy Joel twice. Billy Joel! It shows you that they don't really like New York people. I'm from the old school. I think they ran out of people early on — Little Richard, Jerry Lee Lewis, Everly Brothers, Elvis, Ricky Nelson... Those are the rock and roll heroes in my book.

I think they made a mistake trying to produce their own album. That last album was great. **GOOD TIMES!** Look at the help from all the people they got! They're great guys and a great entertainment!

Mark: Not a song, but Davy doing a poetry recital. Interesting to hear; understandable to see why it was left off **PRESENT**.

It is also included on the **PRESENT DELUXE EDITION** (2013), but listed as an alternate take.

Michael: As far as poetry goes, I liked *Peter Percival Patterson's Pet Pig Porky* better.

MOMMY AND DADDY (Micky Dolenz)

Monkee involvement: Vocals by Micky Dolenz. Piano and drums by Micky Dolenz.
Recording dates: August 1, 1968; August 8, 1968; December 9, 1968; December 28, 1968; January 10, 1969; May 13, 1969; July 1, 1969; July 2, 1969; July 10, 1969; July 22, 1969
Highest chart position: #109 single B-side
Original release date: September 6, 1969 from 7" single and **PRESENT**

Michael: One of my favorite Micky songs. The first version was too controversial for the record company apparently so he had to rewrite the lyrics. ("Ask your mommy and daddy who really killed JFK / Would it matter if the bullet went through my head / If it was my blood spilling on the kitchen floor / would you care a little more?")

Starts off with a kind of cliche Native American beat before settling into the verse, and then Micky does a little scat singing that sounds like what he imagines they'd sing around a campfire or something, then we're into the second verse, building up the energy, which then follows a new part that continues to build on the excitement until we get to the end and the fadeout. Wonderfully produced, always interesting, and over before it ever has a chance to be boring.

Mark: Micky delves into some social commentary and succeeds quite nicely. He certainly put a lot of effort into this considering how many recording sessions he used to achieve just the right sound. It succeeds in building much better than his similar *Bye Bye Baby Bye Bye* off the same album.

It was also the B-side to *Good Clean Fun* and bubbled under briefly.

The alternate version is included as a bonus track on the 1994 CD issue of **PRESENT**. It is basically similar, but contains more drums and some different vocals.

A 1968 stereo mix appears on the **INSTANT REPLAY DELUXE EDITION** (2011). There is also a 1968 mono mix which really sounds different all around. I actually prefer this version.

This song was also included on the **PRESENT DELUXE EDITION** (2013) in a 1969 mono mix. There are also two different July 1969 stereo mixes and the May 13, 1969 stereo mix included, but all of these versions sound pretty similar to the final released version.

The July 10, 1969 mono mix was released as the B-side of a vinyl single included in the package.

MIDNIGHT TRAIN (Micky Dolenz)
Monkee involvement: Vocals by Micky Dolenz
Recording dates: February 1967; June 16, 1969; July 22, 1969
Original release date: June 1970 from **CHANGES**

Mark: Of course, the better songs on **CHANGES** tended to be the ones resurrected from the vaults since the new ones sometimes sank to the lowest levels of cliché. Micky sang this with much more spirit than anything else he sang during the February-April 1970 sessions.

A demo version of this song with Coco Dolenz was released on **MISSING LINKS, VOLUME 3** (1996) and later on **HEADQUARTERS SESSIONS** (2000) and on **HEADQUARTERS DELUXE EDITION** (2007). **MISSING LINKS** dates these demos from February 1967.

This song was also included on the **PRESENT DELUXE EDITION** (2013) in a TV mix mono version, which has a very different ending than the **CHANGES** version.

Michael: I wish Micky had written more songs, as I said previously. His are some of my favorites.

It's a great production, with wonderful talking/singing from Micky, an exciting banjo pushing the energy forward, and a great harmonica giving it that "train" sound. The best song on **CHANGES**. I know, that's not saying much...

For the TV show, they took the guitar lick that ends the song and added it to the beginning as well as on the end, but this was mostly done to fit the time needed. After all, the show was in reruns on Saturday morning around this time, and since Colgems wanted to sell the new albums, they'd replace the songs that appeared in the first run of the show with the new songs. Sometimes they'd speed them up or repeat bits to fill the time needed. *Oklahoma Backroom Dancer*, for instance, repeated the solo twice on the TV show.

BYE BYE BABY BYE BYE (Micky Dolenz/Ric Klein)
Monkee involvement: Vocals by Micky Dolenz. Backing vocals by Davy Jones.
Recording dates: July 16, 1969; July 22, 1969
Original release date: October 1, 1969 from **PRESENT**

Michael: Another good Micky song, although the lyrics aren't up to his standards. It has a lot of the same feel as *Midnight Train* and even *Mommy and Daddy*, so I can kind of see why they left *Midnight Train* for the next album.

Mark: Micky's attempt to do something meatier on **PRESENT**. He succeeds quite well as the song builds as it goes along.

This song was also included on the **PRESENT DELUXE EDITION** (2013) in a mono version. This has some lyric changes. Also included is a July 1969 stereo mix.

MICHIGAN BLACKHAWK (Michael Nesmith)
Monkee involvement: none
Recording dates: June 10, 1969; July 29, 1969
Original release date: August 2013 from **PRESENT DELUXE EDITION**

Mark: The song *Down the Highway* was mistakenly issued under this title on **MISS-ING LINKS, VOLUME 2**. The real *Michigan Blackhawk* exists as an upbeat instrumental that has a Chuck Berry vibe and was finally released in 2013 as a backing track, take 4.

IF I KNEW (Davy Jones/Bill Chadwick)
Monkee involvement: Vocals by Davy Jones
Recording dates: June 27, 1969; July 1, 1969; July 11, 1969; August 4, 1969
Original release date: October 1, 1969 from **PRESENT**

Michael: This starts off pleasantly enough with a few chords that remind me of *Here, There and Everywhere* but then changes to a nice jazzy progression. Compared to the other songs Davy was giving us at the time, this is quite good. No syrupy strings or muted horns! Wonderful vocals and harmonies, and then it ends when it should, at just over two minutes.

Not a hit song, would never be a single, won't ever make a "Monkees Greatest" collection, but it works well as an album filler.

Mark: A nice, pleasant tune by Davy. It's not bad, but not terribly memorable, either. There is some nice, light guitar and piano. Nice is definitely the best word to describe this.

This song was also included on the **PRESENT DELUXE EDITION** (2013) as Bill and Davy's stereo mix and as a mono TV mix and take 11. They all basically sound the same, but take 11 is incomplete.

PILLOW TIME (Janelle Scott/Matt Willis)
Monkee involvement: Vocals by Micky Dolenz. Zither and acoustic guitar by Micky Dolenz.

Recording dates: March 14, 1967; August 14, 1969
Original release date: October 1, 1969 from **PRESENT**
Significant other versions: Micky Dolenz

Mark: This nursery rhyme tune was a favorite of Micky's as he re-recorded it many years later for his own **MICKY DOLENZ PUTS YOU TO SLEEP** (1991). I don't really know how well it fit onto a Monkees album, but I guess Micky wanted to have a song similar to *Good Night* which closed **THE BEATLES** (a.k.a. **THE WHITE ALBUM**). Incidentally, Janelle Scott is Micky's mother. She married Robert Scott in 1965, two years after Micky's father's death.

A demo version from March 14, 1967 appears on the 1995 Rhino CD version of **HEADQUARTERS** as a bonus track sans any instrumental embellishment. This version also appears on **HEADQUARTERS SESSIONS** (2000) and on the **HEADQUARTERS DELUXE EDITION** (2007). This is a continuation of *Micky in Carlsbad Caverns*.

Takes 8 and 9 of this song also appears on the **PRESENT DELUXE EDITION** (2013), which feature a vocal flub by Micky.

Michael: I, too, also always thought of *Good Night* whenever I'd hear this, especially since it also ends the album in the same way *Good Night* ended the White Album. However, the theme is where the similarity ends, as this has more of a 30s jazz feel. Micky's vocals, as usual, are excellent. Warm and soothing like a lullaby should be.

FRENCH SONG (Bill Chadwick)
Monkee involvement: Vocals by Davy Jones.
Recording dates: June 27, 1969; July 1, 1969; July 9, 1969; July 11, 1969; August 14, 1969
Original release date: October 1, 1969 from **PRESENT**

Michael: Another song where Davy tries his best to distance himself as far away from a rock and roll band as possible. It's pleasant enough as these things goes, but seriously, can you imagine any of the songs Davy sang since the TV show ended ever being accepted by the show? Kirshner would have laughed them out of the studio, and Chip Douglas would have said, "That's very nice Davy, but why don't you do a solo album with all of these? We're making a rock and roll album here."

And come on, look at these lyrics. A girl goes out walking, she meets a guy, they talk, and then she's gone. So f'ing what? Why should I care?

Mark: A different-sounding Monkees track considering the instruments used: organ, flute, marimba and vibes. Unfortunately, with all that going for it, it is still a very bland song and unmemorable.

This song was also included on the **PRESENT DELUXE EDITION** (2013) in a version identified as the LP master with alternate ending with raindrop sound effects added, which kind of sounds like pissing, which I'm sure is why it was later removed. The TV mono mix is also included on this collection as is a rough mono mix. Take 3 has more prominent bass.

LITTLE GIRL (Micky Dolenz)
Monkee involvement: Vocals by Micky Dolenz
Recording dates: August 14, 1969
Original release date: October 1, 1969 from **PRESENT**

Mark: A groovy little tune composed by Micky with some backing vocals by sister Coco and some crazy drums and flamenco guitar.

The Monkees were to release another song with this title on **GOOD TIMES!**, but there is no relation to this one. Ironically, the later one was by Peter Tork, who was not with the group at the time of Micky's track.

Take 7 is included on the **PRESENT DELUXE EDITION** (2013), which just sounds like the final released version, but with some different lyrics. The take is incomplete.

Michael: While I really like Micky's songs, it didn't occur to me until now how similar the ones from this era are. They all have the same sort of feel to them. That's not necessarily a good thing.

And let's talk about the use of the phrase "little girl." This was a common form of endearment in the 60s heard on plenty of songs, but doesn't it sound so dated and somewhat sexist these days? It doesn't age well. And yet, 40-something years later with **GOOD TIMES!**, we find another *Little Girl* song... and by then, it gets really creepy.

THE MONKEES PRESENT
Original release date: October 1, 1969
Highest chart position: #100
Weeks on chart: 7

Little Girl
Good Clean Fun
If I Knew
Bye Bye Baby Bye Bye
Never Tell a Woman Yes

Looking for the Good Times

Ladies Aid Society
Listen to the Band
French Song
Mommy and Daddy
Oklahoma Backroom Dancer
Pillow Time

Michael: I never knew if this album should be pronounced The Monkees Present — as in past, present, and future (or maybe "Here's a birthday present for you!") or if it should be pronounced The Monkees Present — as in "Presenting for your entertainment, The Monkees!"

Each Monkee gets four songs, and if you moved *Mommy and Daddy* up one notch, it would follow a specific pattern: Micky / Mike / Davy / Micky / Mike / Davy for side one, Davy / Mike / Micky / Davy / Mike / Micky for side two.

I have a feeling that was the plan, and had Mike not left, what we would have seen with the follow-up album. However, this sold even worse than **HEAD**, only reaching #100 on the charts. A terrible number for a band that had been at #1 just two years earlier, and sad, because it's not a bad album, and certainly better than **INSTANT REPLAY**.

However, this doesn't necessarily make a good *Monkees* album. This doesn't feel at all like a group effort, because it isn't. It's literally Mike with his own people, Davy with his own people, and Micky with his own people. It's three solo albums patched together onto one record. The only song that even has more than one Monkee on it is *Ladies Aid Society* which was originally recorded back during the **MORE OF THE MONKEES** sessions!

Mark: To answer Mike's question, the title of the album should be pronounced "THE MONKEES pre-SENT", not as a birthday present or past-present-future. Proof of this comes from *The Monkees Present Radio Promo*, included as a bonus track on the 1994 CD issue of **PRESENT** and also on the **PRESENT DELUXE EDITION** (2013). For this book, we have agreed to use **PRESENT** for short.

For lack of a better place to mention it, this **DELUXE EDITION** also includes a cheesy ad for **THE MONKEES GREATEST HITS**, which did nothing to help so-

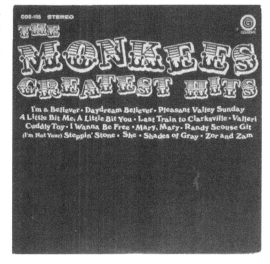

lidify The Monkees as a mature-sounding group designed to appeal to older teens and adults, since they have kids discussing scraping their money together in order to buy the compilation, which was released on June 9, 1969. I'm sure Michael Nesmith would have been disgusted with this if he had heard it at the time.

As for **PRESENT**, it seems that The Monkees without Peter were really trying to make one last go of it with this album and tour before hanging it up. If they succeeded in attaining another hit record, The Monkees as a trio may have lasted into 1972 or 1973 when their contracts were up and perhaps beyond that. If it failed, The Monkees would call it a day.

We all know what happened. **PRESENT** performed even worse than **INSTANT RE-PLAY** and **THE MONKEES GREATEST HITS,** Michael left the group, and Micky and Davy soldiered on to do one more contractually-obligated album before they too called it quits.

It really is too bad, as **PRESENT** is a much stronger album than **INSTANT REPLAY**. If there are any weak spots, it is Davy's fault as he relied on older material and his new material wasn't that strong or memorable. Fortunately, Davy doesn't dominate the album, as this really is Michael's album and his springboard for his initially-successful solo career.

I NEVER THOUGHT IT PECULIAR (Tommy Boyce/Bobby Hart)
Monkee involvement: Vocals by Davy Jones
Recording dates: October 28, 1966; July 24, 1969; September 5, 1969; September 12, 1969
Original release date: June 1970 from **CHANGES**

Mark: A nice, bouncy song that always has qualified as an interesting also-ran in the Boyce and Hart song catalog. Interestingly, after sitting in the can, it finally made its debut as the final new album track during The Monkees' original run and a nice way to sign off. The Monkees had indeed come full circle with Davy getting the last word since according to Michael Nesmith, "The Monkees were Davy's band."

This song was also included on the **PRESENT DELUXE EDITION** (2013) as an August 1969 version with no strings or backing vocals and a 1969 mono mix without overdubs. They sound exactly as described. Also included is a September 1969 mono mix with overdubs adds a lots of brass and violins which were reeled back by the time of final release on **CHANGES**.

Michael: An old song resurrected to fill the contractual obligation album. It's a pleasant little thing, and the perfect Davy song, with that old vaudeville kind of feel that gave Herman's Hermits much success. It's also interesting how the middle eight switches into 3/4 time and then the whole thing slows to half time for the lead. These things keep the song moving along well. One of the better songs on **CHANGES,** and I'm glad they used this instead of one of Davy's Broadway ballads.

IF YOU HAVE THE TIME (Davy Jones/Bill Chadwick)
Monkee involvement: Vocals by Davy Jones
Recording dates: May 1, 1969; August 6, 1969; November 11, 1969
Original release date: July 1987 from **MISSING LINKS**

Mark: A nice, bouncy song, that is strongly reminiscent of the *Sesame Street Theme*, which is strange since *Sesame Street* didn't make its TV debut until November 1969, so did *Sesame Street* rip off Davy?

This song was also included on the **PRESENT DELUXE EDITION** (2013) as a November 1969 stereo mix. The synthesizer is much more prominent on this version. There is also a 1969 mono mix without Moog on this collection, which makes the piano more prominent, making it sound even more like the *Sesame Street Theme*. And there's the 1969 mono mix with Moog as well as the take 4 version (missing some vocals and adding some scat) which begs the question on these latter-day Monkees Deluxe Edition collections: do we really need so many versions of the same song that basically sound the same?

Michael: While this has the same kind of beat and backing from the *Sesame Street Theme*, the actual melody is completely different. It's not a bad Davy song. Unlike many of Davy's songs at the time, this one is happy, poppy, and energetic. And it's short, too, which is good — if they had repeated the verse again completely, I think it would have started to drag.

This is better than any of the Andy Kim / Jeff Barry songs chosen for **CHANGES**.

TIME AND TIME AGAIN (Davy Jones/Bill Chadwick)
Monkee involvement: Vocals by Davy Jones
Recording dates: May 1, 1969; August 6,1969; November 11, 1969
Original release date: July 1987 from **MISSING LINKS**

Michael: And now we're back to the same old Davy songs. You know, Colgems could have put out a Davy solo album with all of these. After all, they'd already been recorded, so the major expense was already done. Instead, in 1971, Davy had a solo album which had a different feel altogether with songs like *Rainy Jane* (much better than any of these). I guess even the record company knew these weren't good enough to release.

This song is so forgetful, that when I later saw a reference to it online, I went "Oh, hey, we forgot to include that one in the book!" and then I went back and saw that I had written the above paragraph already. I'm sure in another few months, I'll forget it even existed again. And again, and again, and again, and again.

Mark: This plodding song was also included on the **PRESENT DELUXE EDITION** (2013) as a November 1969 stereo mix. There is a little chimey sound that is added to this version, which is also on the **MISSING LINKS** version. The November 1969 mono mix does not have this chime, and is also included on this collection as well as take 1, which has Davy singing "and again" ad infinitum.

They also added this song as a bonus track on the 1994 CD issue of **CHANGES**. I would have preferred a different track added since this was just on **MISSING LINKS**, and bonus tracks on **CHANGES** were sparse anyway. I know it says in the liner notes that this song was originally in the **CHANGES** song lineup, but really? C'mon guys, there's still one or two things left in the vaults that could have been placed here.

STEAM ENGINE (Chip Douglas)
Monkee involvement: Vocals by Micky Dolenz
Recording dates: May 12, 1969; July 8, 1969; August 28, 1969; November 21, 1969
Original release date: First release on the Australian **MONKEEMANIA** album (1979); First US album release on **MONKEE BUSINESS** (1982); First CD release from **LISTEN TO THE BAND** (1991).

Mark: This song was also included on **PRESENT DELUXE EDITION** (2013) as a November 1969 stereo mix. Some of the brass sounds are different on this version and is probably the best-sounding version of the song. There is also a mono version that sounds like the **MISSING LINKS** version and there is a 1969 rough stereo mix that has much double tracking of vocals and more backing vocals.

The **MONKEEMANIA / MONKEE BUSINESS** version sounds like it was recorded off a TV set broadcast and was originally aired on syndicated prints of "The Monkees on Tour" episode of the TV series.

The **MISSING LINKS, VOLUME 3** (1996) version is listed as a previously unissued alternate mix than the **LISTEN TO THE BAND** version..

Michael: I bought that **MONKEEMANIA** album when it came out primarily for this song and *Love to Love*. The sound quality was so poor, I hardly ever listened to it. However, underneath all that there is a very good song here, and recent releases are of much better quality.

I can understand why they didn't want to release this on the same album as a similarly-themed *Midnight Train*, but I really like this. It's great to see that Chip Douglas was back, and I only wish they had used him to produce **CHANGES** — I'm sure it would have been much better. I've read that there were some contractual and copyright problems that prevented this from being released.

And you know, I have to ask: What's the obsessions with trains? *Last Train to Clarksville*, *Midnight Train*, *Steam Engine*... not to mention the train references in *What Am I Doing Hangin' 'Round?*, *Tomorrow's Gonna Be Another Day* and *Cuddly Toy*. Or **THE WICHITA TRAIN WHISTLE SINGS**. (Did I miss any?)

TELL ME LOVE (Jeff Barry)
Monkee involvement: Vocals by Micky Dolenz
Recording dates: February 5, 1970
Original release date: June 1970 from **CHANGES**

Michael: And now we're getting into the Jeff Barry / Andy Kim **CHANGES** sessions where basically these two songwriters made an album and then brought in Micky and Davy one day to add vocals. I'm not kidding — look at the recording dates. These songs are so simple they brought in the musicians, taught them the songs, and had them recorded almost instantly.

Jeff Barry was a well-established songwriter, famous mostly for *Do Wah Diddy Diddy* and a bunch of early 60s Phil Spector hits like *Chapel of Love*, *Be My Baby*, *Leader of the Pack* and *Then He Kissed Me*. Andy Kim worked with Barry to write songs for The Archies, including one The Monkees had previously rejected, *Sugar Sugar*.

Somewhere, Don Kirshner was perfecting his evil laugh.

The two of them threw together some of their songs that apparently were rejected from the Archies sessions, all of which seem to have lyrics that were unimaginative and written on the spot, and we end up with **CHANGES**.

Tell Me Love is one of the more boring of them.

Mark: I've got a ticket for a ferry ride... oh whoops, this is a different song, or is it? In any case, it's just as boring as the other one, mixed with some syrupy sounding male chorus in the background: A-ha-ha-haaaa.

OH MY MY (Jeff Barry/Andy Kim)
Monkee involvement: Vocals by Micky Dolenz
Recording dates: February 5, 1970
Highest chart position: #98 single
Original release date: April 1, 1970 from 7" single and **CHANGES**

Michael: Probably the best of the Barry / Kim songs, but that's not saying much. Micky's vocals, once again, are the saving grace and they make the song at least listenable.

Mark: One thing that I can say about The Monkees, excepting *D.W. Washburn,* they really knew how to pick the best track on the album for the single, or in the case of the earlier albums, one of the best tracks on the album. *Oh My My* is one of these. It's deceptively simple, starting with a basic guitar lick, but graduates to quite a funky song and it really should have charted better. Perhaps this single should have also been released as a Micky Dolenz and Davy Jones single, or a Micky Dolenz solo single and The Monkees should have just called it a day after Nesmith left.

Welcome to the world of contractual obligations. A music video of Micky and Davy riding motorcycles and such didn't seem to help a more deserving song.

Ringo Starr had a big hit with a song with this title in 1973. His song has nothing to do with this one and vice-verse.

I LOVE YOU BETTER (Jeff Barry/Andy Kim)
Monkee involvement: Vocals by Micky Dolenz. Backing vocals by Davy Jones.
Recording dates: February 5, 1970
Highest chart position: uncharted single B-side
Original release date: April 1, 1970 from 7" single and **CHANGES**

Mark: Not a bad track, beat-wise, but lum-dooly-ally-day? Really? Didn't Jeff and Andy know how to write *any lyrics*? If I was Micky I would have protested and asked if I could help add some lyrics to some of these **CHANGES** songs. I guess they were defeated by this point, but it's a sad state of affairs that The Monkees (all two of them) lost every ounce of independence that they fought for just three years earlier.

Michael: Meh. Very simple. The kind of melody anyone with basic understanding of music could write in their sleep. And those lyrics! "I once went with a belly dancer / once around I didn't stand a chance - uh" Huh? First of all, "once around" doesn't seem to fit there at all, and geez, if you can't find a rhyme for dancer, you don't use "chance - uh". Spend a few seconds and rewrite the damn lyrics already.

YOU'RE SO GOOD TO ME (Jeff Barry/Bobby Bloom)
Monkee involvement: Vocals by Davy Jones
Recording dates: March 25, 1970
Original release date: June 1970 from **CHANGES**

Michael: Another song with unimaginative lyrics and music. I give Davy credit here, though — he puts a good effort to make this rise above its mediocrity.

Mark: Davy comes to the rescue to help save **CHANGES**, but essentially fails as well. Did anyone know how to write any good lyrics anymore? At least it has a funky sort of beat and soul groove, which helps it a bit, sort of. This definitely has Archies written all over it!

TICKET ON A FERRY RIDE (Jeff Barry/Bobby Bloom)
Monkee involvement: Vocals by Micky Dolenz
Recording dates: March 25, 1970
Original release date: June 1970 from **CHANGES**

Michael: Hey Jude was a huge hit for The Beatles a year and half earlier, and it has a really long fade out where they repeat something over and over again, so if we do that, the song will be really good! Uh, no. Repeating something boring over and over again doesn't erase the boring (see also: *Take My Love* from Davy's 1971 album).

This is a real sleeper of a song. And, seriously, if you haven't heard this before, go play it and see if you can't predict exactly where the song will go next. There are absolutely no surprises whatsoever.

Also, allow me to say how worried I am that Mark here seems to know so much about The Archies' music.

Mark: After a bright opening with *Oh My My*, **CHANGES** grinds to an immediate halt with Micky singing about having a ticket on a ferry zzzzzzzzz. He doesn't even ride the damn thing, just pines over *not* riding it! And why is Micky hurting anyway, the banality of the song?

WHICH WAY DO YOU WANT IT? (Jeff Barry/Bobby Bloom)
Monkee involvement: unknown
Recording dates: March 25, 1970

RIDE BABY RIDE (unknown)
Monkee involvement: unknown
Recording dates: March 26, 1970

Mark: Things certainly got sloppy in the waning days of the original Monkees sessions. These two songs were apparently actually recorded for **CHANGES**, and then lost!

Michael: Apparently a mercy killing.

ALL ALONE IN THE DARK (Steve Soles/Ned Albright)
Monkee involvement: Vocals by Micky Dolenz
Recording dates: March 26, 1970
Original release date: June 1970 from **CHANGES**

Mark: Gag.

Michael: Soles and Albright also were part of the Barry / Kim songwriting pantheon, and were just as influential in helping to kill off The Monkees. This song is rather embarrassing and even features a kazoo solo, and Micky treats it with the respect this song deserves. I always thought it was a song about masturbation, actually (I mean, if he's "all alone" that means she's not there, right? And he's just imagining all this?). I don't think that was the intention of the song. After all, that would have made it interesting.

Anyway, Davy has said that **CHANGES** was originally an Andy Kim album and then they just erased his vocals and added Micky and Davy's instead. Here, that seems more obvious because Micky shares lead vocals with someone and that someone isn't even Davy. It's like he just overdubbed his voice onto an already existing track, and that's probably exactly what happened.

DO YOU FEEL IT TOO? (Jeff Barry/Andy Kim)
Monkee involvement: Vocals by Davy Jones
Recording dates: March 26, 1970
Original release date: June 1970 from **CHANGES**

Michael: This is all right, I guess. When I was young, I'd play this album every once in a while, but now that I'm relistening for this book, I hardly remember it. I think I might forget it again after this is over.

Mark: Remarkably, this song is a little bit better than the average song on **CHANGES**. It almost could be a song that could have appeared on an earlier Monkees album, had it been recorded. It has a nice beat and you can dance to it. Had *Oh My My* been a bigger hit, this would have been my vote for a second single.

ACAPULCO SUN (Steve Stoles/Ned Albright)
Monkee involvement: Vocals by Micky Dolenz
Recording dates: April 2, 1970
Original release date: June 1970 from **CHANGES**

Mark: The songs counts in "Uno, dos, tres" and I feel that we're in for a Monkees version of *Wooly Bully*, which would have been preferable to this Mexican homage. I have never really liked songs like this that try to evoke a mood of a culture that an artist is not normally associated with. And, is it the 1994 CD remastering, or on the original recording, there is audible hiss on the track! Terrible.

Michael: The other Stoles/Albright song on the album. At least it doesn't really sound too much like the Barry/Kim songs. The backing vocals are grating to the point where I can't stand to listen. And couldn't they get Davy and Micky together for a few songs? Hearing Davy's vocals in the background would have helped, and also would have made it seem a little more like a Monkees album.

IT'S GOT TO BE LOVE (Neil Goldberg)
Monkee involvement: Vocals by Micky Dolenz
Recording dates: April 2, 1970
Original release date: June 1970 from **CHANGES**

Mark: Well, Michael was no longer in the group, so Micky had to take over the requisite country-sounding song spot. What, you want the Manchester boy to do it? It's a decent, if unmemorable song.

Michael: Seriously, I used to play this album as a kid, not knowing any better, but here I am more than 45 years later and hearing this song now is like hearing it for the first time. It left absolutely no impression on me.

But hey, Micky sure has a nice voice, doesn't he?

CHANGES
Original release date: June 1970
Highest chart position: #152
Weeks on chart: 4

Oh My My
Ticket on a Ferry Ride
You're So Good to Me
It's Got to be Love
Acapulco Sun
99 Pounds

Tell Me Love
Do You Feel it Too?
I Love You Better
All Alone in the Dark
Midnight Train
I Never Thought it Peculiar

Michael: The Monkees sing The Archies! Also known as "The Contractual Obligation Album."

I'll bet Mike and Peter heard this and wiped their foreheads in a comical manner while saying "Boy, I got off that sinking ship just in time." And the cover doesn't make it any better, with Davy and Micky dressed in semi-tuxedos playing percussion instruments. Hardly inspires a rock and roll attitude and certainly goes against everything The Monkees had been trying to do over the past few years, to convince everyone to take them seriously as a "real band."

On the other hand, Davy and Micky had always been actors first, so with Mike and Peter out of the band, they may not have really cared.

(Ironically, the real picture used for the album cover includes Mike, but he's been cropped out. You can see the shadow of his guitar just over Davy's head.)

This didn't even make the top 200 chart when it was released, but for some unknown reason, during the 1986 reunion when The Monkees were all over MTV, it got as high as #152. The big mystery is why **CHANGES** showed up on the charts in 1986 while **HEAD, INSTANT REPLAY** and **PRESENT** were nowhere to be found. The world may never know.

Mark: Just like The Archies' **THIS IS LOVE**, The Turtles' **WOODEN HEAD**, The Mamas and the Papas' **PEOPLE LIKE US** and Monty Python's **CONTRACTUAL OBLIGATION ALBUM**, this album was the last gasp by the original lifetime of The Monkees to breathe life into some new material before disbanding. Even that wasn't it, as Micky and Davy even cut a further single after this album's release, which was eventually added to the CD version of **CHANGES**.

DO IT IN THE NAME OF LOVE (Bobby Bloom/Neil Goldberg)
Monkee involvement: Vocals by Micky Dolenz and Davy Jones.
Recording dates: September 22, 1970

Highest chart position: uncharted single A-side
Original release date: April 1971 from 7" single. First CD appearance as **CHANGES** bonus track (1994).

Mark: The Monkees don't know when to quit, do they? In hindsight, it seems like The Monkees never broke up; just had small breaks between tours and albums, but at the time (1970), Micky and Davy just kept plugging away as long as anyone would have them in the studio. This is why Micky said, "It just kind of wound down. There wasn't any great last moment."

As for this song, it's pleasant. That's my code word (if you haven't noticed) for saying that something is not very good, but not downright unlistenable. It is unknown as to whether this song and *Lady Jane* were intended for anything more than a single, or the beginnings of yet another Monkees album session with Davy and Micky for 1971 release.

What *did* happen next is more of a letdown. The two songs were released as a single in April 1971 under the name "Mickey Dolenz & Davy Jones" in the US. Yes, with Micky's name misspelled! The single was released under The Monkees' name in other countries, but with the same dismal results. It's interesting that the two songs were *not* included on **BARREL FULL OF MONKEES**, a two-disc compilation album released in March 1971 as a last gasp from Colgems Records. That could have been an added sales incentive.

BARREL FULL seems to have had its genesis as **THE MONKEES GREATEST HITS, VOLUME 2**, which was a 14-song compilation that would have appeared in 1971, but somehow was expanded to the 20-song, two-disc set that **BARREL FULL** eventually became.

Do It and *Lady Jane* were released on Bell Records, which became the home for The Monkees' next compilation with **RE-FOCUS**, released in 1972. *The Monkees* TV series was still being aired on Saturday Mornings until 1973 and compilations seemed to fill the contractual bill rather than have Micky, Davy or anyone go in to record any more new material or raiding the vaults.

Michael: Well, I hope Micky and Davy got paid up front.

This is an interesting attempt to build a kind of gospel-sounding Motown-ish song, but it never really goes anywhere. The only good thing I can say about it is that it's nice to hear both Davy and Micky singing together, sharing verses. Also, it's nice and short.

As long as we're discussing **BARREL FULL OF MONKEES** here, let me say how much of a rip off it was. Only five songs per side when every other Monkees album had six songs a side? Come on, the average length of a Monkees song is less than three minutes. You could fit seven or eight songs on a side and it would still be shorter than the average Beatles album of the time.

LADY JANE (Jeff Barry)
Monkee involvement: Vocals by Micky Dolenz and Davy Jones.
Recording dates: September 22, 1970
Highest chart position: uncharted single B-side
Original release date: April 1971 from 7" single. First CD appearance as **CHANGES** bonus track (1994).

Michael: Once more, it's nice to hear Micky and Davy sharing verses. Other than that, there is really nothing to recommend this song. It just keeps repeating the same basic hook over and over, and that gets boring *real* fast.

Mark: This song seems to be sort of a springboard of what would happen next for Davy more than Micky, even though both share lead vocals.

This song has a funky groove and probably would have fit nicely onto the **DAVY JONES** album, which was released around May 1971. Interestingly, **DAVY JONES** has a song called *Rainy Jane*, which was released as a single a month after this song. This caused me much confusion in earlier years before Monkees history was straightened out.

Ultimately, this single and those associated with **DAVY JONES** as Bell Records focused all of their attention on their new big TV series based act: The Partridge Family.

This *Lady Jane* has nothing to do with The Rolling Stones' *Lady Jane*.

CHRISTMAS IS MY TIME OF YEAR
(Howard Kaylan/Chip Douglas)
Monkee involvement: Vocals by Micky Dolenz and Davy Jones. Backing vocals by Peter Tork.
Recording dates: 1976
Original release date: December 1976 from 7" single. First CD appearance on **A T.V. FAMILY CHRISTMAS** (1992).
Significant other versions: Christmas Spirit (a/k/a The Turtles)

Mark: Straight from the Dolenz, Jones, Boyce and Hart reunion tour, Chip Douglas managed to get three of the four Monkees into the recording studio in 1976 to record this Davy Jones Fan Club single. The B-side was Davy Jones' solo version of *White Christmas*. Rumor has it that Michael Nesmith appears on the record as well, but I feel that that was wishful thinking as Mike was still in the midst of his solo

195

recording career and really didn't want anything to do with his former group. It would be another 10 years before he would finally venture on stage with the other three.

This rarity finally got a proper release in 1992. It is very similar in sound and structure to the original version done by Christmas Spirit, a 1960s supergroup consisting of Howard Kaylan of The Turtles and Linda Ronstadt among others.

In both cases, the 7" singles are difficult to find and very expensive when found, but are easily available to listen to on album compilations and streaming.

Incidentally, the year 1976 also saw the reissue of **RE-FOCUS** with a much more palatable title **THE MONKEES GREATEST HITS**, and it finally saw chart action, rising as high as #58, their highest-charting compilation so far. Reasons for this had to do with the pseudo-Monkees reunion tour of Dolenz, Jones, Boyce and Hart, the better compilation title, and the marketing push of Arista Records, the successor to Bell Records and the new Monkees home for the next decade.

Michael: This is an excellent Christmas song, with a kind of Beach Boys sound. Micky and Davy share lead vocals again, which is a good idea. It's too bad this wasn't a hit, as it would be pleasant to hear this every year instead of, say, McCartney's dreadful *Wonderful Christmastime*.

The original version of this is now available on The Turtles CD **ALL THE SINGLES**.

ANYTIME, ANYPLACE, ANYWHERE (Bobby Hart/Dick Eastman)
Monkee involvement: Vocals by Micky Dolenz and Peter Tork.
Recording dates: May 30, 1986
Original release date: July 7, 1986 from **THEN AND NOW...THE BEST OF THE MONKEES**

Michael: Now we skip ahead ten years. The Monkees show is popular again on MTV and Colgems is now called Arista. They're anxious to cash in, so they want to release an album of greatest hits but wish to stick on a few new songs to grab the fans that already have all the old stuff.

This is a pretty good song, but here's where we get into the problem of the reunion albums other than **GOOD TIMES!** — instead of recreating The Monkees sound and bringing back what we loved, they decide to try to match current trends. This is a typical 80s pop song with that 80s drum and synthesizer sound. It's actually a very good song, but absent Micky's vocals, there's no way you'd say "Oh, that sounds like a Monkees song."

Still, it's great that they got Bobby Hart back!

Mark: This was supposed to be the follow-up single to *That Was Then, This is Now*. It's sounds a lot like something that Starship (*We Built This City*) was doing at the time with synthesized marimba. Davy did not participate and once *That Was Then* was a hit, balked at the idea of a second hit single that he would not receive and royalties or credit from.

Instead, a remixed version of *Daydream Believer* was released as a follow-up single, which killed any sort of momentum The Monkees had to become a viable group again in the 80s. They tried to rebound with **POOL IT!**, but like the 1960s for The Monkees, 1986-1989 became a repeat of 1966-1969 of declining interest and record sales and concert attendance. I was now a confirmed Monkees fan at this point and was saddened by The Monkees' second quick fall from grace.

This has nothing to do with the similarly-titled Who song called *Anyway, Anyhow, Anywhere*.

KICKS (Barry Mann/Cynthia Weil)
Monkee involvement: Vocals by Micky Dolenz and Peter Tork.
Recording dates: May 30, 1986
Original release date: July 7, 1986 from **THEN AND NOW...THE BEST OF THE MONKEES**
Significant other versions: Paul Revere and the Raiders

Mark: Micky does a great job covering the Raiders classic. For some reason, it has never been included on any subsequent Monkees compilation, making the now out of print **THEN AND NOW** album a necessity for one who would want a complete Monkees song collection in CD format.

Michael: Why they chose to cover an old song like this is beyond me. Surely, there were plenty of new songs available, no? My guess is that they just wanted to get something out quick. After all, all three of these new songs were recorded in one day.

THAT WAS THEN, THIS IS NOW (Vance Brescia)
Monkee involvement: Vocals by Micky Dolenz and Peter Tork.
Recording dates: May 30, 1986
Highest chart position: #20 single
Original release date: June 27, 1986 from 7" single and **THEN AND NOW...THE BEST OF THE MONKEES**
Significant other versions: The Mosquitoes

Mark: This one is easily the best of the three, but now sounds very 80s with its synthesized drums and guitars. I still enjoy it, and Micky's voice is in great shape, but it doesn't really have the traditional Monkees sound. This was a complaint heard most about the upcoming **POOL IT!** and later reunion album, **JUSTUS**.

Davy didn't appear on the track (or the other two from these sessions) and later was resentful about it, leaving the stage during concert performances. He changed his tone in later years and by 2001 can be seen singing and performing the song on stage with the others.

This song has nothing to do with the similarly titled ABC 1983 single called *That Was Then, But This is Now.*

Michael: Another cover, this one from the group The Mosquitos, recorded less than a year earlier. It wasn't a hit for them (obviously) so most people didn't realize The Monkees had become a cover band.

Here's the ironic part: The Mosquitos was part of that "new wave" sound that attempted to go back to the pop feeling of the 60s. The Monkees took this and added synthesizers and otherwise "updated it" to match other pop songs of the 80s. As a consequence, The Mosquitos version sounded more like The Monkees than The Monkees' version.

THEN AND NOW...THE BEST OF THE MONKEES
Original release date: July 1986
Highest chart position: #21
Weeks on chart: 34

(Theme From) The Monkees
Last Train to Clarksville
Take a Giant Step
(I'm Not Your) Stepping Stone
She
A Little Bit Me, A Little Bit You
I'm a Believer
Look Out (Here Comes Tomorrow)
Sometime in the Morning
The Girl I Knew Somewhere
Randy Scouse Git
You Just May Be the One
For Pete's Sake
Pleasant Valley Sunday
What Am I Doing Hangin' 'Round
Words
Goin' Down
Daydream Believer
Valleri
D.W. Washburn
Porpoise Song (Theme from Head)
Listen to the Band

That Was Then, This is Now
Anytime, Anyplace, Anywhere
Kicks

Mark: Normally, we aren't paying attention to compilation albums in this book, but this particular one is significant in a few ways. First, it was the first to compile a number of Monkees tracks left off of albums in the past and more significantly, the first appearance for many of these tracks on the new compact disc format. Ultimately, it was the inclusion of three brand-new recordings by The Monkees (alright, Micky and Peter) that warrants its inclusion here. It charted well (#21) and spawned a hit single with *That Was Then, This is Now* (#20), which were the greatest chart actions for the boys since 1968. It's also the only place one can find the elusive *Kicks*.

This compilation was released during The Monkees' successful 20th anniversary tour and MTV's successful airing of the original TV series. All of the older Monkees albums were reissued by Rhino Records and they all charted again! **CHANGES**, which originally didn't chart in 1970, actually made its way to #152!

This collection is a good catch-all for the various Monkees single A-sides and B-sides that except for *A Little Bit Me, A Little Bit You,* had never appeared on CD before. Most had never even appeared on an LP until 1982 and 1983 compilations! So, here is where you can get *A Little Bit Me, The Girl I Knew Somewhere, Goin' Down* and *D.W. Washburn* in one compilation along with the hits and three brand new tracks. One quibble: the non-appearances of *It's Nice to Be With You,* which would not appear on CD until 1991, and *Someday Man,* which would not appear on CD until 1995!

Michael: 1986 was an interesting year for Monkees fans. For a few weeks in November, there were seven Monkees albums on the top 200 chart: The first five albums, this one, and, for reasons known only to the Illuminati, **CHANGES**.

The vinyl version of this album only has 14 songs, three of them being the new ones:

SIDE ONE:
(Theme From) The Monkees
Last Train to Clarksville
Take a Giant Step
I'm a Believer
(I'm Not Your) Stepping Stone
A Little Bit Me, A Little Bit You
Anytime, Anyplace, Anywhere

SIDE TWO:
That Was Then, This is Now
The Girl I Knew Somewhere
Pleasant Valley Sunday
What Am I Doing Hanging Round
Daydream Believer
Valleri
Kicks

MGBGT (Peter Tork)
Monkee involvement: Vocals by Peter Tork. Backing vocals by Micky Dolenz and Davy Jones. Guitar by Peter Tork.
Recording dates: 1986
Highest chart position: uncharted single B-side
Original release date: August 1987 from 7" single and **MICKY DOLENZ DAVY JONES PETER TORK LIVE!** (1986) and later **POOL IT!** bonus track (2012).
Significant other versions: Peter Tork

Michael: To capitalize on the new interest in The Monkees, work began immediately on a new album. For some reason, this song was not recorded in the studio so we only get a live version.

This is a pretty good song, actually! Peter gets to sing, and he does a fine job of it. It's never boring.

Mark: Easily the best new song to come out of this period of renewed Monkeemania. Strangely, The Monkees only regaled us with this live version which was first released on a limited edition live album only sold at 1987 (and some later) reunion tour concerts. I really like the upswell of screams on the live version.

The bouncy song about Peter's car finally got a little bit more mainstream release as the B-side of The Monkees upcoming *Heart and Soul* single in 1987.

Still later, it was added to the **POOL IT!** 2012 reissue as a bonus track.

To hear a studio version, pick up Peter Tork's first solo album **STRANGER THINGS HAVE HAPPENED** (1994), which also has the almost complete Monkees reunion track *Milkshake* (see below). Here, the song is titled as *MG-BGT* and Nesmith appears doing backing vocals!

CHRISTMAS MEDLEY '86 (various)
Monkee involvement: Vocals by Micky Dolenz, Davy Jones, Peter Tork and Michael Nesmith.
Recording dates: December 5, 1986
Original release date: Aired on MTV on December 5, 1986. Never officially released.
Significant other versions: Anyone who's ever done a Christmas song.

Mark: 1986 was *The* Monkees reunion year, especially on MTV, who reran the series and tried to have the boys er, uh, *men* on their network as much as possible that year. One of the final things they did was have them sing a live Christmas Medley of *We Wish You a Merry Christmas / Winter Wonderland / Jingle Bell Rock / I Saw Mommy Kissing Santa Claus / Happy Christmas (War is Over) / We Wish You a Merry Christmas (Reprise)* along with some of the various MTV VJs and their families including

Martha Quinn, Downtown Julie Brown and Santa Claus. At the end, Santa takes off his sunglasses, hat and white beard to reveal that it's Michael Nesmith!

It has never been officially released to LP, 45 or CD or other format, but you can view it easily on YouTube.

Michael: The video is typical Christmas stuff, but if you catch it on YouTube, the fun is in watching it knowing that Santa is actually Mike and then seeing him reveal himself at the end.

COUNTING ON YOU (Alan Green)
Monkee involvement: Vocals by Davy Jones
Recording dates: May 22, 1987; June 11, 1987; July 2, 1987
Original release date: August 1987 from **POOL IT!**

Michael: And now we're getting into the **POOL IT!** sessions, which were not that different from the **CHANGES** sessions: A bunch of musicians quickly record some songs and then individual Monkees come in and sing their parts. There's not even a song on this album with more than one Monkee on it. And this could have been much more — producer Roger Bechirian had worked for Elvis Costello and Squeeze (two of my favorites) and you'd think he'd understand the right sound for The Monkees, given that those bands also were trying to recapture the fun of 60s pop in their own way. Didn't quite work out that way.

I tried to look up who Alan Green was, since he wrote this song, and found a web page where he mentions he wrote songs for John Denver and about how he had been influenced by "The Beetles." Uh huh.

Anyway, this is a typical 80s power ballad that starts off low-key but builds and goes nowhere. It's not bad, but nothing great, and as Mark points out, the lyrics are obnoxious. It's also a terrible way to end an album.

Mark: After literally counting one, two, three, etc., Davy sings that he is "counting" on you. Clever! Sell this to *Sesame Street* and get Davy some better material. Another sappy ballad from Davy to close out a highly uneven album.

Fan Thoughts

I was at The Monkees convention in 1987 in Teaneck, NJ with my friends, and we attended Davy Jones' Q&A session. At the end of the rowdy session, Davy sang a couple of songs. He started with Hippy Hippy Shake, *which got the entire crowd on its feet. Then a new song started playing — a slow song. One I hadn't heard before. As Davy started the countdown, the crowd slowly sat. I was so rapt listening to the song, I didn't notice I was the only one left standing...until he looked right at me. — Kerry Gans*

DON'T BRING ME DOWN (Bill Teeley/Glenn Wyka)
Monkee involvement: Vocals by Micky Dolenz
Recording dates: May 22, 1987; June 11, 1987; July 2, 1987
Original release date: August 1987 from **POOL IT!**
Significant other versions: Tommy James

Michael: Here's where I start to wish that The Monkees had been wise enough to do what worked so well for them when they first began — get the best songwriters in the country and pick from their top submissions. I'm so very glad they did that for **GOOD TIMES!** (Thanks Andrew!) but for now, we have to look at these songwriters and go, "Who the heck is that?"

With that said, this is pretty good, and is a cover of a Tommy James song from a few years earlier, which sounds just as dated today. The original is a bit slower and instead of the guitar doing the little hook, it has a synthesizer that makes it sound kind of Ghostbustery. (My interview with Tommy James, elsewhere in this book, shows that he was quite proud that The Monkees covered this.)

The problem with The Monkees' version is the production. The echoey drums and vocals, that synthesizer background, that whole 80s feel dates this to the point where, if Micky wasn't singing, you'd never know it was a Monkees song. Underneath all of this is a good song that would have been improved by doing a simple two guitars, bass and drum combo.

Mark: No relation to the ELO song of the same name. This casually-paced song is one of the better showcases for Micky with a nice, jingly beat and some heavy echo. Much better than *(I'd Go the) Whole Wide World.*

EVERY STEP OF THE WAY (Mark Clarke/Ian Hunter)
Monkee involvement: Vocals by Davy Jones
Recording dates: May 22, 1987; June 11, 1987; July 2, 1987
Highest chart position: uncharted single A-side
Original release date: August 1987 from 7" single and **POOL IT!**

Mark: This second single stiffed from **POOL IT!** I have strong mixed feelings about this song and Davy's performance, even in these reviews. Ultimately, I think it would have been a good album track, but it doesn't work as the all-important follow-up single to the highly catchy *Heart and Soul* single, which was sorely needed as The Monkees no longer had MTV to rely on to promote their latest works.

The single version has a different mix and vocals and is included on the 2012 **POOL IT!** reissue. There was also a music video produced that was included in the 1988 *Heart and Soul* VHS special that was also included on DVD on the 2012 reissue.

Michael: This is kind of song that bands with long, long hair would play live in front of stacks of Marshall amps while the audience screams along. In other words, the kind of band that The Monkees never were. It's not even the type of song Mott the Hoople would play, even though their leader Ian Hunter co-wrote it. And I *like* Mott the Hoople, who had songs much more creative than this.

It's a very simple melody containing absolutely nothing to surprise, with very predictable progression. Yawn. A terrible choice for a follow-up single.

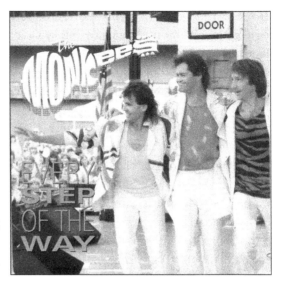

GETTIN' IN (Peter Tork)
Monkee involvement: Vocals by Peter Tork. Guitar by Peter Tork.
Recording dates: May 22, 1987; June 11, 1987; July 2, 1987
Original release date: August 1987 from **POOL IT!**

Michael: This is more like it. I mean, if The Monkees are going to sound like they're an 80s band, do it right! This is like Devo-meets-Brian Ferry or something, unique enough to make it interesting. Easily my favorite song on the album. It's got that catchy kind of hook that made *Ghostbusters* and *Pop Music* hits. Maybe it was never released as a single because the record company thought no one would recognize Peter's voice?

And unlike the other songs on this album, this one is more than just a Monkee coming into the studio, singing their bit, and then leaving. Peter actually wrote this and played guitar on it as well.

Mark: Why, oh why wasn't this released as a single, or at least a B-side? I remember when **POOL IT!** came out that this and *Heart and Soul* would get more listens on my programmable CD player. So, when *Every Step of the Way* was issued as the second single, I cried, "No! No! No!" *Gettin' In* is highly catchy and very commercial and has one thing going for it that many of the **POOL IT!** songs don't, it stands up well to repeat listens. Peter sings it in a somewhat David Byrne-Talking Heads mode. In fact, you could hear Talking Heads easily covering this.

HEART AND SOUL (Andrew Howell/Simon Byrne)
Monkee involvement: Vocals by Micky Dolenz
Recording dates: May 22, 1987; June 11, 1987; July 2, 1987
Highest chart position: #87 single
Original release date: August 1987 from 7" single and **POOL IT!**

Mark: This song was released with a cool video where The Monkees (well, three of them. I guess Mike melted.) are being defrosted after being on ice for the past 20 years. It is the best song on the album and it is a shame that the rest of the songs don't come up to muster as well as this one. Tork's songs come closest and *Gettin' In* should have been the second single off of this album instead of Davy's shrieking *Every Step of the Way*.

The video was included on the 1988 *Heart and Soul* VHS tape special which also appeared as a DVD bonus with the **POOL IT!** 2012 reissue.

Michael: This is a good song, but it still has that dated 80s sound I never really liked. It still doesn't sound much like a Monkees song, which is depressing given how many good songwriters were writing Monkees-like songs at the time. Imagine if they had asked Elvis Costello, or Andy Partridge, or Joe Jackson, or Joey Ramone, or some of the other pop songwriters of the time to contribute? For that matter, you know who wrote some great pop songs in the late 70s who was available? A little songwriter named Michael Nesmith.

(I'D GO THE) WHOLE WIDE WORLD (Eric Goulden)
Monkee involvement: Vocals by Micky Dolenz
Recording dates: May 22, 1987; June 11, 1987; July 2, 1987
Original release date: August 1987 from **POOL IT!**
Significant other versions: Wreckless Eric

Michael: See? Like this. Wreckless Eric was one of those new wave songwriters with Stiff Records back in the late 70s, along with Elvis Costello and Nick Lowe and Lene Lovich and so many others that became my favorites. This is a cover of a song he had a small hit with ten years previously. I was the program director of my college radio station in the late 70s and I'd play this every once in a while. Wreckless Eric didn't have a very good voice, though, and compared to Micky's wonderful voice, well, The Monkees' version is better even with all its 80s trappings.

This song fits better than many of the other 80s type of songs on **POOL IT!** but still, if you're going to do a cover of a new wave song from years earlier, I have so many other suggestions. I mean, come on, this song is just two chords over and over again. Not much to it. There are so many other great new wave songs they could have taken on and made their own.

Mark: Not a bad song, but not that great. It honestly sounds like a **CHANGES** out-take, because it sounds like a song that's almost complete, like it's missing something. I can't put my finger on it.

(I'LL) LOVE YOU FOREVER (Davy Jones)
Monkee involvement: Vocals by Davy Jones
Recording dates: May 22, 1987; June 11, 1987; July 2, 1987
Highest chart position: uncharted single B-side
Original release date: August 1987 from 7" single and **POOL IT!**

Mark: Sap, sap, sap. I try to be kind to Davy as he does have a wide-ranging singing voice and certainly produced a good amount of excellent Monkees songs over the years, even ones penned by him. He can growl with the rest of them and get really raunchy (see *Every Step of the Way* of which this song is also the B-side of), but he was given a whole lot of sappy songs to sing over the years. Whether this was by choice or by design, I think Davy should have gotten a little more coaching about this when it came to group efforts. Save stuff like this for your solo records.

The guitar solo in this definitely saves this from total obscurity.

And why is "I'll" in parentheses?

Michael: Corny cliched lyrics hiding behind a predictable and boring melody. It's well produced, though — the instruments sound great, and the guitar solo does bring the song out of its stupor. And I will at least give it credit for having been written by a Monkee.

LONG WAY HOME (Dick Eastman/Bobby Hart)
Monkee involvement: Vocals by Davy Jones
Recording dates: May 22, 1987; June 11, 1987; July 2, 1987
Original release date: August 1987 from **POOL IT!**

Michael: This is another song with nothing in the lyrics or the music to grab attention and keep it. It's fine as it is, but, well, nothing I'd put on my music player to hear again later.

Mark: Typical Davy-type song and on that level it succeeds quite well and why not, since Bobby Hart (of Boyce and Hart), was one of the writers. Davy sings it well, too, and I like the little castanets.

MIDNIGHT (David)
Monkee involvement: Vocals by Micky Dolenz
Recording dates: May 22, 1987; June 11, 1987; July 2, 1987
Original release date: August 1987 from **POOL IT!**

Mark: A nice, moody song that has a different pace and feel than many of the other songs on the album. Some eerie sounding vocals accompany Micky, but they're probably synthesized as well.

Michael: I kind of like this one. It has a nice feel to it, although as I've said previously, not a Monkees sound. Of course, once it's over, I can hardly remember a thing about it.

Who the heck is the songwriter? One name? David? Is that a first name or a last name?

SECRET HEART (Brian Fairweather/Martin Page)
Monkee involvement: Vocals by Micky Dolenz
Recording dates: May 22, 1987; June 11, 1987; July 2, 1987
Original release date: August 1987 from **POOL IT!**

Michael: Songwriter Brian Fairweather led a British synth-pop group called Q-Feel. Yeah, I'd never heard of them either until I looked him up. This song just moves along, doesn't build at all. There are no dynamics — you know, where the musicians get quiet and then build and make the song come alive (take, for example, *Goin' Down*). It just plods along and then fades out without ever having accomplished anything of note. (Of note! Ha! I made a pun.)

Mark: A generally upbeat song a little bit too layered with synthesizers. This, from an album that is already heavy with synthesizers. Nothing specific about it to recommend it. Micky sings it well and it makes for pleasant listening, but it is not memorable. A sax solo sort of breaks up the monotony.

SHE'S MOVING IN WITH RICO (Andrew Howell)
Monkee involvement: Vocals by Davy Jones
Recording dates: May 22, 1987; June 11, 1987; July 2, 1987
Original release date: August 1987 from **POOL IT!**

Mark: Almost universally considered the worst released Monkees song ever. I think it has more to do with the title of the song than anything else. It has a nice, reggae beat and is very catchy on that level, but just on that level. Since it does have that title and lyrics, it's honestly pretty stupid and stoops to the level of *Gonna Buy Me a Dog*, but it's not as funny, and that's saying a lot!

I knew a guy named Rico at the time this came out, so I still think of him whenever I hear this song. This Rico was gay so moving in with him wouldn't have been such a threat.

Michael: See, I'm much more interested in hearing a song called *She's Moving In With Rico* than I am with *Secret Heart* or *Midnight* or any other cliché. I mean, I'll bet there are a hundred songs called *Midnight*, but have you ever heard of another song called *She's Moving In With Rico*? Originality counts.

With that said, there's not much to recommend to this song, but it's surely not the worst Monkees song ever. That honor belongs to *The Day We Fall in Love*. This is a reggae-influenced song that actually has lyrics that aren't variations on "Baby I love you." Davy is upset that his girl broke up with him but to make it worse, she's moving in with Rico, everybody's hero. Come on, that at least makes the lyrics somewhat interesting. Give it points for trying.

SINCE YOU WENT AWAY (Michael Levine)
Monkee involvement: Vocals by Peter Tork
Recording dates: May 22, 1987; June 11, 1987; July 2, 1987
Original release date: August 1987 from **POOL IT!**

Mark: After a *Eight Days a Week*-type fade-in, Tork surprises and delights again with another catchy song, although he didn't write this one. It's the one song on the album that has the best and the funniest lyrics about breaking up. A true highlight.

Michael: This is the kind of song The Beatles would give to Ringo (or maybe what The Monkees would give to Peter. Hmm). This is actually one of the best on the album, with interesting lyrics. When you find out there's a song called *Since You Went Away* you expect a sad love song but instead you get "Things are much better / Since you went away." This is the alternate version of *She's Moving in With Rico* — same theme, different emotion. ("When I was younger I was told without another I'd be incomplete and deflated / My chosen one has chosen to befriend another and to my surprise I'm elated!")

POOL IT!
Original release date: August 1987
Highest chart position: #72
Weeks on chart: 4

Heart and Soul
(I'd Go the) Whole Wide World
Long Way Home
Secret Heart
Gettin' In
(I'll) Love You Forever

Every Step of the Way
Don't Bring Me Down
Midnight
She's Movin' in With Rico
Since You Went Away
Counting On You

Mark: *Heart and Soul*, as a teaser for the upcoming all-new reunion album, was the song that promised great things. It was not entirely to be.

While I am not as harsh as Andrew Hickey is in his book, claiming that **POOL IT!** was ruined by tons of synthesizers and synsonic drums, this album does has its moments. I actually like it better than the full reunion album made ten years after this with all four, **JUSTUS**.

If you compare what The Monkees were doing in comparison to other hot acts of 1986-1987, they represent well, but in the 80s, there was a certain ageist creepiness afoot about hearing men in their forties trying to be relevant to teenagers, when The Monkees should have crafted an album that sounded more like their best in the 60s.

But even The Monkees' contemporaries were releasing heavily-synthesized albums like this at this time with differing results: Chicago, Starship, The Beach Boys, The Rolling Stones, The Bee Gees, Paul McCartney, George Harrison, The Moody Blues, The Kinks, Brian Wilson, CSNY, etc.

Strangely, it was current hot 80s acts like Prince, The Bangles, The Go-Go's, Talking Heads, XTC, OMD, Duran Duran, etc., that were doing retro-sounding stuff and embracing psychedelia, while The Monkees were totally ignoring it.

One could argue that this album was no more a Monkees album than **DOLENZ, JONES, BOYCE AND HART** (1976), since they didn't sing on each others songs and technically they were billed as "Peter Micky Davy - The Monkees".

I do wish the three 1986 reunion tracks were included on this album, or at least on the 2012 expanded reissue, but I guess licensing issues prevented this.

Michael: You know how you can tell what is possibly a good album? Look at the song titles. Do they stand out? Are they interesting in and of themselves? Now compare the titles from **POOL IT!** or **CHANGES** to the titles on **HEADQUARTERS** or

PISCES. If you knew nothing about the band or the music and had to choose one album to listen to, which one catches your interest?

Seriously, the only title that even grabs my attention is *She's Moving in With Rico* which clearly is not a masterpiece.

The problem with this album is that, as Mark points out, this is the era where you have that new wave sound that is trying to get back to the fun pop of the 60s and The Monkees could have fit right in perfectly. Hell, their first five albums had made the chart just months before, and that showed that even kids who were just now being exposed to The Monkees liked the music enough to buy it. So the clear and obvious thing to do would be to make an album that recaptures that style of music — through the recent sales of those early albums, we had absolute proof that is what people wanted.

But noooooooooooooooooo. Instead, someone decides to update their sound to match what the bands of the 80s were doing, and why would anyone need to buy a Monkees album if it just sounds like everyone else? Is that all The Monkees know how to do — impersonate whatever the sound of the day is? (Insert the humorous band Gruppo Sportivo's line from their song *Blah Blah Magazines*: "Yes, it's true, we're like The Monkees / We've got no ideas of our own.")

It's sad that it took till **GOOD TIMES!** for them to realize what people wanted from a Monkees album. Instead, we get something that sounded dated almost instantly and does not stand the test of time. Maybe if the songs were better, it wouldn't matter as much, but most are quite forgettable.

And can we talk for a minute about the title and cover? What does **POOL IT!** mean? Is it a pun? Some expression I don't know? And who wants to see these guys in a pool? You're not twenty years old any more, gentlemen. The only good thing about the cover is that they brought back The Monkees logo, which hadn't been seen on a cover since **PISCES**. Smart marketing move.

MILKSHAKE (Martin Briley)
Monkee involvement: Vocals by Peter Tork. Backing vocals by Micky Dolenz and Michael Nesmith.
Recording dates: 1994
Original release date: 1994 from Peter Tork solo album **STRANGER THINGS HAVE HAPPENED**

Mark: The line-up of the 2012-2014 version of The Monkees makes its debut on this Peter Tork solo album. It's a fun song and is only included here as there is no other solo album track out there that

features three of The Monkees. Micky and Mike are very audibly represented, unlike the 1986 reunion tracks which supposedly feature Peter on them, but you'd be hard-pressed to hear him on the resulting tracks.

The 2012 reissue includes the live *MGBGT*, a remix single version of *Every Step of the Way* and a second disc featuring the DVD debut of *Heart and Soul - The Official Monkees Videography*, which was originally released on VHS only in 1988.

Michael: It's not a bad song, but it's fun to hear Mike and Micky in the background. The lyrics are funny and not your typical love song. And you know what, if **POOL IT!** had this kind of feel it would have been much better. I'm disappointed to discover that Peter didn't write this.

Mark and I debated whether to include this since we didn't include things like **DO-LENZ, JONES, BOYCE & HART,** but when Mark said, "Yes, but this is the only one that has *three* Monkees on it!" I agreed.

ADMIRAL MIKE (Michael Nesmith)
Monkee involvement: Vocals by Micky Dolenz; Backing vocals by Peter Tork, Davy Jones and Michael Nesmith; Drums by Micky Dolenz; Bass and keyboard by Peter Tork; Percussion by Davy Jones; Guitars by Michael Nesmith.
Recording dates: May 10, 1996-August 5, 1996
Original release date: October 15, 1996 from **JUSTUS**

Michael: And now we move forward another ten years to the next reunion. Over a period of a few months, the pre-fab four recorded a bunch of songs. We don't have the information as to which songs were recorded on which dates so we're listing them here alphabetically.

This time, The Monkees are in charge, writing all the songs and playing all the instruments — something they didn't even do back when they demanded full control!

Unfortunately, the experiment doesn't quite work. For one thing I never understood, the most prolific and talented songwriter among them only contributes one new song — this one — and he doesn't even sing it.

I wonder what happened to Mike? He didn't release any music in the 80s, and only two albums in the early 90s. After **JUSTUS**, there were some instrumental things, and then just one more song for **GOOD TIMES!**

Anway, *Admiral Mike* is not autobiographical (nor is it about me!). It's based on a true story about an Admiral who killed himself after the press reported that he had done something wrong and had ruined his life. It's not about the poor admiral's life, though, but instead is an opportunity for Mike to go after the press for being irresponsible.

Mike used to give us clever lyrics, often full of wordplay and colorful images, and now we're getting insults: "Go back to Hell you giddy fools... You slimy toad... You stupid twit ... "

This particular song has no bridge and no lead, but underneath it all, there's a pretty good melody. I guess I'm disappointed because I know Mike is capable of so much more.

But the other problem with this album is that they didn't learn the lesson from **POOL IT!** and once more are trying to match the sound of the times instead of sounding like The Monkees. The heavy grunge guitars, the lack of harmonies — without Micky's voice, you'd never know who this was.

Mark: Michael Nesmith's *other* major contribution to **JUSTUS**, but he doesn't sing lead. I would *love* to hear a demo or something with Michael singing lead. Micky sings it well and strongly, but Michael's vocals are sorely missing on this album and not having him perform his own self-penned tune is a major missed opportunity and a letdown to his fans. Fortunately, Michael participated more strongly vocally on their next album, **GOOD TIMES!** (2016).

CIRCLE SKY Version 2 (Michael Nesmith)
Monkee involvement: Vocals by Michael Nesmith. Backing vocals by Micky Dolenz, Peter Tork, Davy Jones. Drums by Micky Dolenz. Bass, keyboards by Peter Tork. Percussion by Davy Jones.
Recording dates: May 10, 1996-August 5, 1996
Original release date: October 15, 1996 from **JUSTUS**

Mark: And so we come to the big head-scratcher of the album. The big highlight of **JUSTUS**, besides the fact that The Monkees were playing and producing themselves, was that Michael Nesmith was back in the group as a studio recording unit for the first time since 1969 (1967 if count them *actually* playing together on the same tracks). This highlight was muted completely when Nesmith's songwriting contributions totaled two and his vocal contributions was just this one — a remake no less.

It would have been fine if it was a remake of something that was obscure or was previously a solo item like Davy had done, but *Circle Sky* had been done before and done well. It was prominently featured as both a live and studio recording on the **HEAD** album and in the movie as well with actual footage of The Monkees performing it, so the re-recording was absolutely unnecessary.

A Monkees version of something like *Joanne* or *Different Drum* would have been much more welcome if Nesmith was going to be this lazy. Heck, I would have even welcomed a Monkees version of *Cruisin'*.

A video was made for the song on the *Justus* VHS (1997), included on DVD with the 2013 **JUSTUS** reissue.

Michael: This is so disappointing. Only two Nesmith songs on the album, and one is a remake of a song that didn't need a remake. And it's not even a different version. I mean, had they done it with horns or added a lead or done it as a tango, I would be much more willing to cheer this on.

DYIN' OF A BROKEN HEART (Micky Dolenz)
Monkee involvement: Vocals by Micky Dolenz; Backing vocals by Peter Tork, Davy Jones and Michael Nesmith; Drums by Micky Dolenz; Bass and keyboard by Peter Tork; Percussion by Davy Jones; Guitars by Michael Nesmith.
Recording dates: May 10, 1996-August 5, 1996
Original release date: October 15, 1996 from **JUSTUS**

Michael: The rest of the songs on **JUSTUS** were written by the other Monkees, and while Micky and Peter have indeed written wonderful songs in the past, the ones here just don't reach the heights of some of their earlier compositions. For one thing, look at the titles of the songs on this album. With the exception of Mike's two contributions, they're all pretty bland and forgettable. Like **POOL IT!**, if you read these titles on an album cover, there's nothing that makes you say "Wow, that sounds interesting; I can't wait to hear that song!"

Anyway, on to *Dyin' of a Broken Heart*. It has a different feel from the rest of the album and is quite listenable. Micky's vocals once again raise any song above its original level. And the lyrics are a bit more than what the title may tell you: Micky sees his doctor and his psychiatrist who (of course) first ask for money and then do tests to determine that his problem is that he's dyin' of a broken heart (reminiscent of Ringo's *Oh My My* in some ways). However, Micky should survive, and his doctor tell him not to worry since he "lived through Nixon and a drug or two."

Mark: A nice, catchy calypso beat highlights this track. Once again, as with all Monkees projects, it is Micky Dolenz that seems to put forth 110%, a claim that cannot be made for any of the others on every Monkees album. Granted, there are albums where Davy, Mike or Peter shine brightly, but Micky is *always* prominently there.

I BELIEVE YOU (Peter Tork)
Monkee involvement: Vocals by Peter Tork; Backing vocals by Micky Dolenz, Davy Jones and Michael Nesmith; Drums by Micky Dolenz; Bass and keyboard by Peter Tork; Percussion by Davy Jones; Guitars by Michael Nesmith.
Recording dates: May 10, 1996-August 5, 1996
Original release date: October 15, 1996 from **JUSTUS**

Michael: Aha! Another Monkees song with "believe" in the title. Surely it will be a hit! Now if only he had included a train...

Actually, this weird little ditty gets repetitious very quickly, mostly because Peter repeats the line "I believe you" over and over again. I admire the fact that it's not trying to sound like the 90s grunge sound, with a more jazzy feel in 3/4 time, but meh, it doesn't do much for me. I do like the way the vocals come in every now and then really heavy and powerful, overdubbed a bunch of times to create a real chorus. But basically this song just moves along, doesn't know where it's going, and then just fades out.

Mark: Usually, as with **HEAD** and **POOL IT!**, Peter comes up with the best material on the album when he composes. However, this song truly misses the mark. It's sung averagely and it's a tad boring, as well. Ok, we get it, I believe you. The middle section almost saves it, but overall, it's too maudlin.

IT'S MY LIFE (Micky Dolenz)
Monkee involvement: Vocals by Micky Dolenz; Backing vocals by Peter Tork, Davy Jones and Michael Nesmith; Drums by Micky Dolenz; Bass and keyboard by Peter Tork; Percussion by Davy Jones; Guitars by Michael Nesmith.
Recording dates: May 10, 1996-August 5, 1996
Original release date: October 15, 1996 from **JUSTUS**

Mark: After Peter bores you with *I Believe You*, Micky picks up the slack and bores again with a song that probably would have been better suited for Davy to sing. It is a problem with this album, the lack of 12 songs of consistent quality, when The Monkees' strength was to always rely on outside writers to pick up the slack on an album. They learned this lesson when they did **GOOD TIMES!**, and the results were infinitely superior.

Michael: A slow piano-driven song with pretty introspective lyrics. "And I listen to the songs / And I read all the words / And I seem to remember something that I heard / Of a fire and a cave and shadows on the wall." This is one of the better songs on the album, well played and (of course) well sung. I would have loved to hear how a good producer would have built this up, perhaps with strings and horns and everything, but of course that would have gone against the idea of the "just us" album.

IT'S NOT TOO LATE (Davy Jones)
Monkee involvement: Vocals by Davy Jones; Backing vocals by Peter Tork, Micky Dolenz and Michael Nesmith; Drums by Micky Dolenz; Bass and keyboard by Peter Tork; Percussion by Davy Jones; Guitars by Michael Nesmith.

Recording dates: May 10, 1996-August 5, 1996
Original release date: October 15, 1996 from **JUSTUS**

Mark: And now it's Davy to the rescue. While not Davy's best moment on **JUSTUS** or even with The Monkees, this song was superior the two that preceded it, and a solemn way to end the album considering that it was Jones' final appearance on a new Monkees album before his death in 2012. It's nice to hear all four singing together at the end, proving they had harmony once again.

Michael: **JUSTUS** doesn't have many bad songs, but none on the album really shine to the point where you could imagine them as hit singles or anything. This one is much better than the stuff Davy was writing back in the late 60s, and it's fun to hear all four of The Monkees harmonizing. Lyrically, there's not much there, though.

MANCHESTER BOY (Davy Jones/Doug Trevor)
Monkee involvement: Vocals by Davy Jones; Backing vocals by Peter Tork, Micky Dolenz and Michael Nesmith; Drums by Micky Dolenz; Bass and keyboard by Peter Tork; Percussion by Davy Jones; Guitars by Michael Nesmith.
Recording dates: May 10, 1996-August 5, 1996
Original release date: unreleased
Significant other versions: Davy Jones

Mark: A known reject from the **JUSTUS** album. There are two different solo versions out there recorded by Davy, one with a ukelele and one without, that can give the listener an inkling of what The Monkees version may have sounded like. I suppose it was rejected because it was a bit too personal for a group album such as this, but it's too bad that they couldn't have included it on the 2013 **JUSTUS** reissue, especially since the reissue has no bonus tracks and the fact that Davy had passed away in 2012.

Monkee Business Fanzine said it was rejected when it was discovered that Davy was the CO-author of this song, thus breaking the rules of "just us".

Michael: All four Monkees did a version of this, but they've never released it so we can only look at the Davy versions to see what this would be like.

NEVER ENOUGH (Micky Dolenz)
Monkee involvement: Vocals by Micky Dolenz; Backing vocals by Peter Tork, Davy Jones and Michael Nesmith; Drums by Micky Dolenz; Bass and keyboard by Peter Tork; Percussion by Davy Jones; Guitars by Michael Nesmith.
Recording dates: May 10, 1996-August 5, 1996

Original release date: October 15, 1996 from **JUSTUS**

Mark: Harder-rocking than most things Monkees, but harder-rocking doesn't necessarily mean better. It almost sounds like a 90s version of *(I'd Go the) Whole Wide World* from **POOL IT!** What I said there applies here.

Michael: A slow plodding rocker that sounds nothing like a Monkees song. There's a good song here, but had it been produced like, say, a Cars song, it would have been much better.

This goes back to the importance of having a producer. Sometimes you need someone objective to look at your work and say "You know what this needs?" I certainly appreciate the editors I've had who have made my novels so much better, and in general, I've found that musicians that produce their own albums rarely reach the potential that a good producer can give them.

OH, WHAT A NIGHT (Davy Jones)
Monkee involvement: Vocals by Davy Jones; Backing vocals by Peter Tork, Micky Dolenz and Michael Nesmith; Drums by Micky Dolenz; Bass and keyboard by Peter Tork; Percussion by Davy Jones; Guitars by Michael Nesmith.
Recording dates: May 10, 1996-August 5, 1996
Original release date: October 15, 1996 from **JUSTUS**

Michael: When I first read this on the song list, I assumed they were doing a cover of the Frankie Valli song.

Not a bad little pop song here. Fairly predictable music and lyrics. One of the problems with this song — and many of the songs on this album — is that there are no dynamics. In other words, the song has the same basic energy from beginning to end. Compare this to *Goin' Down* which is probably the best Monkees example, where a simple two-chord progression becomes exciting and interesting as the musicians quiet themselves at certain points and then build to a crescendo at others. (You know who does this best? Elvis Costello. Listen to how often he has the first verse of a song at a specific energy level, then builds for the chorus, drops back down

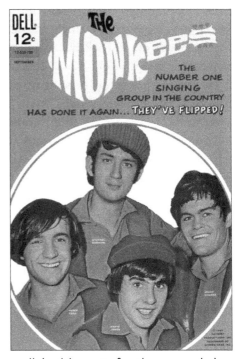

for the second verse while adding something small, builds again for the second chorus, goes all out for the bridge and lead, and then drops to practically nothing for the third verse so that when the chorus comes back in again, it is so powerful in comparison that it pounds excitement into you. I tried to follow this formula as much as possible in my songwriting days, and you could tell that it really made a difference in the audience reaction. You can't do this with every song — some work better to have a steady energy level throughout — but dynamics should always be something a good musician pays attention to.)

Micky says "I forgot the crash at the end!" which is his version of "I got blisters on my fingers" I guess.

Mark: One of the best songs on the album, amazingly, because usually Davy's songs come across as very sappy ballady things, but this one features strong backing vocals where you can definitely hear Micky and Michael. Even though Davy wrote this one, it actually sounds like a Nesmith solo song, especially when you hear him sing.

REGIONAL GIRL (Micky Dolenz)
Monkee involvement: Vocals by Micky Dolenz; Backing vocals by Peter Tork, Davy Jones and Michael Nesmith; Drums by Micky Dolenz; Bass and keyboard by Peter Tork; Percussion by Davy Jones; Guitars by Michael Nesmith.
Recording dates: May 10, 1996-August 5, 1996
Original release date: October 15, 1996 from **JUSTUS**

Mark: Even *more* harder rocking than *Never Enough* comes this song that should have been released as a single for no other reason as to show the world how hard The Monkees could rock out when given the chance, but singles were all but non-existent in the world of 1996, so this song and the album were quickly forgotten.

A video was made for the song on the *Justus* VHS (1997), included on DVD with the 2013 **JUSTUS** reissue.

Michael: At last, a song title that hasn't been used a hundred times before. This is a pretty standard rocker without surprises, about kids who move to the big city expecting fame and fortune and end up working at Burger King or something. But it's kind of dismissive of their dreams and also a bit insulting. What did these people do to deserve your anger, Micky? What's wrong with chasing your dream?

RUN AWAY FROM LIFE (Peter Tork)
Monkee involvement: Vocals by Davy Jones; Backing vocals by Micky Dolenz, Peter Tork and Michael Nesmith; Drums by Micky Dolenz; Bass and keyboard by Peter Tork; Percussion by Davy Jones; Guitars by Michael Nesmith.
Recording dates: May 10, 1996-August 5, 1996
Original release date: October 15, 1996 from **JUSTUS**

Michael: This has an interesting melody, but the production doesn't live up to the potential. Too much heavily distorted guitar. I'd love to hear this more keyboard-oriented, sort of like *All of Your Toys*.

Mark: I think this is a first: a song written by Peter, given to Davy to sing. The results turn out quite well. It's definitely a Peter-sounding type song, with uncharacteristic vocals by Davy, but Davy stands up to the plate and hits a homerun.

UNLUCKY STARS (Micky Dolenz)
Monkee involvement: Vocals by Micky Dolenz; Backing vocals by Peter Tork, Davy Jones and Michael Nesmith; Drums by Micky Dolenz; Bass and keyboard by Peter Tork; Percussion by Davy Jones; Guitars by Michael Nesmith.
Recording dates: May 10, 1996-August 5, 1996
Original release date: October 15, 1996 from **JUSTUS**

Mark: Micky takes a stab at a 50s-sounding song replete with heavy, heavy echo that makes it strongly reminiscent of the 50s section on the *33 1/3 Revolutions Per Monkee* special from 1969. Perhaps that was the goal. Micky sounds vaguely Elvis-like and one can almost picture him as Fonzie singing this on *Happy Days*, a role that Micky lost out to Henry Winkler back in 1973.

Michael: One of the good things The Monkees did on this album is try not to have all the songs sound alike. This 50s style rocker is done pretty well, but, well, there are plenty of 50s songs already. We didn't necessarily need a new one. Micky's vocals, however, are always great to listen to.

The first time I heard this, when Micky sings "deserve to cry," I heard "Jesus Christ" (at 0:19) and I thought "Well, that's something you never heard in a 50s song…"

YOU AND I (Micky Dolenz/Davy Jones)
Monkee involvement: Vocals by Davy Jones; Backing vocals by Peter Tork, Micky Dolenz and Michael Nesmith; Drums by Micky Dolenz; Bass and keyboard by Peter Tork; Percussion by Davy Jones; Guitars by Michael Nesmith.
Recording dates: May 10, 1996-August 5, 1996
Original release date: October 15, 1996 from **JUSTUS**
Significant other versions: Dolenz, Jones, Boyce and Hart

Mark: A remake that makes sense, unlike *Circle Sky*, since The Monkees never officially recorded it before and the lyrics actually are pertinent since they seem to be commenting on the entire Monkees experience. Davy takes the lead, unlike the **DOLENZ, JONES, BOYCE AND HART** version where Micky takes the lead. I would have to say that this is the superior version. Sorry, Micky.

This version of *You and I* also appears on the **HEY HEY WE'RE THE MONKEES** CD-Rom game, released at the same time as **JUSTUS**.

A video was made for the song on the *Justus* VHS (1997), included on DVD with the 2013 **JUSTUS** reissue.

Michael: I'm frustrated by The Monkees not being able to come up with new titles for different songs. Davy had already co-written a song called *You and I*. Couldn't they have named this something else? *It was You and I*, maybe? Or

they could have asked Mike to name it for them, but then again, he'd probably come up with *Tangerine Buffalo* or something.

Anyway, this is a pleasant little song. I really like the bass — it very much pushes the song along well. Kudos to Peter again.

I like Micky's vocals better in general, but The Monkees version is less sappy sounding than the Dolenz, Jones, Boyce & Hart version. Ironic, no? You'd expect the Davy version to be the sappy one. This version definitely improves on the original.

JUSTUS
Original release date: October 15, 1996

Circle Sky
Never Enough
Oh, What a Night
You and I
Unlucky Stars
Admiral Mike

Dyin' of a Broken Heart
Regional Girl
Run Away From Life
I Believe You
It's My Life
It's Not Too Late

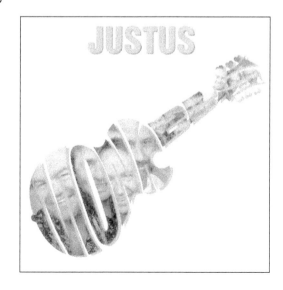

Mark: This highly-anticipated album (at least by me) turned out to be highly-aggravating and a major letdown. While many regard **CHANGES** or **POOL IT!** as The Monkees worst album, I would have to give the nod to this, only because of so many missed opportunities.

The reason why **CHANGES** and **POOL IT!** are regarded so badly are due to weak material and the complete absence of Michael Nesmith, but the remaining Monkees make do with what they have.

Here we *have* Michael Nesmith, and the material is *still* weak! Part of it is Mike's fault, for not composing more material or singing more material. This leaves us with a **POOL IT!**-like album with a **HEAD**-era track tacked on.

It's **POOL IT!** with grunge guitars instead of synthesizers.

It's also the only album of original material by The Monkees to not chart in the Billboard Top 200. **CHANGES** didn't either, originally, but did upon the album's reissue in 1986, it did a respectable #152 considering that the album didn't receive any airplay or promotion and was 16 years old.

There were no bonus tracks, but the *Justus* VHS (1997), was included on DVD with the 2013 **JUSTUS** reissue.

Michael: Overall, it's not a bad album, really – better than **POOL IT!** in my opinion, but still ultimately disappointing. If they had not been so determined to write all the songs and play all the instruments and produce it, it would have been even better. If they had brought back Chip Douglas and a few outside musicians from time to time, it could have been really great, even with these songs.

GIRL (Charles Fox/Norman Gimbel)
Monkee involvement: Vocals by Davy Jones
Recording dates: March 2001
Original release date: 2001 from **2001: LIVE FROM LAS VEGAS!**
Significant other versions: Davy Jones

Mark: After so many reunion tours, it was bound to happen that The Monkees would tire of performing the same 20 hits, so by 2001, they incorporated more solo material and deeper album cuts in order to change it up a bit. **2001: LIVE FROM LAS VEGAS!** (sold only at concerts) features much of this solo material designed to perform something different or to give the other Monkees a much needed break while one is performing. Doing a two-plus hour show is not as easy when you are in your fifties, sixties and seventies as it was when you are in your twenties.

This, and the next few entries will cover these "new" tracks. The first one is *Girl*, the infamous Davy Jones track that Davy performed on the "Getting Davy Jones" episode of *The Brady Bunch* back in 1971 and then again in 1995 in *The Brady Bunch Movie*. It's a great, catchy song, and would have been a welcome addition to The Monkees catalog had they still been recording together in 1971. It might have even been a hit for them.

Another live version of this song also appears on the **MONKEEMANIA 2002 LIVE IN TORONTO** CD, also available for sale only at concerts.

Michael: I never heard these live tracks before now, coming from such an obscure CD, but these are very well recorded which is unusual for live records from anyone. The album features Micky, Davy and Peter and a nice horn section that works very well.

It's cool to hear new versions of some of the old songs, though — Davy does a harmony on *Randy Scouse Git* that wasn't in the original, and Micky's scat singing sounds a lot like he's trying to capture the spirit of Louis Armstrong. The horns on *I'm a Believer* are a nice addition. An acoustic version of *Papa Gene's Blues* is also welcome! And a more stripped-down *Porpoise Song* works very well, actually, and then instead of jumping to the long fadeout, they jump into *Listen to the Band*.

However, I don't like the addition of these non-Monkees songs. In any event, I've never been a fan of *Girl*. It's only known because of that *Brady Bunch* episode. I wish he had sung *Rainy Jane* on the show instead, which is a much better song. Still, compared to doing covers of old songs or Broadway tunes, at least this is a song associated with one of The Monkees!

IS YOU IS OR IS YOU AIN'T MY BABY? (Louis Jordan/Billy Austin)
Monkee involvement: Vocals by Davy Jones
Recording dates: March 2001
Original release date: 2001 from **2001: LIVE FROM LAS VEGAS!**
Significant other versions: Louis Jordan, Diana Krall, Andrews Sisters

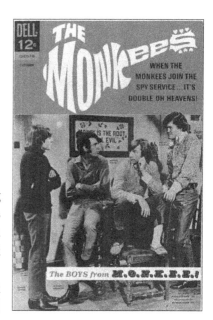

Mark: Davy does a spirited version of this song most famously performed by Louis Jordan and fills it with a little comedic patter throughout. Possibly, more than any other, this song is the most furthest removed from The Monkees' typical repertoire.

Michael: A very fast version of this old classic, but you know, once more, not sure why people would want to hear this at a Monkees concert.

LUCILLE (Albert Collins/Richard Penniman)
Monkee involvement: Vocals by Peter Tork
Recording dates: March 2001
Original release date: 2001 from **2001: LIVE FROM LAS VEGAS!**
Significant other versions: Little Richard

Mark: Peter Tork takes his turn doing the Little Richard classic. While Peter's intentions are admirable, it would have been better suited for Micky to take on vocally.

Michael: Peter starts off by mentioning 33 1/3 and saying "This is the kind of music that changed my life." He then says "It goes a little bit like this... Actually, it goes exactly like this, except for the mistakes." A fun little rock and roll song that Peter performs well, and while Micky would have done this better, I can see why Peter chose this for his solo section of the concert. It's better than the banjo stuff he used to do in his section.

OLIVER MEDLEY (CONSIDER YOURSELF, I'D DO ANYTHING, WHO WILL BUY?) (Lionel Bart)
Monkee involvement: Vocals by Davy Jones
Recording dates: March 2001
Original release date: 2001 from **2001: LIVE FROM LAS VEGAS!**

Mark: Davy's biggest success prior to The Monkees was playing the Artful Dodger in stage versions of *Oliver!* As mentioned before, he even performed on *The Ed Sullivan Show* on the same night that The Beatles made their US stage debut, performing some of these same songs.

These are great songs and Davy still performs them with gusto after all of these years as this is and was his first love – the stage.

Another live version of this medley also appears on the **MONKEEMANIA 2002 LIVE IN TORONTO** CD, also available for sale only at concerts.

Michael: Another example why Davy never really fit in with The Monkees music. He does a great job with these songs but you know, so what? If I wanted to hear this kind of music, I'd get a soundtrack album, not a Monkees album. They're not even trying to do anything different with it.

Notice that I dodged any reference to Davy's Broadway fame as a major character in *Oliver!*. I was pretty artful at it, too. Guess you can call me... Michael, the dodgy guy who is artful at it.

TOMMY JAMES (*Crimson and Clover, Mony Mony, Hanky Panky, I Think We're Alone Now***)**

I worked with them in Atlanta at the baseball stadium. We opened for them, and it was great. Not only did they play, but the screaming! I've never heard screaming like this in my life. I mean, we got our share of screams but when The Monkees hit the stage — it made you sick at your stomach. I don't mean because you were getting screamed at, I mean that the sound went right through you. Like a real loud horn or something that rattles you from the inside. It was like an explosion.

I'll never get over playing with them at the peak of their career. What a thrill it was. That screaming just blew me away!

We became friends. And then later on, when they got back together in '87, they did one of my songs. They did *Don't Bring Me Down* on the **POOL IT!** album. I've worked several times over the years with Micky and Davy. I performed at Davy's memorial at BB King's.

I saw Peter's group — he's a good guitar player! He has a blues group and he played locally here in North Jersey and I went to see him. He was really good. We weren't bosom buddies or anything, but we'd get together every now and then.

We met in the airport after they had done the **POOL IT!** album and after they had done my song and they really redid it in a very different way. It was very creative. So Peter came up to me and thanked me for the song.

When we were having hits at the same time as The Monkees, 66 and 67, we were both having very poppy hits. They sure had a hell of a team! I liked their singles a lot, but I can't really say I knew any of their albums until the one where they started doing their own stuff. I understand their frustration of not being able to play and do their own thing and being kept in their place.

I always felt kind of sorry for them after things went negative. They were put together but they had the will to better themselves as musicians and so forth, and it's almost like the business wouldn't let them.

SINCE I FELL FOR YOU (Buddy Johnson)
Monkee involvement: Vocals by Micky Dolenz
Recording dates: March 2001
Original release date: 2001 from **2001: LIVE FROM LAS VEGAS!**
Significant other versions: Dinah Washington, Barbra Streisand, Lenny Welch, Bonnie Raitt

Mark: Micky does a brief snippet of *Some Enchanted Evening* in operatic voice — a song his father, George, had performed — before singing this heartfelt ballad from his youth.

Another live version of this song also appears on the **MONKEEMANIA 2002 LIVE IN TORONTO** CD, also available for sale only at concerts.

Michael: A great song that Micky does a fine version of. Once more, I'm not sure this belongs on a Monkees album. I mean, come on, there are some good slow Monkees songs he could have sung instead.

(YOUR LOVE KEEPS LIFTING ME) HIGHER AND HIGHER (Gary Jackson/Carl Smith)
Monkee involvement: Vocals by Peter Tork. Backing vocals by Micky Dolenz and Davy Jones. Banjo by Peter Tork. Maracas by Davy Jones.
Recording dates: March 2001
Original release date: 2001 from **2001: LIVE FROM LAS VEGAS!**
Significant other versions: Jackie Wilson, Peter Tork, Rita Coolidge, Bruce Springsteen, The Dells

Mark: Peter performed this song for decades as a solo artist before including it in The Monkees act. Unlike *Lucille*, Peter's voice is much better suited for a song like this. He accompanies himself on the banjo.

On this live version, Peter gives a brief, comedic history of the banjo before going into the song.

Michael: Ah, there's the banjo. Now, mind you, Peter is very talented on this instrument but maybe they should have done *You Told Me* instead. With that said, this is a very different and unusual arrangement of this old Jackie Wilson song, and that's what I like. I'm never impressed with a band doing a cover of a great song where all they do is replace the vocals with their own. However, when they take a song and make it their own, with a new feeling completely, then you have my interest. Peter does that here, and it's the best cover on this album.

WHATEVER'S RIGHT (Tommy Boyce/Bobby Hart)
Monkee involvement: Vocals by Micky Dolenz and Michael Nesmith. Keyboards by Peter Tork.
Recording dates: July 26, 1966; February-March 2016
Original release date: May 27, 2016 from **GOOD TIMES!**

Michael: And now we jump ahead another fifteen years to the very successful **GOOD TIMES!** Sessions.

Whatever's Right has that old feel that The Monkees were trying to recapture for this album, and duh, that's because it *is* an old song from those days. Catchy and over in less than two minutes, like a good 60s pop song should do. (And of course, they had to include at least one Boyce/Hart song.)

Here's the ironic part of all of this: When music changed from the early days of The Monkees to 1968 or so, a song like this would seem so dated had it appeared on **THE BIRDS BEES AND THE MONKEES** and I would have complained about it in the same way I did about *Valleri* and *Tear Drop City*. But here, fifty years later, that doesn't matter. Recapturing that basic era was the goal, and it was accomplished.

Mark: Like *Wasn't Born to Follow*, *Good Times* and *Gotta Give it Time*, The Monkees and Adam Schlesinger wisely scoured The Monkees' vaults to find any good Monkees recordings that didn't have their vocals added to them. The result made songs like this fifty-year-old gem sound brand new, but also authentic. A promising start for the **GOOD TIMES!** sessions.

GOTTA GIVE IT TIME (Jeff Barry/Joey Levine)
Monkee involvement: Vocals by Micky Dolenz
Recording dates: January 21, 1967; February 2016
Original release date: May 27, 2016 from **GOOD TIMES!**

Mark: This great Monkees song was sitting in the vaults without a vocal since virtually the beginning of Monkeedom. Micky finally gives it a vocal almost 50 years later, but you wouldn't know it, since Micky sounds so youthful singing this. Although it doesn't say, I could swear Nesmith is singing backing vocals.

Michael: This is a pretty boring song, in my opinion. Oh, look — it's Jeff Barry, who pours out songs in a minute without a thought for lyrics or originality. Still, it fits the concept of the album, since it's an old recording brought back to life. The fact that they included this on the basic album while leaving off much better songs like *Love's What I Want* is a mystery to me. I guess they wanted to emphasize the old songs from the vaults.

GOOD TIMES (Harry Nilsson)
Monkee involvement: Vocals by Micky Dolenz. Electric guitar by Michael Nesmith.
Recording dates: January 10, 1968; February 2016
Original release date: May 27, 2016 from **GOOD TIMES!**

Michael: Not one of Nilsson's greatest songs, but it is so damn cool to hear him doing a duet with his old friend Micky! In some ways, it's kind of weird to hear them trading verses since Nilsson was never a Monkee, but hey, who's complaining?

Before the instrumental solo, you can hear Harry say "Instrumental!" It reminded me of Nilsson's own *Good for God*, which was on his **DUIT FOR MON DEI** album. Micky appears in pictures on that album's inner sleeve and I think he may have even sang backup on *Good for God* along with Ringo Starr, but I can't seem to confirm this. Anyway, when I first got that album, I was reading the lyrics while the song played and between a couple of choruses, the lyric sheet said "Instrumental." However, when it got to that part, Harry just said "instrumental" and then went right into the next chorus without even the hint of an instrumental break. It cracked me up, and now I'm wondering if Micky left that comment in on *Good Times* because of that... Probably not, but it's fun to speculate.

Mark: Dolenz sings a posthumous duet with the late, great Harry Nilsson, who passed away in 1994 and the results are outstanding. Isn't technology great? It really sounds that Micky and Harry are singing together on the same mic. No one would ever know that the vocals were recorded 48 years apart if it didn't say so in the liner notes.

WASN'T BORN TO FOLLOW (Gerry Goffin/Carole King)
Monkee involvement: Vocals by Peter Tork
Recording dates: March 9, 1968; February 2016
Original release date: May 27, 2016 from **GOOD TIMES!**
Significant other versions: The Byrds

Mark: Peter's turn. Peter adds vocals to this 1968 outtake by Goffin and King. It's slightly weaker than the other songs on the album. Slightly. There's so much wealth on this album, it's crazy.

The 1968 backing track appears on **THE BIRDS, THE BEES AND THE MONKEES DELUXE EDITION** (2010) and was called *I Wasn't Born to Follow*.

Michael: This is the weakest song on the album. Usually, I gush over Carole King songs, but there's a reason they never finished this. It's just kind of there, rambles on a bit, and then fades out.

And, to make matters worse, the Byrds eventually did their own version, so this is now a cover. To make matters even worse again, the Byrds' version was used in the film *Easy Rider* so it's pretty well known. To make matters worse a third time, *Easy Rider* was produced by Bert Schneider and Bob Rafelson, who got their start producing a weird TV show known as *The Monkees*. The Byrds' version is more country-influenced and has wonderful harmonies.

There's a banjo in The Monkees' mix there somewhere. I assume that's Peter playing it, but that doesn't seem to be mentioned in any of the materials.

I KNOW WHAT I KNOW (Michael Nesmith)
Monkee involvement: Vocals by Michael Nesmith
Recording dates: February 2016
Original release date: May 27, 2016 from **GOOD TIMES!**

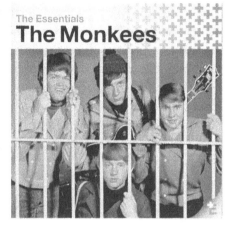

Michael: Here's where I once more ponder what happened to Michael Nesmith. He used to write so many songs, many of which became classics. For **GOOD TIMES!**, all he brings to us is just this one, which hardly sounds like anything we'd expect from him. I mean, if they were really trying to recapture the feel of the old Monkees albums, they should have done at least one country-flavored song.

I read that Mike was surprised that Adam Schlesinger (the producer of the album and the leader of the band Fountains of Wayne — go out and buy all their albums now! You won't regret it!) picked this song to go on the record, so maybe we can't blame Mike completely for its inclusion. It's a nice song, but perhaps we're being harsh because we know Mike is capable of so much more.

Mark: I tend to agree with Michael above. Nesmith sounds like he has run out of ideas. The lyric "what I have is nothing" is telling, indeed. Probably the weakest spot in an abundant album. Fortunately, Nesmith put his energies into singing the other songs that are very well-suited for him.

Fan Thoughts

Another instant classic from Papa Nez. I'll admit that I don't like the solo piano banging the same chord over and over through the majority of this song, but the lyrics more than make up for it. When I got married in 1993, I used some of the lyrics to Nez's solo song Harmony Constant *in my vows. I believe I will be using some of the lyrics of this song for my 25th anniversary.* — Randall Buie

---

LITTLE GIRL (Peter Tork)
Monkee involvement: Vocals by Peter Tork. Acoustic guitar by Peter Tork.
Recording dates: February 2016
Original release date: May 27, 2016 from **GOOD TIMES!**

Mark: This song is totally unrelated to the same-titled song from **PRESENT**. Peter is in great vocal form and this is a great song especially to his dismal contributions for the **JUSTUS** album. Everyone was really on board with this album and is in great form.

Michael: "Little girl" is a phrase heard often in old songs but it sounds rather creepy these days, especially when sung by a man in his 70s — unless it's actually sung to a little girl.

Anyway, this one is another of Peter's 3/4 jazz pieces. I worry that Peter is more interested in showing off his talent than writing a pop song. And he'd probably say, "I don't care, Michael so-called Ventrella, this is the kind of music I like and who are you to tell me what I can play?" And while I can always respect artists of all sorts who make the art they want regardless of what the public wants, they have to understand that's the risk they take: that people like me won't like it.

It's a pleasant enough song but it sure doesn't fit the feel of the rest of the album, which is trying to capture the kind of sound from the 60s.

OUR OWN WORLD (Adam Schlesinger)
Monkee involvement: Vocals by Micky Dolenz. Backing vocals by Michael Nesmith and Peter Tork. Keyboards by Peter Tork.
Recording dates: February 2016
Original release date: May 27, 2016 from **GOOD TIMES!**

Michael: Now this is more like it. We're starting to get into the songs others have written specifically for The Monkees. And you know, if you looked at a list of my favorite bands, they'd include Fountains of Wayne, Weezer, Oasis, and XTC — so you can see why I was so happy when the list of songwriters for this album was released.

Adam Schlesinger is the leader of Fountains of Wayne, and they have plenty of great songs other than *Stacy's Mom* and if you don't know that, go find out now! He's also written songs for the Stephen Colbert Christmas special, and he wrote music for the films *Cry Baby* and *That Thing You Do!* (among many other achievements). He was the perfect choice to produce this album, and this song feels like it was written just for The Monkees, and it was!

This is the kind of catchy song that would have easily been a hit single in 1967, but then again this album is full of those kinds of songs. The bridge and the lead are very Beatle-ish, and then there's another chorus and and then it ends, no third verse, which was something missing from **POOL IT!** and **JUSTUS**. It was one of the things I admired from the early albums but it's a trend few songs today meet — they feel like they have to do more and make the song longer when sometimes short and sweet is best.

Mark: **GOOD TIMES!** producer Adam Schlesinger contributes this great song that is similar in vein to the other preview songs. Schelinger "gets" The Monkees and this resulting song and album prove this. Backing vocals by Mike and Peter are strongly reminiscent of Brian Wilson.

SHE MAKES ME LAUGH (Rivers Cuomo)
Monkee involvement: Vocals by Micky Dolenz. Backing vocals by Peter Tork and Michael Nesmith. Banjo by Peter Tork. Guitar by Michael Nesmith.
Recording dates: February 2016
Original release date: May 27, 2016 from **GOOD TIMES!**

Mark: The first teaser song and video released to promote the upcoming **GOOD TIMES!** album, this was released on April 28, 2016. They really hit the nail on the head with this one. It perfectly captures the essence of what makes a great Monkees song and it wasn't just relegated to this one release. The entire album features gems such as this.

The video cleverly uses panels from the old Monkees Dell comic book.

Michael: Rivers Cuomo leads Weezer and they have some wonderful pop songs that I always wanted to redo without all the distorted guitar. The problem with Weezer is that production-wise, almost every song sounds alike, but underneath there are some really great melodies and words. Their latest album as of this writing (the white one) moves away from that constant fuzzy guitar sound and I wonder if working on **GOOD TIMES!** had an influence on Rivers.

Anyway, Rivers was always a Monkees fan, apparently — Weezer even did a cover of *I'm a Believer* that was used on *The Simpsons* TV show.

This is a very clever and catchy song and Peter even gets to play banjo! Definitely one of the best songs on the album. I would have loved to hear more from Rivers.

TERRIFYING (Zach Rogue)
Monkee involvement: Vocals by Micky Dolenz. Guitar by Michael Nesmith. Keyboards by Peter Tork.
Recording dates: February 2016
Original release date: May 27, 2016 from **GOOD TIMES!** digital download and the **GOOD TIMES! PLUS!** 10" (2016).

Michael: One of the better songs on the album, but it didn't make the main release. This one is written by someone named Zach Rogue who apparently has a band called Rogue Wave that I had never heard of before. I checked them out, and they're not bad. Nowhere near as fun as The Monkees, though; lots of mid-tempo songs, well played and well written but not real exciting.

Terrifying is similar. A good tune, but not a high energy song. I kept wanting it to kick in and build, and it never does. With a production by Adam Schlesinger, it has that good 60s feel that brings it from the background, and I still like this more than the old songs they dug up from the 60s.

The part that goes "So much information / when no words are spoken" reminds me so much of Barenaked Ladies' *Bull in a China Shop* that I half expect the Ladies to come singing next. Barenaked Ladies — now *that* would have been a great band to ask to write a Monkees song! (Or *me* — you can always ask me to write one!) Get on it for the follow-up, guys.

Mark: It must have been hell deciding what to keep and what to discard from this album, but this one apparently didn't make the final cut, possibly only due to one too many Micky lead vocals. There's certainly nothing wrong with this tune.

BIRTH OF AN ACCIDENTAL HIPSTER (Noel Gallagher/Paul Weller)
Monkee involvement: Vocals by Michael Nesmith, Micky Dolenz.
Recording dates: February 2016-March 2016
Original release date: May 27, 2016 from **GOOD TIMES!**

Mark: This has a jangly Oasis-like sound to it and no wonder, considering its composers. This, like *Me and Magdalena* again sounds like something that Nesmith could have composed, but didn't. It also has an early Pink Floyd sound to it.

Michael: This one's written by Noel Gallagher from Oasis and Paul Weller from the Jam. How cool is that? It's one of those songs with lots of different parts like *Shorty Blackwell* or the kind of songs The Beatles liked to do. When it works, it's great. I love the way Mike and Micky both sing and how their vocals overlap especially when it merges from Mike's part to Micky's "Do you know where we go" — but when it cuts to the Micky-led piano part, it just doesn't work as well. Sounds too much like a second song plugged into the first where it doesn't really belong. Kind of jarring — it doesn't flow smoothly.

But you know, I'm not really complaining. I'm just all smiles while this entire album plays. This is a wonderful song, and while it may not be a masterpiece, it is absolutely one of my favorites.

And so well-produced. Wonderful sound — jangly guitars, perfect echo on Mike's voice, tinkly piano. And congrats to Adam for not allowing this to turn into a typical Oasis song lasting nine minutes and ending with nothing but feedback.

ME AND MAGDALENA (Benjamin Gibbard)
Monkee involvement: Vocals by Michael Nesmith and Micky Dolenz. Guitar by Michael Nesmith.
Recording dates: February 2016-March 2016
Original release date: May 27, 2016 from **GOOD TIMES!**

Michael: Benjamin Gibbard is the leader of the band Death Cab for Cutie, which is named after a song by the Bonzo Dog Band, who performed the song in the film *Magical Mystery Tour* with The Beatles, who were the inspiration for The Monkees. (How's that for degrees of separation?) Death Cab for Cutie is another band that was a good choice for writing for The Monkees. I enjoy some of their stuff although I'm not a huge fan (like I am of XTC and Fountains of Wayne and Oasis, for instance).

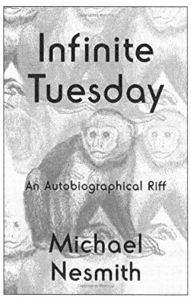

Like *Terrifying*, it's laid back and never quite grabs you like it should, although Mike and Micky's voices blend perfectly. Ironically, there's a second version that's done with an electric guitar opening and a drony bass and heavy drums that add that excitement I was looking for. If you only have one version, get this second one. Why they ignored it for the album is beyond me, because it's much better.

Mark: The third and final song released to preview the excellent **GOOD TIMES!** album. This debuted on May 20, 2016, just days before the album was officially released. Nesmith is in great vocal form here, with Micky singing great harmonies. It sounds like a song he could have written, but didn't.

The alternate version a.k.a. *Version Two* first appeared on record on the **GOOD TIMES! PLUS!** 10" from November 2016. This version is more upbeat and full than the standard album version. I agree with Michael on this one. This, rather than the sparser version, should have been on the album.

YOU BRING THE SUMMER (Andy Partridge)
Monkee involvement: Vocals by Micky Dolenz. Backing vocals by Michael Nesmith and Peter Tork. Guitar by Michael Nesmith. Organ by Peter Tork.
Recording dates: February 2016-March 2016
Original release date: May 27, 2016 from **GOOD TIMES!**

Michael: I am such a big XTC fan. What an underrated band that deserves more attention! When I heard that Andy Partridge was writing songs for The Monkees, I practically screamed. I almost wish he had written the entire album for them.

This song is wonderful, and I'm happy The Monkees used it as one of their signature tunes from the album, making a major video for it and everything. Now, mind you, it sounds exactly like an XTC song and I could hear Andy singing it easily, but then again, maybe XTC just sounds a lot like The Monkees at times.

Andy Partridge had written about his love for The Monkees before. Back in the 80s, I was a member of the XTC fan

club and they'd put out a booklet every few months (this was pre-internet, obviously) called "The Little Express." In one issue, Andy shared a drawing he had done of Micky Dolenz from when he was younger and damn it was good. He's a good artist, too.

Back to the song: It really feels like an XTC song that would have fit on their 60s-style albums as their alter egos The Dukes of Stratosphear. Remove Micky's voice and replace it with Andy and you'd never tell. And then at the end to hold that note and build the end vocals and the backwards guitar — just perfect. Beach Boys meet psychedelica.

Also, note in the video where The Monkees pose for all the album covers and right after **THE BIRDS THE BEES AND THE MONKEES** pose comes the line "the birds and the bees will fly around me." Clever!

Mark: The second song released with a video on May 2, 2016, to promote the upcoming **GOOD TIMES!** album, which was every bit as good as *She Makes Me Laugh*. These two songs set the stage for an excellent and welcome comeback album which every Monkees fan was anticipating since at least 1970.

The video has cartoon versions of The Monkees that look very similar to the Rock Band versions of The Beatles.

A BETTER WORLD (Nick Thorkelson)
Monkee involvement: Vocals by Peter Tork; Backing vocals by Micky Dolenz; Guitar and percussion by Peter Tork.
Recording dates: March 7, 2016; March 29, 2016
Highest chart position: uncharted single B-side
Original release date: May 27, 2016 from 7" single and **GOOD TIMES!** FYE Edition bonus track and **GOOD TIMES! PLUS!** 10".

Mark: Peter's brother Nick contributes this fine song that also didn't make the final cut of the main album. I suppose it's because that a typical Monkees album doesn't have many Peter vocals and this one is the weakest of the three he contributed vocally to the project. It's still a good song and performance, however!

Michael: This certainly feels like a 60s hippie anthem, a sort of sequel to *For Pete's Sake*. But there's not that much there, really. I feel guilty saying I'm not that impressed, because had this appeared on **POOL IT!** or **JUSTUS**, I'd be saying some nicer things about it. But with the great songs on **GOOD TIMES!** it's kind of weak in comparison.

LOVE'S WHAT I WANT (Andy Partridge)
Monkee involvement: Vocals by Micky Dolenz
Recording dates: March 25, 2016; March 29, 2016
Highest chart position: uncharted single A-side
Original release date: May 27, 2016 from 7" single and **GOOD TIMES!** Japanese edition and **GOOD TIMES! PLUS!** 10".

Michael: I'm so glad Andy had two songs during these sessions and, as I said previously, I'd be happy to have him write the entire album.

I like this one better than *You Bring the Summer* but I can see how *Summer* is more of a "hit" song. This one is is much more XTCish. Andy is fond of picking a note that is completely unexpected and jarring the first time you hear it which then sounds absolutely perfect every following listen. Here, it's in the chorus (that opens the song): "It's all we have to give" — Note how *give* is the note that then pulls up to its correct spot after a beat or two. The verses themselves remind me of XTC's *Omnibus* which, if you don't have, you should. If you like great pop music, you should have all of XTC's albums. Go buy them now. This book will still be here when you get back, and you'll thank me.

And then, when you think this song is over, Andy does another Beach Boys thing where there are harmonies over a pounding drumbeat to build the song as it heads to the fade, and to add to the fun, Micky starts singing "Why don't you be like me? Why don't you stop and see?" and we're having a great *Randy Scouse Git* nostalgia. Ah, when I first heard that, after smiling so hugely over such a great song, I was in heaven. When I played it for my wife, she laughed and clapped. Just perfect.

Mark: I suppose if you had to choose between this and *You Bring the Summer* (also written by Andy Partridge), I would give *You Bring the Summer* the nod to be on the album, but oh, is this a good song. In the final assessment, I would have preferred a 17-song album and hang the bonus tracks.

I WAS THERE (AND I'M TOLD I HAD A GOOD TIME) (Micky Dolenz/Adam Schlesinger)
Monkee involvement: Vocals by Micky Dolenz. Drums by Micky Dolenz.
Recording dates: February 2016; April 2016
Original release date: May 27, 2016 from **GOOD TIMES!**

Mark: The final song on a great album. Micky's oft-repeated quote prior to performing *Randy Scouse Git* in concert finally gets a song of its own. It's a great way to end the album and to sum up The Monkees experience if this is indeed the final Monkees go round. It ends with Micky doing his best Harry Nilsson imitation and saying, "I dropped my stick."

Michael: Musically, there's not much to this song. It kind of feels like *Why Don't We Do It In The Road?* but with a few more lyrics. As Mark says, it's a great way to end the album. After all, we start with *Good Times* and we end with Micky singing "We are here and we're going to have a good time" bringing the whole thing to a full circle. He then sings "like we did before — supposedly." And if you didn't laugh the first time you heard that last line, you need to check your funny bone!

GOOD TIMES!
Original release date: May 27, 2016
Highest chart position: #14
Weeks on chart: 3

Good Times
You Bring the Summer
She Makes Me Laugh
Our Own World
Gotta Give it Time
Me & Magdalena

Whatever's Right
Love to Love
Little Girl
Birth of an Accidental Hipster
Wasn't Born to Follow
I Know What I Know
I Was There (and I'm Told I Had a Good Time)

Mark: If this is truly the final new album contribution by the collective entity known as The Monkees, it is a fine, fine way to do it and go out with a bang and not a whimper. It is leaps and bounds above the previous two reunion albums, **POOL IT!** and **JUSTUS**, and even better than the latter-day original Monkees albums **CHANGES** and **INSTANT REPLAY**.

Micky, Peter, Mike and all of those involved really put their best foot forward to make the best album they could. I only wish there was a 17-track version of this that incorporated all of the leftover tracks that were released as singles, bonus tracks and downloads. Perhaps this is coming, but at least all 17 known tracks are released. I am unsure of any outtakes.

There are weak spots on the album to be sure, but overall the album is excellent. The biggest misstep in my honest opinion is the inclusion of *Love to Love*, which was probably included just so that they could say that Neil Diamond contributed to the album. While it is nice that the other three gave Davy representation, the track was already readily available on the **MISSING LINKS** collections among other places and as such, is a major letdown. A better choice would have been a more obscure unreleased track or even a more obscure *released* track. Perhaps, The Monkees' version of *Manchester Boy*, the unreleased outtake from **JUSTUS**. Or, the other Monkees could have done a Beatles *Free As a Bird*-type deal and recorded vocals over an obscure Davy Jones solo recording. A Monkees studio version of *Girl*, anyone?

All this is nitpicking as they could have done far worse than *Love to Love*, or even ignored Davy completely, and not included anything by him.

If you are reading this and haven't picked up this fine, final album, do so immediately.

Michael: It appears that the original idea for this was to take old Monkees songs that had never been finished and then finish them, so we get *Whatever's Right*, *Love to Love*, *Wasn't Born to Follow*, and *Good Times*. But here's the thing: The new songs are much much better and in many ways, sound more like Monkees songs than the old rejected ones.

Grabbing the best songwriters of the day and asking them to contribute to The Monkees was a stroke of genius, because that's exactly the reason the early Monkees albums were so good. You could take certain XTC songs or Fountains of Wayne songs and have Micky sing them, and they would fit perfectly on a Monkees album, so it's no wonder this works so well.

It's interesting to see how different the *Billboard* charts are these days. Back in the 60s, they relied mostly on things like radio play and reports from a few random record stores to estimate where on the chart an album should be placed. These days, with most sales coming from downloading, they can get instant numbers. Radio play is kind of meaningless, and so what we get is a huge number of people buying the album in its first week and having it debut at #14, but within a few weeks, it's off the charts completely. Still, I think it's safe to say that this album sold better than **JUSTUS** or **POOL IT!**

Here's hoping they decide to make a follow-up and get many of these same writers to contribute, ignoring the old songs from the 60s. And then we can do an updated version of this book!

The Monkees TOUR DATES
by Mark Arnold

The following lists all known musical performances or personal appearances by at least two of The Monkees. The list is considered complete except for dates from 1970 and from 1977. Special thanks to *Monkee Business Fanzine*, Andrew Sandoval and MonkeesLiveAlmanac.com for help in compiling this list.

1966 PROMOTIONAL TOUR:
September 1: Screen Gems, Hollywood, California
September 6: Chicago, Illinois
September 7: Boston, Massachusetts
September 8: New York, New York
September 9: Broadway Theatre, New York, New York
September 11: Del Mar & Los Angeles, California

THE 1966-1967 TOUR:
December 3: Honolulu International Centre Arena, Honolulu, Hawaii
December 26: Auditorium Arena, Denver, Colorado
December 27: Mid-South Coliseum, Memphis, Tennessee
December 28: Freedom Hall, Louisville, Kentucky
December 29: Memorial Coliseum, Winston-Salem, North Carolina
December 30: Civic Arena, Pittsburgh, Pennsylvania
December 31: Cincinnati Gardens, Cincinnati, Ohio
January 1, 1967: Municipal Auditorium, Nashville, Tennessee
January 2: Civic Center Arena, Tulsa, Oklahoma
January 14: Olympia Stadium, Detroit, Michigan
January 15: Public Hall, Cleveland, Ohio
January 21: Memorial Coliseum, Phoenix, Arizona
January 22: Cow Palace, San Francisco, California

April 1: The Arena, Winnipeg, Manitoba, Canada
April 2: Maple Leaf Gardens, Toronto, Ontario, Canada
May 6: W.S.U. Field House, Wichita, Kansas

1967 US & BRITISH TOUR: (* = with The Jimi Hendrix Experience as opening act)
June 9: Hollywood Bowl, Los Angeles, California
June 30: Empire Pool, Wembley, London, England
July 1: Empire Pool, Wembley, London, England (2 shows)
July 2: Empire Pool, Wembley, London, England (2 shows)
July 8: The Coliseum, Jacksonville, Florida *
July 9: Convention Hall, Miami Beach, Florida*
July 11: The Coliseum, Charlotte, North Carolina *

July 12: Coliseum, Greensboro, North Carolina *

July 14: Forest Hills Stadium, New York, New York *

July 15: Forest Hills Stadium, New York, New York *

July 16: Forest Hills Stadium, New York, New York *

July 20: Memorial Auditorium, Buffalo, New York

July 21: Civic Center, Baltimore, Maryland

July 22: Boston Garden, Boston, Massachusetts

July 23: Convention Hall, Philadelphia, Pennsylvania

July 27: War Memorial, Rochester, New York

July 28: Cincinnati Gardens, Cincinnati, Ohio

July 30: Chicago Stadium, Chicago, Illinois

August 4: St. Paul Auditorium Arena, Minneapolis, Minnesota

August 5: Kiel Auditorium, St. Louis, Missouri

August 6: Veterans Memorial Auditorium, Des Moines, Iowa

August 9: Memorial Auditorium, Dallas, Texas

August 10: Sam Houston Coliseum, Houston, Texas

August 11: State Fair Coliseum, Shreveport, Louisiana

August 12: Municipal Auditorium, Mobile, Alabama

August 13: Olympia Stadium, Detroit, Michigan

August 17: Mid-South Coliseum, Memphis, Tennessee

August 18: Assembly Center Arena, Tulsa, Oklahoma

August 19: Coliseum, Oklahoma City, Oklahoma

August 20: Denver Coliseum, Denver, Colorado

August 25: Seattle Center Coliseum, Seattle, Washington

August 26: Memorial Coliseum, Portland, Oregon

August 27: The Coliseum, Spokane, Washington

1968 HEAD ORIGINAL MOTION PICTURE CONCERT:
May 17: Valley Music Hall, Salt Lake City, Utah

1968 AUSTRALIA & JAPAN TOUR:

September 18: Festival Hall, Melbourne, Australia (2 shows)

September 19: Festival Hall, Melbourne, Australia (2 shows)

September 21: Sydney Stadium, Sydney, Australia (2 shows)

September 23: Festival Hall, Brisbane, Australia (2 shows)

September 27: Centennial Hall, Adelaide, Australia (2 shows)

September 28: Sydney Stadium, Sydney, Australia (2 shows)

September 29: Sydney Stadium, Sydney, Australia (2 shows)

October 3: Budokan Hall, Tokyo, Japan (2 shows)

October 4: Budokan Hall, Tokyo, Japan

October 5: Kokusai Hall, Kyoto, Japan

October 7: Festival Hall, Osaka, Japan

October 8: Festival Hall, Osaka, Japan

1968 HEAD INVITATIONAL PREMIERE:
November 18: Vogue Theatre, Hollywood, California

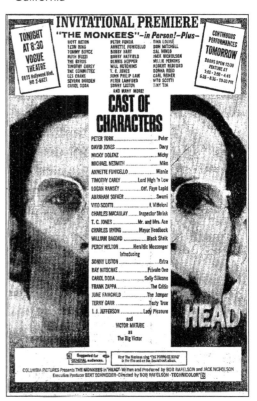

1969 NORTH AMERICAN TOUR (Dolenz, Jones and Nesmith)::

March 29: Pacific Coliseum, Vancouver, BC, Canada

March 30: Seattle Center Coliseum, Seattle, Washington

April 11: Municipal Auditorium, Birmingham, Alabama

April 12: Civic Center Arena, Charleston, West Virginia

April 13: Bell Auditorium, Augusta, Georgia

April 19: Honolulu International Center Arena, Honolulu, Hawaii

April 26: Auditorium Theatre, Chicago, Illinois

May 3: Jackson Coliseum, Jackson, Mississippi

May 4: Civic Auditorium, Houston, Texas

May 9: Civic Auditorium, Albuquerque, New Mexico

May 10: Century II Convention Center, Wichita, Kansas

June 11: Charlotte Coliseum, Charlotte, North Carolina

June 12: City Stadium, Richmond, Virginia

June 13: Dome, Virginia Beach, Virginia

June 20: The Coliseum, Eastern States Expo, West Springfield, Massachusetts

June 22: Milwaukee Pop Festival, Milwaukee, Wisconsin

July 18: Dane County Fair, Madison, Wisconsin

July 19: Majestic Bandstand, Majestic Hills, Wisconsin

July 24: The Forum, Mexico City, Mexico

July 25: The Forum, Mexico City, Mexico

July 26: The Forum, Mexico City, Mexico

July 27: Plaza Monumental, Jalisco, Mexico

July 27: The Forum, Mexico City, Mexico

July 28: The Forum, Mexico City, Mexico

July 29: The Forum, Mexico City, Mexico

August 1: Curtis Hixon Hall, Tampa, Florida

August 2: Mollenkopf Stadium, Warren, Ohio (2 shows)

August 25: Grandstand, Canadian National Exhibition, Toronto, ON, Canada (2 shows)

August 28: Colorado State Fair, Pueblo, Colorado (2 shows)

August 29: Colorado State Fair, Pueblo, Colorado (2 shows)

September 4: California State Fair, Sacramento, California

September 6: Duluth Auditorium, Duluth, Minnesota (2 shows)

October 17: Dorton Arena, North Carolina State Fair, Raleigh, North Carolina (2 shows)

October 18: Greenville Memorial Auditorium, Greenville, South Carolina (2 shows)

October 19: Civic Coliseum, Knoxville, Tennessee

November 3: Memorial Coliseum, Phoenix, Arizona (2 shows)

November 30: Oakland Coliseum, Oakland, California

December 6: Salt Palace, Salt Lake City, Utah

LIVE IN 1970 (Dolenz and Jones): (incomplete)

May 15-17: Roosevelt Mall, Philadelphia, Pennsylvania

June 13: Cleveland, Ohio

September 5-7: Steel Pier, Atlantic City, New Jersey (promoted as The Monkees, but probably Jones solo)

November 21: Valley REC Center, Van Nuys, California (with Peter Tork)

Date unknown: The Troubadour, Los Angeles, California (Dolenz and Tork)

1975-1976 THE GREAT GOLDEN HITS OF THE MONKEES (Dolenz, Jones, Boyce & Hart):

June 21: Six Flags Over Mid-America, Eureka, Missouri

June 22: Bel Rae Ballroom, New Brighton, Minnesota

June 24-25: Spectrum Club, Madison, Wisconsin

June 26: Gibbons Ballroom, Gibbons, Minnesota

June 27: Paradise Ballroom, Maconia, Minnesota

July 4: St. Louis, Missouri (incorrect date and city of June 21, 1975 concert)

July 27: Country Aire, Appleton, Wisconsin

August 17: Magic Mountain, Valencia, California

August 19: Houston Music Hall, Houston, Texas

August 21: Baton Rouge, Louisiana

August 29: Marshfield, Wisconsin

August 31: Idora Park, Youngstown, Ohio

September 12-13: Knott's Good Time Theatre, Buena Park, California

October 8: Mar Vista High, Imperial Beach, California

October 11: De Anza College, Cupertino, California

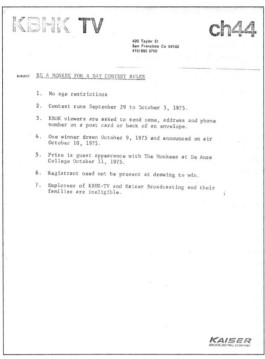

KBHK TV ch44

420 Taylor St
San Francisco Ca 94102
415/885 3750

SUBJECT: BE A MONKEE FOR A DAY CONTEST RULES

1. No age restrictions

2. Contest runs September 29 to October 3, 1975.

3. KBHK viewers are asked to send name, address and phone number on a post card or back of an envelope.

4. One winner drawn October 9, 1975 and announced on air October 10, 1975.

5. Prize is guest appearance with The Monkees at De Anza College October 11, 1975.

6. Registrant need not be present at drawing to win.

7. Employees of KBHK-TV and Kaiser Broadcasting and their families are ineligible.

KAISER BROADCASTING COMPANY

October 15: Santa Maria High, Santa Maria, California
October 16: Roosevelt High, Fresno, California
October 17: Barstow High, Barstow, California
October 18: San Luis Obispo High, San Luis Obispo, California
October 20: Chico High, Chico, California
October 21: Shasta High, Redding, California
October 22: Sheldon High, Eugene, Oregon
October 23: McNairy High, Salem, Oregon
October 24: Yakima Valley, Yakima Valley, Washington
October 28: Spokane Community College, Spokane, Washington
October 29: University of Idaho, Moscow, Idaho
October 31: Brigham Young College, Provo, Utah
November 4: Dixie College, St. George, Utah
November 5: Northern Arizona University, Flagstaff, Arizona
November 6: Yuma High School, Yuma, Arizona
November 8: University of California, Santa Barbara, California
November 22: Swing Auditorium, San Bernadino, California
December 15: Mt. Horeb, Wisconsin
December 20: Cable, Wisconsin
December 21: Chicago Theater, Chicago, Illinois
December 25: Bel Rae Ballroom, New Brighton, Minnesota
December 26: Northstar Ballroom, Carlton, Minnesota
December 28: Paradise Ballroom, Waconia, Minnesota
December 31: Chase Park Plaza Hotel, St. Louis, Missouri
January 2-3, 1976: Disneyland, Anaheim, California
April 12-17: Six Flags Over Texas, Arlington, Texas
April 20-25: Riverboat, New York, New York
April 16-May 2: The Golden Banana, Peabody, Massachusetts
May 30: Armadillo World Headquarters, Austin, Texas
June 1-5: Six Flags Great Adventure, Jackson, New Jersey
June 9: Tomorrow Theatre, Youngstown, Ohio
June 10: Agora Theatre, Cleveland, Ohio
June 11: Masonic Temple, Scranton, Pennsylvania
June 12: Calderone Theatre, Hempstead, New York
June 13: Pine Knob Music Theatre, Detroit, Michigan
June 26-27: Worlds of Fun Amusement Park, Kansas City, Missouri
July 4-9: Disneyland, Anaheim, California
July 19: Shimizu City Hall, Shizuoka, Japan
July 20: Yubin Chokin Hall, Tokyo, Japan
July 23: Koseinenkin Hall, Osaka, Japan
July 24: Suzuran Park, Nagoya, Japan
July 29: Singapore
July 30-31: Dusit Thani Hotel, Bangkok, Thailand
August 23-27: Six Flags Over Mid-America, Eureka, Missouri
Date unknown: The Col Ballroom, Davenport, Iowa

1977 THE GREAT GOLDEN HITS OF THE MONKEES DOLENZ & JONES SHOW: (incomplete)
March 7: Starwood Club, Hollywood, California (with Peter Tork)
Date unknown: Cape Cod, Massachusetts

1977 *TOM SAWYER* (Dolenz and Jones):
August 22-28: Sacramento Civic Theater, Sacramento, California

1977-1978 *THE POINT* (Dolenz and Jones):
December 22-February 23: Mermaid Theatre, London, England

1986 'SOUND OF THE MONKEES'
AUSTRALIAN TOUR (Jones and Tork):
February 25: Port Macquarie, New South Wales, Australia
February 26: Twin Towns Services Club, Tweed Heads, Australia
February 27: Twin Towns Services Club, Tweed Heads, Australia
February 28: Twin Towns Services Club, Tweed Heads, Australia
March 1: Twin Towns Services Club, Tweed Heads, Australia
March 2: Twin Towns Services Club, Tweed Heads, Australia
March 4: Newcastle Club, New South Wales, Australia
March 5: Hellenic Club, Canberra, Australia
March 6: Gosford Central Club, New South Wales, Australia
March 7: Manly Warringah Club, New South Wales, Australia
March 8: Rooty Hill Club, New South Wales, Australia
March 9: Ingleborn Club, New South Wales, Australia
March 14: St. George Leagues Club, Sydney, Australia
March 15: St. George Leagues Club, Sydney, Australia

March 17: The Venue, Melbourne, Australia
March 18: The Venue, Melbourne, Australia
March 19: The Venue, Melbourne, Australia

1986 20th ANNIVERSARY REUNION TOUR (Dolenz, Jones and Tork):
May 24: Concord Hotel, Kiamesha Lake, New York
May 30: Tropicana, Atlantic City, New Jersey
May 31: Tropicana, Atlantic City, New Jersey
June 1: Tropicana, Atlantic City, New Jersey
June 3: Warner Theatre, Erie, Pennsylvania
June 4: Stanley Theatre, Utica, New York
June 5: Samuel Clemens Theatre, Elmira, New York
June 6: Great Arena, Great Adventure, Jackson, New Jersey
June 7: State Theatre, Cleveland, Ohio
June 8: Woodlands, Wilkes-Barre, Pennsylvania
June 10: Newport Music Hall, Columbus, Ohio
June 11: Newport Music Hall, Columbus, Ohio
June 12: Santa Teresa Country Club, Santa Teresa, New Mexico
June 13: Fort Bliss Army Base, El Paso, Texas
June 14: Civic Auditorium, Omaha, Nebraska
June 15: Nebraska Land Days, North Platte, Nebraska
June 17: Cotillion Ballroom, Wichita, Kansas
June 18: Sandstone, Kansas City, Missouri
June 19: Riverfront Amphitheatre, Hannibal, Missouri
June 20: Steamboat Days, Burlington, Iowa
June 21: Civic Center, Des Moines, Iowa
June 22: Arlington Stadium, Arlington, Texas
June 24: Bayfront Arena, Corpus Christi, Texas
June 25: Sunken Gardens, San Antonio, Texas
June 26: Frank Erwin Center, Austin, Texas
June 27: Southern Star Amphitheatre, Houston, Texas
June 28: Civic Center, Beaumont, Texas
June 29: Audubon Zoo, New Orleans, Louisiana
July 1: Mud Island Amphitheatre, Memphis, Tennessee
July 2: Starwood Amphitheatre, Nashville, Tennessee
July 3: Civic Center, Albany, Georgia
July 4: Robarts Arena, Sarasota, Florida
July 5: Ruth Eckerd Hall, Clearwater, Florida

July 6: Flagler Greyhound Track, Miami, Florida

July 8: Wolftrap Park, Vienna, Virginia

July 9: Civic Center, Pittsburgh, Pennsylvania

July 10: Blossom Music Festival, Cuyahoga Falls, Ohio

July 11: Chautauqua Institute, Chautauqua, New York

July 12: Ontario Place, Toronto, Ontario, Canada

July 13: Ottawa Congress Center, Ottawa, Ontario, Canada

July 14: Fingerlakes Center, Lake Canandaigua, New York

July 17: Jones Beach Theatre, Wantagh, New York

July 18: Warwick Musical Theatre, Warwick, Rhode Island

July 19: South Shore Music Circus, Cohasset, Massachusetts

July 20: Oakdale Music Theatre, Wallingford, Connecticut

July 21: Cape Cod Melody Tent, Hyannis, Massachusetts

July 22: Pier 84, New York, New York

July 23: Performing Arts Center, Saratoga Springs, New York

July 25: Great Arena, Great Adventure, Jackson, New Jersey

July 26: Jones Beach Theatre, Wantagh, New York

July 29: Club Casino, Hampton Beach, New Hampshire

July 30: Club Casino, Hampton Beach, New Hampshire

July 31: Wolftrap Park, Vienna, Virginia

August 1: Pier Six Pavilion, Baltimore, Maryland

August 2: Garden State Arts Center, Holmdel, New Jersey

August 3: Mann Music Center, Philadelphia, Pennsylvania

August 5: Pine Knob Music Theatre, Clarkston, Michigan

August 6: Pine Knob Music Theatre, Clarkston, Michigan

August 7: Poplar Creek Music Theatre, Hoffman Estates, Illinois

August 8: Riverbend, Cincinnati, Ohio

August 9: Mulligan's Hollow, Grand Haven, Michigan

August 10: Wisconsin State Fair, Milwaukee, Wisconsin

August 12: Rockland County Fair, Suffern, New York

August 13: Powell Hall, St. Louis, Missouri

August 15: Douglas County Fair, Waterloo, Nebraska

August 16: Brown County Fair, Aberdeen, South Dakota

August 17: Hall County Fair, Grand Island, Nebraska

August 19: Sioux Empire Fair, Sioux Falls, South Dakota

August 20: Carlton Celebrity Theatre, Bloomington, Minnesota

August 21: Carlton Celebrity Theatre, Bloomington, Minnesota

August 27: Red Rocks Amphitheatre, Denver, Colorado

August 29: The Lagoon, Salt Lake City, Utah

August 30: Civic Stadium, Portland, Oregon

August 31: Marriott's Great America, Santa Clara, California

September 1: Marriott's Great America, Santa Clara, California

September 4: Pacific Amphitheatre, Costa Mesa, California

September 5: Greek Theatre, Los Angeles, California

September 6: Greek Theatre, Los Angeles, California

September 7: Greek Theatre, Los Angeles, California (with Michael Nesmith)

September 8: Hilton Hotel, Las Vegas, Nevada

September 9: Hilton Hotel, Las Vegas, Nevada

September 10: Hilton Hotel, Las Vegas, Nevada

September 11: Hilton Hotel, Las Vegas, Nevada

September 12: Hilton Hotel, Las Vegas, Nevada

September 13: Hilton Hotel, Las Vegas, Nevada

September 14: Hilton Hotel, Las Vegas, Nevada

September 15: Memorial Coliseum, Phoenix, Arizona

September 17: Dane County Arena, Madison, Wisconsin

September 18: Marketplace Arena, Indianapolis, Indiana

September 19: Oklahoma State Fair, Oklahoma City, Oklahoma

September 20: Veterans Stadium, Philadelphia, Pennsylvania

September 21: Valley Forge Music Fair, Devon, Pennsylvania

September 23: Bloomsburg Fair, Bloomsburg, Pennsylvania

September 24: War Memorial Arena, Buffalo, New York

September 25: Civic Center, Hartford, Connecticut

September 26: Sullivan Stadium, Foxboro, Massachusetts

September 27: Trump Plaza, Atlantic City, New Jersey

September 28: Westbury Music Fair, Westbury, New York

September 29: Broome City Arena, Binghamton, New York

September 30: Landmark Theatre, Syracuse, New York

October 8: Civic Center, Pittsburgh, Pennsylvania

October 9: Cambria War Memorial Coliseum, Johnstown, Pennsylvania

October 10: Rensselaer Polytechnic Institute Fieldhouse, Troy, New York

October 11: Patriot Center, Fairfax, Virginia

October 12: Scope Convention Center, Norfolk, Virginia

October 14: Brendan Byrne Arena, Meadowlands, Secaucus, New Jersey

October 15: Civic Center, Baltimore, Maryland

October 16: Richmond Coliseum, Richmond, Virginia

October 17: Dean Dome, University of North Carolina, Chapel Hill, North Carolina

October 18: The Omni, Atlanta, Georgia

October 19: O'Connell Center, Gainesville, Florida

October 22: Superdome, New Orleans, Louisiana

October 23: Jackson Coliseum, Jackson, Mississippi

October 24: Mobile Municipal Auditorium, Mobile, Alabama

October 25: Barton Coliseum, Little Rock, Arkansas

October 26: Louisiana Tech, Ruston, Louisiana

October 29: Chattanooga Arena, University of Tennessee, Chattanooga, Tennessee

October 30: Civic Coliseum, Knoxville, Tennessee

October 31: University of Dayton Arena, Dayton, Ohio

November 1: Roberts Stadium, Evansville, Indiana

November 2: Rosemont Horizon, Rosemont, Illinois

November 4: Kiel Auditorium, St. Louis, Missouri

November 5: Civic Center, Peoria, Illinois

November 6: Five Seasons Center, Cedar Rapids, Iowa

November 7: La Crosse Center, La Crosse, Wisconsin

November 8: Duluth Arena, Duluth, Minnesota

November 10: Fort Wayne Coliseum, Fort Wayne, Indiana

November 11: Athletic Center, Notre Dame University, South Bend, Indiana

November 12: Browne County Arena, Green Bay, Wisconsin

November 14: Centennial Hall, Toledo, Ohio

November 15: Wing Stadium, Kalamazoo, Michigan

November 16: Silverdome, Pontiac, Michigan

November 17: Richfield Stadium, Cleveland, Ohio

November 20: The Centrum, Worcester, Massachusetts

November 21: Cumberland County Civic Center, Portland, Maine

November 22: Bangor Auditorium, Bangor, Maine

November 23: Civic Center, Providence, Rhode Island

November 24: Utica War Memorial, Utica, New York

November 25: Rochester War Memorial, Rochester, New York

November 28: Hershey Arena, Hershey, Pennsylvania

November 29: Civic Center, Roanoke, Virginia

November 30: Charlotte Coliseum, Charlotte, North Carolina

December 1: Civic Center Arena, Charleston, West Virginia

December 3: Stabler Arena, Bethlehem, Pennsylvania

1987 'SOUND OF THE MONKEES' AUSTRALIAN TOUR (Jones and Tork):

February 10-15: The Venue, Victoria, Australia

February 17: Ballina Club, New South Wales, Australia

February 18-22: Twin Towns Services Club, New South Wales, Australia

February 24: Rumours Nightclub, Toowoomba, Queensland, Australia

February 25-27: Sheraton Breakwater Casino, Townsville, Queensland, Australia

February 28: Rockhampton Pilbeam Theatre, Queensland, Australia

March 1: Melanesia Village Entertainment Centre, Hervey Bay, Queensland, Australia

March 5: Revesby Club, New South Wales, Australia

March 6-7: St. George Leagues Club, New South Wales, Australia

March 8: Ingleburn Club, New South Wales, Australia

March 10: Newcastle Club, New South Wales, Australia

March 11: Hornsby Club, New South Wales, Australia

March 12: Seven Hills Club, New South Wales, Australia

March 13: Manly Leagues Club, New South Wales, Australia

March 14: Rooty Hill Club, New South Wales, Australia

March 15: Penrith Club, New South Wales, Australia

March 17: Auburn Club, New South Wales, Australia

March 18: Castle Hill Club, New South Wales, Australia

March 19: Selinas, Coogee, New South Wales, Australia

March 20: Manly Leagues Club, New South Wales, Australia

March 21: Shellharbour Workers Club, New South Wales, Australia

March 22: St. George Leagues Club, New South Wales, Australia

March 24-25: Stallions, Parramatta, New South Wales, Australia

March 26: The Lady Bay, Warrnambool, Australia

March 27: The Venue, Melbourne, Australia

March 28: The Excelsior, Thomastown, Victoria, Australia

March 29: Adelaide, Australia

April 4: St. George Leagues Club, New South Wales, Australia

April 5: Canterbury, Sydney, Australia

1987 NORTH AMERICAN 'HERE WE COME AGAIN' TOUR (Dolenz, Jones and Tork):

July 1: Community Center Arena, Tucson, Arizona

July 2: Arizona State University, Tempe, Arizona

July 3: Silverbowl, Las Vegas, Nevada

July 4: Weber State College Stadium, Ogden, Utah

July 7: Red Rocks Amphitheatre, Denver, Colorado

July 9: Kansas Coliseum, Wichita, Kansas

July 10: Rosenblatt Stadium, Omaha, Nebraska

July 11: Veterans Memorial Auditorium, Des Moines, Iowa

July 12: Poplar Creek Music Theatre, Hoffman Estates, Illinois

July 14: Sandstone Amphitheatre, Kansas City, Missouri

July 15: Allsports Stadium, Oklahoma City, Oklahoma

July 17: Park Central Amphitheatre, Dallas, Texas

July 18: Southern Star Amphitheatre, Houston, Texas

July 19: Mississippi Gulf Coast Coliseum, Biloxi, Mississippi

July 21: Ruth Eckerd Hall, Clearwater, Florida

July 22: Sunrise Musical Theatre, Sunrise, Florida

July 23: Orange County Civic Center, Orlando, Florida

July 24: Civic Center, Augusta, Georgia

July 25: Oak Mountain Amphitheatre, Birmingham, Alabama

July 26: Chastain Park, Atlanta, Georgia

July 29: The Gardens, Louisville, Kentucky

July 30: Riverbend, Cincinnati, Ohio

July 31: Sports & Music Center, Indianapolis, Indiana

August 1: Castle Farms, Charlevoix, Michigan

August 4: Ionia Fair, Ionia, Michigan

August 6: Merriweather Post Pavilion, Columbia, Maryland

August 7: Merriweather Post Pavilion, Columbia, Maryland

August 8: Mann Music Center, Philadelphia, Pennsylvania

August 9: Garden State Arts Center, Holmdel, New Jersey

August 10: Coliseum Theatre, Latham, New York

August 12: Great Woods, Mansfield, Massachusetts

August 13: Great Woods, Mansfield, Massachusetts

August 14: Fingerlakes Center, Lake Canandaigua, New York

August 15: Melody Fair, North Tonawanda, New York

August 16: Molson Park, Toronto, Ontario, Canada

August 18: Oakdale Music Theatre, Wallingford, Connecticut

August 19: Jones Beach Theatre, Wantagh, New York

August 20: The Pier, New York, New York

August 21: Stabler Arena, Bethlehem, Pennsylvania

August 25: Blossom Music Center, Cleveland, Ohio

August 26: Pine Knob Music Theatre, Clarkston, Michigan

August 27: Pine Knob Music Theatre, Clarkston, Michigan

August 28: Holiday Star Theatre, Merrillville, Indiana

August 29: Marcus Amphitheatre, Milwaukee, Wisconsin

August 30: Minnesota State Fair, Como Station, Minnesota

September 1: Fox Theatre, St. Louis, Missouri

September 5: Mahoning County Fair, Canfield, Ohio

September 6: The Naval Base, Quonset, Rhode Island

September 7: Great Arena, Great Adventure, Jackson, New Jersey

September 12: Washington State Fair, Puyallup, Washington

September 13: Washington State Fair, Puyallup, Washington

September 14: Spokane, Washington

September 16: Concord Pavilion, Concord, California

September 18: Shoreline Amphitheatre, Mountain View, California

September 19: Cal Expo Amphitheatre, Sacramento, California

September 20: Pacific Amphitheatre, Costa Mesa, California

September 21: Greek Theatre, Los Angeles, California

September 22: Greek Theatre, Los Angeles, California

September 23: Greek Theatre, Los Angeles, California

September 25: Harrah's, Lake Tahoe, Nevada

September 26: Harrah's, Lake Tahoe, Nevada

September 27: Harrah's, Lake Tahoe, Nevada

September 28: Harrah's, Lake Tahoe, Nevada

September 29: Harrah's, Lake Tahoe, Nevada

September 30: Harrah's, Lake Tahoe, Nevada

October 1: Harrah's, Lake Tahoe, Nevada

October 24: Lowry Park, Tampa, Florida

1988 AUSTRALIAN TOUR (Dolenz, Jones and Tork):

August 20: Vic Theatre, Chicago, Illinois

September 21-25: Twin Towns Services Club, Tweed Heads, Australia

September 27-30: Burswood Convention Centre, Perth, Australia

October 1: Queens Park Theatre, Geraldton, Australia

October 4: Alexanders, Melbourne, Australia

October 5: Goulburn Valley, Shepparton, Australia

October 6: Alexanders, Melbourne, Australia

October 7: Entertainment Centre, Melbourne, Australia

October 8: Festival Hall, Adelaide, Australia

October 9: Lady Bay, Warrnambool, Australia

October 13: State Theatre, Sydney, Australia

October 14: Tiffany's, Sydney, Australia

October 15: State Theatre, Sydney, Australia

1989 EUROPEAN TOUR (Dolenz, Jones and Tork):

March 17: Harrogate International Centre, Harrogate, England

March 18: Liverpool Empire, Liverpool, England

March 19: Edinburgh Playhouse, Edinburgh, Scotland

March 20: Aberdeen Capitol Theatre, Aberdeen, Scotland

March 21: Newcastle City Hall, Newcastle, England

March 23: Gloucester Leisure Centre, Gloucester, England

March 24: Newport Leisure Centre, Newport, Wales

March 25: Royal Albert Hall, London, England (2 shows)

March 26: Oxford Apollo, Oxford, England

March 27: Brighton Dome, Brighton, England

March 28: Exeter Plaza Centre, Exeter, England

March 29: Bournemouth International Centre, Bournemouth, England

March 31: Fairfield Halls, Croydon, England

April 1: Colston Hall, Bristol, England

April 2: Portsmouth Guildhall, Portsmouth, England

April 3: Corn Exchange, Cambridge, England

April 5: Royal Concert Hall, Nottingham, England

April 6: Sheffield City Hall, Sheffield, England

April 7: Hull City Hall, Hull, England

April 8: Manchester Apollo, Manchester, England

April 9: The Hippodrome, Birmingham, England

April 10: DeMontfort Hall, Leicester, England

April 12: Crawley Leisure Centre, Crawley, England

April 13: The Wintergardens, Margate, England

April 14: The Opera House, Blackpool, England

April 15: Carlisle Sands Centre, Carlisle, England

April 17: Glasgow Pavillion Theatre, Glasgow, Scotland

April 20: Hammersmith Odeon, London, England

April 21: Amsterdam, Holland

April 22: International Leisure Centre, Brentwood, England

April 23: Theatre Royal, Hanley, England

April 24: Rivermead Centre, Reading, England

1989 RADIO APPEARANCES (all four Monkees):

June 28: KLOS-FM, Los Angeles, California

June 30: KIIS-FM with Rick Dees, Los Angeles, California

1989 NORTH AMERICAN & JAPANESE TOUR (Dolenz, Jones and Tork):

July 1: Red River Fair, Winnipeg, MB, Canada

July 4: Fiddlers Green, Denver, Colorado

July 6: Celebrity Theatre, Phoenix, Arizona

July 7: Humphreys, San Diego, California (2 shows)

July 8: Celebrity Theatre, Anaheim, California

July 9: Universal Amphitheatre, Los Angeles, California (with Michael Nesmith)

July 10: Hollywood Star Walk of Fame Ceremony, Hollywood, California (with Michael Nesmith)

July 11: McCallum Centre, Palm Desert, California (2 shows)

July 12: Circle Star Theatre, San Carlos, California

July 16: Sun Marina, Okinawa, Japan

July 18: Kudan Kaikan Hall, Tokyo, Japan

July 20: Ink Stick Shibaura Factory, Tokyo, Japan

July 22: Kosei Nenkin Hall, Shinjuku, Tokyo, Japan

July 29: Valley Forge Music Fair, Devon, Pennsylvania

July 30:Westbury Music Fair, Westbury, New York (2 shows)

July 31: Garden State Arts Center, Holmdel, New Jersey

August 1: Cape Cod Melody Tent, Hyannis, Massachusetts

August 3: Club Casino, Hampton Beach, New Hampshire

August 4: Starlite Music Theatre, Latham, New York

August 5: Lake Compounce, Bristol, Connecticut

August 7: Ontario Place, Toronto, Ontario, Canada (2 shows)

August 8: Ontario Place, Toronto, Ontario, Canada

August 9: Wolftrap, Vienna, Virginia

August 10: Great Woods, Mansfield, Massachusetts

August 11: New Jersey State Fair, Cherry Hill, New Jersey (2 shows)

August 13: Melody Music Fair, North Tonawanda, New York

August 14: Lulu's Roadhouse, Kitchener, Ontario, Canada

August 16: Mosque Auditorium, Richmond, Virginia

August 17: Southern Star, Six Flags Over Georgia, Atlanta, Georgia

August 18: Saenger Theatre, New Orleans, Louisiana

August 19: Southern Star Amphitheatre, Houston, Texas

August 20: Starplex Amphitheatre, Dallas, Texas

August 24: Indiana Fairgrounds, Indianapolis, Indiana

August 25: Entertainment Complex, Stevens Point, Wisconsin

August 26: Masonic Hall, Toledo, Ohio

August 27: Meadowbrook Music Festival, Rochester, Michigan

August 29: Ohio Theatre, Columbus, Ohio

August 30: Front Row Theatre, Cleveland, Ohio

September 1: Walworth Fair, Elkhorn, Wisconsin (2 shows)

September 2: Holiday Star Theatre, Merrillville, Indiana (2 shows)

September 3: Six Flags Amusement Park, Eureka, Missouri

1994 MICKY & DAVY TOGETHER AGAIN:

July 19: Casino Magic, Bay St. Louis, Mississippi

July 20: Casino Magic, Bay St. Louis, Mississippi

August 5: Star Plaza Theatre, Merrillville, Indiana

August 6: Three Rivers Regatta, Point State Park, Pittsburgh, Pennsylvania

August 18: Milwaukee A La Carte, Milwaukee, Wisconsin

August 19: Treasure Island Casino, Minneapolis, Minnesota

August 20: Treasure Island Casino, Minneapolis, Minnesota

September 2: Sands Hotel, Las Vegas, Nevada (2 shows)

September 3: Sands Hotel, Las Vegas, Nevada (2 shows)

September 4: Sands Hotel, Las Vegas, Nevada (2 shows)

September 17: Worlds of Fun Park, Kansas City, Missouri

September 18: Worlds of Fun Park, Kansas City, Missouri

January 5, 1995: The Hard Rock Cafe, Hollywood, California (all four Monkees)

1995 MICKY & DAVY TOGETHER AGAIN:

June 10: KOOL-Radio Concert Series, Mile High Stadium, Denver, Colorado

July 3: Aloha Tower, Honolulu, Hawaii

August 3: Tobin Plaza, World Trade Center, New York, New York

August 4: Frontier City Park, Oklahoma City, Oklahoma

August 5: City Hall Plaza, Boston, Massachusetts

August 11: Treasure Island Casino, Minneapolis, Minnesota

August 12: Treasure Island Casino, Minneapolis, Minnesota

August 13: FallFest, Oakton Park, Skokie, Illinois

August 20: Humphreys Concerts by the Bay, San Diego, California

August 26: Taste of Blue Ash City Festival, Blue Ash, Ohio

August 31: Pine Knob Music Theatre, Clarkston, Michigan

September 2: Cooper Stadium, Columbus, Ohio

September 3: State Fair, Syracuse, New York (2 shows)

September 10: Worlds of Fun Park, Kansas City, Missouri

September 20: Oneida Casino, Green Bay, Wisconsin

September 21: Oneida Casino, Green Bay, Wisconsin

October 7: Sunrise Musical Theatre, Miami, Florida

1996 LET THE GOOD TIMES ROLL:
April 12: Flint Center, Cupertino, California (Jones and Tork)

1996 30th ANNIVERSARY REUNION TOUR (Dolenz, Jones and Tork):
June 8-9: Ramada, Laughlin, Nevada

June 15: Riverport Amphitheatre, St. Louis, Missouri

June 19: Reno Hilton Amphitheatre, Reno, Nevada

June 20: Universal Amphitheatre, Los Angeles, California

June 21: Las Vegas Hilton, Las Vegas, Nevada

June 22: Huntsman Center, Salt Lake City, Utah

June 27: Orpheum Theatre, Minneapolis, Minnesota

June 28: Sec Taylor Stadium, Des Moines, Iowa

June 29: Zoo Amphitheatre, Oklahoma City, Oklahoma

June 30: Sandstone Amphitheatre, Bonner Springs, Kansas

July 1: Edmonton Stadium, Edmonton, Alberta, Canada

July 4: Music Mill Amphitheatre, Arlington, Texas

July 5: Sea World, San Antonio, Texas

July 6: Tim McCarver Stadium, Memphis, Tennessee

July 8: Brady Theatre, Tulsa, Oklahoma

July 12: Star Lake Amphitheatre, Pittsburgh, Pennsylvania

July 13: Nautica Stage, Cleveland, Ohio

July 14: Warner Theatre, Erie, Pennsylvania

July 15: Coors Pavilion, Cincinnati, Ohio

July 17: Interlochen Center, Interlochen, Michigan

July 18: Pine Knob Music Theatre, Clarkston, Michigan

July 19: Columbus Amphitheatre, Columbus, Ohio

July 20: Claridge Casino, Atlantic City, New Jersey

July 22: Molson Amphitheatre, Toronto, Ontario, Canada

July 24: Melody Fair Theatre, North Tonawanda, New York

July 25: Foxwoods, Ledyard, Connecticut

July 26: Hershey Park Amphitheatre, Hershey, Pennsylvania

July 27: North Shore Music Theatre, Beverly, Massachusetts

July 28: Cape Cod Melody Tent, Hyannis, Massachusetts

July 30: Hampton Beach Casino, Hampton Beach, New Hampshire

July 31: Oakdale Musical Theatre, Wallingford, Connecticut

August 1: Warwick Musical Theatre, Warwick, Rhode Island

August 2: South Shore Music Circus, Cohasset, Massachusetts

August 3: Valley Forge Music Fair, Devon, Pennsylvania

August 4: Westbury Music Fair, Westbury, New York

August 5: Anderson Center, Binghamton, New York

August 7: Classic Amphitheatre, Richmond, Virginia

August 8: Virginia Beach Amphitheatre, Virginia Beach, Virginia

August 10: Walnut Creek Amphitheatre, Raleigh, North Carolina

August 11: Blockbuster Pavilion, Charlotte, North Carolina

August 14: Mankato Civic Center, Mankato, Minnesota

August 15: Bayfront Park, Duluth, Minnesota

August 16: Star Plaza Theatre, Merrillville, Indiana

August 17: Metrocentre, Rockford, Illinois

August 18: Mark Of The Quad Cities, Moline, Illinois

August 21: Stanley Theatre, Utica, New York

August 22: Fingerlakes Center, Lake Canandaigua, New York

August 23: Kirby Center, Wilkes Barre, Pennsylvania

August 24: Patriot Center, Fairfax, Virginia

August 25: Mid-Hudson Civic Center, Poughkeepsie, New York

August 30: Taste Of Iowa Festival, Cedar Rapids, Iowa

August 31: Maritime Days Festival, Milwaukee, Wisconsin

September 8: Street Scene Festival, San Diego, California

September 13: Salt Lake City, Utah (Private Show)

September 20: Los Angeles, California (Private Show)

November 1: Vanderburgh Auditorium, Evansville, Indiana

November 20: Billboard Live Club, Los Angeles, California (with Michael Nesmith)

November 21: Braden Auditorium, Normal, Illinois

November 22: Rosemont Theatre, Rosemont, Illinois

November 23: Eagles Ballroom, Milwaukee, Wisconsin

November 29-30: Tropicana, Las Vegas, Nevada

December 31: Tempe Tostitos Block Party, Fiesta Bowl, Tempe, Arizona

January 17, 1997: South Florida Fairgrounds, West Palm Beach, Florida

January 19: Ruth Eckerd Hall, Clearwater, Florida

1997 UNITED KINGDOM JUSTUS TOUR (all four Monkees)

March 7: Newcastle Arena, Newcastle, England

March 8: Scottish Exhibition and Conference Centre, Glasgow, Scotland

March 9: Waterfront Hall, Belfast, Northern Ireland

March 10: The Point, Dublin, Republic Of Ireland

March 12: International Arena, Cardiff, Wales

March 14: Sheffield Arena, Sheffield, England

March 15: Nynex Arena, Manchester, England

March 16: International Centre, Bournemouth, England

March 18: National Exhibition Centre, Birmingham, England

March 19: Wembley Arena, London, England

March 20: Wembley Arena, London, England

1997 US TOUR (Dolenz, Jones and Tork):

June 20: Candlestick Park, San Francisco, California

July 4: Sunset Station, Las Vegas, Nevada

July 5: Del Mar Fair Grandstand, Del Mar, California

July 19:   Celebrity Theatre, Phoenix, Arizona

July 25:   Funfest, Kingsport, Tennessee

July 26:   Cardinal Stadium, Louisville, Kentucky

July 27:   Palace Theatre, Cleveland, Ohio

August 1: Star Plaza Theatre, Merrillville, Indiana

August 2: Rosemont Theatre, Rosemont, Illinois

August 3: Cincinnati Music Hall, Cincinnati, Ohio

August 6: Pine Knob Music Theatre, Detroit, Michigan

August 8: Crystal Grand Music Theatre, Wisconsin Dells, Wisconsin

August 9: State Theatre, Minneapolis, Minnesota

August 16: Mount Airy Lodge, Mount Pocono, Pennsylvania

August 17: Mann Music Center, Philadelphia, Pennsylvania

August 21: Hammerstein Ballroom, Manhattan Centre, New York

August 22: Thunder Ridge, Patterson, New York

August 23: The 9:30 Club, Washington, D.C.

August 24: North Shore Music Theatre, Beverly, Massachusetts

August 26: Westbury Music Fair, Westbury, New York

August 27: Casino Ballroom, Hampton Beach, New Hampshire

August 29: South Shore Music Circus, Cohasset, Massachusetts

August 30: Cape Cod Melody Tent, Hyannis, Massachusetts

August 31: Clovis Ballroom Expo, Clovis, California

September 6: Mile High Stadium, Denver, Colorado

September 13: Doheny Days Festival, Dana Point, California

September 15: Western Washington Fair, Puyallup, Washington

September 18: Palace Theatre, Myrtle Beach, South Carolina

September 19: Peace Centre for Performing Arts, Greenville, South Carolina

September 20: Chastain Park Amphitheatre, Atlanta, Georgia

September 22: Mid-South Fair, Main Stage, Memphis, Tennessee

September 24: Bloomsburg Fair, Bloomsburg, Pennsylvania

September 27: Frank Erwin Center, Austin, Texas

October 4: Golden Eagle Casino, Horton, Kansas (2 shows)

October 11: WBMX Mixfest, Boston, Massachusetts

October 21: Arizona State Fair, Phoenix, Arizona

November 8: Universal Amphitheatre, Los Angeles, California

November 19: Harley-Davidson Cafe, Las Vegas, Nevada (Private Show)

November 28: Mount Airy Lodge, Mount Pocono, Pennsylvania

November 29: The Concord, Kiamesha Lake, New York

November 30: Palace Theatre, New Haven, Connecticut

December 22: State University Pavilion, Boise, Idaho

December 31: Walt Disney World, Orlando, Florida (Private Show)

1998 AUSTRALIAN TOUR (Dolenz, Jones and Tork): (all dates canceled)

February 27-28: Kewadin Casino, Saulte Ste. Marie, Michigan

March 5-8: Crown Casino, Melbourne, Australia

March 10-11: Southport RSL, Southport, Australia

March 13: Fairfield RSL, Sydney, Australia

March 14: Rooty Hill RSL, Sydney, Australia

March 15: Newcastle Civic Theatre, Newcastle, New Zealand

March 16: Wellington Town Hall, Wellington, New Zealand

March 17-18: Metropolis Concert Club, Perth, Australia

2001 US TOUR (Dolenz, Jones and Tork): (* = no Peter Tork)

March 1: Ruth Eckerd Hall, Clearwater, Florida

March 2: House of Blues, Orlando, Florida

March 3: Pompano Beach Amphitheatre, Fort Lauderdale, Florida

March 4: Florida Theatre, Jacksonville, Florida

March 6: Centre Stage Theatre, Atlanta, Georgia

March 8: State Theatre, Easton, Pennsylvania

March 9: Lowell Memorial Auditorium, Lowell, Massachusetts

March 10: Oakdale Theatre, Wallingford, Connecticut

March 11: Westbury Music Fair, Westbury, New York

March 14: 9:30 Club, Washington, D.C.

March 15: Kahuna Concert Hall, Wilmington, Delaware

March 16: Xanadu Theater, Atlantic City, New Jersey

March 17: Xanadu Theater, Atlantic City, New Jersey

March 18: Mohegan Sun, Uncasville, Connecticut

March 21: Turning Stone Casino, Verona, New York

March 22: Palace Theatre, Columbus, Ohio

March 24: Sam's Town Casino, Tunica, Missouri

March 25: Star Plaza Theatre, Merrillville, Indiana

March 29: MGM Grand, Las Vegas, Nevada

March 30: MGM Grand, Las Vegas, Nevada

March 31: MGM Grand, Las Vegas, Nevada

April 1: MGM Grand, Las Vegas, Nevada

April 2: MGM Grand, Las Vegas, Nevada

April 3: MGM Grand, Las Vegas, Nevada

April 4: MGM Grand, Las Vegas, Nevada

April 5: Kiva Auditorium, Albuquerque, New Mexico

April 6: Celebrity Theatre, Phoenix, Arizona

May 26: Burke Lakefront, Cleveland, Ohio

May 27: Applebee's Park, Lexington, Kentucky

June 8: Fox Theatre, St. Louis, Missouri

June 9: Midland Theatre, Kansas City, Missouri

June 10: Lied Center for the Performing Arts, Lincoln, Nebraska

June 12: House Of Blues, Chicago, Illinois

June 13: Embassy Center, Fort Wayne, Indiana

June 15: Red River Valley Fair, Fargo, North Dakota

June 16: Midwest Wireless Civic Center, Mankato, Minnesota (canceled)

June 17: Steamboat Days, Burlington, Iowa

June 18: Nebraskaland Days, North Platte, Nebraska

June 20: Coronado Theatre, Rockford, Illinois

June 22: Country Jam, Grand Junction, Colorado

June 23: Greeley Independence Stampede, Greeley, Colorado

June 24: Pikes Peak Theatre, Colorado Springs, Colorado

June 28: Kewadin Casino, Sault Ste. Marie, Michigan (2 shows)

June 29: Freedom Hill Amphitheatre, Sterling Heights, Michigan

June 30: Allegheny Fair, South Park, Pennsylvania

July 1: Bryce Jordan Center, State College, Pennsylvania

July 3: Bay Center, Dewey Beach, Delaware

July 5: House Of Blues, Myrtle Beach, South Carolina

July 6: Tennessee Theatre, Knoxville, Tennessee

July 7: Harbour Centre, Portsmouth, Virginia

July 10: Portland Expo Center, Portland, Maine

July 12: PNC Bank Arts Center, Holmdel, New Jersey

July 13: Cape Cod Melody Tent, Hyannis, Massachusetts

July 14: Hatch Shell, The Esplanade, Boston, Massachusetts

July 15: Westbury Music Fair, Westbury, New York

July 16: Westbury Music Fair, Westbury, New York

July 19: Calvin Theatre, Northampton, Massachusetts

July 20: Meadowbrook Farm Musical Arts, Gilford, New Hampshire

July 21 (day show): Buffalo Bisons Stadium, Buffalo, New York

July 21 (night show): Trump Marina, Atlantic City, New Jersey

July 22: Wolf Trap Filene Centre, Vienna, Virginia

July 24: Regency Park Amphitheatre, Raleigh, North Carolina

July 26: King Center, Melbourne, Florida

July 27: Barbara Mann Performing Arts Hall, Fort Myers, Florida

July 28: Van Wezel Performing Arts Hall, Sarasota, Florida

August 3: Johnny Mercer Theatre, Savannah, Georgia (canceled)

August 16: Bank of America Center, Boise, Idaho

August 18: The Fillmore, San Francisco, California

August 19: Amphitheatre at California State University, Bakersfield, California

August 22: House of Blues, Los Angeles, California

August 23: House of Blues, Los Angeles, California

August 26: Mandalay Bay, Las Vegas, Nevada

August 30: San Diego Civic Auditorium, San Diego, California

August 31: Sun Theatre, Anaheim, California

September 7: Redmond Recreation Complex, Bensenville, Illinois *

September 8: Lone Star Park, Grand Prairie, Texas *

October 13: Veterans Stadium, Philadelphia, Pennsylvania *

December 1: Walton Arts Center, Fayetteville, Arkansas *

2002 MONKEEMANIA TOUR: THE MONKEES featuring Micky Dolenz and Davy Jones:

January 11: Casino Rama, Rama, Ontario, Canada

January 12: Casino Rama, Rama, Ontario, Canada

January 25: Grand Casino Mille Lacs, Onamia, Minnesota (two shows)

March 21: Clyde Auditorium, Glasgow, Scotland

March 23: Telewest Arena, Newcastle, England

March 24: Sheffield Arena, Sheffield, England

March 26: Manchester Arena, Manchester, England

March 27: NEC, Birmingham, England

March 28: Wembley Arena, London, England

March 30: Vicar Street, Dublin, Ireland

April 5: B.B. King Blues Club, New York, New York

April 6: B.B. King Blues Club, New York, New York

April 7: Westbury Music Fair, Westbury, New York

April 9: Celebrity Theatre, Phoenix, Arizona

April 12: Providence Performing Arts Center, Providence, Rhode Island

April 13: Hampton Beach Casino Ballroom, Hampton Beach, New Hampshire

April 14: Fairmont Copley Plaza Hotel, Boston, Massachusetts (private show)

May 25: Louisville Zoo Amphitheater, Louisville, Kentucky

May 26: Soldiers Memorial Plaza, St. Louis, Missouri

May 31: Star Plaza Theatre, Merrillville, Indiana

June 1: Meadowbrook Music Festival, Rochester Hills, Michigan

June 2: Paramount Kings Island Theme Park, Kings Mills, Ohio

June 8: Mohegan Sun, Uncasville, Connecticut

June 9: Brookhaven Amphitheatre, Farmingville, New York

June 13: Galaxy Theatre, Santa Ana, California (two shows)

June 14: House of Blues, Los Angeles, California

June 15: Fillmore, San Francisco, California

June 22: The Odeon, Cleveland, Ohio

June 23: Heinz Field, Pittsburgh, Pennsylvania

June 29: Paramount Arts Centre, Aurora, Illinois

July 5: Beau Rivage Casino, Biloxi, Mississippi

July 9: Fort Erie Racetrack, Fort Erie, Ontario, Canada

July 10: Hiawatha Casino, Sarnia, Ontario, Canada

July 11: Windsor Slots, Windsor, Ontario, Canada

July 12: Colonial Downs, New Kent, Virginia

July 13: Hatch Shell, Boston, Massachusetts

July 20: Billy Bob's Texas, Fort Worth, Texas

August 16: Sportsdome, Brewster, New York

August 17: North Shore Music Theatre, Beverly, Massachusetts

August 21: Disneyland, Anaheim, California

August 22: Disneyland, Anaheim, California

August 23: Disneyland, Anaheim, California

August 25: Ventura Theatre, Ventura, California

August 30: Sam's Town Live, Las Vegas, Nevada

September 7: Electric Factory, Philadelphia, Pennsylvania

September 8: Oyster Festival, Norwalk, Connecticut

September 14: Benson Auditorium at Harding University, Searcy, Arkansas

2011 AN EVENING WITH THE MONKEES: The 45th Anniversary Tour (Dolenz, Jones and Tork):

May 12: Echo Arena, Liverpool, England

May 14: O2 Apollo, Manchester, England

May 15: City Hall, Newcastle, England

May 16: Clyde Auditorium, Glasgow, Scotland

May 19: Royal Albert Hall, London, England

May 20: Sheffield City Hall, Sheffield, England

May 21: NIA Academy, Birmingham, England

May 23: Pavilions, Plymouth, England

May 24: Cardiff International Arena, Cardiff, Wales

May 25: The Royal Centre, Nottingham, England

June 3: Chastain Park Amphitheatre, Atlanta, Georgia

June 4: Ruth Eckerd Hall, Clearwater, Florida

June 5: Pompano Beach Amphitheatre, Pompano Beach, Florida

June 6: Florida Theatre, Jacksonville, Florida

June 8: Innsbrook Pavilion, Glen Allen, Virginia

June 9: Mayo Performing Arts Center, Morristown, New Jersey

June 10: Mohegan Sun, Uncasville, Connecticut

June 11: Avalon Ballroom Theatre, Niagara Falls, Ontario, Canada

June 12: Avalon Ballroom Theatre, Niagara Falls, Ontario, Canada

June 15: Lowell Memorial Auditorium, Lowell, Massachusetts

June 16: Beacon Theatre, New York, New York

June 17: NYCB Theatre at Westbury, Westbury, New York

June 18: Borgata Music Box, Atlantic City, New Jersey

June 19: Filene Center at Wolf Trap, Vienna, Virginia

June 20: Hershey Theatre, Hershey, Pennsylvania

June 22: Stage AE, Pittsburgh, Pennsylvania

June 23: Fox Theatre, Detroit, Michigan

June 24: Lifestyle Communities Pavilion, Columbus, Ohio

June 25: Aronoff Center for the Arts, Cincinnati, Ohio

June 26: Murat Theatre, Indianapolis, Indiana

June 28: Morris Performing Arts Center, South Bend, Indiana

June 29: Genesee Theatre, Waukegan, Illinois

June 30: Star Plaza Theatre, Merrillville, Indiana

July 1: Weesner Amphitheater, Minneapolis, Minnesota

July 2: Weesner Amphitheater, Minneapolis, Minnesota

July 3: Stir Concert Cove, Council Bluffs, Iowa

July 5: Paramount Theatre, Denver, Colorado

July 8: Pantages Theater, Tacoma, Washington

July 9: Sleep Country Amphitheater, Ridgefield, Washington

July 10: Mountain Winery Amphitheatre, Saratoga, California

July 13: Fox Theater, Bakersfield, California

July 14: Samala Showroom, Santa Ynez, California

July 15: Morongo Events Center, Cabazon, California

July 16: Greek Theatre, Los Angeles, California

July 21: Seaside Summer Concert Series, Brooklyn, New York

July 23: Marcus Amphitheater, Milwaukee, Wisconsin (Davy Jones' final Monkees show)

The following shows originally scheduled for this tour were canceled:

August 26: NYCB Theater at Westbury, Westbury, New York

August 27: Cape Cod Melody Tent, Hyannis, Massachusetts

August 28: Hampton Beach Casino Ballroom, Hampton Beach, New Hampshire

August 31: Tower Theater, Upper Darby Township, Pennsylvania

September 1: Durham Performing Arts Center, Durham, North Carolina

September 2: Big Sandy Superstore Arena, Huntington, West Virginia

September 4: Jacobs Pavilion at Nautica, Cleveland, Ohio

September 7: Bergen Performing Arts Center, Englewood, New Jersey

September 8: State Theatre, New Brunswick, New Jersey

September 9: Times Union Center, Albany, New York

September 10: Poconos Mountains Performing Arts Center, Bushkill, Pennsylvania

September 12: Family Arena, St. Charles, Missouri

September 23: Red Robinson Show Theatre, Coquitlam, Canada

2012 DAVY JONES MEMORIAL CONCERT (Dolenz and Tork):

April 3: New York City, New York

2012 AN EVENING WITH THE MONKEES (Dolenz, Nesmith and Tork):

November 8: California Center for the Arts, Escondido, California

November 9: Arlington Theatre, Santa Barbara, California

November 10: Greek Theatre, Los Angeles, California

November 11: Flint Center for the Performing Arts, Cupertino, California

November 15: State Theatre, Minneapolis, Minnesota

November 16: Chicago Theatre, Chicago, Illinois

November 17: Lakewood Auditorium, Cleveland, Ohio

November 18: The Center For The Arts, Buffalo, New York

November 29: Keswick Theatre, Philadelphia, Pennsylvania

November 30: State Theatre Regional Arts Center, New Brunswick, New Jersey

December 1: The Paramount, Huntington, New York

December 2: Beacon Theatre, New York, New York

2013 A MIDSUMMER'S NIGHT WITH THE MONKEES (Dolenz, Nesmith and Tork):

July 15: Capitol Theatre, Port Chester, New York

July 16: Citi Performing Arts Center, Boston, Massachusetts

July 17: Count Basie Theatre, Red Bank, New Jersey

July 19: NYCB Theatre at Westbury, Westbury, New York

July 20: Mann Music Theatre, Philadelphia, Pennsylvania

July 21: Warner Theatre, Washington, D.C.

July 23: Memorial Auditorium, Raleigh, North Carolina

July 24: Ryman Auditorium, Nashville, Tennessee

July 26: St. Augustine Amphitheatre, St. Augustine, Florida

July 27: Mizner Park Amphitheatre, Boca Raton, Florida

July 28: Ruth Eckerd Hall, Clearwater, Florida

July 31: Long Center, Austin, Texas

August 1: Arena Theatre, Houston, Texas

August 2: Verizon Theatre, Grand Prairie, Texas

August 3: Brady Theater, Tulsa, Oklahoma

August 5: Paramount Theatre, Denver, Colorado

August 9: Mesa Arts Center, Mesa, Arizona

August 10: Green Valley Events Center, Henderson, Nevada

August 11: Humphreys, San Diego, California

August 13: Terrace Theatre, Long Beach, California

August 14: Mountain Winery, Saratoga, California

August 15: Uptown Theatre, Napa, California

August 17: Benaroya Hall, Seattle, Washington

August 18: Arlene Schnitzer Concert Hall, Portland, Oregon

THE 2014 MONKEES TOUR (Dolenz, Nesmith, and Tork):

May 22: Hampton Beach Casino Ballroom, Hampton, New Hampshire

May 23: Borgata Music Box, Atlantic City, New Jersey

May 24: New Jersey Performing Arts Center, Newark, New Jersey

May 25: The Paramount, Huntington, New York

May 27: Sands Bethlehem Event Center, Bethlehem, Pennsylvania

May 28: The Palace Theater, Greensburg, Pennsylvania

May 30: Fox Theatre, Detroit, Michigan

May 31: Star Plaza Theater, Merrillville, Indiana

June 1: Riverside Theater, Milwaukee, Wisconsin

June 2: Weesner Amphitheater, Minneapolis, Minnesota

June 4: Uptown Theater, Kansas City, Missouri

June 5: Fox Theatre, St. Louis, Missouri

June 6: PNC Pavilion at Riverbend Music Center, Cincinnati, Ohio

June 7: Hard Rock Live, Cleveland, Ohio

2015 AN EVENING WITH THE MONKEES Featuring Micky Dolenz and Peter Tork:

March 27: Fantasy Springs Events Center, Indio (Palm Springs), California

April 22: River Cree Resort & Casino, Enoch, Alberta, Canada

April 24: Casino Rama, Rama, Ontario, Canada

April 25: Casino Rama, Rama, Ontario, Canada

July 31: Nashville Symphony, Nashville, Tennessee

August 1: River City Casino and Hotel, St. Louis, Missouri

August 27: Mayo Performing Arts Center, Morristown, New Jersey

August 28: American Music Theatre, Lancaster, Pennsylvania

August 29: NYCB Theatre at Westbury, Westbury, New York

September 4: Hammersmith Eventim Apollo, London, England

September 6: Moseley Folk Festival, Birmingham, England

2016 GOOD TIMES 50th ANNIVERSARY TOUR (Dolenz and Tork; Special Appearances by Nesmith):

May 18: Barbara B. Mann Performing Arts Hall, Fort Myers, Florida

May 19: King Center for the Performing Arts, Melbourne, Florida

May 20: Ruth Eckerd Hall, Clearwater, Florida

May 21: Frederick Brown Jr. Amphitheater, Atlanta, Georgia

May 24: Blumenthal PAC - Belk Theater, Charlotte, North Carolina

May 26: Warner Theatre, Washington, D.C.

May 27: The Wilbur Theatre, Boston, Massachusetts

May 28: Keswick Theatre, Philadelphia, Pennsylvania

May 29: Count Basie Theatre, Red Bank, New Jersey

June 1: The Town Hall, New York, New York (with Michael Nesmith via Skype)

June 3: Casino Rama - Entertainment Centre, Toronto, Ontario, Canada

June 4: The Colosseum at Caesars Windsor, Windsor, Ontario, Canada

June 5: Hard Rock Live Northfield Park, Cleveland, Ohio

June 7: Foellinger Theatre, Fort Wayne, Indiana

June 8: Frederik Meijer Gardens & Sculpture Park, Grand Rapids, Michigan

June 10: Louisville Palace Theatre, Louisville, Kentucky

June 11: The Venue At Horseshoe Casino, Hammond, Indiana

June 12: Murat Theatre at Old National Centre, Indianapolis, Indiana

June 14: Rose Music Center at The Heights, Dayton, Ohio

June 16: Red Butte Garden Amphitheatre, Salt Lake City, Utah

June 28: AT&T PAC — Winspear Opera House, Dallas, Texas

June 30: Hard Rock Hotel & Casino — The Joint, Tulsa, Oklahoma

July 1: Prairie Band Casino & Resort — Grand Lakes Ballroom, Mayetta, Kansas

July 14: Ottawa Bluesfest, Ottawa, Ontario, Canada

July 16: Hampton Beach Casino Ballroom, Hampton Beach, New Hampshire

July 22: Oaklawn Racing and Gaming — Finish Line Theater, Hot Springs, Arkansas

July 24: Bell Auditorium, Augusta, Georgia

August 5: Golden State Theatre, Monterey, California (with Michael Nesmith)

August 6: Grand Sierra Resort and Casino, Reno, Nevada

August 11: The Bomb Factory, Dallas, Texas (Special Live Concert for AXS TV)

September 4: Pacific National Exhibition, Vancouver, British Columbia, Canada

September 14: Fox Tucson Theatre, Tucson, Arizona (with Nesmith substituting for Tork)

September 15: Mesa Arts Center — Ikeda Theater, Phoenix, Arizona (with Nesmith substituting for Tork)

September 16: Pantages Theatre, Los Angeles, California (with Michael Nesmith)

September 17: Primm Valley Casino Resorts — Star of the Desert Arena, Las Vegas, Nevada

September 20: The Warfield, San Francisco, California

September 21: Gallo Center For The Arts, Modesto, California

September 23: Chinook Winds Casino Resort, Lincoln City, Oregon

September 24: Chinook Winds Casino Resort, Lincoln City, Oregon

September 25: The Moore Theatre, Seattle, Washington

September 29: Paramount Theatre, Austin, Texas

October 1: Hard Rock Live Biloxi, Biloxi, Mississippi

October 3: Welk Resort Theatre, Branson, Missouri (canceled)

October 7: Tilles Center for the Performing Arts, Brookville, New York

October 19: Velma V. Morrison Center for the Performing Arts, Boise, Idaho

October 21: Grove of Anaheim, Anaheim, California

October 22: Vina Robles Amphitheatre, Paso Robles, California

October 26: State Theatre, New Brunswick, New Jersey

October 28: Harrah's Resort, Atlantic City, New Jersey

October 29: Shippensburg University — H. Ric Luhrs PAC, Shippensburg, Pennsylvania

November 4: Genesee Theatre, Waukegan, Illinois

November 5: The Family Arena, St. Charles, Missouri

November 19: Twin River Event Center, Lincoln, Rhode Island

November 20: Bergen Performing Arts Center, Englewood, New Jersey

November 29: Isaac Theatre, Christchurch, New Zealand

November 30: ASB Theatre, Auckland, New Zealand

December 2: QPAC, Brisbane, Australia

December 5: Wrest Point, Hobart, Australia

December 7: Palais Theatre, Melbourne, Australia

December 9: Llewellyn Theatre, Canberra, Australia

December 10: State Theatre, Sydney, Australia

December 11: Thebarton Theatre, Adelaide, Australia

December 13: Perth Concert Hall, Perth, Australia

December 15: Enmore Theatre, Sydney, Australia

December 16: Jupiters, Gold Coast, Australia

2017 WIZARD WORLD COMIC CON (Dolenz and Tork):

March 17-19: Huntington Convention Center, Cleveland, Ohio

April 7-9: St. Louis, Missouri

May 5-7: Minneapolis, Minnesota

May 19-21: Des Moines, Iowa

TV APPEARANCES
by Mark Arnold

Amazingly enough, The Monkees didn't really make that many TV appearances during their 1960s heyday apart from their weekly TV series, and it is with that show, apart from the music, that we typically remember them. By the 1980s and on, The Monkees seemed to appear on every show either in an interview or a performance or both. The following is a list of every known TV show to feature at least two of The Monkees or features documentary footage in discussion about the group. Special thanks to *Monkee Business Fanzine*, IMDB and YouTube for help in compiling this list.

The Today Show - August 15, 1966

The Monkees - September 12, 1966-March 25, 1968 (primetime repeats through September 9, 1968; Saturday repeats from September 13, 1969-August 25, 1973; syndication from September 1975-present; MTV: February 23, 1986-1987; Nick at Nite: November 1986-September 1987, 1988; June 27. 1995, 1997)

Kellogg's Commercials - 1966-1968

Yardley Black Label Commercials - 1966-1968

Where the Action Is - September 26, 1966

American Bandstand - December 17, 1966

Tienerklanken - May 29, 1967

The 19th Annual Primetime Emmy Awards - June 4, 1967

Top of the Pops - July 6, 1967

The Joey Bishop Show - April 24, 1968

The Hy Lit Show - November 1968

Head (theatrical release) - November 6, 1968

The Hollywood Squares - December 23-27, 1968

The Glen Campbell Goodtime Hour - February 5, 1969

Happening '69 - March 22, 1969

33 1/3 Revolutions Per Monkee - April 14, 1969

The Joey Bishop Show - April 24, 1969

The Tonight Show Starring Johnny Carson - June 16, 1969

The Johnny Cash Show - July 19, 1969

Rowan and Martin's Laugh-In - October 6, 1969

Kool-Aid Commercials - 1969-1970

Oh My My Promotional Film - June 1970

Upbeat - June 13, 1970

The CBS Late Movie: Head (1968) (first TV broadcast) - December 30, 1974; repeat: July 7, 1975

Dinah! - January 12, 1976

Rock Concert - February 14, 1976

The Mike Douglas Show - February 27, 1976

American Bandstand - March 13, 1976

The Great Golden Hits of The Monkees - 1976 (broadcast 1977)

The Tomorrow Show - September 1, 1977

Entertainment Tonight - May 2, 1984

MTV Guest VJ - May 3, 1986

MTV Sunday Special: I Was a Teenage Monkee - May 4, 1986

Showbiz Today - May 28, 1986

The Today Show - May 29, 1986

Entertainment Tonight - June 2, 1986

Good Morning America - July 25, 1986

CBS News Nightwatch - July 16, 1986

MTV Music Video Awards - September 5, 1986

MTV Interviews at the Greek Theatre - September 7, 1986

Entertainment Tonight - September 8, 1986

Solid Gold - October 11, 1986

Macy's Thanksgiving Day Parade - November 27, 1986

MTV Monkees Christmas Medley '86 - December 1986

MTV Superbowl TV Party - January 25, 1987 (canceled)

The 14th Annual American Music Awards - January 27, 1987

Good Morning America - June 26, 1987

The Morning Program - August 20, 1987

Sally Jessy Raphael - August 31, 1987

Solid Gold - October 15, 1987

PM Magazine - November 24, 1987

Heart and Soul - February 14, 1988

The Factory - October 1988

Saturday Morning Live - October 1988

Midday - October 1988

Aspel & Company - January 4, 1989

Daytime Live - February 1, 1989

The Steve Wright Show - February 3, 1989

Good Morning Britain - March 8, 1989

TV AM - March 8, 1989

Entertainment Tonight - May 9, 1989

AM Los Angeles - June 29, 1989

The Pat Sajak Show - June 30, 1989

USA Today - July 9, 1989

People Are Talking - August 3, 1989

Nashville Now - August 15, 1989

Midday - August 30, 1989

Rhino Records Hard Rock Cafe Ceremony - January 5, 1995

The Brady Bunch Movie (theatrical release) - February 17, 1995

Entertainment Tonight - June 29, 1995

Pizza Hut Commercial - June 29, 1995

Entertainment Tonight - November 17, 1995

Boy Meets World - November 17, 1995

The Today Show - June 10, 1996

The Tonight Show with Jay Leno - June 17, 1996

The Rosie O'Donnell Show - July 24, 1996

Miss Teen USA Pageant - August 21, 1996

Hey Hey We're The Monkees CD-ROM Video Game - October 29, 1996

Justus Release Concert at Billboard Live! - November 20, 1996

Good Morning America - November 21, 1996

Showbiz Today - November 21, 1996

E! News in Review - January 5, 1997

This Morning - January 10, 1997

Breakfast News - January 10, 1997

Noel's House Party - January 11, 1997

Hey, Hey We're The Monkees - January 22, 1997

Hey, Hey, It's The Monkees - February 17, 1997

The Big Breakfast - March 3, 1997

The Clive James Show - March 4, 1997

Kenny Live - March 10, 1997

Justus - June 17, 1997

Access Hollywood - July 11, 1997

The Today Show - August 22, 1997

E! True Hollywood Story - August 1, 1999

Behind the Music - June 25, 2000

Daydream Believers: The Monkees' Story - June 28, 2000

Entertainment Tonight - January 6, 2001

Live! with Regis and Kelly - May 29, 2001

The Early Show - May 31, 2001

The Early Show - June 18, 2001

The Tonight Show with Jay Leno - August 21, 2001

The Monkees: Live Summer Tour - November 12, 2002

Biography - December 19, 2007

The Ed Bernstein Show - August 12, 2008

Making The Monkees - January 10, 2009

From The Monkees to Head - November 23, 2010

The One Show - February 21, 2011

The Today Show - May 14, 2011

Loose Women - May 18, 2011

The Today Show - August 17, 2011

The Guys Who Wrote 'Em - February 12, 2014

The Wrecking Crew! - March 13, 2015

Loose Women - September 2, 2015

BBC Breakfast - September 4, 2015

Good Times! Electronic Press Kit - May 23, 2016

CBS News Sunday Morning - May 29, 2016

Good Morning America - June 1, 2016

Studio 10 - June 5, 2016

AXS TV Concerts The Monkees Live at The Bomb Factory - August 11, 2016

BILLBOARD CHARTS
by Michael A. Ventrella

Looking over the charts is fascinating in some regards, but you have to take them with a proverbial grain of salt for many reasons: The ones in the 60s were largely based on radio play as opposed to sales, for one thing, and when they did use sales figures, they were from the record companies who had an incentive to exaggerate. Secondly, the position on the chart is only important as compared to other songs on the chart that week — a #1 hit could sell a million copies one week and only half a million the second week yet still remain at #1 if others sold less. Similarly, a song could be at #2 and sell more than the #1 song the week before.

Anyway, they're still fun to examine and can give us a better picture of how The Monkees music would have been heard on the radio at the time.

The charts below also include the few solo songs and albums that hit the chart. Just in case you're curious, the Micky single was one he recorded pre-Monkee that was re-released after the show started. Davy had one pre-Monkees song that barely charted (*What Are We Going to Do*) and one post-Monkees song (*Rainy Jane*). Mike, of course, had a few post-Monkees singles and albums that made the charts.

To compare how well the songs did, I took their position on the chart and assigned a number, so that a #1 song gets 100 points, #2 gets 99, and so on. I then added all the numbers up so that the higher a song got and the longer it stayed on the charts, the higher its score. Here, then are The Monkees singles that made the chart, with their scores in parenthesis:

SINGLES

1. *I'm a Believer* (1373)
2. *Daydream Believer* (1268)
3. *Last Train to Clarksville* (1252)
4. *A Little Bit Me, A Little Bit You* (878)
5. *Pleasant Valley Sunday* (830)
6. *Valleri* (806)
7. *That Was Then, This is Now* (738)
8. *Joanne* [MN] (733)
9. *Words* (645)
10. *I'm Not Your Steppin' Stone* (503)
11. *D.W. Washburn* (480)
12. *Silver Moon* [MN] (381)
13. *Rainy Jane* [DJ] (371)
14. *Tapioca Tundra* (311)
Tie. *It's Nice to Be With You* (311)
16. *The Girl I Knew Somewhere* (256)
17. *Tear Drop City* (254)

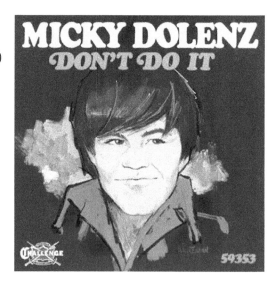

18. *Porpoise Song* (207)
19. *Listen to the Band* (181)
20. *Don't Do It* [MD] (98)
21. *Nevada Fighter* [MN] (76)
22. *Good Clean Fun* (36)
Tie. *Someday Man* (36)
24. *Heart and Soul* (24)
25. *What Are We Going to Do* [DJ] (17)
26. *Oh My My* (5)

For the albums, there is a top 200 chart, so #1 gets 200 points. Albums can stay on the chart for years, leave, and come back, so the numbers here are much higher than on the singles chart. Pretty much all of The Monkees albums stayed on the chart while the TV show was active. (When you have a half hour commercial for your albums on prime time TV every week, that will happen.) Once the show went off the air, the albums disappeared from the chart. This means the older albums had a bit of a head start and longer chart life than the later ones.

ALBUMS

1. *The Monkees* (14589)
2. *More of The Monkees* (12571)
3. *Headquarters* (9455)
4. *Pisces Aquarius Capricorn and Jones Ltd.* (6967)
5. *The Birds The Bees and The Monkees* (5738)
6. *Then and Now* (4705)
7. *Greatest Hits* [Arista] (2841)
8. *Instant Replay* (1866)
9. *Head* (1465)
10. *Greatest Hits* [Colgems] (987)
11. *Present* (538)
12. *Pool It!* (483)
13. *Good Times!* (370)
14. *The Best of The Monkees* (334)
15. *The Wichita Train Whistle Sings* [MN] (320)
16. *Infinite Rider on the Big Dogma* [MN] (305)
17. *Magnetic South* [MN] (165)
18. *Loose Salute* [MN] (131)
19. *Changes* (125)

1965

1965	8/14	8/21	8/28
What Are We Going to Do (DJ)	100	93	93

1966

1966	9/10	9/17	9/24	10/1	10/8	10/15	10/22	10/29	11/5	11/12	11/19	11/26	12/3
Last Train to Clarksville	67	43	26	18	6	4	3	2	1	2	4	7	10
THE MONKEES					121	29	18	6	2	1	1	1	1

1966	12/10	12/17	12/24	12/31
Last Train to Clarksville	27	43		
THE MONKEES	1	1	1	1
I'm a Believer	44	8	3	1
(I'm Not Your) Steppin' Stone		77	48	32

1967

1967	1/7	1/14	1/21	1/28	2/4	2/11	2/18	2/25	3/4	3/11	3/18	3/25	4/1
THE MONKEES	1	1	1	1	1	2	2	2	2	2	3	3	3
I'm a Believer	1	1	1	1	1	1	2	4	10	21	43		
(I'm Not Your) Steppin' Stone	32	20	28	28	40								
MORE OF THE MONKEES					121	1	1	1	1	1	1	1	1
Don't Do It (MD)											80	76	75
A Little Bit Me A Little Bit You												32	19
The Girl I Knew Somewhere												65	51

1967	4/8	4/15	4/22	4/29	5/6	5/13	5/20	5/27	6/3	6/10	6/17	6/24	7/1
THE MONKEES	3	3	5	6	6	7	7	7	9	13	14	16	21
MORE OF THE MONKEES	1	1	1	1	1	1	1	1	1	1	4	7	8
Don't Do It (MD)	75												
A Little Bit Me A Little Bit You	9	5	3	2	4	5	20	33					
The Girl I Knew Somewhere	48	39	48										
HEADQUARTERS										197	6	1	2

1967	7/8	7/15	7/22	7/29	8/5	8/12	8/19	8/26	9/2	9/9	9/16	9/23	9/30
THE MONKEES	20	17	30	32	35	35	38	37	37	34	34	44	46
MORE OF THE MONKEES	8	9	10	10	17	15	17	17	18	18	19	24	28
HEADQUARTERS	2	2	2	2	2	2	2	2	2	2	3	4	5
Pleasant Valley Sunday			51	24	9	4	3	3	8	13	25	40	
Words			78	46	34	24	15	15	11	12	29		

1967 (cont.)

1967	10/7	10/14	10/21	10/28	11/4	11/11	11/18	11/25	12/2	12/9	12/16	12/23	12/30
THE MONKEES	53	54	61	62	63	67	94	95	96	98	91	88	86
MORE OF THE MONKEES	38	39	39	37	36	34	34	31	39	54	51	47	44
HEADQUARTERS	6	7	8	10	10	13	15	15	18	24	25	28	28
Daydream Believer							33	5	1	1	1	1	3
PISCES, AQUARIUS								29	1	1	1	1	1

1968

1968	1/6	1/13	1/20	1/27	2/3	2/10	2/17	2/24	3/2	3/9	3/16	3/23	3/30
THE MONKEES	85	83	76	75	69	66	62	58	61	63	63	102	108
MORE OF THE MONKEES	42	38	33	49	50	48	45	47	51	53	75	79	92
HEADQUARTERS	27	25	24	29	29	32	34	35	35	37	40	40	41
Daydream Believer	2	3	6	8	24								
PISCES, AQUARIUS	3	3	3	3	4	6	6	18	23	34	33	32	34
Valleri										24	8	7	3
Tapioca Tundra										73	49	49	34

1968	4/6	4/13	4/20	4/27	5/4	5/11	5/18	5/25	6/1	6/8	6/15	6/22	6/29
MORE OF THE MONKEES	106	127	151	156	157	191	191	193	193				
HEADQUARTERS	41	50	57	85	133	134	134	132					
PISCES, AQUARIUS	45	53	53	56	58	65	67	66	91	104	109	110	114
Valleri	3	9	13	45	45	47							
Tapioca Tundra	45	45											
BIRDS BEES AND MONKEES						80	3	3	3	3	4	4	7
D.W. Washburn											61	29	29
It's Nice to Be With You											84	54	54

1968	7/6	7/13	7/20	7/27	8/3	8/10	8/17	8/24	8/31	9/7	9/14	9/21	9/28
PISCES, AQUARIUS	115	117	112	112	110	109	118	124	154	163	160	160	166
BIRDS BEES AND MONKEES	7	10	15	16	31	29	33	33	43	46	46	64	67
D.W. Washburn	19	19	31	39									
It's Nice to Be With You	51	51	51	51									
WITCHITA TRAIN WHISTLE (MN)					161	160	144	144	157	157	164		

1968	10/5	10/12	10/19	10/26	11/2	11/9	11/16	11/23	11/30	12/7	12/14	12/21	12/28
PISCES, AQUARIUS	181	192											
BIRDS BEES AND MONKEES	67	80	80	88	101	105	105	106	106	113	120	132	132
Porpoise Song		89	62	62	62	62	62						
HEAD												168	158

1969

1969	1/4	1/11	1/18	1/25	2/1	2/8	2/15	2/22	3/1	3/8	3/15	3/22	3/29
BIRDS BEES & MONKEES	127	133	136	136	151								
HEAD	132	127	116	98	46	45	45	55	104	108	114	114	120
Tear Drop City								87	68	62	56	56	58
INSTANT REPLAY									111	70	67	36	33

1969	4/5	4/12	4/19	4/26	5/3	5/10	5/17	5/24	5/31	6/7	6/14	6/21	6/28
Tear Drop City	66												
INSTANT REPLAY	33	32	38	44	54	90	114	113	148	166			
Someday Man						85	81						
Listen to the Band									97	97	91	73	67
GREATEST HITS													163

1969	7/5	7/12	7/19	7/26	8/2	8/9	8/16	8/23	8/30	9/6	9/13	9/20	9/27
Listen to the Band	64	63	75										
GREATEST HITS	99	97	95	89	94	95	93	128	155	155	162		
Good Clean Fun												100	99

1969	10/4	10/11	10/18	11/1	11/8	11/15	11/22	11/29	12/6	12/13
Good Clean Fun	97	91	82							
PRESENT				187	116	108	108	103	100	147

1970

1970	6/6	6/13	8/8	8/15	8/22	8/29	9/5	9/12	9/19	9/26	10/3	10/10
Oh My My	99	98										
Joanne (MN)			86	67	51	45	36	30	28	23	21	21

1970	10/17	10/24	10/31	11/28	12/5	12/12	12/19	12/26
Joanne (MN)	27	44						
MAGNETIC SOUTH (MN)	149	143	146					
Silver Moon (MN)				92	75	59	56	45

1971

1971	1/2	1/9	1/16	1/23	4/17	4/24	5/1	5/8	6/19	6/26	7/3
Silver Moon (MN)	43	42	51	65							
LOOSE SALUTE (MN)	173	171	170	159							
Nevada Fighter (MN)					173	171	170	159			
Rainy Jane (DJ)									83	69	62

1971	7/10	7/17	7/24	7/31	8/7	8/14
Rainy Jane (DJ)	58	55	54	52	52	53

1976

1976	8/7	8/14	8/21	8/28	9/4	9/11	9/18	9/25	10/2	10/9	10/16	10/23	10/30
GREATEST HITS	125	112	102	92	80	80	69	59	58	63	62	136	156

1976	11/6	11/13	11/20
GREATEST HITS	156	148	149

1979

1979	8/4	8/11	8/18	8/25	9/1	9/8	9/15	9/22	9/29
INFINITE RIDER (MN)	179	168	158	151	151	175	175	174	173

1986

1986	5/3	5/10	5/17	5/24	5/31	6/7	6/14	6/21	6/28	7/5	7/12	7/19	7/26
GREATEST HITS	180	160	121	107	89	80	71	70	70	69	82	77	136
That Was Then This is Now										88	68	57	46
THEN & NOW													71

1986	8/2	8/9	8/16	8/23	8/30	9/6	9/13	9/20	9/27	10/4	10/11	10/18	10/25
GREATEST HITS	165												
That Was Then This is Now	36	29	25	21	20	23	36	62	75	90			
THEN & NOW	45	42	31	27	24	22	21	21	22	25	28	31	33
THE MONKEES			139	126	109	101	101	117	107	107	104	99	92
MORE OF THE MONKEES			143	134	110	108	120	121	115	115	111	104	96
HEADQUARTERS			160	157	127	121	121	134	134	142	134	134	131
PISCES AQUARIUS			177	154	140	124	124	141	135	135	132	137	145
BIRDS BEES & MONKEES							185	165	149	149	145	151	148

1986	11/1	11/8	11/15	11/22	11/29	12/6	12/13	12/20	12/27
THEN & NOW	41	41	38	48	55	60	61	69	74
THE MONKEES	92	97	99	113	122	132	151	163	179
MORE OF THE MONKEES	96	105	110	126	134	158	154	165	183
HEADQUARTERS	142	143	151	184	195	197			
PISCES AQUARIUS	145	147	163	183	193	200			
BIRDS BEES & MONKEES	148	158	160	189					
Daydream Believer (remix)	90	79	79	89					
CHANGES		174	154	152	199				

1987

1987	1/3	1/10	1/17	1/24	1/31	2/7	2/14	2/21	2/28	3/7	3/14	9/19
THEN & NOW	74	68	68	77	85	95	115	139	143	172	163	
THE MONKEES	179	179	178	195								
MORE OF THE MONKEES	183	176	181	193	199	200						
POOL IT!												97

1987	9/26	10/3	10/10
POOL IT!	80	72	72
Heart and Soul	89	89	

2003

2003	5/17	5/24	5/31	6/7	6/14	6/21
THE BEST OF THE MONKEES	51	106	155	177	192	191

2016

2016	6/18	6/25	7/2
GOOD TIMES!	14	77	142

BIBLIOGRAPHY

Baker, Glenn A., with Tom Czarnota and Peter Hogan, **Monkeemania: The True Story of The Monkees**, St. Martin's Press, New York, NY, 1986, 2000

Bronson, Harold, **Hey, Hey, We're The Monkees**, General Pub Group, 1996

Dolenz, Mickey, and Mark Bego, **I'm a Believer: My Life of Monkees, Music and Madness**, Hyperion, New York, NY, 1993, 2004

Eck, Marty, **The Monkees Collectibles Price Guide**, Antique Trade Books, Iola, WI, 1998

Finn, Ed and T. Bone, **The Monkees Scrapbook**, Last Gasp, San Francisco, CA, 1986

Hart, Bobby, with Glenn Ballantyne, **Psychedelic Bubble Gum: Boyce & Hart, The Monkees, and Turning Mayhem Into Miracles**, SelectBooks, New York, NY, 2015

Hickey, Andrew, **Monkee Music**, Andrew Hickey, Amazon Digital Services, Seattle, WA, 2011

Jones, Davy, and Alan Green, **Mutant Monkees Meet the Masters of the Multi-Media Manipulation**, Samuel French Trade, Los Angeles, CA, 1992

Jones, Davy, with Alan Green, **They Made a Monkee Out of Me**, Dome Press, Beaverton, PA, 1987, 2014

Lefcowitz, Eric, **Monkee Business: The Revolutionary Made-for-TV Band**, Retrofuture Products, Port Washington, NY, 2010, 2011, 2013

Lefcowitz, Eric, **The Monkees Tale**, Last Gasp, San Francisco, CA, 1985, 1986, 1989

Livingston, Scot P., **The Monkees: A Many Fractured Image**, Createspace, North Charleston, SC, 2015, 2016

Masingill, Randi L., **Total Control: The Monkees' Michael Nesmith Story**, Flexquarters.com, Las Vegas, NV, 1997, 2005

McManus, Maggie, **Monkee Business Fanzine**, Trenton, NJ, #35, December 1985 - #101, June 2002

Mills, Peter, **The Monkees, Head and the 60s**, Jawbone Press, London, England, 2016

Mitchell, Melanie, **Monkee Magic: A Book About a TV Show About a Band**, CreateSpace, North Charleston, SC, 2013

Nesmith, Michael, **Infinite Tuesday: An Autobiographical Riff**, Crown Archetype, New York, NY, 2017

Reilly, Ed, **The Monkees: A Manufactured Image**, Pierian Press, Ypsilanti, MI, 1990

Sandoval, Andrew, **The Monkees: The Day-by-Day Story of the '60s TV Pop Sensation**, Thunder Bay Press, San Diego, CA, 2005

Velez, Fred, **A Little Bit Me, A Little Bit You: The Monkees From a Fan's Perspective**, CreateSpace, North Charleston, SC, 2014

Welch, Rosanne, **Why The Monkees Matter: Teenagers, Television and American Pop Culture**, McFarland Press, Jefferson, NC, 2016

Wincentsen, Edward, **The Monkees: Memories & the Magic**, Wynn Publishing, Pickens, SC, 2000

SONG AND ALBUM INDEX:

About the Authors

Mark Arnold is a comic book and animation historian. He has written for various magazines including *Back Issue, Alter Ego, Hogan's Alley, Comic Book Artist* and *Comic Book Marketplace.* He is the author of many other books including two about Harvey Comics, two about *Cracked Magazine*, and others

about TTV (Underdog), The Beatles, Disney, DePatie-Freleng (The Pink Panther), Dennis the Menace, and helped Craig Yoe with a book about Archie Comics. He has also performed interviews and commentary for the Underdog, Tennessee Tuxedo and Casper DVD sets for Shout Factory and the DePatie-Freleng DVD sets from Kino Lorber and has given public speeches and interviews about many of these diverse subjects and more. He lives in Eugene, Oregon.

Michael A. Ventrella writes witty adventure novels like *Bloodsuckers: A Vampire Runs for President* and *The Axes of Evil.* He is the editor of the *Baker Street Irregulars* anthologies (along with NY Times Bestselling author Jonathan Maberry) as well as the *Tales Of Fortannis* fantasy anthologies. His short stories have appeared in many collections, including *The Ministry of Peculiar Occurrences Archives* and the *Heroes In Hell* series. Michael is one of the founders of the biggest fantasy medieval live action role-playing groups in North America, Alliance LARP. He is also the founder of *Animato* magazine which, in the late '80s, was the first major magazine dedicated to animated films. His website is www.michaelaventrella.com. He lives in the beautiful Pocono Mountains of Pennsylvania with his wife, award-winning artist Heidi Hooper, and four spoiled cats. In his spare time, he is a lawyer.

About the Cover Artist

For more than forty-five years, Scott Shaw! has written and drawn underground comix (*Fear and Laughter, Gory Stories Quarterly*), kids' comic books (*Captain Carrot and His Amazing Zoo Crew!, Sonic the Hedgehog, Simpsons Comics*), comic strips (*Bugs Bunny, Woodsy Owl*), graphic novels (*Annoying Orange*), TV cartoons (*Jim Henson's Muppet Babies, The Competely Mental Misadventures of Ed Grimly, Camp Candy*), toys (McFarlane Toys' line of Hanna-Barbera and Simpsons action figures), and advertising (Pebbles Cereal commercials starring the Flintstones). His work has garnered him has four Emmy Awards, an Eisner Award and a Humanities Award. Scott also is known for presentations of "the craziest comic books ever published", *Oddball Comics Live!* and his regular participation in *Quick Draw!* with Mark Evanier and Sergio Aragonés. He was also one of the kids who created what is currently known as Comic-Con International: San Diego. His most recent projects have been illustrating Dark Horse's *How to Win at Life...by Cheating at Everything!*, designing and art directed a mobile app game featuring Topps' *Garbage Pail Kids* and designing, drawing and art-directing Gerrish Press' *Marooned Lagoon*, a children's picture book. Fascinated by the clash between art and commerce, Scott's been a fan and close observer of the Monkees since the broadcast of their show's first episode on NBC. He has also designed two of their album covers for Rhino, *A Barrel Full of Monkees* and *Just Us*.

List of Covers Characters

Front cover:
Mike Nesmith
Peter Tork
Micky Dolenz
Davy Jones
Mr. Babbit (Henry Corden)
Don Kirshner
Mr. Schneider
Mr. Daggart (Stan Freberg)
Girls

Back Cover:
Zelda (Joy Harmon)
Sonny Liston
"Gonna Buy Me A Dog"
Evil Wizard Glick (Rip Taylor)
April Conquest (Julie Newmar)
Loopy De Loop
Whyte Out bottle
PBS logo
The Texas Prairie Chicken
Sock Monkey
Lenny (Lon Chaney, Jr.)
Sea Captain
Captain Crocodile (Joey Forman)
Ronnie Farnsworth (George Furth)
Mike Nesmith (Frank Zappa)
Jack Nicholson
Baron Von Klutz
Dr. Mann (Jerry Colonna)
Hubbell Bensen (Carl Ballantine)
"Porpoise Song"
Black Bart
Rocky Rhino
The Monkeemobile
FRODIS The Alien
The MTV logo
"Peter Percival Patterson's Pig Porky"
"Teeny Tiny Gnome"
Mendrek the magician (Hans Conried)
S. Zero AKA The Devil

"Your Auntie Grizelda"
Minnie (Annette Funicello)
Corky the Circus Boy (Micky Dolenz)
Joey the Clown (Noah Beery, Jr.)
Bimbo the elephant
5,000 FINGERS OF DR. T cap
"Apples, Peaches, Bananas and Pears"
Jimi Hendrix
Snap, Crackle and Pop
Testy True (Terri Garr)
Sea Monkey
Lord High 'n' Low (Timothy Carey)
Thursday (Rupert Crosse)
The Penguin (Burgess Meredith)
Colonel Pshaw (Monty Landis)
Kamba the jungle boy (Burt Mustin)
Scott Shaw!
Mr. and Mrs. Ace (T.C Jones)
The Big Man (Rose Marie)
Y. A. Tiddle
Princess Betina
Archduke Otto
Sigmund
"Zor and Zam"
Frankie Catalina (Bobby Sherman)
Mexican banditos
Boris
Madame
Count Myron
Shah-Ku
The Count's Monster
The Count
Lorelei
The Wolfman
Mildred Witherspoon (Ruth Buzzi)
Henry Witherspoon
Madame Roselle
Coca-Cola machine
Kool-Aid Man
Dragon Man (Joey Forman)
Toto

Chang
The Jolly Green Giant
Furious George
Princess Colette
Vidaru
"The Last Train To Clarksville"
Farmer Fisher and his racehorse
The Chubber Clan

The Weskitt Clan
"Swami — Plus Strings, Etc."
The Big Victor (Victor Mature)
The Black Box
Police
Gangsters
Girls

Printed in the USA
CPSIA information can be obtained
at www.ICGtesting.com
LVHW010725011123
762414LV00050B/20